Corruption and Crime in Finance

Corruption and Crime in Finance: Legal and Economic Perspectives

EDITED BY

LUAN VARDARI

University "Ukshin Hoti" Prizren, Republic of Kosovo

AND

ADELINA RAKAJ

University "Ukshin Hoti" Prizren, Republic of Kosovo

emerald
PUBLISHING

United Kingdom – North America – Japan – India – Malaysia – China

Emerald Publishing Limited
Emerald Publishing, Floor 5, Northspring, 21-23 Wellington Street, Leeds LS1 4DL

First edition 2026

British Library Cataloguing in Publication Data
A catalogue record for this book is available from the British Library

ISBN: 978-1-83708-171-4 (Print)
ISBN: 978-1-83708-170-7 (Online)
ISBN: 978-1-83708-172-1 (Epub)

Printed and bound by CPI Group (UK) Ltd, Croydon, CR0 4YY

INVESTOR IN PEOPLE

Contents

About the Contributors

Dafina Abdullahu is a teaching assistant in the department Business and Management at the University "Ukshin Hoti" Prizren, Kosovo. She earned both her Bachelor's and Master's degree from the University of Prizren, Business Administration Department, with a specialization in accounting and auditing. She is a PhD Candidate at the University of Osijek—Croatia in the Department of Management. Her research interests are in accounting, auditing, finance, and operation management. She has worked in a bank as a Commercialist and Credit Analysts and also she worked as a teacher in high school in Prizren, in Economics field. She has attended some conferences, seminars, trainings and has published several scientific articles.

Firas Jamil Alotoum is currently an Associated Professor in the faculty of business at ASU in Jordan. Dr Alotoum received his undergraduate degrees as well as his PhD degree from the west of Timisoara University, Romania. Dr Alotoum published a number of papers in preferred journals and chapters in books. He also presented various academic as well as research-based papers at several national and international conferences. His scientific fields of interest include: business administration, marketing management, e-marketing, consumer behavior, and smart business. Dr Alotoum is an authorized trainer in human development and marketing from Ilm, United Kingdom.

Naim Baftiu is a recognized expert in the field of Computer and Electrical Sciences, with an extensive academic and professional portfolio that includes numerous peer-reviewed publications and university textbooks such as *E-Business and Management Information Systems*. He currently serves as the Vice Dean at the University of Prizren "Ukshin Hoti." In addition to his academic role, Dr Baftiu is the CEO of the INKOS Institute SH.A in Prishtina and continues to contribute as a journal reviewer and lead project designer in the field of computer science.

Halim Bajraktari is an Associate Professor at Ukshin Hoti University in Prizren. Kosovar nationality. He received his PhD in European Legislation and Institutions from the Institute of European Studies at the University of Tirana, Albania, in 2014. He is a Professor at the Faculty of Law in the field of international human rights law. His research and teaching focus on International Criminal Law, European law, where he explores legislation, integration, EU challenges and the national and international aspects of Kosovo's membership,

Security, cyber warfare and terrorism in Kosovo. Human Rights Advocacy: He is actively engaged in the promotion of human rights, especially in identifying hate crimes on social media. He is the editor of a book, Exploring AI in Contemporary Legal Systems, Artificial Intelligence a "right" or "violation" of Human Rights and Freedoms in the 21st Century. His dedication to advancing knowledge in various legal fields makes him a valuable contributor to academia and the legal community.

Nehir Balcı is an Assistant Professor at Dokuz Eylül University, Türkiye. She received her PhD in Business Administration from Dokuz Eylül University in 2019. Her research focuses on artificial intelligence in finance, clean energy and climate finance, financial market integration, stock market volatility and spillover effects, risk management, Islamic finance, financial performance analysis, health economics and economic modelling, with a particular emphasis on sustainability and environmental outcomes. Dr Balcı has published numerous articles in peer-reviewed journals such as *Journal of Environmental Management*, *Sustainable Development*, and *International Journal of Health Governance*. Dr Balcı teaches courses on financial risk management, corporate finance, international finance, mathematics and statistics. Her current research explores volatility spillover effects, risk perception in financial markets.

Chirag Balyan is an Associate Professor of Law at DY Patil School of Law, Navi Mumbai. He is on lien from Maharashtra National Law University Mumbai, where he is a founding faculty member. He teaches criminal law, criminal procedure, evidence law, white-collar crimes, and international arbitration. He also founded the Center for Research in Criminal Justice at the university. His report titled *Commercial Sexual Exploitation in Maharashtra: A Survey of Public Prosecutors* was published by the Department of Women and Child Development, Government of Maharashtra, in collaboration with the International Justice Mission. His doctoral thesis, *Antinomies in the Criminal Justice System: A Normative Critique of the Pre-Trial Detention Laws*, offers a critical analysis of the contradictions inherent in liberal criminal law theory. His recent publications include *Criminalization: Politics and Policies and Criminalization: Where Do We Go From Here?* both published by Brill in 2025. His earlier work, *Revisiting Reforms in the Criminal Justice System in India*, was published by Thomson Reuters in 2020.

Enver Buçaj is an Associate Professor at the Faculty of Law of the "Ukshin Hoti" University in Prizren. He specializes in criminal law, terrorism, and cybercrime. He graduated from the Faculty of Law in 1992, completed his Master's studies in criminal law in 2008, and earned his Doctorate in Criminal Law at the University of "Hasan Prishtina" in Prishtina in 2013. Between 2008 and 2014, he served as a lecturer of criminal law at both public and private universities, as well as a coordinator and an academic director for the establishment of the University of Prizren. From 2014 to 2016, he was a Counselor and the Deputy Head of Mission at the Embassy of Kosovo in Stockholm, covering several countries including Finland, Norway, Estonia, Lithuania,

Latvia, and Iceland. From 2016 to 2021, he served as a Minister Counselor and the Deputy Head of Mission at the Embassy of Kosovo in Montenegro. He has also worked as a legal advisor and a lecturer on topics related to economic crime and applicable laws in Kosovo and European Union international law. He served as a Senior Program Manager for the Finnish–UNHCHR Human Rights Support Program in Kosovo. Since 2014, he has been an Assistant Professor at the Faculty of Law at "Ukshin Hoti" University in Prizren, contributing to academic and research work for over 30 years. He has published scientific papers, monographs and books in well-known international journals.

Adila Haidari is a research scholar at the Faculty of Economics and Business, Universitas Islam Internasional Indonesia. She holds a Master's degree in Economics from the same institution and a Bachelor's in Law and Political Science from Rana University, Afghanistan. Her research focuses on gender economics, labor economics, economic growth, and sustainable development. She has published in peer-reviewed journals, contributing to policy-oriented economic research emphasizing inclusive growth and evidence-based analysis.

Fidan Haliti currently holds the rank of Captain and is the Head of the Organized Crime Investigation Unit in the Kosovo Police. Since 2005, he has worked in the Directorate for the Investigation of Economic Crimes and Corruption in Pristina, as the Head of the Corruption Crime Investigation Unit. He specializes in the investigation of corruption, economic, financial, and organized crime. He completed his doctoral studies at the Faculty of Philosophy, University of Pristina, and also completed his specialist and Master's studies at the University of Sarajevo, Faculty of Criminalistics, Criminology and Security Studies, and holds the title of Mr.sc. in Criminalistics and Security Studies. In addition, he has also completed studies in the field of Political Science at the University of Pristina. He is a lecturer at the UBT College in Pristina in subjects from the field of economic crime and corruption. He has completed many trainings and specializations in the field of corruption and economic and financial crime investigations in various international agencies such as the Guarda de Financa, Federal Bureau of Investigation, and has collaborated in this field with many international partner agencies, and has published scientific papers and monographs in well-known international journals.

Safiullah Junejo is a research fellow in economics at the Faculty of Economics and Business, Universitas Islam Internasional Indonesia, where he also serves as a lab assistant for the financial econometric course. He holds a Master's degree in Economics from Universitas Islam Internasional Indonesia and a Bachelor's from Shah Abdul Latif University, Pakistan. His research interests include financial crime, economic growth, renewable energy, trade policy, and sustainable development. He has contributed to academic discourse through conference presentations and publications in peer-reviewed journals, focusing on policy-oriented economic analysis.

Serdar Karaağın: With an Associate's degree in Accounting and Tax Applications from Dokuz Eylül University and a Bachelor's degree in Business Administration from Celal Bayar University, Serdar Karaagın is a member of the Turkish Chamber of Certified Public Accountants. He is an independent auditor licensed by the Capital Markets Board of Turkey (SPK) and the Public Oversight, Accounting and Auditing Standards Authority (KGK). Since 2006, he has worked as a manager and a tax and audit specialist for various CPA and independent audit firms in Turkey, providing tax and audit services. In addition to accounting, taxation, and financial reporting, his key areas of competence are audits and reporting related to renewable energy subsidies. As the head of the company's tax and advising division in Turkey, he is currently responsible for overseeing the implementation of Crowe HSY's quality management system and providing tax consulting services.

Funda Karakoyun is a qualified lecturer with 30 years of teaching experience and a professionally trained financial advisor and independent auditor. She has received assistant, associated and full professorship degrees in 2011, 2020 and 2025, respectively, as a faculty member at Dokuz Eylul University in Izmir. In addition, she has served as an expert witness in independent courts in the field of financial law. Her books and book chapters are generally on the subjects of taxation, security of tax receivables, tax criminal jurisdiction, and penal assessment in the field of public finance. She is currently a member of the Izmir Chamber of Certified Public Accountants (CPA), the Public Oversight and Audit Authority, and the Concordat Commissariat.

Amani Mohammad Said Khdair holds a Master's degree in Smart Business Technologies and currently serves in an administrative role at the Social Security Corporation of Jordan. With a strong background in business intelligence and digital transformation, she plays an integral part in enhancing operational efficiency and supporting data-driven decision-making within the institution. Her professional interests include smart governance, innovation in public service, and the application of intelligent systems in administrative frameworks.

Alban Kryezi is a teaching assistant from the Republic of Kosovo. Born in 1998, he is widely recognized for his research contributions in the field of law. He earned his Bachelor's degree in Law Studies from the University of Prizren in 2020 and later completed his Master's degree in Criminal Law at South-East European University in 2022. He began his academic career in 2022, gaining recognition for his contributions to the University of Prizren. Alban is particularly passionate about legal research, and his work has been featured in several prominent academic journals. In addition to his professional achievements, he is known as a hard-working, highly motivated, and professional member of the Faculty of Law at "Ukshin Hoti" University. He continues to be active in both teaching and research and is currently based in Prizren. He is currently pursuing his doctoral studies in Criminal Law at the South East European University.

Anuj Kumar works as the Head of Research and an Associate Professor at Rushford Business School, Switzerland. He is also associated with INTI International

University, Malaysia, as a Research Fellow (Honorary Role). His significant thrust areas are marketing, international business, and general management. He has completed an M.Sc. in International Business from University College Dublin, Michael Smurfit Graduate Business School, Ireland (Ranked among the top 200 colleges of the world—QS World ranking). He has completed a PhD from Aligarh Muslim University (Central University). He has published research papers in reputed SCOPUS/Web of Science/SCI/ABDC/UGC Care Journals. Dr Kumar has over a 100 publications. He also has three e-books and five book chapters to his credit (two are Scopus-indexed). He has published several cases in *Emerald Emerging Case Studies* (Scopus), *International Social Science Journal* (ABDC-B and Scopus), *Small Enterprise Research* (Scopus and Web of Science), *Case Centre-UK*, and other reputed Scopus, ABDC, and Web of Science journals. He has three internationally granted patents by South Africa and one patent granted by the Indian Government.

Ish Kumar is a transport planning researcher with a focus on urban freight logistics, spatial planning, and sustainable last-mile delivery systems. His work explores the intersection of logistics infrastructure, institutional design, and mobility governance, particularly in the context of E-commerce and Q-commerce. He has served as an Assistant Professor at the School of Planning and Architecture, Delhi, and actively contributes to academic and policy discourse through peer-reviewed publications and collaborative research. Dr Kumar is a reviewer for leading journals and conferences including Transport Geography, Transportation Research Interdisciplinary Perspectives, CTRG, CTSEM, and WCTR. He was awarded Best Paper at CTSEM 2025; RATE 2022. He also serves as Papers' Referee for the WCTRS-Y 2026 Mini-Conference. Dr Kumar is a member of the WCTR Society, ITPI, and COA.

Vinay Maitri is a transport expert with over 38 years of academic and professional experience. A former Professor and Dean (Student Affairs) at the School of Planning and Architecture, Delhi, he holds a PhD in Mathematical Statistics from IIT Delhi. His work spans Intelligent Transport Systems (ITS), transport economics, and sustainable urban mobility. Dr Maitri has authored seven books and over 25 research papers and has presented at international platforms including the TRB Annual Meeting in Washington, D.C. He has led major consultancy projects with institutions such as the World Bank and the Government of India and has played a pivotal role in integrating ITS and GIS into transport planning education and practice.

Hakan Özkaya is an Associate Professor of Accounting in the International Trade Department at Dokuz Eylül University in İzmir, Türkiye, where he also received his PhD. His research interests focus on cost and management accounting, international accounting, and financial accounting.

Ashwani Panesar, presently, working as an Associate Professor with Chitkara Business School, Chitkara University, Rajpura, Punjab, India. Previously, worked as an Associate Professor in Mittal School of Business, Lovely Professional University, Punjab (India) for 16 years till 2025; Dr. Ashwani Panesar has a rich teaching experience of over 13 years, taking up various business management subjects at university level. Having worked closely with the sales aspect of the pharmaceutical industry (8 years), he had pursued his Doctorate in pharmaceutical marketing strategies from Jaipur National University, Rajasthan (India). He has a number of quality Research Papers in the field of marketing and Book Chapters in various journals of repute of Scopus. His interest areas include Pharmaceutical Marketing, Distribution and supply Chain Management, etc.

Venus W. Samawi is a Professor in the Department of Management Information Systems/Smart Business at Isra University, where she teaches in the Master's program. She is a member of the IEEE Society. Dr Samawi earned her Bachelor of Science degree from the University of Technology in 1987, followed by her Master's and PhD degrees in Computer Science from Al-Nahrain University in 1992 and 1999, respectively. She supervises numerous PhD and Master's theses focusing on system programming, pattern recognition, network security, and text classification. Additionally, she leads and teaches courses at both the undergraduate and graduate levels in computer science, including programming courses. Dr Samawi has also served as a reviewer for various conferences and journals, including IEEE Access. Her primary research areas include pattern recognition, evolutionary computing, image processing, and natural language processing. Recently, she has shifted her primary research interest to the Internet of Things (IoT).

Rohit Sood, Assistant Professor at Lovely Professional University, Phagwara, Punjab (India), Department of Finance, has an extensive academic and professional experience of more than 14 years. He has presented numerous papers in national and international conferences and 10 papers are published in reputed international referred journals with high impact factor and indexing Google Scholar, Scopus, BEIESP, Open J Gate, DOAJ, get CITED, dig, Higher Education Forum, Cite Factor, Index Copernicus, Search Sight, Scirus, UK Index, New Jour, Research Gate. Apart from this, he has attended various conferences, workshops, and seminars in different colleges. He has attended 10+ relevant training and courses for continuous learning and has attended more than 10 Faculty Development Programs. He is a life member of Society of FSP and Global Risk Community.

Ankit Srivastava is an Assistant Professor of Law at Rajiv Gandhi National University of Law, Punjab, and a visiting faculty at Indian Institute of Management, Rohtak. He is a distinguished academic with a PhD in Competition Law. He is a Member of the Network for Indian Competition Experts at the Competition Commission of India and has over nine years of experience. He has authored 25+ papers on various domains of Corporate Law and has edited a book on Corporate Criminal Liability.

Arsim Thaçi has been serving in the Kosovo Police since 1999 and is currently working in the Regional Unit for the Investigation of Economic Crimes and Corruption in Prizren, under the Directorate for the Investigation of Economic Crimes and Corruption in Pristina. He specializes in criminal law, criminalistics, criminology, and areas related to economic crime, financial crime, and corruption. He graduated from the Faculty of Law in 2010, completed his Master's studies in Criminal Law in 2015, and earned the academic title *Doctor of Legal Sciences – Criminal Law* at the South East European University in North Macedonia on September 6, 2023. From 2016 to 2020, he served as an assistant and lecturer in criminal law and criminalistics at the Faculty of Law of the University "Ukshin Hoti" in Prizren, where he contributed to academic teaching and research for over nine years. He has participated in numerous international projects organized by the European Union and the U.S. Department of Justice and has published scientific papers and monographs in well-known internationally recognized journals.

Dardan Vuniqi is an Assistant Professor at the Faculty of Law of the "Ukshin Hoti" University of Prizren. He specializes in constitutional and administrative law. He graduated from the Faculty of Law in 2012, completed his Master's studies in constitutional-administrative law in 2014 and earned his Doctorate in Governance and Public Administration at the South East European University in North Macedonia, in 2019. Between 2015 and 2021, he was an assistant in constitutional-administrative subjects at the Faculty of Law of the "Ukshin Hoti" University in Prizren, the "Haxhi Zeka" University in Peja, and the "Kadri Zeka" University in Gjilan, coordinator of the Legal Clinic at the USAID for Justice Affairs National Center for the State Court, Head of Teaching, Vice Dean and Acting Dean of the Faculty of Law - "Ukshin Hoti" University, Prizren, Acting Vice Rector for Budget, Finance and Infrastructure of the "Ukshin Hoti" University in Prizren and since 2021 he has been an assistant professor at the University, where he has contributed in the academic and research fields for mnb ore than 9 years. He has published scientific papers and monographs in well-known international journals.

Şebnem Yaşar completed her undergraduate education at Boğaziçi University, Department of Political Science and International Relations, received her Master's degree in Business Administration from İzmir University of Economics, and her PhD in Business Administration from Dokuz Eylül University. She was awarded the title of Associate Professor in Accounting in 2018 and currently serves as a Professor at Dokuz Eylül University, İzmir Vocational School, Accounting and Tax Applications Program. Her academic areas of expertise include cost accounting, management accounting, and accounting theory, and she teaches associate, undergraduate, and graduate courses in these areas. In addition, as an academic who attaches importance to interdisciplinary studies, she has national and international academic publications focusing on the interactions between accounting and areas such as finance, economics, financial crimes, and corporate transparency.

Ismail Zejneli is a Full Professor at the Faculty of Law of the South East European University in North Macedonia. He specializes in criminal law, criminology, and criminalistics as well as other areas of juvenile delinquency, penology, and criminal policy. He completed his undergraduate studies in Law and received his Master's degree in Criminal Law and the title of Doctor of Law at the Faculty of Law of the University "Hasan Prishtina" in Prishtina, in 2001. His areas of expertise cover Criminal Law and other crime-related subjects. He has actively contributed to research and scientific work at the university for more than 30 years. He has participated in various projects focused on criminal law and has published monographs, lot of books, and research papers in internationally recognized journals.

Chapter 1

The Financial Crime Landscape: Scope, Impact, and Evolution

Safiullah Junejo[a,b] *and Adila Haidari*[a]

[a]Universitas Islam Internasional Indonesia, Indonesia
[b]Xi'an Jiaotong University, China

Abstract

Financial crime constitutes a metastasizing threat to global economic integrity, with illicit flows estimated to exceed $2.2 trillion annually, undermining institutions, distorting markets, and exacerbating inequality. This chapter dissects the anatomy of modern financial crime through three critical dimensions: its expanding scope (from fraud and money laundering to cyber-enabled schemes and crypto-based networks), its corrosive multi-sector impact (eroding public trust, enabling organized crime, and diverting resources from development), and its accelerating evolution (fueled by regulatory fragmentation, digitalization, and globalization). The authors expose systemic vulnerabilities where legal frameworks—such as anti-money laundering (AML) directives and extradition treaties—clash with economic realities like offshore havens, anonymous shell companies, and Artificial Intelligence (AI)-driven market manipulation. Through case studies like the Danske Bank scandal and emerging ransomware economies, the authors reveal how criminal enterprises exploit jurisdictional gaps and technological asymmetries. Crucially, this analysis pioneers an integrated legal–economic diagnostic framework, mapping how regulatory arbitrage and illicit profit incentives interact to perpetuate crime ecosystems. This chapter concludes by advocating synchronized countermeasures: harmonized transnational legislation, AI-enhanced forensic accounting, and "follow-the-money" public–private partnerships. By linking legal accountability to economic disincentives, the authors offer policymakers a blueprint to disrupt financial crime's lifecycle, transforming reactive enforcement into proactive systemic resilience.

Corruption and Crime in Finance, 1–26

Published under exclusive licence by Emerald Publishing Limited
doi:10.1108/978-1-83708-170-720261003

Keywords: Transnational financial crime; illicit financial flows; regulatory arbitrage; forensic economics; cyber-enabled fraud

1. Introduction

In today's hyperconnected world, money moves at the speed of code, and digital footprints are the new currency of power. Financial systems that once relied on face-to-face transactions, paper trails, and human oversight have evolved into sprawling, borderless infrastructures fueled by algorithms, machine learning, and blockchain protocols. While this transformation has brought unprecedented efficiency and convenience from contactless payments to real-time global transfers, it has also opened the floodgates to a darker parallel world where financial crime operates invisibly, strategically, and with growing impunity. Imagine an international banking system where illicit money flows seamlessly across jurisdictions, shielded by layers of shell companies and encrypted transactions. In such a system, criminals no longer need to rob banks physically; instead, they can exploit smart contracts, hack decentralized finance (DeFi) platforms, or deploy deepfake audio to impersonate CEOs and authorize fraudulent transfers. Within this digital maze, financial crime has not only survived but thrived, morphing into a trillion-dollar global industry that often outpaces regulatory attempts to contain it (WEF, 2024).

Financial crime, traditionally defined as unlawful acts committed to gain financial or professional advantage, such as money laundering, tax evasion, fraud, and embezzlement (Europol, 2023), is no longer confined to dusty ledgers and white-collar offices. Increasingly, it is being conducted over cyberspace, using an arsenal of tools including malware, ransomware, crypto wallets, and Artificial Intelligence (AI)-powered bots. The line between financial fraud and cyberattack has blurred so significantly that scholars have begun referring to this emerging domain as financial cybercrime, an umbrella term for crimes committed digitally for illegal financial gain (Kuzior et al., 2024). This includes not only stealing money but also manipulating markets, laundering proceeds, or financing terrorism through anonymized networks. What makes financial cybercrime particularly insidious is its stealth and scalability. With a few lines of malicious code, a cybercriminal can exploit a vulnerability in a bank's server in New York, mask their trail through anonymizing browsers in Amsterdam, and launder the stolen funds via cryptocurrency mixers in Singapore, all within minutes. And with each leap in technology, whether in AI-generated deepfakes or quantum-proof encryption, criminals acquire new tools to exploit and evade. In contrast, law enforcement often tends to employ a reactive approach, which is hampered by regulatory fragmentation, jurisdictional mismatches, and outdated investigation tools.

The consequences are not abstract. In past years, globally, the economy has endured several high-profile financial crime scandals, demonstrating how systemic and institutional shortcomings could be exploited. The Danske Bank money laundering scandal includes over €200 billion in suspicious transactions from Russia to Estonian accounts. This is just one example of how legitimate banking systems are co-opted for illicit purposes (Reuters, 2022). The Wirecard scam, which calibrated a fintech poster child of Germany, which collapsed under revelations of mission billions and forged balance in various countries. Likewise, ransom attacks such as the Colonial Pipeline breach in the United States, interrupted the petroleum supply chain and showed the power of cybercriminals to extort millions of dollars through encrypted crypto payments while escaping traceability (FBI, 2021). The emergence of DeFi, although revolutionary, yet has led to additional layers of opacity and complexity. Smart contracts and decentralized marketplaces operate without any central body; this makes them a perfect vehicle for money laundering and fraud (Kamps & Kleinberg, 2018). With the proliferation of nonfungible tokens (NFTs), privacy coins, and also synthetic identities, the financial crime landscape resembles a digital conflict between innovation and regulation.

Efforts to combat these crimes are underway, yet remain uncoordinated and uneven. The Financial Action Task Force (FATF) has established global anti-money laundering (AML) and combating the financing of terrorism (CFT) frameworks, and countries are forced to enforce Know Your Customer (KYC) and beneficial ownership regulations (FATF, 2023). Still, loopholes exist. Offshore financial centers continue to protect corrupt actors behind opaque trusts. National regulators lack coordination, and even within countries, agencies often operate in silos. This patchwork response creates what experts call regulatory arbitrage, the exploitation of legal asymmetries between jurisdictions by criminals to maximize profits and minimize detection (Zetzsche et al., 2020).

Compounding the problem is the technological asymmetry between threat actors and defenders. Criminals increasingly utilize graph neural networks, autoencoders, and generative adversarial networks (GANs) to automate fraud and obfuscate transaction patterns (Johora et al., 2024). Meanwhile, many regulators still rely on outdated monitoring systems or manually flagged suspicious activity reports that cannot keep up with the pace and volume of modern financial crime (Demetis, 2010). It is within this context that this chapter seeks to intervene. Rather than treating financial crime as merely a legal or technical issue, we propose an integrated legal–economic diagnostic framework that maps how regulatory failures, economic incentives, and technological innovation interact to create fertile ground for crime. This framework not only identifies vulnerabilities but also provides a roadmap for systemic resilience, balancing enforcement with prevention, and regulation with technological adaptability. We organize our analysis along three critical dimensions:

(1) Scope—What are the typologies of contemporary financial crime, and how are they evolving with technology?
(2) Impact—How do these crimes affect institutions, markets, public trust, and development outcomes?
(3) Evolution—What structural and technological changes are accelerating the sophistication and spread of financial crime?

Each section draws on real-world case studies, current literature, and empirical insights to unpack the micro-dynamics of criminal behavior and the macro-level consequences for global finance. We conclude with forward-looking recommendations aimed at fostering coordinated, technology-enhanced, and policy-informed responses. These include AI-powered forensic tools, public–private intelligence-sharing frameworks, and international legislative harmonization. In sum, the financial crime of the 21st century is no longer a niche concern for forensic accountants or compliance officers. It is a rapidly expanding, tech-driven ecosystem that threatens the stability of markets, the integrity of institutions, and the security of nations. To confront it effectively requires nothing less than rethinking how we diagnose, disrupt, and defend against financial exploitation in the digital era.

2. Expanding Scope of Financial Crime

2.1 Traditional and Emerging Typologies

Traditional crimes such as fraud, smuggling, extortion, corruption, and robbery continue to serve as foundational predicate offenses for money laundering and terrorist financing (Patel et al., 2023; Simser, 2012). These crimes manifest in various ways. Deceptive practices, such as securities fraud, generate illicit capital (Georgiou, 2017; Ranjan, 2015). Smuggling, particularly across borders, facilitates the covert transfer of wealth and assets. Corrupt extortion and institutional corruption significantly drain public resources and erode trust in governance structures (Katica, 2024). However, these criminal activities are no longer restricted to physical environments. In recent years, digitization and globalization have enabled the emergence of new typologies that transcend traditional boundaries. For example, cyber-enabled fraud now includes ransomware attacks—as seen in the Colonial Pipeline case—phishing schemes, and AI-driven social engineering.

Moreover, the rise of virtual assets like cryptocurrencies has provided new avenues for laundering money and financing terrorism, given their potential for anonymity and lack of centralized control (Samantha Maitland Irwin et al., 2011). Trade-based money laundering has also become prevalent, involving the manipulation of invoices and supply chains to disguise the movement of illicit funds (Chelliah & Prasad, 2017). Similarly, cross-border payment systems are increasingly abused through shell companies and complex jurisdictional arrangements that obscure the origin and destination of illicit financial flows (IFFs) (Rowley, 2024). Another critical trend is proliferation finance, in which illicit networks are used to mislead financial practices for supporting weapons of mass destruction (WMD) projects (Stewart et al., 2020). This integration of traditional and digital tactics has resulted significantly in hybrid threats. Traditional typologies, for instance, now involve crypto-based bribes, whilst profits from smuggling activities are laundered by forged trade documentations. These transforming typologies highlight the need for adaptive legal and regulatory frameworks to combat more complex financial crimes worldwide.

These shifts are not just theoretical but observable in real-world crime trends, especially within cryptocurrency markets. As Fig. 1.1 illustrates, the transaction volumes associated with various types of crypto-related crimes have shifted over recent years, revealing evolving criminal priorities and the dynamic impact of market conditions.

Notably, while most categories of crypto crime have seen declining transaction volumes, stolen funds saw a year-over-year increase. This reflects not only the adaptability of criminal actors but also the role that speculative market cycles play in shaping illicit financial behavior. It also underscores how even in bear markets, specific typologies (like hacking and asset theft) remain resilient due to low technical barriers and high rewards.

2.2 Technological Enablers

Technology acts as both a catalyst and force multiplier for financial crime, increasing criminal conduct's scope, speed, and stealth (Europol, 2021). AI has evolved into a powerful tool for manipulation. Generative Adversarial Network (GANs) generate synthetic identities or deepfake documents to avoid KYC inspections (Caldarelli & Ellul, 2021). Meanwhile, algorithmic trading approaches are employed for market manipulation by spoofing or pump-and-dump tactics, specifically in unregulated contexts such as the cryptocurrency market (Foley et al., 2019). Crypto "rug pulls" are prominent examples of developers disappearing after attracting investor funds under false pretenses (Glaeser et al., 2022).

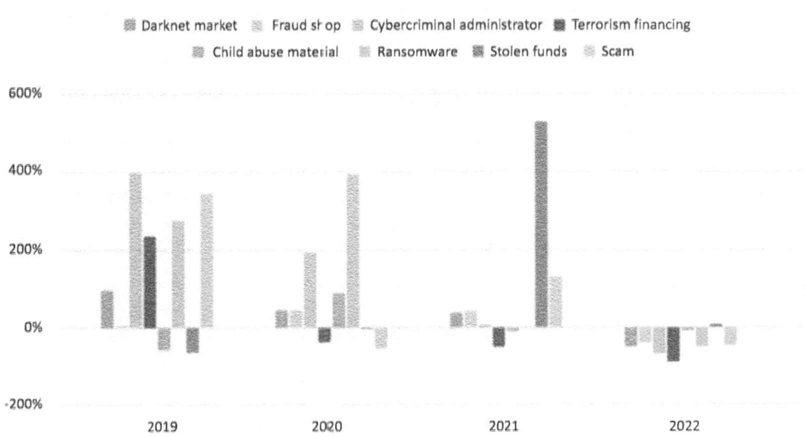

Fig. 1.1. YoY Percent Change in Value Received by Crime Type, 2019–2022. *Source*: Crypto Crime Report (2023), Chainalysis

Anonymity infrastructure encourages crime by obscuring digital footprints. The dark web, privacy-focused cryptocurrencies such as Monero and Zcash, and encrypted browsing tools like Tor enable malicious individuals to conduct illicit transactions with minimal traceability. These technologies are being used for ransomware payments, illegal arms sales, and drug trafficking (see Fig. 1.2). DeFi has brought a new dimension of risks. Through smart contracts, DeFi platforms enable automated and jurisdiction-less financial activity, often bypassing traditional regulatory oversight (Kamps & Kleinberg, 2018). This opens the door to various crimes, from unregulated lending to instantaneous asset mixing and laundering. The $3.8 billion Euler Finance hack in 2023 is a striking example of how DeFi can be exploited through sophisticated code-based attacks, underscoring the sector's inherent vulnerabilities (Chainalysis, 2023). These technological enablers challenge conventional regulatory tools and demand innovative, tech-savvy responses from policymakers and financial watchdogs.

3. Impact of Financial Crime

Financial crime is not an individual malpractice or an isolated rare event but a systemic danger that vibrates through economies, institutions, and societies. Its effects are not one-dimensional—it destabilizes economically, delegitimizes institutions, and hinders social progress. As such, financial crime leads to various aspects such as fraud and money laundering, leading to market disruption and discouraging investment. Hence, it decreases the credibility and public trust in

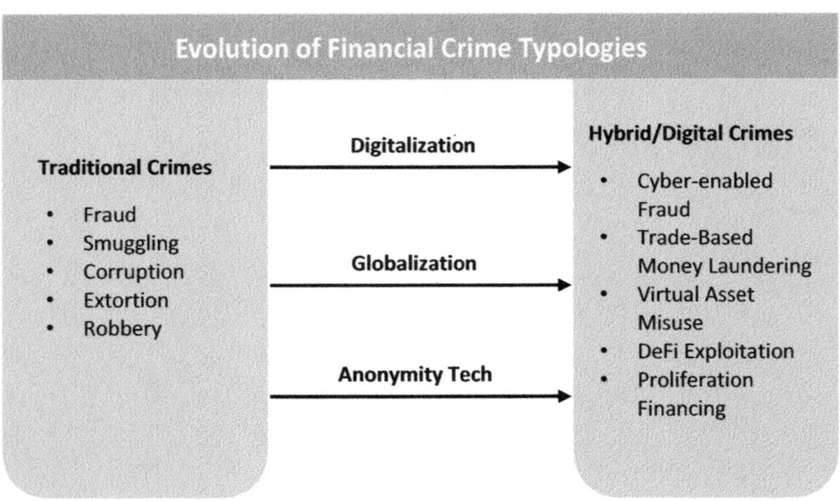

Fig. 1.2. Evolution From Traditional to Digital Financial Crime Typologies. *Source*: Author's work.

public and private institutions. Such effects are especially sharp in the age of accelerated technological transformation and financial globalization, when the scale of illegal participants can exceed the resources of policymakers and law enforcement services. The section will explain the financial crime costs in four key dimensions, including economic, institutional, social, and developmental costs, based on recent statistics and cases around the world.

3.1 Economic and Institutional Effects

The foundation of any financial system is the public trust. When the Illicit financial activity is systemic and widespread, or when prominent financial controversies arise, the credibility and social confidence in the institutions (i.e., banks, regulators, and even governments) can be heavily undermined. A Danske Bank scandal in 2020, where more than 200 billion euros in suspicious transactions took place, resulted not only in regulatory fines but also in the sudden drop of trust in the European banking system (Reuters, 2022). Likewise, the German fintech company Wirecard went bankrupt after its fraud-related business practices were in the spotlight, highlighting the fragility of regulatory regimes and undermining the communal spirit of trust in corporate and governmental governance.

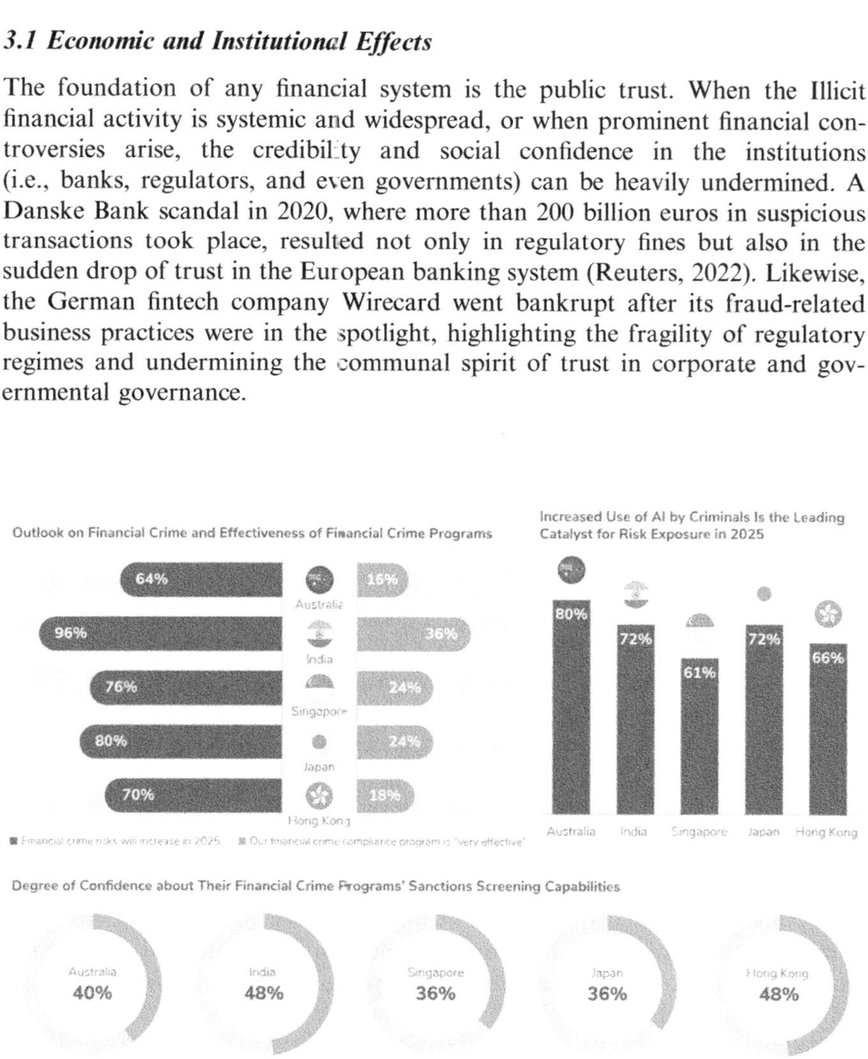

Fig. 1.3. Financial Crime Risk Perception and Sanctions Screening Confidence by Country (2025). *Source*: FCR (2025).

The trust undermining is not only a matter of reputation but also has economic ramifications. The depositors can withdraw funds, investors' confidence may erode, and the cost of capital in affected institutions can increase dramatically. A survey by the WEF (2024) found that 67% of financial executive respondents said that the most significant negativity brought about by financial crime was the loss of public trust, even more than the direct loss of funds (see Fig. 1.3). Financial crime distorts markets by introducing illicit funds, manipulating asset prices, and undermining fair competition. One example is money laundering, which can cause the overheating of real estate markets, drive out legitimate purchasers, and develop asset bubbles, as witnessed in cities such as London, Vancouver, and Dubai. Any scheme of manipulating the market, including the pump-and-dump schemes in cryptocurrency exchanges, undermines investors' faith and destabilizes any emerging market.

Trade and investment patterns are also distorted due to IFFs. UN Office on Drugs and Crime (UNODC) estimates that IFFs represent up to 5% of the global GDP, with a disproportionate rate of effect in the developing economies (UNODC, 2022). Such an unjust allocation of resources also hinders effective investment and innovation, as legitimate businesses find it challenging to compete with those who are favored with the proceeds of crime. Low- and middle-income countries are severely impacted by the financial costs resulting from illicit financial activities, which impede a nation's growth efforts and financial stability. Illegal financial outflows, tax evasion, and corruption deprive states of resources that could be used to develop infrastructure, healthcare, and education. Global Financial Integrity (2023) estimates that developing economies lose over $1 trillion annually to IFFs. This figure often exceeds foreign direct investment and official development assistance. This financial outflow weakens the state and creates further chains of economic stagnation. The total amount of sub-Saharan Africa's illicit financial outflows between 2000 and 2020 exceeded external debt obligations by the region and thus eroded much of the fiscal capacity to support developmental projects like infrastructure, health, and education (GFI, 2023). The outcome is perpetual underfinancing of crucial public services and a diminished capacity to react to economic shocks.

3.2 Social and Developmental Costs

The World Bank stated that the diversion of funds from critical societal services is the most apparent manifestation of the social cost of financial crime. The numbers alone prove that corruption is a significant contributor to that cost. The embezzlement of state finances and the acceptance of bribes by officials means that funds intended for healthcare, education, and infrastructure are redirected to personal profit. Increase the cost of basic public services by up to 20%, placing the greatest burden on the poorest sections of society. This deviation is not restricted to direct stealing. Tax evasion and money laundering erode the tax base, leaving governments with the option of reducing services or increasing taxes on law-abiding citizens. The outcome is the vicious circle of worsening service quality, citizen deception, and enhanced openness to additional corruption.

Organized crime and terrorism are multiplicators of financial crime. This is the case with the profits made through fraud, smuggling, and online crime that are then returned to the wider criminal activities by financing acts of drug trafficking, human trafficking, and even terrorist groups (Europol, 2023). This offers a circular environment of financial crime, as financial crime not only creates illegitimate finance but also supports and promotes other illicit activities. Criminal networks have also been complemented by the adoption of new technologies, like cryptocurrencies and DeFi, which increases the scale and persistence of the criminal networks. For example, law enforcement agencies report that ransomware attacks are also increasingly used to finance transnational criminal organizations (FATF, 2023).

One of the most dangerous effects of financial crime is probably that it leads to inequality and governance decay. Financial crime maintains power disparities and undermines the rule of law by absconding with the responsibility of elites and criminal subjects. In nations where corruption and other money laundering are endemic, people lose trust in the democratic institutions, and there is a lack of social mobility as well. According to the IMF (2023), economies with high financial crime rates have poorer economic growth, increased inequality, and poorer human development indicators. This is not a loss of income alone but a loss of opportunity, social cohesion, and legitimacy of the state.

Fig. 1.4 presents a highly shocking reality where USD 3.1 trillion a massive amount coming from illegal sources, mainly divided into three key categories, including money laundering (47.42% – USD 1.47 trillion), fraud (15.66% – USD 485.6 billion), and other crimes (25.25% – USD 782.9 billion). While these numbers are alarming on their own, beyond these numbers, it is essential to understand what this costs us as a global society, particularly in low- and

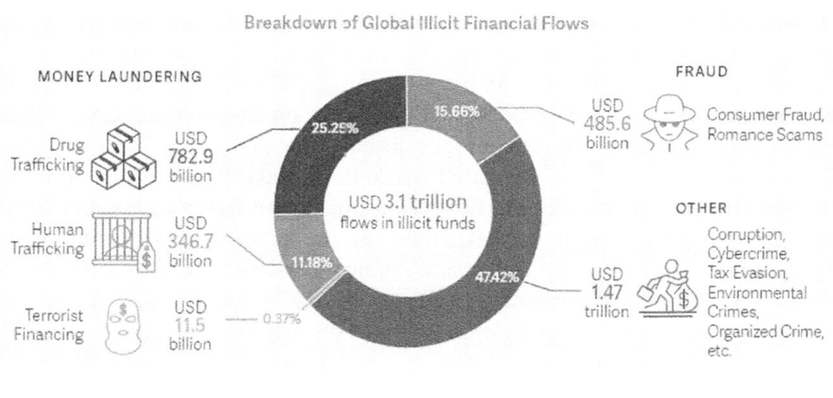

Fig. 1.4. Illicit Financial Flows. *Source*: Global Financial and Economic Crime Outlook 2025

middle-income countries. These illicit flows have a negative impact on domestic resources, leading to a decreased ratio of resources that could otherwise be used for public services. According to UNCTAD (2020), Africa loses USD 88.6 billion annually through IFFs—nearly 3.7% of the continent's GDP—affecting its ability to fund its development. These flows weaken state capacity, exacerbate inequality, and hinder the achievement of the SDGs (Souza, 2021). In addition, human costs are another element that gets impacted by this illicit finance, including exploitation and suffering in terms of Human trafficking (USD 346.7B) involves forced labor, child exploitation, and sexual slavery, and drug trafficking (USD 782.9B) devastates communities by fueling addiction, gang violence, and overburdened health systems.

4. Legal and Systemic Vulnerabilities

Financial crime persists not simply due to individual malfeasance but because of a deeper, systemic architecture that enables and sometimes even incentivizes illicit behavior. This architecture is characterized by fragmented regulation, gaps in jurisdictional cooperation, and technological asymmetries that collectively form a fertile environment for criminal exploitation. This section critically examines the legal and institutional blind spots that financial criminals exploit—not as isolated oversights but as interconnected structural deficiencies that demand a systemic diagnostic lens.

4.1 Regulatory Fragmentation and Jurisdictional Gaps

Despite the awareness and years of reform, AML and financial system transparency remain stubbornly compartmentalized. The lack of unity, both a legal jurisdictions and regulatory bodies as well as in technological systems, provides a breeding ground for exploitation. The international AML system is very uneven. Although there is an internationally accepted set of standards given by the FATF, adoption is not consistent. As an illustration, although FATF has highlighted the necessity of regulating digital assets, in 2023, only 35% of the jurisdictions had enacted strong AML controls on cryptocurrencies (FATF, 2023). This fragmentation encourages jurisdiction shopping, where criminal organizations find the least regulated markets to make illegal deals. Although consolidated economies, like the European Union, are trying to combat collection efforts through common AML strategies, enforcement gaps, mainly focusing on nonresident banking and online finance, persist in devaluing the overall effects of such unification (see Fig. 1.5).

The limitations of international extradition treaties further hamper the prosecution of financial crime. Political considerations, legal technicalities, and procedural delays often result in safe havens for white-collar criminals. A recent INTERPOL report indicates that over 60% of Red Notices related to financial crime have experienced significant delays or outright refusals in extradition, undermining the deterrent capacity of international law (INTERPOL, 2022).

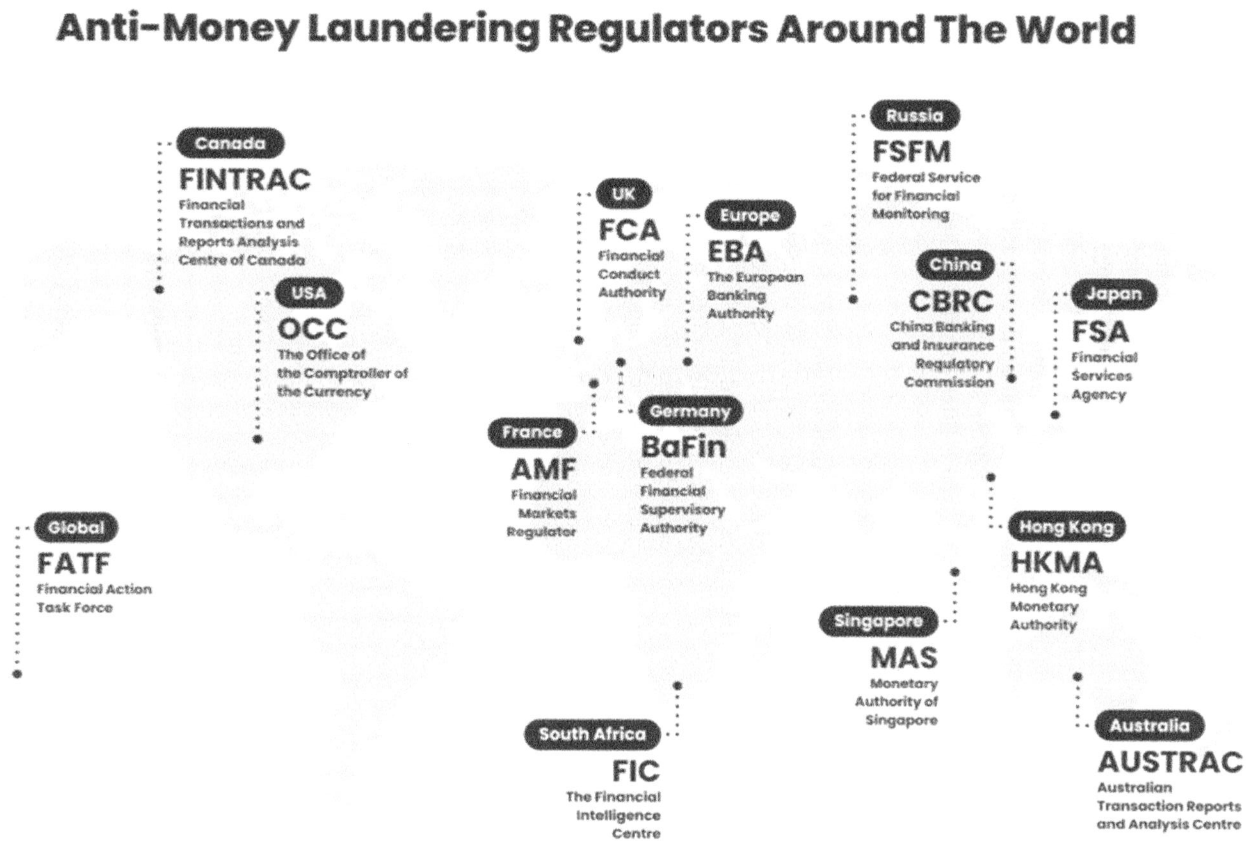

Fig. 1.5. Global Landscape of Anti-money Laundering (AML) Regulators. *Source*: Anti-money laundering regulators around the world. SEON.

Cases involving whistle-blowers or controversial developers, such as the Tornado Cash incident, reveal how these treaties can be entangled in geopolitics rather than legal clarity.

Perhaps the most potent weapon in the arsenal of financial criminals is the legal yet opaque world of offshore financial vehicles. Anonymous trusts, shell corporations, and layered ownership structures—often domiciled in jurisdictions like the British Virgin Islands or Delaware—make it nearly impossible to identify the true beneficial owners of assets. The Pandora Papers (ICIJ, 2021) revealed that over 68% of identified shell company structures involved US or British-linked jurisdictions, many of which were used in major fraud schemes, including Danske Bank's notorious €200 billion laundering operation through Estonian nonresident accounts (EBA, 2019). As the TJN (2023) succinctly put it: "The difference between a tax haven and a crime haven is often just the quality of paperwork."

4.2 Case Studies

Table 1.1 shows the high-profile case studies from 2007 to 2021. We examine a series of high-profile case studies to understand how these systemic weaknesses play out in practice. Each example underscores a specific set of vulnerabilities and demonstrates how these gaps are exploited at scale.

Fig. 1.6 visualizes a framework that illustrates how disparate weaknesses—often treated as isolated policy problems—are mutually reinforcing. Fragmented legal regimes allow jurisdictional arbitrage, further compounded by the technological lag in surveillance and enforcement tools. Criminal networks do not merely adapt to these conditions; they flourish because of them.

These case studies collectively demonstrate that financial crime is not an aberration within the system but a consequence of the system's current design. From laundering billions through Estonian accounts to exploiting regulatory silos in Europe, the recurring theme is that governance structures—laws, treaties, and institutions—are being systematically repurposed to serve illicit ends. The rise of crypto-enabled financial crime, opaque offshore vehicles, and politicized extradition processes reveals a troubling dynamic: laws meant to protect the public interest often become loopholes that endanger it. As we transition into the next section, we pivot from diagnosis to design. Section 5 develops a framework to map these vulnerabilities systematically and proposes reengineering tools that match the scale and sophistication of financial crime.

5. Toward an Integrated Diagnostic Framework

5.1 Legal–Economic Diagnostic Mapping

Financial crime is not a random anomaly, it's the predictable output of a broken system. For decades, policymakers and scholars have treated its symptoms in isolation: legal scholars dissect regulatory gaps, economists model criminal incentives, and technologists chase digital threats. Yet this siloed approach misses the synergy between these forces—a synergy that criminals exploit with

Table 1.1. Case Studies From 2007 to 2021.

No	Case	Vulnerability	Exploitation	Systemic Lesson
1	Danske Bank Scandal (2007–2015)	Weak EU AML directives and Estonia's permissive oversight of nonresident accounts.	> €200 billion in suspicious transactions were routed through Danske Bank's Estonian branch, largely involving Russian oligarchs and politically exposed persons (Bohr, 2018).	Even when supranational regulations exist, inconsistent enforcement at the national level can collapse the entire compliance framework.
2	Wirecard Collapse (2020)	Regulatory capture and prioritization of market stability by BaFin, Germany's financial watchdog.	Wirecard falsely declared over $2.1 billion in assets held in Asian subsidiaries, bolstered by forged audit statements (EY, 2020).	A siloed regulatory environment—where oversight bodies fail to question cross-border financial flows—can facilitate prolonged deception.
3	Colonial Pipeline Ransomware Attack (2021)	Absence of mandatory Know Your Customer (KYC) checks on decentralized crypto exchanges.	The ransomware group DarkSide was able to extract 75 Bitcoin (valued at $4.4 million) without triggering red flags on the blockchain (FBI, 2021).	Technological asymmetries undermine traditional monitoring systems, where criminals adapt faster than regulators.
4	Pandora Papers Leak (2021)	Legal opacity surrounds beneficial ownership in over 50 jurisdictions.	The leak revealed that over 35 heads of state and government officials had concealed approximately $11.3 trillion in offshore accounts (ICIJ, 2021).	This case exemplifies "regulatory arbitrage," where systemic gaps are not merely exploited but actively engineered into profit-making strategies.

(Continued)

Table 1.1. *(Continued)*

No	Case	Vulnerability	Exploitation	Systemic Lesson
5	Cryptocurrency "Rug Pulls" (e.g., BBC News, 2021)	Lack of oversight in the decentralized finance (DeFi) space, including unaudited smart contracts and anonymous developer teams.	The Squid Game Token fraud saw developers abscond with \$3.3 million after crashing the token's value to zero following a staged sell-off (Chainalysis, 2022).	The combination of anonymity, low regulation, and high return creates an asymmetry where risk is socialized while reward is privatized—an imbalance explored in Section 5.2.
6	FTX Collapse (2022–2023)	Regulatory fragmentation in crypto oversight (SEC vs. CFTC turf wars; Bahamas' lax governance).	\$8B customer funds misappropriated via unregulated "backdoor" transfers between FTX and Alameda Research (U.S. DOJ, 2023).	Jurisdictional arbitrage is enabled by registering in "crypto-friendly" havens with weak supervision.
7	Binance \$4.3B Settlement (2023)	Inconsistent AML enforcement across jurisdictions (e.g., no KYC for Iranian and Syrian users).	>100K illicit transactions processed, including \$899M for ransomware and darknet markets (FinCEN, 2023).	Global exchanges exploit "weakest-link" jurisdictions to evade oversight.
8	ABLV Bank Liquidation (2022–Present)	The EU banking passport system allows high-risk entities to operate cross-border.	Latvian bank laundered \$2B + for Russian missile procurement networks via shell companies (ECB, 2022).	Harmonized markets ≠ harmonized risk controls.

9	OFAC Sanctions Evasion Network (2023)	Opacity in trade finance and shipping registries.	$2B Russian oil sold via "ghost fleet" of tankers using forged bills of lading and UAE shell companies (OFAC, 2023).	Trade-based laundering adapts to sanctions using multi-jurisdictional layering.
10	Russian Oil Price Cap Evasion (2023–2024)	Lack of global shipping registry verification.	"Shadow fleet" of 1,800+ unflagged tankers moved $15B + sanctioned oil using Cyprus/Greek intermediaries (IMF, 2024).	Illustrates "regulatory arbitrage" at the maritime-law level (Section 5.1).

Source: Author's work.

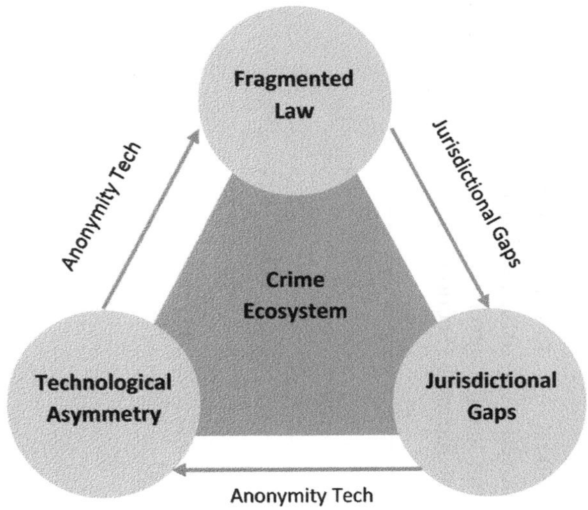

Fig. 1.6. The Vulnerability Triad. *Source*: Author's work.

surgical precision. Our integrated diagnostic framework bridges this divide, mapping how regulatory architecture, profit incentives, and technological enablers coalesce into self-sustaining crime ecosystems. Consider "regulatory arbitrage"—the art of exploiting jurisdictional asymmetries. Traditional views framed it as a legal loophole (e.g., setting up shell companies in Delaware or the British Virgin Islands). But this misses its economic engine. When Danske Bank funneled €200B through Estonia (Section 4.2), it wasn't just dodging EU directives—it was leveraging cost-benefit calculus: the profit from moving illicit funds outweighed the negligible risk of detection. Similarly, crypto "rug pulls" thrive where anonymous DeFi developers face zero accountability but reap millions (BBC News, 2021). This is not mere lawbreaking; it's a rational business model built on imbalanced risk-reward equations.

Our framework's ability to move beyond static categorization and offer a dynamic, systems-based analysis of financial crime makes it novel. Unlike traditional models that treat vulnerabilities as isolated flaws, our approach identifies dynamic feedback loops—how regulatory actions unintentionally incentivize innovation in illicit tools. For example, the emergence of privacy coins such as Monero directly followed FATF's tightening of cryptocurrency surveillance, offering bad actors new avenues for money laundering under the guise of decentralization and anonymity. Another distinguishing feature is our vulnerability triangulation model, illustrated in Fig. 1.7. This conceptual visualization shows how financial crime thrives at the intersection of three converging forces: regulatory gaps, profit incentives, and technological asymmetries. These vectors are not abstract—each has measurable manifestations. Regulatory weaknesses, such as lax KYC protocols, create openings; staggering profit potential, such as ransomware's reported 2,620% return on investment in 2023, draws in opportunists; and

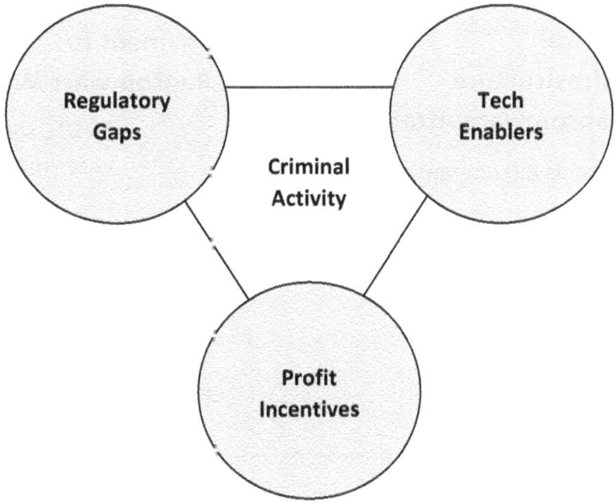

Fig. 1.7. The Legal–Economic–Technological Nexus.
Source: Author's work.

technological disparities, like the rise of AI-generated "synthetic identities," consistently outpace existing verification frameworks.

Crucially, the framework also introduces a predictive dimension. By quantifying the relationships among these elements, we move from a reactive paradigm to one of proactive risk modeling. For instance, INTERPOL data suggest that a mere 1% drop in extradition effectiveness corresponds with a 15% rise in cross-border fraud. This empirical linkage allows policymakers to model the downstream consequences of inaction or poorly coordinated reforms, thereby reorienting financial crime prevention from episodic enforcement to anticipatory governance.

Critically, this framework exposes why past interventions failed. While well-intentioned, the FATF's AML standards ignored how fragmentation becomes a commodity, traded by criminals who strategically "shop" for weak jurisdictions. Meanwhile, economists overlooked how illicit markets mimic legitimate ones: ransomware now operates franchise models with customer service desks, while darknet platforms offer Yelp-style vendor ratings.

5.2 Role of Forensic Economics

If Section 5.1 diagnoses the disease, forensic economics delivers the cure. This emerging discipline—where data science meets financial investigation—transforms abstract frameworks into actionable intelligence. Forget dusty ledgers; modern forensic economists wield AI-driven network analysis, blockchain forensics, and behavioral econometrics to trace illicit flows through layers of obfuscation. Fig. 1.8 presents, why this framework matters

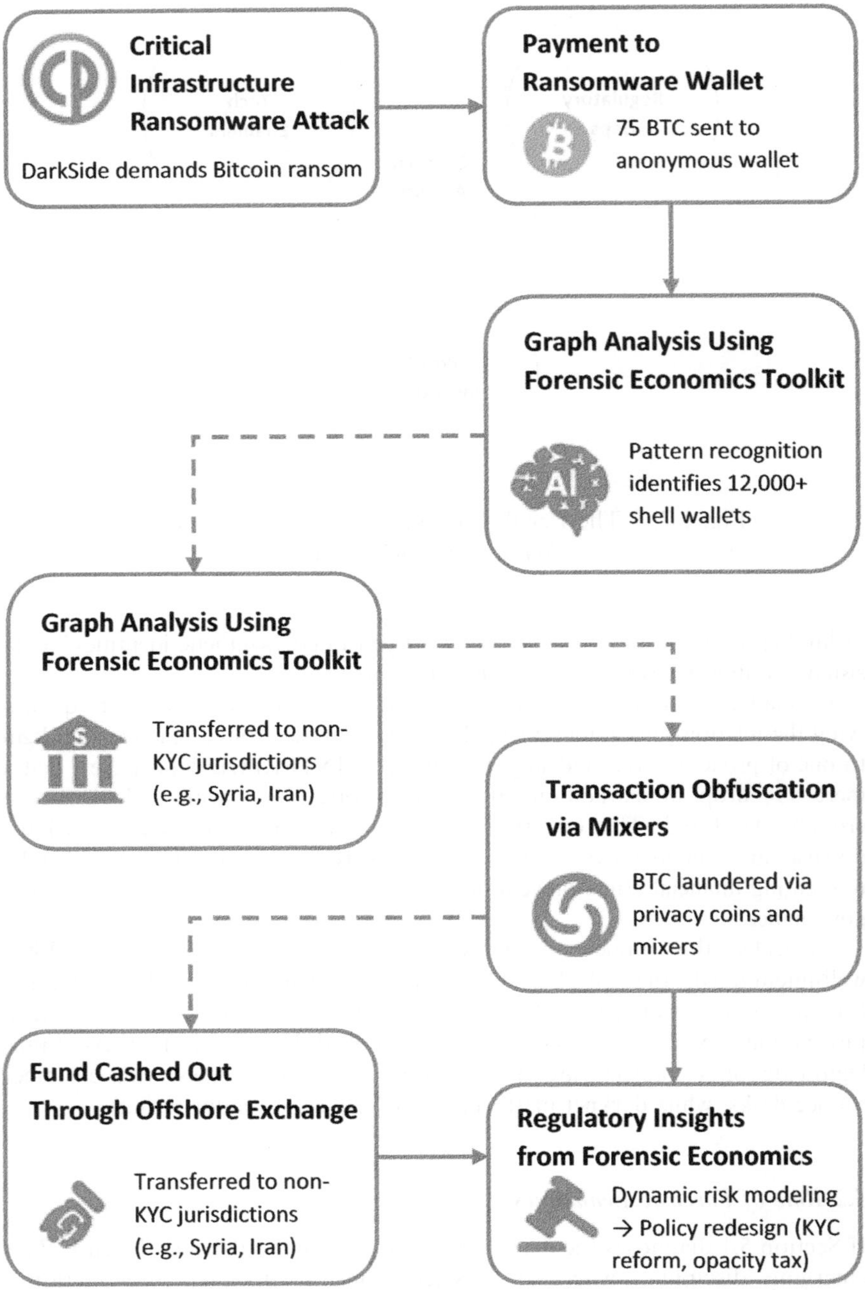

Fig. 1.8. Forensic Economics in Action. *Source*: Author's work.

lies in its capacity to unmask the complexity and interconnectedness of modern financial crime. Take, for example, the case where $4.3 billion flowed through Binance without undergoing Know Your Customer (KYC) checks (as explored in Section 4.2). Traditional audits interpreted these as isolated transactions. However, a deeper forensic economic analysis using graph algorithms uncovered a broader pattern: funds were funneled through over 12,000 shell wallets, many of which clustered around unregulated exchanges and traced back to users in sanctioned jurisdictions like Iran and Syria. This illustrates how systemic vulnerabilities can remain hidden without multi-dimensional mapping tools.

Moreover, the framework empowers predictive risk modeling. We can detect emerging patterns long before they scale by training machine learning models on historical laundering operations, such as the Danske Bank case and its Estonian nonresident corridors. One current example is the evasion of Russian oil sanctions via so-called "ghost fleets," which our model flagged using trade and maritime data before it reached international headlines (IMF, 2024). This proactive capability transforms regulatory responses from reactive crackdowns to strategic preemption. Lastly, the model provides behavioral insights into the decision-making logic of criminal actors. Criminal networks do not act randomly; instead, they strategically allocate resources across tools like crypto mixers, hawala networks, and trade misinvoicing depending on the relative enforcement strength in different regions. Agent-based simulations reveal these adaptive behaviors, identifying where legal, technological, or diplomatic interventions would have the highest impact. This level of behavioral granularity ensures that financial crime prevention is more intelligent, targeted, and cost-effective.

Traditional law enforcement viewed financial crime through a legal lens—prosecuting individuals after the fact. Forensic economics adopts a systemic view: treating illicit networks as adaptive organisms. For example, by applying epidemiological models to the Pandora Papers leak, we identified how "infection" (corruption) spreads fastest where transparency thresholds fall below 40% (e.g., Seychelles trusts). This is not just academic—it enables surgical policy: strengthening ownership registries in high-risk hubs. The critical blind spot our framework addresses is the overemphasis on detection at the expense of disruption. While prior research has focused heavily on AML algorithms and compliance systems, we shift the lens toward making financial crime structurally unprofitable. If regulatory arbitrage turns certain jurisdictions into "crime havens," then forensic economics can be used to starve them out economically. For example, implementing dynamic risk pricing—such as taxing jurisdictions with opacity scores above 60% (based on the Tax Justice Network index)—helps offset the global costs of monitoring hidden flows (see Fig. 1.9). Likewise, incentive inversion strategies, like rewarding whistleblowers with 10–30% of recovered assets (as demonstrated in the $200 million Binance settlement), harness insider knowledge to undermine criminal networks from within.

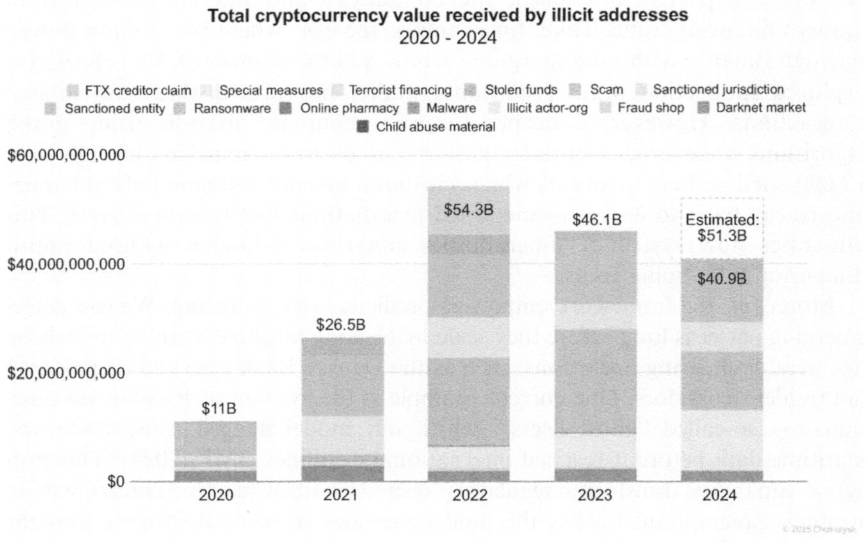

Fig. 1.9. Cryptocurrency Flows to Illicit Addresses (2020–2024). *Source*: The Crypto Crime Report Chainalysis (2025).

6. Policy Recommendations

Financial crime in the 21st century does not exist in the shadows, but rather in the structural blind spots of globalization, regulatory balkanization, and technological asymmetry. To this end, our recommended suggestions support a triad approach based on legal harmonization, technological innovation, and shared governance. Collectively, these tackle the symptoms of financial crime and the structural facilitators of that crime. This section outlines three interconnected policy recommendations that aim to build long-term resilience: (1) harmonizing legal frameworks, (2) leveraging technological innovation, and (3) fostering public–private partnerships. Together, these pillars offer a path toward transforming vulnerability into vigilance.

6.1 Harmonization of Legal Frameworks

It is the exposure of the insufficiency of national silos in enforcement and legislation due to the spread of cross-border financial crime. The lack of uniformity in national legal systems is one of the priority issues that must be addressed today. Similar standards exist at the international level, such as the FATF standards, where enforcement differs significantly. This opens the door to regulatory arbitrage, whereby illegal actors can merely process their money through the least resistant parts of the global chain. To respond to the same, nations must shift toward internationally accepted and enforceable global standards, particularly in essential spheres like AML, regulation of cryptocurrencies, and beneficial ownership transparency. Introducing a multilateral treaty obliging countries to regulate digital assets and share data across borders would be a first step. Similarly to how the OECD's (CRS) revolutionized the landscape of tax compliance, an analogous model would greatly benefit the landscape of financial crime enforcement, bringing the much-needed clarity and consistency.

Some areas have laws in place; however, they tend to fail in practice. In secrecy jurisdictions, most financial crimes use lawful vehicles such as anonymous shell companies or offshore trusts. Such structures enable criminals to operate under the guise of legitimacy. Through these structures, criminals can work under the guise of legitimacy. Governments should require open registries of beneficial ownership, impose universal KYC standards, and launch automatic cross-border information exchange. The initial point is the establishment of transparency universally, i.e., commonly applied to a standard like the CRS of the OECD, along with the public availability of beneficial ownership data. Moreover, failure by jurisdictions to adhere to the international standards of transparency continuously ought to have consequences, including restrictions on access to global markets or sanctions. Nationally, reform efforts must strive to enable financial regulators to conduct extraterritorial investigations, especially in cases of crypto-crimes that occur across international borders and digital asset laundering schemes. Unless the following measures are taken, genuine legal structures will remain subverted by the loopholes in the system.

6.2 Technological Solutions

As the techniques of criminal acts change, so must the methods, tools, and technology used. The volume and rapid pace of modern financial crime are incomparable to the traditional compliance systems that have significantly depended on manually marked suspicious transactions. In this regard, Artificial Intelligence is essential. Complex networks and hidden patterns in illicit flows are necessary to detect, and artificial intelligence-powered forensic analytics play a crucial role in this process. As an example, machine learning algorithms can be pretrained around historical typologies of fraud and behavioral modeling to detect anomalous activity within the banking system and blockchain networks. These tools have proven helpful in monitoring cryptocurrency-related crimes and complicated webs of shell entities already.

Nevertheless, few countries use them widely because of insufficient infrastructure or policy endorsement. To fill this gap, regulators have to invest in a national-level forensic analytics center and collaborate with the private sector to have access to state-of-the-art systems. Such initiatives should also be backed by frequent audits and ethical control to avoid abuse. Although blockchain was initially viewed as a place of anonymous crime, it has also provided significant detection tools. Tools such as Chainalysis, CipherTrace, and Elliptic can track illicit crypto transactions through transaction clustering, heuristics, and cross-chain analytics. All transactions are saved indefinitely, so even intricate laundering schemes involving numerous wallets and exchanges can be traced by an investigator with the appropriate tools. The government and regulators should embrace blockchain forensics platforms that detect real-time activity through clustering algorithms and transaction heuristics. It is also important to develop legal requirements so that virtual asset service providers (VASPs) have to incorporate such tools into their compliance activities. Moreover, smart contract auditing should be the new standard in DeFi platforms to prevent predatory scams, such as the so-called "rug pulls."

6.3 Public–Private Partnerships

Financial crime is often detected not by law enforcement, but by private firms, banks, fintech companies, and even social media platforms. Yet many actors operate in isolation, with limited channels for sharing intelligence or collaborating on investigations. A robust public–private intelligence framework modeled after the UK's Joint Money Laundering Intelligence Taskforce (JMLIT) is essential, as it fosters real-time data exchange between law enforcement and financial institutions.

We propose the creation of "Follow-the-Money Taskforces"—cross-sectoral teams embedded within financial hubs to jointly map IFFs, disrupt shell structures, and proactively monitor high-risk sectors (e.g., real estate, high-end art, or luxury goods). Siloed enforcement efforts are ill-suited for agile criminal networks. Instead, interoperability between regulators and institutions must be achieved through shared financial intelligence platforms. This includes real-time suspicious transaction reports (STRs), jointly maintained risk registries, and confidential whistleblower channels supported by legal protections and monetary incentives.

Private firms must also take ownership through self-regulation and certification schemes, where compliance with AML tech standards and ethical auditing protocols becomes a mark of industry leadership. Encouraging compliance through fines and reputational incentives, such as public transparency scores, could create market-based accountability. Trust and communication between stakeholders are crucial. Financial crime networks are agile and decentralized, so our responses must be the same. This enables the secure and confidential exchange of information between financial institutions, regulators, and enforcement agencies.

One practical step is the creation of shared intelligence platforms—databases where red flags, risk profiles, and transaction data can be securely shared. Strong legal safeguards would be necessary to protect privacy and ensure accountability; however, the benefits of coordinated action far outweigh the risks of continued fragmentation. Additionally, using insider knowledge, encouraging whistle-blower protections and rewards, as seen in the US Securities and Exchange Commission's approach—can help bring hidden crimes to light.

7. Conclusion

With the rapid expansion of financial crime, its scope has become broader and complex, driven by technological innovation and global interconnectedness. Financial crimes extend beyond traditional and basic fraud and embezzlement. The advanced methods of financial crimes include ransomware schemes, cryptocurrency-enabled money laundering, trade misinvoicing, and exploiting shell entities. Several factors contribute to the success of the illicit financial crimes, which are the (i) fragmented legal landscape, where laws are not the same across countries and don't work well together, (ii) technological advancements in contrast to regulatory frameworks lag, and (iii) inefficiency in the coordination between authorities across institutions. As reflected in this chapter, the financial crime ecosystem is not merely evolving: it is altering and moving faster than existing enforcement tactics. According to these developments, it is not just a law enforcement issue but a crisis of structure in governance. The existing strategies, which are mostly reactionary and disjointed, were insufficient to deal with agile, adaptive criminal networks. Low-level reform of law, scattered changes to regulation, and sluggish investigation processes tend to trail behind the speed of criminal innovation. Consequently, the financial system's vulnerability to failure does not lie entirely in the failure of regulation but lies in the absence of coordinated and anticipatory resilience.

This chapter holds forth a paradigm shift to proactive and systemic resilience-based enforcement to counter this. Systemic resilience refers to the ability of legal, technological, and organizational institutions to predict, absorb, and adjust to the changing environment of financial crimes. It combines synchronized international legal norms, AI-based forensic analytics, blockchain tracking, and built-in intelligence-sharing platforms. They are not discrete solutions but interconnected elements of a comprehensive defense architecture. Proactive governance models focus more on Prevention than punishment, as well as Intelligence-based intervention rather than investigation. Their goal is to interfere with existing crime systems on the structural level by changing the risk-reward assessment of financial crime and sealing problematic legal and technological loopholes.

On the other hand, reactive models tend to leave crimes unchecked, cause immense damage, after which they are almost impossible to reverse financially or on an institutional basis. Finally, financial crime cannot be perceived as an external aberration, but rather as a systemic consequence of regulatory, economic, and technological asymmetries worldwide. It will entail equally systemic solutions, solutions that are synchronized, evidence-based, and solutions based on the future. Only with such a proactive, deliberate policy framework can integrity, transparency, and the stability of the global financial system be ensured in the decades to come.

References

BBC News. (2021, November 2). *Squid Game cryptocurrency collapses in apparent scam*. BBC. https://www.bbc.com/news/technology-59109033

Bohr, H. (2018). *Almost periodic functions* (H. Cohn, Trans.). Dover Publications.

Caldarelli, G., & Ellul, J. (2021). The blockchain oracle problem in decentralized Finance—A multivocal approach. *Applied Sciences*, *11*(16), 7572. https://doi.org/10.3390/APP11167572

Chainalysis. (2022). *Crypto crime report 2022*. Chainalysis Inc. https://go.chainalysis.com/2022-crypto-crime-report.html

Chainalysis. (2023). *The 2023 crypto crime report*. https://www.chainalysis.com/

Chelliah, J., & Prasad, A. (2017). South Pacific transnational money laundering typologies. *Journal of Money Laundering Control*, *20*(4), 345–353. https://doi.org/10.1108/JMLC-11-2016-0045

Demetis, D. S. (2010). *Technology and anti-money laundering: A systems theory and risk-based approach*. Edward Elgar Publishing.

European Banking Authority. (2019). *Annual report 2019*. Publications Office of the European Union. https://eba.europa.eu/sites/default/files/document_library/885450/EBA%20Annual%20Report%202019.pdf

European Central Bank. (2022). *Annual report 2022*. European Central Bank. https://www.ecb.europa.eu/home/html/index.en.html

Europol. (2021). *Internet organised crime threat assessment (IOCTA)*. https://www.europol.europa.eu/cms/sites/default/files/documents/internet_organised_crime_threat_assessment_iocta_2021.pdf

Europol. (2023). *Consolidated annual activity report 2023*. Europol. https://www.europol.europa.eu/publications-events/publications/consolidated-annual-activity-report-caar-2023

Federal Bureau of Investigation. (2021). *Crime in the United States, 2021*. U.S. Department of Justice. https://www.hsdl.org/c/fbi-releases-2021-crime-statistics/

Financial Crimes Enforcement Network. (2023). *Beneficial ownership information reporting rule*. U.S. Department of the Treasury. https://www.fincen.gov/beneficial-ownership-information-reporting-rule

FATF. (2023). *Anti-money laundering and counter-terrorist financing measures*. https://www.fatf-gafi.org/publications/fatfrecommendations/

Foley, S., Karlsen, J. R., & Putnins, T. J. (2019). Sex, drugs, and bitcoin: How much illegal activity is financed through cryptocurrencies?. *Review of Financial Studies*, *32*(5), 1798–1853. https://doi.org/10.1093/RFS/HHZ015

Georgiou, G. C. (2017). Unintended consequences of anti-money laundering and combating the financing of terrorism (AML/CFT). *International Finance and Banking*, *4*(2), 16. https://doi.org/10.5296/IFB.V4I2.11375

Glaeser, N., Maffei, M., Malavolta, G., Moreno-Sanchez, P., Tairi, E., & Thyagarajan, S. A. K. (2022). Foundations of coin mixing services. In *Proceedings of the ACM conference on computer and communications security* (pp. 1259–1273). WGROUP:STRING:ACM. https://doi.org/10.1145/3548606.3560637

Global Financial Integrity. (2023). *Financial statements and independent auditor's report FY23*. Global Financial Integrity. https://gfintegrity.org/wp-content/uploads/2024/08/GFI-Final-Audit-Report-FY23.pdf

International Consortium of Investigative Journalists. (2021, October 3). *Pandora papers*. International Consortium of Investigative Journalists. https://www.icij.org/investigations/pandora-papers/

International Monetary Fund. (2023). *World economic outlook, October 2023*. IMF. https://www.imfconnect.org/content/imf/en/meetings/AM23/docs-pubs.html

International Monetary Fund. (2024). *Annual report 2024: Resilience in the face of change*. IMF. https://www.imf.org/external/pubs/ft/ar/2024/?trk=public_post_comment-text

INTERPOL. (2022). *Global crime trend summary report 2022*. INTERPOL. https://primarynewssource.org/sourcedocument/2022-the-international-criminal-police-organization-interpol-global-crime-trend-summary-report/

Johora, F. T., Hasan, R., Farabi, S. F., Alam, M. Z., Sarkar, M. I., & Al Mahmud, M. A. (2024). AI advances: Enhancing banking security with fraud detection. In *Proceedings - 2024 1st international conference on technological innovations and advance computing* (pp. 289–294). TIACOMP 2024. https://doi.org/10.1109/TIACOMP64125.2024.00055

Kamps, J., & Kleinberg, B. (2018). To the moon: Defining and detecting cryptocurrency pump-and-dumps. *Crime Science*, *7*(1). https://doi.org/10.1186/S40163-018-0093-5

Katica, A. (2024). Money laundering and terrorism financing in Bosnia and Herzegovina: A review of the legislative framework and current situation. *Kriminalističke Teme*, *24*(1–2), 63–78. https://doi.org/10.51235/KT.2024.24.1-2.63

Kuzior, A., Tiutiunyk, I., Zielińska, A., & Kelemen, R. (2024). Cybersecurity and cybercrime: Current trends and threats. *Journal of International Studies*, *17*(2), 220–239. https://doi.org/10.14254/2071-8330.2024/17-2/12

Office of Foreign Assets Control. (2023). *Annual report 2023*. U.S. Department of the Treasury. https://ofac.treasury.gov

Patel, S., Kasztelnik, K., & Zelihic, M. (2023). Global overview of modern financing typologies to mitigate financial risks in developed countries. *SocioEconomic Challenges*, *7*(2), 54–66. https://doi.org/10.21272/SEC.7(2).54-66.2023

Ranjan, R. (2015). Typologies in Canadian securities fraud: An impact assessment on investor protection, money laundering and the financing of terrorism (AML/CFT), and risk management through problem-oriented policing (POP). *SSRN Electronic Journal*. https://doi.org/10.2139/SSRN.2647578

Reuters. (2022). *Danske bank pleads guilty to U.S. fraud charges in Estonia case*. https://www.reuters.com/business/finance/danske-bank-pleads-guilty-us-fraud-charges-estonia-case-2022-12-13/

Rowley, C. (2024). Leveraging the legal entity identifier to mitigate the risk of financial crime and enhance fraud prevention in cross-border payments. *Journal of Payments Strategy & Systems*, *18*(1), 39–50. https://doi.org/10.69554/FUMW3631

Samantha Maitland Irwin, A., Raymond Choo, K. K., & Liu, L. (2011). An analysis of money laundering and terrorism financing typologies. *Journal of Money Laundering Control*, *15*(1), 85–111. https://doi.org/10.1108/13685201211194745

Simser, J. (2012). Money laundering: Emerging threats and trends. *Journal of Money Laundering Control*, *16*(1), 41–54. https://doi.org/10.1108/13685201311286841

Souza, A. F. (2021). A review of the structure and dynamics of Araucaria mixed forests in southern Brazil and northern Argentina. *New Zealand Journal of Botany*, *59*(1), 1–28. https://doi.org/10.1080/0028825X.2020.1810712

Stewart, I. J., Viski, A., & Brewer, J. (2020). Combating the financing of proliferation: Challenges and new tools. *Journal of Financial Crime*, *27*(4), 1107–1121. https://doi.org/10.1108/JFC-06-2019-0082

Tax Justice Network. (2023). *State of tax justice 2023*. Tax Justice Network. https://taxjustice.net/wp-content/uploads/SOTJ/SOTJ23/English/State%20of%20Tax%20Justice%202023%20-%20Tax%20Justice%20Network%20-%20English.pdf

UNCTAD. (2020). *Tackling illicit financial flows for sustainable development in Africa*. https://unctad.org/system/files/official-document/aldcafrica2020_en.pdf

United Nations Office on Drugs and Crime. (2022). *Annual report 2022: Global programme on crimes that affect the environment*. UNODC. https://digitallibrary.un.org/record/4047872?v=%5B%22%5B%27pdf%27%5D%22%5D

U.S. Department of Justice. (2023). *Annual performance report FY 2023*. U.S. Department of Justice. https://www.justice.gov/doj/justice-management-division/annual-performance-report

World Economic Forum. (2024, September 9). *Annual report 2023–2024*. World Economic Forum. https://www.weforum.org/publications/annual-report-2023-2024/

Zetzsche, D. A., Arner, D. W., & Buckley, R. P. (2020). Decentralized finance. *Journal of Financial Regulation*, *6*(2), 172–203. https://doi.org/10.1093/JFR/FJAA010

Chapter 2

Economic Drivers of Corruptions: Incentives, Power, and Greed

Ish Kumar and Vinay Maitri

School of Planning and Architecture, India

Abstract

Corruption in financial systems is not only present because governments lack strong prosecution or tend to embrace poor morals but also because of embedded economic incentives. This chapter explains how the combination of misaligned incentive systems, institutional power, and the behavioral force of greed perpetuates corruption in both private and public financial institutions. Drawing from institutional economics, behavioral theory, and public choice models, it depicts how corruption can be rationalized as an expected outcome within environments where misbehavior yields greater benefits than the risks of being caught. Using conceptual reasoning and international case studies such as the public banking crisis in India, the 1Malaysia Development Berhad (1MDB) scandal in Malaysia, and London Interbank Offered Rate (LIBOR) manipulation by international banks, this chapter shows how misaligned incentives, power asymmetry, and cultural normalization create systemic vulnerabilities. It emphasizes that corruption transcends geographical and developmental boundaries and thrives where discretion is unchecked and governance becomes a tool for personal gain. This chapter also appraises policy and institutional reform proposals, highlighting the importance of independent oversight, ethical leadership, digital governance tools, and protection for whistleblowers. It argues that innovations in incentive design and behavioral interventions must be reinforced by legal enforcement and organizational transformation. By examining the economic architecture of corruption, this chapter explains why it persists and what structural changes are required to address it. These findings offer insights with implications for national reforms and global anti-corruption efforts aimed at restoring institutional trust and financial integrity.

Corruption and Crime in Finance, 27–46

Published under exclusive licence by Emerald Publishing Limited
doi:10.1108/978-1-83708-170-720261006

Keywords: Institutional corruption; governance reform; financial misconduct; economic incentives; regulatory capture

1. Introduction

Corruption has remained the primary threat to the security and quality of financial systems in our world. It is also its entrenched state in advanced and emerging economies that not only destroys economic growth but also sours confidence of people in regulatory and political institutions. Although it is usually presented as an ethical or a jurist problem, corruption is embedded in economic systems that reward unlawful practices and accept misuse of powers. Corruption, in the financial setting, takes a variety of forms, some of which list embezzlement, money laundering, insider trading, procurement fraud, and regulatory capture. Such practices are not always based on personal malpractice but are in most cases the result of system failures in governance and the existence of economic incentives that supersede possible sanctions.

Corruption has an economic basis, which is usually overwhelmed by stories of governance failure. However, there has been a growing interest in the structural incentives in the financial systems that influence corrupt practices by the scholarly discourse. When the people working in banks, regulatory bodies, government finance, or investment companies view illegal activity as profitable and not likely to be punished, corruption may become a logical, economically rational, and calculated activity. This tendency is particularly strong in the environments with the low level of institutional control, poorly developed transparency procedures, and informal influence networks prevailing over the formal norms of procedures.

Historical and contemporary financial crises have illustrated how the convergence of greed, institutional authority, and skewed incentive structures can facilitate corruption on a systemic scale. The 2008 global financial collapse, for example, revealed how performance-linked bonuses in major financial institutions encouraged high-risk speculation and deceptive practices. As experienced in most of the developing economies, the integration between political leaders and financial institutions would most of the time result in misappropriation of government funds and corruption in procurement practices. This is why it is significant to perceive corruption as not only violation of lawful norms, but, more importantly, a result of the more general economic imbalances and institutional distortions.

A number of theoretical approaches illuminate the prevalence of financial sector corruption. As an example, the Principal-Agent Theory explains the ways in which information differences and incongruent incentives between policymakers and their subordinates or financial managers may provide the path to unethical conduct. This is complemented by Public Choice Theory which considers public servants as people pursuing self-interest, reacting to economic incentives similar to those experienced in markets. These theories also emphasize the importance of systemic rewards combined with unlimited power or monopoly that can slowly erode institutional integrity (Dang et al., 2025).

In most of the locations, especially in the transition and developing world, corruption does not even appear as the case of deviant behavior, but as a rational way of adapting to economic inefficiencies. This is the environment where certain people may need to pay off dusty money to get permission, a loan, or a tax deduction, or where one needs some kind of friendship to acquire a permit or borrow money, so that it is in fact normal in economic transactions to bribe. It complicates anti-corruption work since they must meet structural and social barriers to change.

And, in addition, the economic factor of greed, as well the psychological factor cannot be overestimated. It is preconditioned by the environment, which is fixed by the arrangements of the incentives and power relationships, but, in most situations, people want to find the loopholes, implement workarounds of the rules because they want to make some money or get power. Greed does not occur in this instance as an act of a single individual, but it is an element of a system of limited risk in which the perceived rewards of corruption are compromised against the likelihood risk apprehension and punishment.

This chapter explores the economic foundations of corruption by examining how incentive structures, power dynamics, and individual greed intersect within financial systems to enable and sustain corrupt behavior. Through an integration of theoretical frameworks and illustrative case studies, the discussion highlights the ways in which institutional configurations, performance-based reward mechanisms, and concentrated authority contribute to the persistence of corruption. Furthermore, the analysis extends to the influence of prevailing cultural attitudes and social norms, assessing how they shape the degree of societal tolerance or resistance toward corrupt practices across different financial contexts.

The structure of the chapter is organized as follows. The next section will develop a conceptual framework outlining the economic theories relevant to understanding corruption. This will be followed by an in-depth examination of incentive structures within financial institutions and their role in enabling unethical conduct. Subsequent sections will analyze the effects of power concentration, explore the behavioral economics of greed, and present comparative case studies from both developed and developing contexts. Finally, this chapter will conclude with a discussion on policy responses and reform strategies aimed at reducing corruption by addressing its economic drivers.

This chapter supports the general argument that the anti-corruption mission must balk at the corruption rationale in order to support the argument of larger debate and corruption is structural and systemic issue. Instead of trying to find corrupt practices in some lapse of ethics and conducts and some failures on the part of institutions, it tries to present a more comprehensive view. The critique places corruption as the product of interdependent relationships in the economy that occurs in an environment that is dominated by a large scale of power disparity. Through this, it criticizes the traditional models and advocates the shift toward the models that factor the interaction of the economic incentives, the institution design, and the organization of power.

2. Conceptual Framework of Economic Drivers of Corruption

Understanding the persistence and complexity of corruption in financial systems requires a robust conceptual framework that incorporates insights from economic theory, institutional analysis, and behavioral studies. While corruption is often treated as an ethical or legal anomaly, economic theories reveal how it can emerge as a rational response to systemic incentives and institutional weaknesses. Three key theoretical lenses; Principal-Agent Theory, Public Choice Theory, and Rational Choice Theory offer explanatory power in uncovering the underlying mechanics of corruption, particularly when power and greed interact with structural opportunities (Marino, 2025).

The Principal-Agent Theory has maintained roots in the explanation of corruption development through delegation and asymmetry. Principals (shareholders, regulators or taxpayers) in both the public and the private sphere normally delegate responsibility to their agents (the bank managers, bureaucrats or elected politicians). The agent has more information and discretion of action that may make the agent pursue personal interest other than the objectives of the principal. Corruption comes in when there is no good mechanism of accountability, or the mechanisms are maladjusted in a way that the agent follows personal interests by mean of embezzling, cheating, or conspiracy. The empirical research findings indicate that corruption grows where the supervision is poor, procedures are evasive, and there are superficialities in the governance that increases the principal–agent gap (Groenendijk, 1997).

The Public Choice Theory is further developed on this basis where political and bureaucratic actors are treated as rational utility-maximizers, but not as impartial agents of the public good. This theory argues that those in positions of authority are likely to exploit public office for personal benefit when the costs of doing so are low and the institutional checks are weak. For instance, public procurement systems or regulatory bodies may become vulnerable to influence from private firms through lobbying, bribery, or informal patronage networks. The result is not merely isolated misconduct but systemic policy capture, where institutions serve vested interests over collective welfare (Andrei & Vishny, 1993). This framework helps explain why certain sectors especially banking, construction, and extractives are disproportionately susceptible to corruption due to their high-value transactions and regulatory complexity.

Rational Choice Theory further contextualizes corrupt behavior as a deliberate decision made after evaluating potential rewards and sanctions. In this view, individuals weigh the expected benefits of engaging in corruption against the likelihood and severity of punishment. If enforcement is lax, penalties are minimal, or institutional tolerance is high, the perceived cost of corrupt behavior declines. Consequently, corruption becomes a rational economic strategy rather than a moral deviation. This perspective has been supported by empirical studies showing a negative correlation between corruption levels and judicial effectiveness, regulatory quality, and press freedom (Valverde et al., 2023).

While these theories provide structured explanations, they often operate under assumptions of perfect rationality and static preferences. Behavioral economics introduces nuance by acknowledging that decisions are shaped not only by material incentives but also by cognitive biases, heuristics, and social norms. The role of greed, for instance, cannot be entirely reduced to financial gain. It is also driven by status competition, relative deprivation, and an internalized sense of entitlement. Greed often distorts perceptions of risk, undermines ethical boundaries, and incentivizes repeated offenses, especially when initial corrupt acts go unpunished. Research suggests that individuals in high-powered roles are more prone to unethical behavior when placed in performance-driven or winner-takes-all environments (Marino, 2025; Wawrosz, 2022).

A further explanation using institutional economics is the contribution of formal and informal rules in defining incentives and behavior. In terms of particular contexts, corruption thrives in an environment in which institutional arrangements are over-institutionalized or highly disaggregated so that it is possible to find procedural loopholes or walk between two worlds of formal law and informal practice. There is also a point, as expressed by (North, 1990) explanation of institutions as the rules of the game, where corruption may become an intrinsic characteristic of an economic interplay, when norms that are not legal tend to dominate. As an example, even the risk-averse players in a case where there should be an expectation of informal payments in exchange of basic services or approvals, can react and do as expected not to be delayed or retaliated against.

These theoretical approaches converge on a common insight: corruption is not an aberration, but a predictable outcome in settings where institutional controls are weak, incentives are misaligned, and power is concentrated. The interaction between agents' self-interest and institutional inefficiencies creates fertile ground for corruption to thrive, especially when compounded by greed and limited accountability. Furthermore, the broader political economy shapes these dynamics. In rent-seeking environments, where access to state resources or regulatory favors is highly valuable, competition for influence intensifies, leading to more sophisticated and entrenched forms of corruption.

With this multi-theoretical perspective of corruption, it is necessary to design purpose-based anti-corruption policies. The construed view of the legal deterring or the moral debkoi without looking deeper at economics and the institutionalized means of justifying the maintenance of corruption behavior is faulty. Through the examination of the architecture of incentives, the use of authority, and the functioning of behavioral biases, policymakers and scholars would be able to promote change beyond quick fixes and shift the approach toward deep-seated causes of corruption within the financial systems.

3. Incentive Structures and Corruption in Financial Institutions

The architecture of modern financial institutions is fundamentally shaped by performance-based incentive mechanisms designed to drive profitability and operational efficiency. However, when incentives prioritize short-term financial gains without integrating ethical constraints or accountability mechanisms, they can encourage corrupt behavior across multiple levels of the organization. The misuse of incentive structures has played a central role in some of the most prominent financial scandals of the 21st century, underscoring the link between reward systems, institutional culture, and unethical conduct.

Financial institutions, particularly banks, investment firms, and insurance companies, rely heavily on quantifiable targets such as revenue generation, return on assets, or client acquisition. Employees at all levels, from retail officers to senior executives, are frequently evaluated and rewarded based on performance metrics tied to profitability. While such structures are intended to enhance efficiency and competitiveness, they can create perverse incentives. For example, aggressive sales targets may lead employees to misrepresent financial products, manipulate client data, or forge documents to meet quarterly goals. In this environment, ethical conduct is subordinated to numerical performance.

The case of Wells Fargo cross-selling scandal in the United States is an example of such dynamic. The employees were put under a lot of pressure to achieve unrealistic quota in an attempt to cross-sell more financial products to each customer. Many of them opened false accounts without the permissions of customers to retain their jobs or get bonuses. Such was the case in a number of years, involving thousands of employees and causing regulatory fines and reputation loss. It was found that the incentive scheme at the institution was poorly aligned in addition to promoting a culture of misconducted (Michael Dalde, 2023; Mullen et al., 2023; Tayan, 2019).

Executive compensation structures also play a significant role in encouraging high-risk behavior. Remuneration packages frequently include performance-linked bonuses, stock options, and deferred equity, which are tied to short-term metrics such as quarterly profits or share price movements. These incentive schemes can lead to the manipulation of earnings, window-dressing of balance sheets, and exploitation of regulatory loopholes. Research by Ref (Abascal & González, 2023; Caylor & Lopez, 2013; Gray & Cannella, 1997; Hagendorff & Vallascas, 2011; Peng et al., 2023) found that financial firms with higher executive compensation variability tended to engage in riskier practices that contributed to the 2008 financial crisis.

The design of incentive mechanisms within credit rating agencies has also come under scrutiny. Agencies are typically paid by the issuers of financial instruments rather than the buyers, leading to conflicts of interest and inflated ratings. This pay-to-rate model contributed to the overvaluation of mortgage-backed securities prior to the global financial crisis, enabling the proliferation of toxic assets throughout the financial system (Efing & Hau, 2015; Toscano, 2020). The incentive to retain clients through favorable ratings ultimately undermined the objectivity of the rating process (Jones et al., 2022; Milidonis, 2013).

Corruption linked to incentives is not confined to high-income economies. In several emerging economies, loan officers in public sector banks may receive informal rewards for approving high-risk loans, often under political influence or clientelistic arrangements. These practices lead to nonperforming assets (NPAs), which weaken financial stability and crowd out credit for productive investment.

In India, for instance, the nexus between state-owned banks and politically connected firms has contributed to significant loan defaults, raising concerns about internal incentive mismanagement and external interference (Dang et al., 2025; De Chiara & Manna, 2022).

Another domain where incentive-driven corruption is prevalent is financial auditing and consulting. Auditors are expected to serve as independent watchdogs; however, when auditing firms also offer consulting services to the same clients, the incentives become misaligned. The collapse of Enron and the role of Arthur Andersen demonstrated how compromised independence can lead to the concealment of financial irregularities. Auditors may overlook red flags or manipulate audit findings to retain lucrative contracts, especially when their compensation depends on client satisfaction (Akins et al., 2016).

Incentive structures also intersect with informal institutional practices. In some contexts, informal commissions or success fees are embedded within hiring, promotion, or contract allocation decisions. These practices are especially pervasive in institutions where internal monitoring is weak and ethical norms are not institutionalized. The result is a parallel incentive system that promotes favoritism, nepotism, and transactional decision-making, all of which contribute to systemic corruption (Paganou et al., 2024).

In order to counter these issues, it has been suggested that various policy and institutional reforms should take place. A way of correcting this will be by redesigning incentive systems to achieve a balance between financial and ethical performance. This can come in form of including Clawback bonuses in case of wrong doing, variable pay capping or using long-term measures like compliance score or customer satisfaction to reward employees (Denis et al., 2006). The remedies to unaligned incentives have also been revealed to include governance reforms that increase transparency in compensation practices, enhance board monitoring as well as the incorporation of independent remuneration committees.

Moreover, behavioral interventions, including training and peer accountability systems with feed-back loops to nudge ethical behavior, are becoming more interesting. Organizational culture, or the extent to which the leadership style influences and the incentive schemes strengthens or weaken it, is also significant and important to have a knowledge of whether the employees are subjected to pressure to commit the misconduct or they are provided the power to enact the unethical conducts. The landscape of incentives can be changed by integrating ethics in the performance reviews and encouraging internal whistleblower protection (De Chiara & Manna, 2022).

Ultimately, the misuse of incentive structures in financial institutions underscores a broader failure in institutional design. When rewards are structured without consideration of ethical risks or regulatory boundaries, corruption becomes a rational and even predictable outcome. Addressing these failures requires a combination of economic, institutional, and behavioral strategies that align incentives with transparency, accountability, and sustainability.

4. Power Concentration and Institutional Corruption

Power, when concentrated within a narrow set of individuals or institutions without adequate oversight, becomes a critical enabler of systemic corruption. Unlike transactional forms of misconduct that emerge from individual incentive misalignment, institutional corruption associated with power concentration stems from structural asymmetries that compromise the independence and accountability of public and private actors. The monopolization of decision-making authority often reduces transparency, increases discretion, and weakens external checks, thereby creating an institutional environment where corrupt behavior is not only tolerated but embedded into standard operating procedures.

One of the most obvious consequences of concentration of power is the phenomenon of state capture. In these environments, influential interest groups are closely connected with political or financial elites and dominate policy making, regulatory system and appointments made in institutions. Such power is utilized by the actors to influence the rules and end-results to their own advantage, leading to lopsided public spending, preferential licensing, and compromised stronger enforcement regimes. The conceptualization of state capture by Ref (Hellman et al., 2003) looks like this: it occurs when the laws, policies and regulations are used to serve the needs of the individual parties at the detriment of the common good. The subsequent malformed patterns of governance are especially acute in case of countries in a political or economic transition in that institutional control is yet to mature.

Within the financial sector, the concentration of regulatory authority in politicized or nonindependent institutions can lead to the erosion of oversight and selective enforcement. Regulatory capture occurs when oversight bodies, instead of acting in the public interest, align with the interests of the industries they are meant to regulate. This misalignment compromises the credibility of enforcement mechanisms and allows financial entities to engage in speculative or fraudulent behavior without fear of consequence. In practice, this can lead to the approval of risky financial instruments, the relaxation of capital adequacy norms, or the overlooking of anti-money laundering violations.

Another vivid example of the risks of power concentration is the Petrobras of Brazil, commonly known as Operation Car Wash. The investigation indicated how the top executives of the state-owned oil company conspired with construction companies and political groups in order to raise the contracts and to defraud billions of dollars of state money. The USG culture of impunity was facilitated by the concentration of procurement decisions among a small cluster of executives, which along with limited internal audit presence and political protection gave them an immunized status. This court case sheds light on the weaknesses of state-owned businesses with operational independence followed by less visibility, particularly in cases where political patronage supersedes the institutional responsibility (Abascal & González, 2023; Lima-de-Oliveira, 2020; Tayan, 2019).

In some jurisdictions, financial regulatory authorities are housed within executive ministries or are otherwise subject to political direction, which undermines their functional independence. Such arrangements create a conflict between political goals and regulatory integrity. When regulators rely on discretionary powers without being subject to independent review, the scope for abuse expands significantly. The same applies to public finance institutions that disburse large volumes of credit or manage infrastructure projects, particularly when oversight is weakened by complex bureaucratic structures or limited public access to procurement data.

The concentration of economic and political power is also fostered by oligarchic ownership of the major financial institutions; mainly leading to exclusive control of credit, monopolistic pricing or stifling the competition in the market. In several economies, some few politically well-placed conglomerates have seized huge portions of banking, insurance, as well as capital markets. These players are not only happy to have them favorably treated by a regulator but with them being protected they get a way in stuffing anything that can make them lose their power. This structural inequality leads to distortion of the process of allocating resources as well as undermining institutional legitimacy.

At the global level, similar dynamics are observed in the context of international financial flows and tax havens. When multinational corporations engage in regulatory arbitrage by exploiting jurisdictions with lax oversight, they shift financial activities away from transparent systems. The opacity provided by these jurisdictions, often coupled with legal protections for secrecy, enables large-scale corruption, illicit enrichment, and capital flight. Power in this context is institutionalized through legal and financial engineering rather than explicit political control, yet the outcome remains consistent, accountability is evaded, and the rule of law is undermined.

Power concentration can also become institutional corruption in multilateral financial institutions where the decisions of project approvals, procurement or even sanction regime are driven by the dominant donor countries or the stakeholders of the multilateral financial institutions. Lack of accountability to the people concerned and to a greater extent lack of transparency of decision making, skewed voting right distribution may not only affect the developmental goals of these institutions also the trust of the affected populations would be jeopardized.

The multi-faceted institutional approach will help to solve the risks that were related to the concentration of powers. First, regulatory independence should be ensured and safeguarded through legal frameworks that buffer regulators against political pressure. Secondly, there should be restrictions on the decision-making process including open systems in procurement of goods, assets, and asset declarations as well as participatory budgeting. Thirdly, risks of centralization can be diminished by decentralization of the financial power, and by the strong local control mechanisms. Last but not least, the fact that watchdog institutions such as the judiciary, anti-corruption commissions, and civil society maintain appropriate levels of power counterbalance the existing concentrated institutional power.

In short, power without an accountability mechanism should not be concentrated since it enhances provision of institutional architecture that facilitates the cause of systemic corruption. Whether state capture, regulatory subversion, or elite control, these structures not only reduce the integrity of the financial systems but also limit the success of reform. Sustainable Anti-corruption policy should thus not just combat a single wrong doing action but should also combat the institutional workings which help in entrenching bad behaviors.

5. Greed and Cultural Normalization of Corruption

Corruption does not emerge solely from misaligned incentives or institutional weaknesses; it is also deeply shaped by behavioral drivers, most notably greed, and reinforced by cultural norms that determine how corruption is perceived, tolerated, or resisted. While economic theories explain the conditions under which individuals are likely to engage in corrupt practices, understanding why they choose to do so despite moral or legal prohibitions requires closer attention to psychological and social factors.

As a behavioral dimension, greed is a critical dimension that exists in interaction with institutional settings and is usually referred to as excessive or insatiable desire of wealth, status, or power. It is a driving force that supersedes ethical questions, and it is even more active when the possibilities to enrich a person on their own personal level exist with no severe consequences. In economics, greed leads participants to take advantage of informational leads, evade rules and regulations, and self-interest over institutional accountability. Research on behavioral economics indicates that people tend to be unethically more disposed when they become wealthier or when they move up the hierarchy ladder because they have developed a sense of entitlement and tolerance to risks (Manara et al., 2023; Zafeiriou et al., 2023).

Also, greed is not just an issue of personal pathology, and in many cases, is encouraged by the culture of an institution whereby success and making of money are idealized no matter how. Self-serving behavior may become the norm in most successful corporate settings especially those involving the realm of finance and consulting where reward systems and peer endorsed behavior might make it seem prevalent. He or she develops an institutionalized greed when success is mostly quantified in financial terms, and when individuals who practice corruption are not punished but actually rewarded by being granted promotion, bonuses, or elevated positions. This process is also facilitated by cultural toleration of corruption. Patronage networks and informal payments become part of everyday transactions in many areas, especially in South Asia, Sub-Saharan Africa, and Latin America. These practices are not necessarily viewed as criminal or unethical but as pragmatic strategies for navigating inefficient bureaucracies or securing access to basic services. In such contexts, refusing to participate in corruption can even be seen as naïve or counterproductive.

This normalization is supported by collective experiences and intergenerational transmission of practices. When individuals grow up witnessing routine bribery, nepotism, or manipulation of public resources, such behaviors become culturally embedded. They form part of what Ref (Li et al., 2023; Seuntjens et al., 2016) describe as limited access orders, where social and economic privileges are restricted to elite networks, and participation in informal arrangements becomes essential for survival or advancement. As a result, the distinction between legal and illegal behavior becomes blurred, and corruption is perceived less as a violation of norms and more as a functional aspect of the system.

The role of social learning in corrupt behavior is well documented. People are more likely to engage in unethical actions when they observe their peers, superiors, or mentors doing the same without repercussions. This diffusion of responsibility dilutes individual guilt and reinforces collective impunity. Organizational cultures that lack transparency and accountability mechanisms are especially susceptible to this effect. Over time, corruption becomes routinized and no longer requires active justification; it simply becomes "the way things are done."

Moral these boundaries of corruption can also be determined by religious, historical and sociopolitical factors. In other situations, the religious teachings can be about justice and honesty but the interpretation in institutions might not support and punish corrupt practices. Likewise, bureaucratic systems that did not meet local demands were inherited by postcolonial states thus becoming a source of suspicion between the people and the state. Corruption can actually be justified as a means to overcome systems perceived as unjust, or not accepted as legitimate in such an environment. The problem is that the tolerance of corruption does not mean that the individual is unaware or against it. Most people living in various countries speak of corruption as one of the biggest issues affecting their societies despite not being in a position to address it. Such a contradiction highlights the clash between personal values and group actions. Although corruption is condemnable by many, they can engage in the vice when there are hindrances in accessing the services or the fear of being victimized or subjected to institutional malpractice.

Action against greed and cultural normalization should not be separated with legal changes and restructuring institutions. They need continuously to work at behavioral change interventions, mass education, and norm variation campaigns. Corruption can be better aligned with community good by recruitment of corruption whistleblowing programs, training of corruption whistleblowers, and pressure on managers to become ethical. Additionally, transparency (the availability of open data portals, citizen audit, participatory, budgeting, etc.) has apparent potential to create a culture of accountability by making corruption more visible and less tolerated in society.

In conclusion, greed and cultural acceptance of corruption form an interlinked behavioral and social dimension that sustains corrupt systems even in the presence of formal deterrents. Addressing these forces requires a nuanced understanding of how individual psychology interacts with institutional culture and social norms. Without confronting the deep-rooted normalization of corruption and the role of greed as a motivational engine, efforts at reform are likely to remain superficial and ineffective.

6. Comparative Case Studies of Financial Corruption

Comparative case studies offer a solid comprehension of corruption in the financial systems. These illustrations show how different arrangements of incentives, institutional strength, and cultural norms help to make the corrupt outcomes. Although the elements of corruption like misaligned incentives, concentrated power, institutionalized greed among others are familiar themes, the type and magnitude of corruption differ with governing structures, enforcement of the law, and sociopolitical realities.

6.1 Case 1: India's Banking Sector and the NPA Crisis

The NPAs challenge has plagued the Indian public sector banks on numerous occasions, and much of the problems have been tied to politically motivated loan transactions, lax credit analysis, and regulatory default. These times of crisis were experienced between 2015 and 2019 whereby NPAs increased significantly with several state-owned banks experiencing a gross ratio of NPAs above 10%. Investigations found a common factor of large corporate loan-takers to get a loan on lax due diligence with perceived political backing (Chari et al., 2019).

Among the most notorious example lays the Punjab National Bank (PNB) fraud involving a diamond merchant Nirav Modi, bank employees raised fraudulent letters of undertaking, as a result of which billions could change hands without appropriate collateral or notification to the supervisory authority. The weakness in the level of integration within the banking system, the discretionary control vested on individual officers and a culture of informality working with the understanding among the private beneficiaries and the public officials enabled the scam. The scenario of this case emphasized how the structure of the Indian public banking system was/is prone to corruption and this is evidenced where there were no institutional checks and fails to reward against collusion and negligence (Dimri, 2025; Padhy & Sahoo, 2025).

6.2 Case 2: The 1Malaysia Development Berhad (1MDB) Scandal in Malaysia

The case of 1MDB has become one of the greatest corruption scandals in the recent financial history because more than USD 4.5 billion was taken out of a state-investment fund. Created in 2009 to finance the national development, 1MDB has been used as means of misappropriating the state funds by the senior authorities, including the former Prime Minister Najib Razak. Huge sums of money intended to fund a criminal empire had been laundered through layers of offshore bank accounts, shell corporations, and luxurious goods in several countries (Lim & Yoong, 2023).

The scandal demonstrated how central political powers, lax institutional controls, and lack of transparency of financial dealings present a perfect condition to grand corruption. The participation of international banks and audit companies showed not only the failure at the domestic level of institutions but also the action of international financial mediators who did not notice the warnings on the way to a profit. Another illustrative point discussed in this case was that elite circles in the financial world are rarely governed by compliance but by reputation (Md Ali, 2022; Steiner, 2017).

6.3 Case 3: London Interbank Offered Rate (LIBOR) Manipulation by Global Banks

The LIBOR manipulation scandal, which came to light in 2012, revealed how major financial institutions including Barclays, UBS, and Deutsche Bank colluded to rig benchmark interest rates that influence trillions in global financial contracts. Bank employees submitted false rate estimates to benefit proprietary trading positions or create an illusion of creditworthiness during the global financial crisis.

Unlike conventional corruption involving illegal transfers or bribes, this case involved systemic manipulation rooted in incentive structures and unmonitored discretion. Traders were often rewarded based on their success in influencing benchmark outcomes, with communication via chat rooms and informal networks reinforcing group collusion. The absence of effective oversight by the British Bankers' Association, coupled with weak regulatory frameworks, allowed this misconduct to persist for years. The scandal illustrated how corruption can thrive even in advanced economies when regulatory agencies rely on self-reporting and when market integrity is compromised by unchecked incentive systems (Hou & Skeie, 2014; Lim & Yoong, 2023; Monticini & Thornton, 2013).

6.4 Comparative Insights

Across these diverse cases, several common patterns emerge. First, each involved the abuse of institutional trust and discretionary authority, whether through internal collusion in public banks or through international financial manipulation. Second, all three cases reflected a failure of internal controls, be it technological gaps, lack of independent audits, or overreliance on reputation-based systems. Third, cultural acceptance of certain practices, such as political interference in lending or informal cooperation between competitors, enabled the persistence of corruption even in well-regulated financial ecosystems.

However, the institutional responses varied. India strengthened its bankruptcy code and tightened asset classification norms. Malaysia pursued high-profile prosecutions and launched reforms to strengthen sovereign fund governance. In contrast, the LIBOR scandal led to a restructuring of benchmark rate systems and the eventual transition to alternative reference rates, but penalties were largely monetary, with limited criminal accountability (Hou & Skeie, 2014; Monticini & Thornton, 2013).

These cases demonstrate that corruption is not exclusive to fragile or transitional economies. Even mature financial systems are vulnerable when incentives encourage manipulation, oversight mechanisms are insufficient, and organizational culture favors results over integrity. Importantly, they also highlight that effective reform is possible, but it requires sustained institutional commitment, cross-border cooperation, and alignment between regulatory design and enforcement capacity.

7. Policy Responses and Institutional Reform Measures

Addressing corruption driven by economic incentives, concentrated power, and systemic greed requires a multi-dimensional approach that extends beyond punitive frameworks. While legal enforcement remains essential, durable reforms must reshape the structural, institutional, and behavioral conditions that enable corruption. Effective policy responses focus on realigning incentive mechanisms, strengthening institutional autonomy, promoting transparency, and reinforcing public accountability. These measures must be designed with sensitivity to local political economies while drawing from global best practices and evidence-based interventions.

7.1 Realigning Incentive Structures

The problem of corruption scandals in many states is rooted in systems of incentive that award based on the reward without looking properly into the ethical and procedural implications of attaining the victory. The reconfiguration of such incentive arrangements must emerge in both the state and privately owned financial institutions so that the reformation process should commence with the motive of changing such arrangements. This will entail putting ethical performance indicators within performance evaluation of employees, including compliance with compliance procedures, nonsecrecy concerning client relations, and internal audit ratings.

Executive compensation reforms are particularly crucial. Institutions should adopt mechanisms such as deferred bonuses, clawback clauses, and capped variable pay to disincentivize short-term manipulation of financial outcomes. For instance, after the 2008 financial crisis, several regulatory frameworks in Europe and the United States introduced restrictions on performance-linked compensation in banks, linking remuneration to long-term risk assessments rather than quarterly returns (El-Abiad et al., 2023; Sheedy et al., 2019).

7.2 Strengthening Institutional Autonomy and Oversight

Institutional integrity is compromised when regulatory bodies lack operational independence or when oversight mechanisms are undermined by political or corporate influence. Strengthening institutional autonomy requires clear legal mandates that protect regulatory bodies from executive interference, alongside transparent appointment procedures and sufficient financial resources to conduct independent investigations.

In contexts where state-owned enterprises or public financial institutions dominate, internal governance must be fortified through independent boards, external audits, and public disclosure of operational decisions. Additionally, strengthening the independence of anti-corruption commissions, ombudsman offices, and judicial systems ensures that enforcement is impartial and insulated from retaliation or favoritism.

International experiences demonstrate the value of multi-layered oversight. For example, Singapore's Corrupt Practices Investigation Bureau operates under the Prime Minister's Office but maintains legal independence, enabling proactive investigations with relatively limited political obstruction. This model has contributed to the country's reputation for clean governance and low tolerance for institutional corruption.

7.3 Enhancing Transparency and Digital Governance

Transparency in logistics leads to eradication of corruption. Thus improving the transparency of the financial operations, procurement, and administrative resolutions is the core of the reform. Such transparency initiatives as e-procurement systems, open budgeting, disclosure of beneficial ownership have proven to limit the possibilities of rent-seeking and colluding.

The digital governance systems are specifically useful in breaking the informal networks that promote corruption. Advanced technologies like blockchain, biometrical verification, and digital payments services increase traceability and minimize the discretionary interface between the citizens and the authorities. In India, direct benefit transfer as welfare programs utilizing Aadhaar services has reduced leakage levels considerably because there are no longer ghost benefactors and middlemen (Gilmour et al., 2025). Moreover, the use of real-time data dashboards, audit trails, and automated red-flag systems will enable regulatory bodies to record and make prompt interventions based on the anomalies in the financial behavior. Technology is however not a solution to everything. It cannot be as effective as the basic legal frameworks, cybersecurity systems, and the institutional ability to realize it (Thommandru et al., 2024).

7.4 Strengthening Whistleblower Protections and Internal Controls

Empowering individuals within organizations to report unethical practices requires robust legal protections and procedural safeguards. Whistleblower policies must ensure anonymity, protect against retaliation, and provide accessible reporting channels. Evidence shows that the presence of protected whistleblowing frameworks significantly increases the detection of financial irregularities, particularly in banking and procurement sectors (Eugster et al., 2024).

Internal controls should be designed to minimize discretion and introduce segregation of duties. Regular internal audits, surprise inspections, and independent compliance units act as deterrents by increasing the probability of detection (Arslan & Alqatan, 2020). Integrating behavioral risk assessments into control systems can also help anticipate and mitigate unethical conduct, particularly in high-pressure environments.

7.5 International Cooperation and Legal Harmonization

Since fraudulent financial undertakings tend to have cross-border connections particularly in instances related to illegal flow of capital and multinational companies and tax havens, international collaboration is inevitable. Such coordination can take place at legal level with legal harmonization like that represented by the United Nations Convention Against Corruption (UNCAC), the Financial Action Task Force (FATF) rules, and the OECD anti-bribery standards. The ability of the national agencies to identify and take back illicit gains can be supplemented with cross-jurisdictional information sharing, asset recovery structures, and mutual legal assistance treaties. The International Anti-Corruption Coordination Centre (IACCC) is a good example that shows how joint investigation can be effective in probing elaborate finances.

7.6 Fostering a Culture of Accountability and Ethical Leadership

A culture of accountability, integrity, and ethical leadership is more sustainable to come in and assist in reform measures. Top level leadership should demonstrate that they will pursue clean governance with evident promises of transparent decision making, zero tolerance in application and messaging. Leadership responsibility affects the ethical environment in the institutions and they act to indicate the results of noncompliance.

Public awareness campaigns, civic education, and citizen participation in oversight processes enhance the societal demand for integrity. Mechanisms such as citizen report cards, participatory budgeting, and community monitoring have proven effective in holding institutions accountable in several developing countries.

8. Conclusion

Corruption in financial systems cannot be fully understood or addressed without examining the economic logic that underpins it. As this chapter has demonstrated, corruption is not solely a function of weak morality or poor enforcement; it is often a rational response to distorted incentives, asymmetrical power relations, and permissive institutional environments. When the expected gains from unethical behavior exceed the perceived risks, and when institutional checks are either absent or ineffective, corruption becomes embedded in the decision-making architecture of both public and private financial institutions.

The analysis has emphasized three interrelated drivers: incentives, power, and greed. Misaligned incentives, such as bonus-driven compensation or politically motivated lending, create pathways for individuals and institutions to prioritize short-term gains over long-term accountability. Power concentration, whether in the hands of regulators, political elites, or oligarchic market actors, allows for the manipulation of policies, suppression of oversight, and perpetuation of impunity. Greed, operating as both a personal motive and an institutional culture, further intensifies the tendency to bypass ethical constraints in pursuit of wealth, influence, or competitive advantage.

Case studies from diverse national contexts have revealed that corruption is neither confined to the developing world nor limited to informal practices. Whether in India's public banking crisis, Malaysia's 1MDB scandal, or the LIBOR rate-fixing episode in advanced economies, the patterns are strikingly similar: institutional complacency, discretionary authority, and compromised oversight coalesce to enable large-scale financial misconduct. These examples underline the systemic nature of corruption and challenge the effectiveness of fragmented or punitive reforms.

Effective anti-corruption strategies must therefore address both the structural conditions and behavioral dimensions that sustain corruption. Reforming incentive systems to reward integrity and compliance, decentralizing decision-making authority to dilute monopolistic control, and embedding ethical leadership within organizational culture are necessary steps. At the same time, institutional reforms must be accompanied by robust transparency frameworks, stronger enforcement capacities, and meaningful public engagement to shift societal norms.

Looking forward, future research and policy agendas should focus on five critical areas:

- Empirical evaluation of incentive reforms in financial institutions, particularly in emerging markets.
- Design of behavioral interventions that promote ethical decision-making and counter the normalization of corruption.
- Cross-national comparisons of anti-corruption agency performance to identify replicable models of institutional integrity.
- Integration of digital technologies such as blockchain, AI-driven audit systems, and e-governance platforms in corruption detection and prevention.
- Expansion of international cooperation frameworks to address transnational financial crimes and regulatory arbitrage.

While institutional design and enforcement mechanisms remain foundational, addressing the economic drivers of corruption also demands a transformation in values toward transparency, accountability, and collective responsibility. Only when the systems that reward and protect corruption are dismantled can meaningful progress be achieved in restoring trust in financial institutions and public governance.

References

Abascal, R., & González, F. (2023). What drives risk-taking incentives embedded in bank executive compensation? Some international evidence. *Journal of Corporate Finance*, *79*, 102357. https://doi.org/10.1016/J.JCORPFIN.2023.102357

Akins, B., Dou, Y., & Ng, J. (2016). Corruption in bank lending: The role of timely loan loss recognition. *Journal of Accounting and Economics*, *63*. https://doi.org/10.1016/j.jacceco.2016.08.003

Andrei, S., & Vishny, R. W. (1993). Corruption. *The Quarterly Journal of Economics*, *108*(3), 599–617. https://academic.oup.com/qje/article-abstract/108/3/599/1881822?redirectedFrom=fulltext&login=false

Arslan, M., & Alqatan, A. (2020). Role of institutions in shaping corporate governance system: Evidence from emerging economy. *Heliyon*, *6*(3), e03520. https://doi.org/10.1016/J.HELIYON.2020.E03520

Caylor, M. L., & Lopez, T. J. (2013). Cost behavior and executive bonus compensation. *Advances in Accounting*, *29*(2), 232–242. https://doi.org/10.1016/J.ADIAC.2013.08.001

Chari, A., Jain, L., & Kulkarni, N. (2019). *The origins of India's NPA crisis*.

Dang, T. C., Van, H. V., & Van, D. Le (2025). E-government and corruption in an emerging country: New perspectives from a spatiotemporal approach. *International Review of Economics & Finance*, *100*, 104111. https://doi.org/10.1016/J.IREF.2025.104111

De Chiara, A., & Manna, E. (2022). Corruption, regulation, and investment incentives. *European Economic Review*, *142*, 104009. https://doi.org/10.1016/J.EUROECOREV.2021.104009

Denis, D. J., Hanouna, P., & Sarin, A. (2006). Is there a dark side to incentive compensation? *Journal of Corporate Finance*, *12*(3), 467–488. https://doi.org/10.1016/J.JCORPFIN.2005.08.006

Dimri, A. (2025). Resolution of non-performing assets: Regulatory, supervisory and policy response in India in pre- and post-COVID-19 scenario. *Journal of Banking Regulation*. https://doi.org/10.1057/s41261-025-00275-0

Efing, M., & Hau, H. (2015). Structured debt ratings: Evidence on conflicts of interest. *Journal of Financial Economics*, *116*(1), 46–60. https://doi.org/10.1016/J.JFINECO.2014.11.009

El-Abiad, Z., Braendle, U., & El-Chaarani, H. (2023). Formulation of a corporate governance index for banking sector: The GIB.X62. *Heliyon*, *9*(4), e15253. https://doi.org/10.1016/J.HELIYON.2023.E15253

Eugster, N., Kowalewski, O., & Śpiewanowski, P. (2024). Internal governance mechanisms and corporate misconduct. *International Review of Financial Analysis*, *92*, 103109. https://doi.org/10.1016/J.IRFA.2024.103109

Gilmour, P., Pandey, D., & Goldbarsht, D. (2025). Registers of beneficial owners based on blockchain technology: Implications for the accounting profession. *Technological Forecasting and Social Change*, *214*, 124051. https://doi.org/10.1016/J.TECHFORE.2025.124051

Gray, S. R., & Cannella, A. A. (1997). The role of risk in executive compensation. *Journal of Management*, *23*(4), 517–540. https://doi.org/10.1016/S0149-2063(97)90046-5

Groenendijk, N. (1997). A principal-agent model of corruption. *Crime, Law and Social Change*, *27*, 207–229. https://doi.org/10.1023/A:1008267601329

Hagendorff, J., & Vallascas, F. (2011). CEO pay incentives and risk-taking: Evidence from bank acquisitions. *Journal of Corporate Finance*, *17*(4), 1078–1095. https://doi.org/10.1016/J.JCORPFIN.2011.04.009

Hellman, J. S., Jones, G., & Kaufmann, D. (2003). Seize the state, seize the day: State capture and influence in transition economies. *Journal of Comparative Economics*, *31*(4), 751–773. https://doi.org/10.1016/J.JCE.2003.09.006

Hou, D., & Skeie, D. (2014). LIBOR: Origins, economics, crisis, scandal, and reform. *SSRN Electronic Journal*. https://doi.org/10.2139/ssrn.2423387

Jones, L., Alsakka, R., ap Gwilym, O., & Mantovan, N. (2022). Regulating rating agencies: A conservative behavioural change. *Journal of Financial Stability*, *60*, 100999. https://doi.org/10.1016/J.JFS.2022.100999

Li, X., Dang, J., Liu, L., Liang, Y., Wei, C., & Gu, Z. (2023). Are greedy individuals more corrupt? *Current Psychology*, *42*(1), 165–173. https://doi.org/10.1007/s12144-021-01415-1

Lim, R., & Yoong, D. (2023). Conceptualizing money laundering in the 1MDB scandal: An analysis of metaphors in the Sarawak report. In K. Rajandran & C. Lee (Eds.), *Discursive approaches to politics in Malaysia: Legitimising governance* (Vol. 18, pp. 251–268). Springer Nature. https://doi.org/10.1007/978-981-19-5334-7_13

Lima-de-Oliveira, R. (2020). Corruption and local content development: Assessing the impact of the Petrobras' scandal on recent policy changes in Brazil. *The Extractive Industries and Society*, *7*(2), 274–282. https://doi.org/10.1016/J.EXIS.2019.08.004

Manara, U. M., Nübold, A., van Gils, S., & Zijlstra, R. H. F. (2023). Exploring the path to corruption–An informed grounded theory study on the decision-making process underlying corruption. *PLoS One*, *18*(9), 1–26. https://doi.org/10.1371/journal.pone.0291819

Marino, D. (2025). Dynamics of corruption: Theoretical explanatory model and empirical results. *Physica A: Statistical Mechanics and its Applications*, *658*, 130288. https://doi.org/10.1016/J.PHYSA.2024.130288

Md Ali, A. (2022). 1MDB: The causes! part I. *International Journal of Academic Research in Business and Social Sciences*, *12*. https://doi.org/10.6007/IJARBSS/v12-i11/15770

Michael Dalde, J. A. (2023). Money Mayhem: The Wells Fargo Cross Selling Con Scheme-A Case Study. *International Journal of Advanced Multidisciplinary Studies*, *III*.

Milidonis, A. (2013). Compensation incentives of credit rating agencies and predictability of changes in bond ratings and financial strength ratings. *Journal of Banking & Finance*, *37*(9), 3716–3732. https://doi.org/10.1016/J.JBANKFIN.2013.04.032

Monticini, A., & Thornton, D. L. (2013). The effect of underreporting on LIBOR rates. *Journal of Macroeconomics*, *37*, 345–348. https://doi.org/10.1016/J.JMACRO.2013.02.002

Mullen, D. M., Wheatley, K., & Lamb, N. (2023). Bad apples or poisonous tree? Corporate culture's role in the Wells Fargo scandal. *CASE Journal*, *19*(6), 878–895. https://doi.org/10.1108/TCJ-01-2022-0002

North, D. C. (1990). *Institutions, institutional change and economic performance*. Cambridge University Press. https://doi.org/10.1017/CBO9780511808678

Padhy, Mr S., & Sahoo, R. (2025). A study on NPA dynamics and recovery strategies in Indian PSBs. *International Journal for Research in Applied Science and Engineering Technology*, *13*(5), 6365–6374. https://doi.org/10.22214/ijraset.2025.71676

Paganou, S., Antoniadis, I., Zournatzidou, G., & Sklavos, G. (2024). Investigating the link among corruption, corporate governance and corporate performance in family businesses: A future research agenda. *Administrative Sciences, 14*(7). https://doi.org/10.3390/admsci14070139

Peng, Q. (R.), Sivadasan, P., & Zhang, R. Z. (R. Z). (2023). Executive compensation horizon incentives, performance targets, and auditor risk assessment. *Journal of Accounting and Public Policy*, *42*(6), 107121. https://doi.org/10.1016/J.JACCPUBPOL.2023.107121

Seuntjens, T. G., van de Ven, N., Zeelenberg, M., & van der Schors, A. (2016). Greed and adolescent financial behavior. *Journal of Economic Psychology*, *57*, 1–12. https://doi.org/10.1016/J.JOEP.2016.09.002

Sheedy, E., Zhang, L., & Tam, K. C. H. (2019). Incentives and culture in risk compliance. *Journal of Banking & Finance*, *107*, 105611. https://doi.org/10.1016/J.JBANKFIN.2019.105611

Steiner, K. (2017). Politics and economics: The 1MDB scandal and corruption in Malaysia. In *Illusions of democracy: Malaysian politics and people* (Vol. II, pp. 202–225). SIRD. https://ssrn.com/abstract=3061598

Tayan, B. (2019). *The wells fargo cross-selling scandal.* https://ssrn.com/abstract=2879102

Thommandru, A., Maratovich, F. F., & Saparovna, N. S. (2024). Fortifying Uzbekistan's integrity landscape: Harnessing India's tech-driven anti-corruption strategies. *Sustainable Futures*, *7*, 100206. https://doi.org/10.1016/J.SFTR.2024.100206

Toscano, F. (2020). Does the dodd-frank act reduce the conflict of interests of credit rating agencies? *Journal of Corporate Finance*, *62*, 101595. https://doi.org/10.1016/J.JCORPFIN.2020.101595

Valverde, P., Fernandez, J., Buenaño, E., González-Avella, J. C., & Cosenza, M. (2023). Controlling systemic corruption through group size and salary dispersion of public servants. *Heliyon Journal.* http://arxiv.org/abs/2304.02113

Wawrosz, P. (2022). How corruption is and should be investigated by economic theory. *Economies*, *10*, 326. https://doi.org/10.3390/economies10120326

Zafeiriou, E., Garefalakis, A., Passas, I., & Ragazou, K. (2023). Illicit and corruption mitigation strategy in the financial sector: A study with a hybrid methodological approach. *Sustainability*, *15*(2). https://doi.org/10.3390/su15021366

Chapter 3

Case Studies in Corruption: Key Lessons From High-Profile Scandals

Alban Kryezi and Halim Bajraktari

University "Ukshin Hoti" Prizren, Republic of Kosovo

Abstract

High-profile corruption represents a complex and multidimensional phenomenon that undermines the rule of law, economic development, and public trust in state institutions. Although the phenomenon of corruption has been widely addressed in the literature, specific aspects of corruption at the highest levels of government often remain insufficiently addressed, both within the framework of international legal instruments and in their practical implementation at the national level. This chapter is to analyze the definitions, causes, and consequences of high-profile corruption through the review of well-known international and domestic cases, as well as to assess the institutional approach of the Republic of Kosovo in addressing this phenomenon. This chapter is based on qualitative methodology, using doctrinal analysis of legal sources, the review of concrete judicial cases, and comparative analysis of institutional practices. It addresses international cases such as the "Panama Papers," the case of Riad Salameh and the 1Malaysia Development Berhad (1MDB) scandal, along with domestic cases such as the case of "53 million," "Stenta 2," and the "Pronto" affair. Findings: The research findings indicate a lack of efficiency in the institutional handling of high-profile corruption cases in Kosovo, including procedural delays, political interference, and a lack of professional capacity within the justice system. Such cases reflect not only abuse of official duties but also systemic weaknesses that hinder accountability of political and administrative leadership.

Keywords: High-profile corruption; public officials; scandals; political influence; anti-corruption efforts; Republic of Kosovo

Corruption and Crime in Finance, 47–64

doi:10.1108/978-1-83708-170-720261008

1. Introduction

Corruption has been, and continues to be, one of the greatest challenges for modern states and societies. It undermines the normal and fair functioning of institutions, erodes citizens' trust in the rule of law, and negatively impacts the transparent distribution of public resources. One of the most serious forms of corruption is high-profile corruption, which refers to the phenomenon where high-ranking government and public administration officials abuse their power to pursue private interests using public resources. This type of corruption typically involves large sums of money or critical political and economic decision-making. Its complex nature often hinders investigation and prosecution, especially when the very state mechanisms responsible for ensuring justice are themselves compromised or involved.

Across the globe—and particularly in the region in which we operate—high-profile corruption and political scandals have become a regular feature of national and international media coverage, often implicating key political and institutional figures. Environments plagued by pervasive corruption foster networks of illicit cooperation that facilitate, rather than prevent, the spread of this phenomenon. This not only perpetuates corruption but also heightens the risk of involvement by high-ranking public officials. It is no coincidence that the scale of high-profile corruption has expanded globally, posing a direct threat to the stability of justice and democracy both within the region and beyond. Studies indicate that this form of corruption is present in the majority of countries and, alarmingly, is becoming a "trend"—where, in certain circles, the more corrupt one is, the more they are valued or empowered.

Considering these characteristics, it is essential to study specific cases of high-profile corruption to understand how it occurs in practice, as well as to analyze the eventual failures or successes in its prevention and prosecution. Despite the significance and consequences of high-profile corruption, there is still no clear or universally accepted definition of this phenomenon. In this regard, this chapter aims to examine the concept of high-profile corruption by analyzing its causes and consequences. Specifically, this chapter seeks to provide a clear framework regarding the legal treatment of high-profile corruption, based on concrete cases and an analysis of institutional approaches to the prosecution of high-ranking officials. Through a comparative approach between international practices and those in the Republic of Kosovo, the research aims to uncover existing weaknesses and opportunities for improvement in preventing and combating high-profile corruption.

The importance of this chapter lies in the fact that high-profile corruption affects democratic development and the efficiency of the rule of law. In those countries where punishment for this form of corruption is absent, situations arise that undermine public trust in state institutions. By analyzing the most well-known cases of high-profile corruption, this chapter aims to provide a concrete overview of the challenges faced by judicial institutions. This is particularly important for transitional countries, such as Kosovo, where the building of independent institutions and accountability remain a strategic priority for the rule of law and European integration.

2. Literature Review

2.1 The Concept of High-Profile Corruption

Although corruption is discussed and examined in various ways, it is difficult to provide a single definition due to the complexity of this phenomenon. Regarding the definition of corruption, Ref (Martinsson, 2021, p. 269) states: *"Finding a universal and all-encompassing definition of corruption for corruption scholars would be like finding the Holy Grail: it has not been done yet, and it is highly unlikely it ever will be."* Different concepts may offer different approaches to addressing corruption.

The research approach provides the opportunity to analyze studies that address the concept of corruption from different dimensions. A portion of the literature discusses corruption from legal, economic, and governance perspectives, offering definitions that include elements such as clientelism, abuse of power, state capture, and patrimonialism (Luna-Pla & Nicolás-Carlock, 2020). Another category of research classifies corruption based on its economic scale as grand corruption, structural corruption, systemic corruption, and petty corruption (Andvig et al., 2001). Corruption includes various behaviors and actions, such as bribery, extortion, misuse of information, and abuse of discretion (Graycar, 2015).

In the past, the focus of corruption was primarily on the public sector, and it was defined as the abuse of public office for private gain (Wawrosz, 2022). Today, corruption can affect all areas and sectors of life. It is worth mentioning that the most widely accepted definition of corruption is the one provided by Transparency International, the most prominent nongovernmental organization fighting corruption, which defines it as "*the abuse of entrusted power for private gain*" (Transparency International, 2018). Corruption is considered to be one of the main reasons why many policies aimed at improving living standards fail to achieve their goals (Pozsgai-Alvarez, 2020).

Corruption undermines the proper functioning of institutions and reduces citizens' trust in the legal and political system. While low-level corruption affects the daily lives of citizens, high-profile corruption involves individuals holding important state functions or positions. High-profile corruption is the abuse of power by heads of state, ministers, and high-ranking officials for private gain (González, 2007). It is the form of corruption that permeates the highest levels of a national government, leading to a widespread erosion of trust in good governance, the rule of law, and economic stability (Rose-Ackerman, 1996).

Despite the importance and consequences of high-profile corruption, there is still no legal or universally accepted definition of this phenomenon (OECD, 2024). International legal instruments against corruption—such as the United Nations Convention against Transnational Organized Crime, the United Nations Convention against Corruption, the Council of Europe's Criminal Law

Convention on Corruption, the Council of Europe's Civil Law Convention on Corruption, and the Organization for Economic Cooperation and Development (OECD) Convention on Combating Bribery of Foreign Public Officials in International Business Transactions-do not define high-profile corruption. However, debates continue at both the national and international levels regarding what constitutes high-profile corruption (OECD, 2024).

Transparency International suggests defining high-profile corruption as the commission of any of the criminal acts listed in Articles 15–25 of the United Nations Convention Against Corruption, as part of a scheme involving a high-ranking public official, which results or is intended to result in a significant misuse of public funds or a severe violation of human rights (Transparency International, 2019). The above-mentioned provisions include: Bribery of national public officials; Bribery of foreign public officials and officials of public international organizations; Embezzlement, misappropriation or other diversion of property by a public official; Trading in influence; Abuse of functions; Illicit enrichment; Bribery in the private sector; Embezzlement of property in the private sector; Laundering of proceeds of crime; Concealment; and Obstruction of justice (UNITED NATIONS, 2004).

2.2 Causes and Consequences of Corruption

The reviewed literature discusses three types of causes of high-profile corruption, distinguishing between individual, structural, and contextual factors (Poeschl & Ribeiro, 2015). Individual factors refer to a predisposition toward crime, lack of ethics, and greed, while contextual factors refer to the opportunity to engage in corrupt actions, created by significant government projects, or due to the lack of measures that could prevent corruption (Argandoña, 2001). Structural factors refer to the lack of democracy, underdevelopment, and poverty of nations (Seyf, 2001). In highly corrupt countries, the idea that the state should protect the public interest is underdeveloped, there is a lack of institutional control over abuse of power, as well as a lack of will or ability to address corruption (Shah & Schacter, 2004).

This form of corruption is more prevalent in less developed countries with a weaker democratic tradition and a weaker judicial system, where poverty is widespread (Seyf, 2001). It remains unclear whether an increase in income leads to a reduction in corruption or whether corruption decreases due to an increase in income. The literature provides evidence for both. On one hand, an increase in income may simply open up more opportunities for corruption due to more temptations. At the same time, it is also believed that an increase in income reduces the level of corruption because economic development usually goes hand in hand with political development, democratization, and accountability. On the other hand, an increase in corruption levels is believed to be detrimental to economic growth, particularly certain types of corruption and at specific stages of growth. In much of the literature, corruption is understood as one of the evils caused by economic underdevelopment (Amundsen, 1999).

High-profile corruption causes injustice, inefficiency of services, distrust in government, misuse of public funds, increased poverty, political instability, and limitations in government policy (Poeschl & Ribeiro, 2015). The United Nations defines this form of corruption as one of the causes of undermining democratic institutions, slowing down economic development, and causing government instability (United Nations Office on Drugs and Crime, 2012). The political consequences of high-profile corruption vary significantly depending on the type of governance in a country. In weak states, where the elite in power exercises control over who benefits from what kind of corruption, the legitimacy of the state itself will be undermined due to the lack of service delivery (Amundsen, 1999). The level of high-profile corruption and its political impact in Europe is not comparable to the destructive effects seen in most African and Asian countries. In democratic countries, or more precisely in countries governed by the rule of law where human rights and the separation of powers between institutions and groups are respected and effective, acts of political corruption can be exposed by a free press and other media, by the opposition, by auditing and controlling bodies, or by the police, and offenders can lose their position through legal procedures (Amundsen, 1999).

3. Methodology

This chapter is based on a qualitative, analytical approach aimed at providing a deeper understanding of high-profile corruption and how it is treated in practice. The methodology used in this paper includes doctrinal analysis of legal sources, examination of concrete cases of corruption, and a critical assessment of the institutional and judicial approaches at both the national and international levels. The doctrinal analysis includes the review of theoretical literature, international and national laws, relevant conventions (such as the United Nations Convention Against Corruption), as well as political documents and official guidelines, such as the one issued by the State Prosecutor of the Republic of Kosovo regarding the definition of high-profile corruption.

In the empirical part of this chapter, case studies are used as a key method to analyze different forms of high-profile corruption in various state contexts. Three international cases with wide global impact have been examined: the "Panama Papers," the case of the former Governor of the Central Bank of Lebanon, Riad Salameh, and the 1Malaysia Development Berhad (1MDB) financial scandal in Malaysia. In a comparative manner, three significant cases from Kosovo have also been analyzed: the "53 million" case, "Stenta 2," and "Pronto Affair," which provide a clear view of the systemic challenges and the institutional approach to elite corruption. For each case, the structure of the violation, the role of the involved officials, institutional response, judicial processes, and the final outcome have been examined. Additionally, court decisions at all levels have been reviewed to assess the legal treatment of criminal acts of a corrupt nature.

4. International High-Profile Corruption Cases: An Analysis of the Panama Papers, the Former Governor of the Central Bank of Lebanon Riad Salameh, and the 1MDB Financial Scandal in Malaysia

The "Panama Papers" case represents one of the examples of high-profile corruption and the concealment of assets through offshore structures. The flow of documents known as the "Panama Papers" was first published in April 2016 by the International Consortium of Investigative Journalists. The documents, with a volume of 11.5 million files, were obtained from an anonymous source within the Panamanian law firm Mossack Fonseca. It represents one of the largest cases of using offshore financial structures for purposes such as tax evasion, money laundering, and asset concealment by public figures, politicians, businessmen, and powerful companies (International Consortium of Investigative Journalists, 2016). The case involved current and former heads of state, prominent political figures, powerful businessmen, and individuals closely connected to government elites. Among the most talked-about were the then Prime Minister of Iceland, Sigmundur Davíð Gunnlaugsson (who was forced to resign), as well as figures from the Middle East, Russia, China, Latin America, and the European Union (Harding, 2016).

Despite the consequences and public outcry, this scandal did not lead to severe punishments for those involved in the aforementioned activities. Many countries launched investigations; however, prosecutions were limited due to a lack of political will to address money laundering and tax evasion by public figures implicated in the scandal. Germany issued arrest warrants for Mossack Fonseca lawyers Jürgen Mossack and Ramón Fonseca for tax evasion and operating a criminal organization. In Panama, they faced charges related to the Panama Papers scandal and bribery involving a Brazilian company, for which they spent two months in prison. In June 2024, a Panamanian judge acquitted Mossack and 27 others of money laundering charges related to the Panama Papers case (Molina-Acosta, 2024). This is an example that illustrates how political and economic interests often hinder the achievement of full justice.

Another case of high-profile corruption and lack of transparent management of public finances is that of Riad Salameh, the former Governor of the Central Bank of Lebanon. In 2020, the Swiss foundation Accountability Now filed a criminal complaint in Switzerland against Salameh, raising suspicions of the embezzlement of approximately 300 million US dollars together with his brother, through a company registered in the British Virgin Islands. The funds are suspected to have been transferred through 12 Swiss banks, including well-known names such as HSBC, UBS, Credit Suisse, and others.

In October 2020, the Swiss Prosecutor's Office opened criminal proceedings for money laundering. Switzerland's request for legal assistance led to a parallel investigation in Lebanon, although political interference hindered judicial actions on the ground. The investigations focused on the company Forry Associates, owned by Salameh's brother, which profited from commissions imposed by the central bank on government bond transactions. Investigations were also launched in France and Luxembourg in 2021, and in 2022, Germany, Belgium, and Liechtenstein joined the probe. In March 2022, France, Germany, and Luxembourg froze more than 130 million US dollars in assets. However, the investigations faced obstacles due to domestic political support for Salameh in Lebanon. In 2023, Lebanese authorities formally charged Salameh with embezzlement, money laundering, fraud, and tax evasion. In May of the same year, France and Germany issued international arrest warrants, and Interpol published a Red Notice (Dell, 2023). The former governor was arrested in September of last year and is still in pretrial detention (Bassam & Gebeily, 2025).

The case of Riad Salameh highlights how corruption at the highest institutional levels can have devastating consequences for a country. The lack of transparency and accountability enabled one individual to abuse a central institution like the Central Bank of Lebanon for decades, contributing to a deep economic crisis and a loss of public trust in the banking system. This case underscores the importance of the rule of law, international cooperation in the fight against money laundering, and the need for strong institutions grounded in the principle of accountability (Duparc, 2025).

Another high-profile financial scandal involving corruption and money laundering is the 1MDB case. The Malaysian state fund was established in 2009 to promote development through foreign investment, under the leadership of then-Prime Minister Najib Razak. This fund became the center of one of the biggest corruption scandals in modern history. The US Department of Justice believes that more than $4.5 billion was stolen, making this scandal directly responsible for the collapse of the government and the arrest of Najib, his wife, and several close associates (Abadi, 2021). The leaked financial documents suggest that 1MDB was a hub of fraudulent activity from the very beginning. Large sums were borrowed through government bonds and transferred into bank accounts in Switzerland, Singapore, and the United States. Approximately $731 million appeared in Najib's personal bank account shortly before the 2013 elections and is believed to have been used to pay politicians, cover his credit card bills, and fund his wife's lavish shopping habits. Najib denies the allegations and insists that the money was a donation from a Saudi prince. Abroad, it is suspected that the funds helped finance the extravagant lifestyle of one of the consultants allegedly brought in to oversee 1MDB, Malaysian businessman Jho Low (Jones, 2020).

The alleged embezzlement of 1MDB funds between 2009 and 2012 went unchallenged until 2015. That year, British journalist Clare Rewcastle-Brown, who ran the Sarawak Report website, was handed 227,000 leaked documents detailing the extent of the fraud. The Wall Street Journal also received some of these documents. Malaysia's anti-corruption agency (MACC) launched an investigation and was reportedly preparing to issue an arrest warrant for Prime Minister Najib. However, Najib responded by dismissing the Attorney General leading the investigation, along with the Deputy Prime Minister and four other ministers who had raised concerns about the scandal. His government also refused to cooperate with investigations in the United States, Singapore, and Switzerland.

In 2016, the Attorney General appointed by Najib cleared the prime minister of all wrongdoing, stating that the case was "completely resolved." Not everyone was convinced by Najib's claim of innocence. Mahathir Mohamad, a former prime minister who had helped Najib rise to power, remained committed to the issue. Believing he was the only one capable of taking action, he announced that he would run against Najib in the 2018 general elections. His opposition party was elected for the first time in a historic moment and immediately prioritized 1MDB. Within days of Najib's downfall, properties linked to him were raided by the police, leading to the seizure of millions of dollars' worth of assets (Jones, 2020). In July 2020, Najib was found guilty of abuse of power, breach of public trust, and money laundering. For these charges, he was sentenced to 12 years in prison and a fine of 49 million US dollars. However, in February 2024, Malaysia's Pardons Board decided to reduce his sentence by half, lowering it to 6 years in prison and reducing the fine to 10.6 million US dollars (Ratcliffe, 2022). Najib continues to face other charges.

5. Results of the Fight Against High-Profile Corruption in Kosovo

In terms of the fight against corruption, specifically high-profile corruption, the Republic of Kosovo has made efforts to clarify the concept of high-profile corruption through an official document. What is considered high-profile corruption has been defined through a directive issued by the State Prosecutor, which aims to provide clarity and uniformity in handling cases of this phenomenon, applicable throughout the territory of the Republic of Kosovo. The aforementioned guideline explicitly defines the criminal acts considered high-profile corruption, the individuals holding official positions involved, and the benefits or damages caused by the acts of corruption (Prokuroria Speciale e Republikës së Kosovës, 2013).

A corruption offense will be considered high-profile, regardless of the value or benefit from the committed act, when the person is suspected of committing any of the following criminal acts:

- Conclusion of harmful contracts, aggravated by bribery (Article 285, paragraph 2);
- Escape of a person deprived of liberty, aggravated by bribery (Article 397, paragraph 2);
- Enabling the escape of persons deprived of liberty, aggravated by bribery (Article 398, paragraph 2);
- Abuse of official position or authority (Article 414);
- Embezzlement in office (Article 418);
- Fraud in office (Article 419);
- Unauthorized use of property (Article 420);
- Acceptance of bribery (Article 421);

- Offering bribery (Article 422);
- Offering bribery to a foreign public official or foreign officials (Article 423);
- Exercising influence (Article 424);
- Unlawful issuance of judicial decisions (Article 425);
- Unlawful collection and payment (Article 428);
- Unlawful embezzlement of property during a raid or execution of a court decision (Article 429).

If the person suspected of committing any of the aforementioned criminal acts is:

- The President of Kosovo;
- The President and members of the Parliament of the Assembly of Kosovo;
- The Prime Minister, Deputy Prime Ministers, and Ministers of the Government of Kosovo;
- Mayors of municipalities;
- Judges of the Supreme Court of Kosovo;
- Judges of the Court of Appeals;
- The Chief State Prosecutor;
- The Chief Prosecutors.

The directive has also set out additional conditions regarding when an offense will be considered as high-profile corruption, specifically defining public positions and the value or benefit from the corrupt actions mentioned above.

In this regard, the criminal acts mentioned above will constitute high-profile corruption when the benefit or damage exceeds the amount of 500,000.00 EUR, if the perpetrator is:

- Deputy Minister of the Government of Kosovo;
- Senior Civil Servant (General Secretary or equivalent positions);
- Employee of ministries and public institutions in decision-making or advisory positions.

In addition to the criteria addressed above, the directive also establishes another situation in which high-level corruption is considered to exist. In this specific case, the focus is on financial gain or damage. A corruption offense will be considered high-level corruption in any case where the benefit derived from the criminal act or the damage caused as a result of a particular corruption offense exceeds the amount of 1,000,000.00 EURO.

6. The Case of "53 Million"

The Special Prosecution of the Republic of Kosovo in February 2022 filed an indictment against the former Minister of Infrastructure and former Chairperson of the Inter-Ministerial Steering Committee, Pal Lekaj, as well as his political advisor, Eset Berisha. They are accused of exceeding their official powers in order to cause damage to the budget of the Republic of Kosovo for the benefit of another party. According to the indictment, the abuse occurred when the accused signed, on behalf of the Ministry of Infrastructure as the employer and the company "Bechtel & Enka," an agreement in September 2017 to extend the deadline for the completion of works on the "Arbën Xhaferi" highway, which connects Kosovo with North Macedonia, by an additional 347 days. The completion of the highway, under the base contract signed in 2014, was supposed to occur by January 18, 2018, whereas under the new agreement signed by the accused, the contract would now end in December 2018. The agreement to extend the deadline for completing the works was signed without financial costs, which was in violation of the Public Procurement Law and the Statute and Code of Conduct of the Inter-Ministerial Steering Committee. The signing of the agreement in this manner allowed the contractor to request payment for an additional amount of 63 million euros in November 2017, for the extension of the completion deadline.

The former Minister of Infrastructure, in his capacity as Chairperson of the Inter-Ministerial Steering Committee, without informing or obtaining the consent of the other members of the Steering Committee, had engaged his political advisor to enter into negotiations with the contractor to determine the financial cost. The political advisor, exceeding his authority, held discussions with the contractor, and in full agreement with the former Minister, they decided that, in the name of extending the completion deadline, the Ministry of Infrastructure would pay an additional financial cost of 53,100,000.00 EUR to the company "Bechtel & Enka." The only bodies authorized to conduct negotiations and determine the financial cost were the Inter-Ministerial Steering Committee and the Project Implementation Unit, both of which were completely ignored by the former Minister of Infrastructure.

For the execution of the aforementioned payment, with the assistance of his advisor, the former Minister completely disregarded the opinion of the supervising company for the project, "Hill International." According to this opinion, the reasonable additional cost for extending the completion deadline of the works was 14,778,654.87 EUR. This opinion was not presented in any of the meetings held by the Inter-Ministerial Steering Committee for this purpose.

Continuing with the realization of their goal, the former Minister, in collaboration with his advisor, exerted pressure on the Director of the Legal Department of the Ministry of Infrastructure to change the previous legal opinion, according to which the supervising company for the project, "Hill International," could provide opinions regarding the financial cost requests. The Director of the Legal Department was forced to alter the original version of the first legal opinion and drafted a new version of the legal opinion, which removed the name of the supervising company "Hill International" as the competent party for providing opinions on financial cost requests.

Exploiting these situations, the former Minister of Infrastructure, as the chairperson of the Inter-Ministerial Steering Committee, pressured the other members of the committee, who were presented with false facts, to make a decision recommending the Government of the Republic of Kosovo approve the request of the contractor "Bechtel & Enka" for the payment of the amount of 53,100,000.00 EUR in exchange for extending the completion deadline of the works. Faced with such a situation and the facts presented by the former Minister of Infrastructure, the Government of the Republic of Kosovo decided in June 2018 to approve the payment of the aforementioned amount. The accused for the abuse of official position and authority were also the Secretary General of the Ministry of Infrastructure and the Director of Public Procurement at the Ministry of Infrastructure.

For the corrupt actions mentioned above, the Basic Court in Pristina, in January 2024, issued a verdict in which it sentenced the former minister to a prison term of 3 years and 8 months, as well as an additional penalty of a ban on holding public administrative positions or functions in public services for 3 years and 6 months. His political advisor was sentenced to 3 years and 3 months in prison, along with an additional penalty of a ban on holding public administrative positions or functions in public services for 3 years. The Secretary General was sentenced to 1 year and 8 months in prison, as well as an additional penalty of a ban on holding public administrative positions or functions in public services for 2 years. The Director of Public Procurement was also sentenced to the same prison term and additional penalty.

However, the case "53 million" will be retried at the Basic Court. The Court of Appeals, in February of this year, decided to return the case to the initial point of trial, specifically to retry the sentencing decisions for the individuals mentioned above. This decision was made by the Court of Appeals after approving the appeals filed by the defense lawyers of the defendants in this case.

7. The Case of "Stenta 2"

The Special Prosecution of the Republic of Kosovo, in June 2016, filed an indictment against 37 doctors from the University Clinical Hospital Service of Kosovo for the criminal offense of Abuse of Official Position or Authority. According to the indictment, from 2011 to 2015, they abused their official duties by intentionally and knowingly issuing referral letters to at least 233 individuals as members of the consultative commissions of the Cardiology Clinic, referring them for treatment outside public healthcare institutions even though the individuals had already undergone medical treatment. This was done to enable these individuals to be reimbursed by the Ministry of Health for medical treatment in private institutions. The prosecution claimed that these actions caused financial damage to the budget of the Republic of Kosovo in the amount of €4,555,553.00.

Furthermore, the doctors were reasonably suspected of abusing their official duties and accepting bribes, in that instead of referring patients who came for check-ups at public healthcare institutions to the competent invasive unit at the Cardiology Clinic within the University Clinical Hospital Service of Kosovo, they referred those patients to private hospitals. In return for these actions, they accepted bribes. For each patient sent for stent placement, they received a bribe of €500, and for each coronary angiography, they received €150. As a result, the private hospital was enabled to gain financial profit in the amount of €504,595.00.

In September 2023, the Basic Court in Pristina rendered an acquittal verdict for the doctors accused of the criminal offenses of Abuse of Official Position or Authority and Accepting Bribes. The Court had administered all personal and material evidence proposed by the Special Prosecution, the defendants, and their legal counsels, and assessed that the actions of the accused did not constitute the criminal offenses they were charged with. The Court was unable to establish which individual actions, if any, by the accused caused the alleged damage to the budget of the Republic of Kosovo. According to the verdict, the accused had only provided professional opinions on patient treatment outside public healthcare institutions, but did not make official decisions regarding how much financial support should be allocated for such treatments, which cases should be financially supported, or to what extent such support should be provided from the state budget.

Furthermore, regarding the offense of Accepting Bribes, the Court was not able to verify who had given the bribes or the time at which the bribes were allegedly received by the accused. This acquittal verdict was upheld by the Court of Appeals in March 2025, which rejected as unfounded the appeal submitted by the Special Prosecution within the legal deadline against the acquittal decision of the Basic Court in Pristina.

8. The Case of "Pronto"

The Special Prosecution of the Republic of Kosovo, based on the publication of certain wiretapped conversations by the online newspaper "Insajderi" in August 2016—widely known to the public as the "Pronto" affair—initiated investigations against former MP and head of the parliamentary group of the Democratic Party of Kosovo (PDK), Adem Grabovci. The investigations were conducted for the criminal offense of Violation of the Equal Status of Citizens and Residents of the Republic of Kosovo. According to the Special Prosecution, the former MP had communicated with several public officials regarding the unlawful employment of certain individuals in Kosovo Government institutions and their selection for positions as directors of central public enterprise boards. After concluding the investigation, the Special Prosecution filed an indictment in April 2018 related to the "Pronto" affair for the aforementioned criminal offense.

In addition to the former PDK MP, several other officials holding important positions were also indicted, including the former Minister of the Ministry of Innovation, another former MP, the former Secretary General of the Ministry of Internal Affairs, the former Deputy Minister of the Ministry of Labor and Social Welfare, the former political advisor at the Ministry of Internal Affairs, the former Chairperson of the Board of the Public Enterprise Radoniqi-Dukagjini, the former Chairperson of the Board of the Public Enterprise Hidro-Drini, the former Speaker of the Municipal Assembly of Prizren, and the former Head of the Procurement Unit at the Ministry of Health. Despite the fact that the published wiretapped conversations also involved the then Prime Minister of Kosovo and the former Speaker of the Assembly of the Republic of Kosovo, they were not included in the indictment, neither as defendants nor as witnesses in the case.

According to the indictment, there was well-founded suspicion that the accused had abused their official positions by cooperating with one another to unlawfully grant advantages to certain individuals applying for important state positions, thereby denying the rights of other candidates who had applied for the same positions. The indictment alleges that through their incriminating actions, the accused sought to create privileges or advantages for certain individuals based on their close personal relationships and political affiliation, while discriminating against and denying the rights of other applicants who competed for the positions announced in the aforementioned recruitment processes.

The Basic Court in Pristina, citing lack of evidence, issued a verdict of acquittal in January 2020 for all the defendants in the "Pronto" case. In June 2020, the Court of Appeals partially overturned the first-instance verdict and found former MP Adem Grabovci guilty, sentencing him to a suspended sentence along with a supplementary punishment—disqualification from being elected and a ban on exercising functions in public administration for a period of two years. The former MP filed an appeal with the Supreme Court, which upheld the Court of Appeals' decision regarding the suspended sentence. However, following the submission of a request for protection of legality as an extraordinary legal remedy, in April 2021, the Supreme Court overturned the decision on the suspended sentence and the supplementary punishments, thereby declaring the former MP and former head of the Democratic Party of Kosovo's parliamentary group not guilty.

9. Discussion of Findings

The findings show that the Republic of Kosovo has taken concrete and significant steps in defining the concept of high-profile corruption. The directive issued by the State Prosecutor demonstrates institutional efforts regarding the establishment of clear criteria applicable throughout the country. The content of this directive reflects a combined approach, which on one hand defines the criminal offenses constituting high-profile corruption, while on the other, identifies the categories of state or official positions that present a risk for the abuse of power and illicit benefits through corruption.

However, the definition of public positions and damages or benefits expressed in monetary terms through the directive could create obstacles in the fight against high-profile corruption. In this regard, there may be a risk that some corruption cases committed by individuals outside the positions officially defined in the directive, or with benefits of lower values, may not receive the necessary priority from state authorities. Criminal benefit or harm as a result of corruption does not always reflect the true impact of a criminal act on society. An act that contains elements of corruption may have long-term consequences even if the monetary value of the damage or benefit does not exceed the criteria set forth in the directive.

The case known as the "53 million" is an indicator of the irregularities in the management of the state administration of the Republic of Kosovo. This case represents abuse of official positions and deliberate avoidance of legal procedures, with severe institutional and financial consequences. The main issue is not only the violation of official duties by some high-ranking officials, but also the institutional shortcomings that allowed decision-making without relying on the principles of accountability and transparency. Political interference in professional legal processes through pressures to alter legal opinions and the disregard of recommendations from the supervisory company are signs of the capture of decision-making procedures for the benefit of certain groups. The conviction of officials represents a significant development in the fight against high-profile corruption.

However, the referral of the case for retrial by the Court of Appeals can be interpreted as a procedural weakness that negatively affects the fight against corruption. This may create societal concerns about delayed justice, which could undermine the effectiveness of imposed sentences. This is also reflected in research findings regarding the institutional handling of corruption cases in Kosovo, which indicate that high-profile corruption cases are characterized by prolonged procedures (Fetiu, 2025). Therefore, such cases should be given higher priority in investigation, trial, and the proper sentencing of those involved in this category of offenses in the country.

The "Stenta 2" case highlights several deficiencies in the criminal justice system, specifically in handling high-profile corruption cases within a very sensitive public sector, such as healthcare. The judicial process in this case was characterized by serious and concerning weaknesses in the collection and presentation of evidence. The criminal prosecution was based on a general analysis, without specifying guilt based on the individual principle, without establishing a causal or causal relationship, and without securing convincing and reliable evidence for another form of corruption, such as bribery. These actions created room for the defense to raise doubts about the lack of guilt. The inability to identify the bribe giver, as well as the inability to identify the time or place of the bribe, contributed to the failure of the Special Prosecutor's Office in building this criminal case according to the required standards.

On the other hand, the way in which the Basic Court reasoned its acquittal of the accused shows the restrictive approach to the criminal case. Based on the fact that the doctors had given a professional opinion and did not have decision-making powers for the allocation of financial resources from the public budget, the Court did not deeply analyze the impact of the actions to the detriment of the state financial system. The Court only examined the lack of formal administrative powers, which such an interpretation is technically acceptable in formal terms. However, there was no examination of the factual responsibility of the doctors' actions and their impact on the guidance of patients to private hospital institutions. The fact that the Court of Appeal also confirmed the acquittal shows a lack of critical assessment of the case in the second instance, turning the second instance of the judiciary into another mechanism of impunity. According to research conducted on the efficiency of the second instance of the judiciary, no high-profile corruption case was convicted in the second instance (Bajraktari, 2020).

The "Pronto" case revealed the capture of the public administration by party interests and the use of official positions to distribute political favors. The published wiretaps and the indictment raised by the Special Prosecutor's Office identified the practice of political influence in employment processes, violating the principles of equality and the rule of law. The fact that the Prosecutor's Office did not include high-ranking political figures of that time in the indictment, despite their involvement in the published communications, raises doubts about a lack of objectivity, selective justice, and a lack of will to effectively combat political corruption.

Another concerning issue is that the accused were not prosecuted for the criminal offense of Abuse of Official Position or Authority, but for the offense of Violation of the Equal Status of Citizens and Residents of the Republic of Kosovo. This could be interpreted as an attempt to avoid a harsher criminal prosecution, as the offense they were charged with carries a lighter penalty. The contradictory decisions between the three judicial instances may further diminish the public's trust in Kosovo's justice system. The conclusion of the case with a full acquittal could send a troubling message to society that high-ranking officials' criminal responsibility is often excluded.

From high-profile corruption cases, key lessons can be drawn that it is not only the abuse of official duties that is concerning but also the reflection of institutional weaknesses, including the lack of transparency and effective oversight. Insufficient investigations, inadequate criminal prosecutions, and the narrow approach of courts in handling cases show a system that often fails to prevent political and administrative corruption, where accountability is scarcely applied. From such cases, clear lessons can be drawn that without political will, institutional independence, and the strengthening of the professional capacities of the prosecution and judiciary, the fight against corruption will remain a serious and unavoidable problem for Kosovo's society, especially.

10. Conclusion

The phenomenology of high-profile corruption does not only affect states with weak economic and legal capacities but also those with high standards of the rule of law and democracy. As can be seen, many countries today face this phenomenon, while concrete case studies are clear indicators that both national and international institutions have been involved or accused of involvement in such cases. Research has revealed that there are currently active cases of high-profile corruption, involving high-ranking officials and significant financial amounts.

High-profile corruption continues to be one of the most troubling challenges of contemporary governance, especially in states undergoing democratic transition, such as the Republic of Kosovo. This chapter has analyzed the definitions, forms, and consequences of this phenomenon through a theoretical and comparative approach, examining both well-known international and domestic cases. The analysis of high-profile corruption cases reflects not only individual violations of the law but also failures in the functioning of public institutions and the implementation of principles of criminal accountability. As observed in both international and domestic high-profile corruption cases, political interference and procedural delays are among the factors hindering the punishment of high-ranking officials.

The Republic of Kosovo, despite taking significant steps to define high-profile corruption through the directive issued by the State Prosecutor, the findings indicate that the practical implementation of criteria for prosecution and punishment remains weak. This is due to the lack of professionalism within the prosecution and judiciary, political interference in justice, the absence of transparency and objectivity in investigations and trials, as well as the deliberate application of provisions that grant more favorable positions to public figures in judicial processes. On the other hand, the prolonged duration of proceedings lasting for years, and the even more serious situation where powerful political figures are excluded from indictments, have created a perception of selective justice.

Another element emerging from the analysis of the cases handled is the actions of the second and third levels of the judicial system of the Republic of Kosovo. In many cases, decisions made by these instances have either altered or annulled the decisions of the first instance, resulting in the cases being sent back for retrial or in the complete acquittal of the accused.

Based on such findings, the fight against corruption cannot succeed solely with good laws on paper. Deep structural reforms are recommended, including the independence of the prosecution and judiciary, the expansion of criteria for identifying high-profile corruption beyond the monetary value of harm or benefit and official positions, as well as the enhancement of capacities to investigate complex cases of this phenomenon.

Furthermore, there is a need to increase public transparency and greater citizen engagement in demanding accountability from institutions. Only through institutional and societal commitment can a situation be created where high-ranking officials are held criminally accountable for corrupt actions, and where citizens can trust in the fair governance of the state. The morality of institutional responsibility should be strengthened by ensuring that high-profile officials are removed from public office when they are implicated or convicted of corruption.

This chapter suggests the need for further research in the future that analyzes the long-term impact of high-profile corruption on democratic processes, combining in-depth legal analysis with sociological and economic approaches. Additionally, the paper suggests fostering academic and professional discussions to move from a formal approach to corruption toward a sincere and sustainable effort to build functional and equal justice for all.

References

Abadi, A. M. (2021). Kleptocracy and foreign loan decision-making process: Insights from Malaysia's deals and renegotiations with China. *Journal of Current Southeast Asian Affairs*, *41*(1), 135–158. https://doi.org/10.1177/18681034211058470

Amundsen, I. (1999). *Political corruption: An introduction to the issues*. Bergen: Chr. Michelsen Institute Development Studies and Human Rights. https://open.cmi.no/cmi-xmlui/bitstream/handle/11250/2435773/WP1999.7%20Inge-07192007_3.pdf?sequence=2&isAllowed=y

Andvig, J. C., Fjeldstad, O.-H., Weltzien, Å., Amundsen, I., Sissener, T. K., & Søreide, T. (2001). *Corruption. A review of contemporary research*. Chr. Michelsen Institute; Norwegian Institute of International Affairs. Oslo: Norwegian University of Life Sciences. https://nmbu.brage.unit.no/nmbu-xmlui/handle/11250/2473686

Argandoña, A. (2001). Corruption: The corporate perspective. *Business Ethics: A European Review*, *10*(2), 163–175. https://doi.org/10.1111/1467-8608.t01-1-00227

Bajraktari, L. (2020). *Drejtësia në Shkallë të Dytë*. Instituti i Kosovës për Drejtësi. https://kli-ks.org/wp-content/uploads/2020/03/Gjykata-e-Apelit-Ligji-vs.-Praktika-IKD-24.03.2020-2.pdf

Bassam, L., & Gebeily, M. (2025, April 8). *Lebanon judge paves way for indictment of Ex-central bank chief salameh* Reuters:. https://www.reuters.com/world/middle-east/lebanon-judge-paves-way-indictment-ex-central-bank-chief-salameh-2025-04-08/

Dell, G. (2023). Tackling grand corruption impunity-proposal for a definition and special measures. *Transparency International*. https://images.transparencycdn.org/images/2023-Working-paper-Tackling-grand-corruption-impunity.pdf

Duparc, A. (2025, March 17). *Salameh affair: A major Geneva bank ignores all the money-laundering red flags*. Public Eye:. https://www.publiceye.ch/en/topics/corruption/banks-property-and-lawyer-the-riad-salameh-affair-and-its-swiss-connections/salameh-affair-what-happens-when-a-major-geneva-bank-ignores-all-the-money-laundering-red-flags

Fetiu, D. (2025). *Trajtimi institucional i rasteve të korrupsionit: Sfidat e sistemit gjyqësor gjatë një viti*. Group for Legal and Political Studies. https://www.legal-politicalstudies.org/wp-content/uploads/2024/06/GLPS-Act-Now-Raporit-Vjetor-Trajtimi-Institucional-i-Rasteve-te-Korrupsionit-te-Profilit-te-Larte-ne-Kosove_compressed.pdf

González, A. (2007). *Governance for the 21st century: The fight against corruption in latin America*. Munich: LIT Verlag Münster.

Graycar, A. (2015). Corruption: Classification and analysis. *Policy and Society*, *34*(2), 87–96. https://doi.org/10.1016/j.polsoc.2015.04.001

Harding, L. (2016, April 5). *What are the Panama papers? A guide to history's biggest data leak*. The Gardian:. https://www.theguardian.com/news/2016/apr/03/what-you-need-to-know-about-the-panama-papers

International Consortium of Investigative Journalists. (2016). *The Panama papers: Exposing the rogue offshore finance industry*. https://www.icij.org/investigations/panama-papers/

Jones, D. S. (2020). 1MDB corruption scandal in Malaysia: A study of failings in control and accountability. *Public Administration and Policy*, *23*(1), 59–72. https://doi.org/10.1108/PAP-11-2019-0032

Luna-Pla, I., & Nicolás-Carlock, J. R. (2020). Corruption and complexity: A scientific framework for the analysis of corruption networks. *Applied Network Science*, *5*(1). https://doi.org/10.1007/s41109-020-00258-2

Martinsson, J. (2021). Combatting institutional corruption: The policy-centered approach. *Crime, Law and Social Change*, *7*(3), 267–280. https://doi.org/10.1007/s10611-021-09934-5

Molina-Acosta, C. (2024, June 28). *Panama papers trial concludes with all defendants acquitted of money laundering*. The International Consortium of Investigative Journalists:. https://www.icij.org/investigations/panama-papers/panama-papers-trial-concludes-with-all-defendants-absolved-of-money-laundering-charge/

OECD. (2024). *Combatting high-level corruption in eastern Europe: Insights and solutions*. Paris: OECD Publishing. https://doi.org/10.1787/3c82f87d-en

Poeschl, G., & Ribeiro, R. (2015). Everyday opinions on grand and petty corruption: A Portuguese study. *Corruption, Economic Growth and Globalization*, 57–70. https://www.fep.up.pt/repec/por/obegef/files/wp013.pdf

Pozsgai-Alvarez, J. (2020). The abuse of entrusted power for private gain: Meaning, nature and theoretical evolution. *Crime, Law and Social Change*, *74*(4), 433–455. https://doi.org/10.1007/s10611-020-09903-4

Prokuroria Speciale e Republikës së Kosovës. (2013). *Udhëzim*. Prokurori i Shtetit. https://prokuroria-rks.org/zkpsh/wp-content/uploads/sites/3/2025/02/A.-190-2013-Udhezim-veprat-e-korrupsionit-te-nivelit-te-larte.pdf

Ratcliffe, R. (2022, August 23). *Malaysia's ex–PM Najib sent to prison as final 1MDB appeal lost*. The Guardian:. https://www.theguardian.com/world/2022/aug/23/malaysia-ex-pm-najib-razak-loses-1mdb-appeal

Rose-Ackerman, S. (1996). Democracy and 'grand' corruption. *International Social Science Journal*, *48*(149), 365–380. https://doi.org/10.1111/1468-2451.00038

Seyf, A. (2001). Corruption and development: A study of conflict. *Development in Practice*, *11*(5), 597–605. https://doi.org/10.1080/09614520120085340

Shah, A., & Schacter, M. (2004). Combating corruption: Look before you leap. *Finance & Development*, *41*(4), 40–43.

Transparency International. (2018). *What is corruption?* https://www.transparency.org/en/what-is-corruption

Transparency International. (2019). *Statement submitted by transparency international, a non-governmental organization in consultative status with the economic and social council*. Abu Dhabi. https://www.unodc.org/documents/treaties/UNCAC/COSP/session8/V1911801e.pdf

UNITED NATIONS. (2004). *United nations convention against corruption*. New York. https://www.unodc.org/documents/brussels/UN_Convention_Against_Corruption.pdf

United Nations Office on Drugs and Crime. (2012). *UNODC's action against corruption and economic crime branch*. https://www.unodc.org/corruption/en/about.html

Wawrosz, P. (2022). How corruption is and should be investigated by economic theory. *Economies*, *10*(12), 1–23. https://doi.org/10.3390/economies10120326

Chapter 4

Case Studies in Corruption: Key Lessons From High-profile Scandals—A Case Study of Jordanian Social Security Corporation

Amani Mohammad Said Khdair[a], *Firas Jamil Alotoum*[b], *Venus W. Samawi*[a] *and Anuj Kumar*[c]

[a]Isra University, Jordan
[b]Applied Science Private University, Jordan
[c]Rushford Business School, Switzerland

Abstract

This study examined how intelligent automation (IA) affects the handling of corruption in the Jordanian Social Security General Organization. The 2024 Capital Governorate of Amman study focused on social security staff and service recipients. Both groups received questionnaires, with 29 employees from the Information Systems Department, 30 from the IT Department, and 11 from the Operations Department, totaling 70 under centralized administration at the General Administration office in Amman, excluding branch offices. The study employed quantitative analysis and statistical methodologies to achieve its objectives. The Jordanian social security system had 1,574,291 recipients in the second category. The analysis included 403 random individuals and 40 workers. A quantitative strategy, supported by several statistical methodologies, was employed to accurately achieve the study's goals. The study found statistically significant IA, including robotic process automation, business process management, and data-driven decision-making (DDDM). Service receiver satisfaction was statistically significant in terms of perceived value, reliability/credibility, and responsiveness. These findings demonstrate the link between IA and customer happiness. The study recommended addressing beneficiary service difficulties, reacting quickly to

Corruption and Crime in Finance, 65–82

Published under exclusive licence by Emerald Publishing Limited
doi:10.1108/978-1-83708-170-720261010

inquiries, and incorporating beneficiary feedback into service development. The report also recommended DDDM training and expanding future research to include communications, artificial intelligence, and enterprise resource planning. It also recommended conducting quarterly user surveys, providing improved technical assistance, and implementing IA in other Jordanian governmental organizations to enhance efficiency and service quality.

Keywords: Intelligent automation; robotic process automation; business process management; data-driven decision-making; beneficiary satisfaction; perceived value; reliability; credibility; responsiveness; corruption

Intelligent automation (IA) plays a key role for businesses in today's digital world. This research examines the impact of IA on the work and customer satisfaction of the Jordan Social Security Corporation. IA leverages machine learning (ML) and other advanced technologies to collect, process, and analyze data. This constant flow of information offers new perspectives and ideas on number-based facts related to social security. This helps the company make significant choices. Making choices based on data over and over can make many tasks run smoother (AWS, 2024).

IA combines the brainpower of AI with the strength of automation to transform complex business processes, learn and adapt, and enhance business operations. It enables automation to perform robotic process automation (RPA), business process management (BPM), data-driven decision-making (DDDM), data entry, document processing, and more advanced service recipient responses. A company can utilize AI-based natural language processing and other ML methods to automate customer support and resolve issues (Salameh et al., 2023). An organization can also use IA to process claims paperwork without staff oversight. IA has a significant impact on various areas, but implementing it is challenging and requires careful planning (AWS, 2024).

This study examines how IA enhances service and meets the needs of beneficiaries. Technology can reduce administrative tasks, increase productivity, and improve communication between service recipients and stakeholders (Qafesha et al., 2024). IA that uses AI-based sight, speech, language, and responsiveness can help companies improve their relationships with customers (Salameh et al., 2023), free up workers to handle more complex jobs, provide them with the information they need to make solid decisions in fast-moving business processes, and deliver quicker and more accurate customer service responses using natural language generation.

Training and gaining skills are crucial in IA due to its importance and in-depth nature. The organization must also establish policies and initiatives to promote economic growth and the equitable use of IA.

The value of this study and the subject matter center on tackling key issues (IA and customer satisfaction), which are hot topics that the Jordanian Social

Security Corporation has focused on to boost customer satisfaction. So, we can break down the study's importance like this:

- **Theoretical Value**: It highlights both IA and customer satisfaction, building on the insights gained from earlier research. This topic is one of the few studies conducted at the local and regional levels, to the researcher's knowledge.
- **Scientific Importance**: The Jordanian Social Security Corporation, the focus of this study, is expected to benefit from the anticipated outcomes of the research. This is true, given the push to integrate IA across all its work processes.

This study examines the utilization of intelligent automation at the Jordanian Social Security Corporation and its impact on reducing corruption. The following are the main findings:

- The study shows that men make up 45.2% of recipients, while women account for 54.8%. In the employee group, males represent 47.5% and females 52.5%. Recipients have BA degrees, followed by those with postgraduate qualifications. The employee sample flips this, with postgraduate degree holders leading, and bachelor's degree holders coming in second. Among survey participants, 7.9% are under 30, 29% are in the 30–39 age range, 45.4% fall into the 40–49 bracket, and the rest are 50 or older. For employees, 10% are younger than 30, 40% are 30–39, 45% are in their 40s, and 5% are over 50. Job roles break down as follows: 35% of employees work in IT management, 30% in Information Systems (IS) management, and 17.5% in Operations Management (OM).
- There is a statistical impact or significance of IA in its combined dimensions (RPA, BPM, DDDM) on the satisfaction of service recipients with their combined dimensions (perceived value, reliability/credibility, response) in the Jordanian social security system. This result applies to both the group receiving services and the staff members we surveyed. We see this effect more in the people receiving services than in the employees. Our findings align with the work done by Ruan & Mezei, 2022, as well as that of Gavrila and others in 2023, and with other studies.
- There is a statistical impact or significance of IA in its combined dimensions (RPA, BPM, and DDDM) on the perceived value in the Jordanian social security system. This result is consistent for both the group receiving services and the surveyed employee sample. The results align with the studies by Ruan and Mezei (2022) and Gavrila Gavrila et al. (2023), as well as other research.
- There is a statistically significant impact of IA in its combined dimensions (RPA, BPM, and DDDM) on reliability and credibility in the Jordanian social security system. This result is consistent for both the group receiving services and the surveyed employee sample. The results align with the studies by Ruan and Mezei (2022) and Gavrila Gavrila et al. (2023), as well as other research.

- There is a statistical impact or significance of IA with its combined dimensions (RPA, BPM, DDDM) on the response in the Jordanian social security system. This result is consistent for both the group receiving services and the surveyed employee sample. The results align with the studies by Ruan and Mezei (2022) and Gavrila Gavrila et al. (2023), as well as other research.

1. Introduction

IA plays a key role for businesses in today's digital world. This research examines the impact of IA on the work and customer satisfaction of the Jordan Social Security Corporation. IA leverages ML and other advanced technologies to collect, process, and analyze data. This constant flow of information offers new perspectives and ideas on number-based facts related to social security. This helps the company make significant choices. Making choices based on data over and over can make many tasks run smoother (AWS, 2024).

IA combines the brainpower of AI with the strength of automation to transform complex business processes, learn and adapt, and enhance business operations. It enables automation to perform RPA, BPM, DDDM, data entry, document processing, and more advanced service recipient responses. A company can utilize AI-based natural language processing and other machine learning methods to automate customer support and resolve issues (Salameh et al., 2023). An organization can also use IA to process claims paperwork without staff oversight. IA has a significant impact on various areas, but implementing it is challenging and requires careful planning (AWS, 2024).

Equally important is the use of biometric technology to reinforce the reliability of beneficiary identification. By verifying individuals through unique physical traits like fingerprints, facial features, or iris scans, institutions reduce the likelihood of impersonation or duplicate registrations. When paired with encrypted digital transaction records, these technologies ensure traceability and make it significantly more difficult for fraudulent claims to bypass the system undetected.

Smart surveillance also plays a vital role in fostering organizational accountability (Evrim and others, 2023). AI-enabled monitoring systems equipped with behavioral analytics can observe service interactions in real time, capturing visual evidence of both employee and client conduct. In the event of suspicious activities or complaints, recorded data offers a factual foundation for investigations, helping to eliminate subjectivity or favoritism in decision-making processes:

- **Theoretical Value**: It highlights both IA and corruption, building on the insights gained from earlier research. This topic is one of the few studies conducted at the local and regional levels to the researcher's knowledge.
- **Scientific Importance**: The Jordanian Social Security Corporation, the focus of this study, is expected to benefit from the anticipated outcomes of the

research. This is true, given the push to integrate IA across all its work processes.

The rest of this study is organized into 10 sections. The problem of the study is illustrated in Section 2, while the study hypothesis is introduced in Section 3. In Section 4, the study model is described. In Section 5, the literature review on IA and service recipient satisfaction is presented. The study population and data collection methods are explained in Section 6. Analysis and testing results are illustrated in Sections 7 and 8, respectively. In Section 9, the results are discussed. Finally, the study recommendations are presented in Section 10.

2. The Problem of the Study

Jordanian government bodies have been working on e-government and digital transformation initiatives for years to reduce time, costs, and effort while providing their customers with the best services. Automation has a significant impact on today's fast-moving tech scene, and AI helps speed up new ideas in automation. This study will examine various ways people utilize automation to deal with corruption issues. The Jordanian Social Security Corporation, one of Jordan's largest service providers, handles an increasing number of complex transactions involving many citizens. Through the researcher's work at the Jordanian Social Security Corporation and discussions with the Social Security Affairs Committees.

This method aims to discover that corruption remains a critical threat to the integrity and effectiveness of public sector institutions, particularly those responsible for managing social welfare programs. Social security organizations are especially vulnerable due to the volume of financial transactions, personal data, and discretionary decision-making involved. Traditional oversight mechanisms have often proven insufficient in detecting or preventing misconduct. In response, the emergence of smart security systems offers a promising solution. By integrating advanced technologies such as artificial intelligence (AI), biometric verification, and real-time surveillance, these systems can enhance transparency, reduce human error, and strengthen institutional accountability. This study explores how the implementation of smart security solutions can serve as an effective strategy to combat corruption within social security institutions and ensure the fair distribution of services to eligible beneficiaries.

This leads us to ask: How does an intelligent system for dealing with corruption in society? A case study of the Jordanian Social Security Corporation.

3. Study of Hypotheses

Based on the statement of the study problem and objectives, the research hypotheses are formulated as follows:

The main hypothesis:

H0.1 There is no statistical impact or significance of IA in its combined dimensions (RPA, BPM, DDDM) on the satisfaction of service recipients with their combined dimensions (perceived value, reliability/credibility, response) in the Jordanian social security system.

From which the following sub-hypotheses branch:

H0.1.1 There is no statistical impact or significance of IA in its combined dimensions (RPA, BPM, DDDM) on the perceived value in the Jordanian social security system.
H0.1.2 There is no statistical impact or significance of IA in its combined dimensions (RPA, BPM, DDDM) on reliability or credibility in the Jordanian social security system.
H0.1.3 There is no statistical impact or significance of IA with its combined dimensions (RPA, BPM, DDDM), on the response in the Jordanian social security system.

4. The Study Model

The study model that has been followed includes two variables: the independent variable "Intelligence Automation" and the dependent variable "Service Recipient Satisfaction." The independent variable has three dimensions, including RPA (Al-Abedallat et al., 2021), BPM (Taherdoost & Madanchian, 2023), and DDDM (Elragal & Elgendy, 2024). The dependent variable consists of three dimensions, including Perceived Value (Aguiar-Costa et al., 2022), Reliability/Credibility (Al-Hashedi & Abkar, 2017), and Responsiveness (Al-Hashedi & Abkar, 2017).

5. Literature Review

5.1 Intelligent Automation (IA)

IA utilizes various technologies, including AI, RPA, and low-code process automation (LPA), as well as advanced analytics and automation tools (Parikh, 2021).

IA has a significant impact on how organizations work. It enhances productivity, cuts costs, and sparks new ideas. When companies integrate AI and machine learning, they can refine their processes and deliver greater value to all parties involved (Fontana, 2021). Loten (2020) quotes a computer scientist who knows a lot about AI. This expert believes that IA is transforming the way organizations operate in a significant way. It helps them work and accomplish their tasks more efficiently. Companies use cutting-edge technology to work faster and smarter. IA brings together different technologies to create a system that aims to make operations more efficient and productive.

AI is a key part of this system. It learns from data and improves over time. It utilizes algorithms and machine learning to analyze data and make decisions independently. Feith (2018) discusses RPA. This software automates the boring, repetitive tasks that people used to do, such as entering data or handling requests. This leads to fewer mistakes and quicker work. There is also a concept called LPA. These platforms enable people to create automated apps without writing extensive code. This means that teams who are not tech experts can help come up with solutions. There are advanced automation tools and analytics available. These include a variety of other tools and methods to improve operational efficiency. For example, advanced analytics help understand data and make intelligent choices based on what the data reveals. Advanced automation tools and analytics encompass a range of additional tools and techniques designed to enhance operations, including advanced analytics that facilitate DDDM.

5.1.1 Robotic Process Automation (PRA)

RPA enables the automation of large-scale, complex, and repetitive tasks, used to extract data and provide continuous interaction with applications and systems rapidly and accurately (Aguiar-Costa et al., 2022). Sprint Reply (in 2024) developed the Intelligent Automation Framework. This plan forms the foundation for all business automation rollouts that rely on a combination of AI platforms, RPA, and regular system integration. RPA, combined with AI, can enhance processes and streamline operations. By combining various inputs, the system can make informed choices based on data, leading to improved performance and reduced human error.

5.1.2 Business Process Management (BPM)

Al-Abedallat et al. (2021) developed a system to design, model, improve, and manage processes within and between organizations. This system aims to boost productivity, cut costs, and enhance decision-making by improving the efficiency, visibility, and control of processes. This system is used to enhance productivity, reduce costs, and improve customer satisfaction.

5.1.3 Data-driven Decision-making (DDDM)

In Sarioguz and Miser (2024), DDDM is defined as using facts, metrics, and data to guide strategic business decisions that align with your goals, objectives, and initiatives. People have also described DDDM as using facts, metrics, and data to guide strategic decisions that match your goals, objectives, and plans. When companies maximize the value of their data, they can utilize it to make informed decisions every day. However, this does not happen simply by selecting the right analytical methods to identify the next big opportunity. Companies should make decisions based on data in the usual way and build an environment that promotes asking questions and thinking. People at every level kick off talks with data and improve their ability to handle it through regular use. This requires a setup that allows users to access the necessary data while maintaining security and control. It also requires expertise and providing workers with opportunities to train and develop their data skills. Having big shots and groups that back and make choices based on data will push others to do the same.

5.2 Service Recipient Satisfaction

Customer satisfaction reflects how happy people feel after using a service. It is measured by comparing what customers expect to what they get. The satisfaction of customers plays a key role in demonstrating a company's performance, influencing customer loyalty and retention. Al-Araj et al. (2022) found that this has a significant impact on the success of organizations. Understanding what makes customers satisfied can help improve services and encourage repeat business. Getting customers happy means focusing on these key aspects. When a company improves each of these aspects, customers have a better experience and are more likely to stay loyal, which ultimately benefits the company in the long term.

5.2.1 Perceived Value

Perceived value is what a service is worth in the customer's eyes. It has an influence on the actual price of the service, plus things like how well-known the company is, how good the service is, how easy it is to use, and how it makes people feel. It is a personal judgment customers make based on what they think, believe, and like. Perceived value is the good stuff customers see in a product or service compared to what it costs and plays a significant role in innovative marketing plans (Kopp, 2020).

Customer-perceived value examines what customers believe they will receive from a product or service. This includes things you can touch, such as quality and price, and things you cannot, like the brand's reputation and the level of support you receive after making a purchase. Companies need to do this to keep customers happy and coming back (Kancherla, 2024).

5.2.2 Reliability/Credibility

According to Kedziora and Hyrynsalmi (2023), reliability means that you can count on data and information to be accurate, truthful, or as stated. It is about how well a company can continue to do what people expect, regardless of when or where. Reliability helps build trust, maintain stability, and demonstrate that you can depend on something.

5.2.3 Responsiveness

Responsiveness means that service providers can address customer needs and concerns promptly. It plays a crucial role in customer satisfaction as it affects their overall experience. When service providers remain attentive and efficient, they enhance customer interactions, resulting in higher satisfaction levels. Customers value prompt responses, personal attention, and effective problem-solving (Al-Hashedi & Abkar, 2017; Ruan & Mezei, 2022).

6. Methodology

The researchers employed a quantitative research approach, which they selected and adhered to. They developed two questionnaires, each with two parts. The first section asked about demographic information, while the second contained statements related to each aspect of the study. These statements used a Likert scale ranging from (1) disagree to (5) agree. After creating the surveys, the researchers sent them for academic professors to review.

6.1 Population and Study Sample

The research focuses on employees in key departments of the social security organization, with its main office located in Amman Governorate. It also includes people who receive services from this organization. The study looked at two groups:

(1) A convenient sample of 40 staff members from the LCT, IS, and Operations departments. It is worth noting that the total staff count in these areas is 70.
(2) A random sample of 403 service recipients out of the total number of beneficiaries covered by the provisions of the law (1,574,291).

6.2 Data Collection Methods

In this study, data were collected using two data sources:

(1) **Primary source** → Researchers distributed surveys to selected samples to collect data. This enabled them to examine how IA in the Jordanian Social Security Corporation impacts the satisfaction of service recipients.
(2) **Secondary sources** → For the theoretical part, researchers gathered data from journals, books, other research papers, and various related sources.

7. Analysis

7.1 Results of Demographic Data Analysis

Among those who received it, 45.2% are men and 54.8% are women. For the employees, men make up 47.5%, while women account for 52.5%. Most people who received it have a bachelor's degree, followed by those with postgraduate qualifications. On the other hand, the employee group consists of more individuals with Postgraduate studies at the top, followed by those with bachelor's degrees. Among the surveyed recipients, 7.9% are under 30, 29% are between 30 and 39, 45.4% fall into the 40–49 age group, and the rest are 50 or older. For the employee sample, 10% are under 30, 40% are in the 30–39 range, 45% belong to the 40–49 category, and the remaining are 50 and above.

For the employee sample, 35% work in Information Technology Management, 30% are in Information Systems Management, and 17.5% have jobs in OM.

7.2 Reliability of the Study Tool

The researchers calculated Cronbach's Alpha coefficients to assess the reliability of the research tool. Table 4.1 presents Cronbach's Alpha coefficients, which aid in evaluating the reliability of the study tool. The researchers reported that the Cronbach's alpha coefficient values for both samples exceed 0.7. This shows that the study instrument is reliable (Sekaran & Bougie, 2016).

7.3 Multicollinearity Test

In multiple regression analysis, independent variables should have a strong relationship with the dependent variable but should not be correlated with each other. If they are, it reduces the value of (R) because the independent variables

Table 4.1. Cronbach's Alpha Coefficients for Testing the Reliability of the Study Tool.

Study Variables		**Cronbach Alpha Coefficients (Recipients Sample)**	**Cronbach Alpha Coefficients (Employees Sample)**
Independent variable	Robotic process automation (RPA)	**0.754**	**0.909**
	Business process management (BPM)	**0.849**	**0.844**
	Data-driven decision-making (DDDM)	**0.836**	**0.868**
Dependent variable	Perceived value	**0.878**	**0.927**
	Reliability/ Credibility	**0.877**	**0.911**
	Responsiveness	**0.872**	**0.897**

Source: Authors' own.

Table 4.2. The Results of the Multicollinearity Test for the two Samples.

	Recipients Sample		**Employees Sample**	
	Tolerance	*VIF*	*Tolerance*	*VIF*
Robotic process automation (RPA)	**0.850**	**1.177**	**0.914**	**1.094**
Business process management (BPM)	**0.458**	**2.184**	**0.439**	**2.280**
Data-driven decision-making (DDDM)	**0.473**	**2.114**	**0.440**	**2.275**

Source: Authors' own.

share some of the same information. We performed a Multiple Linear Correlation Test (Multicollinearity) to determine the importance of each independent variable in relation to the dependent variable. Table 4.2 shows that the tolerance coefficients of the independent variables are less than 1 and greater than 0.1. The variance inflation factor (VIF) numbers stayed under 5, suggesting that the independent variables do not have a strong relationship with each other. This also confirms that the data meet the normal distribution requirement before we applied this method.

8. Hypothesis Testing

In this section, we present the testing results for the main and sub-hypotheses for both the recipients' and employees' samples.

8.1 Recipients Sample

The main hypothesis:

H0.1 There is no statistical impact or significance of IA in its combined dimensions (RPA, BPM, DDDM) on the satisfaction of service recipients with their combined dimensions (perceived value, reliability/credibility, and response) in the Jordanian social security system. This is evident from Table 4.3.

Table 4.3. H01 Testing in the Recipient Sample.

Model	**Correlation**	**R^2**	**F**	**Sig.**
1	**0.780**	**0.609**	**206.899**	**0.000**

Source: Authors' own.

The researcher tested the hypothesis using multiple linear regression. The results indicate a strong positive correlation (r = 0.78) between the independent and dependent variables. The independent variables may account for more than 60.9% of the total variation in the dependent variable. Furthermore, it is worth noting the significance of the F-value. This indicates an impact of IA with its combined dimensions (RPA, BPM, and data-driven decision-making) on service recipient satisfaction with its combined dimensions (perceived value, reliability/credibility, and responsiveness) in the Jordanian social security system.

From the main hypothesis, the following sub-hypotheses branch out:

H0.1.1 Table 4.4 shows that there is no statistical impact or significance of IA in its combined dimensions (RPA, BPM, DDDM) on the perceived value in the Jordanian social security system.

Table 4.4. H01.1 Testing in Recipients Sample.

Model	Correlation	R^2	F	Sig.
1	*0.679*	*0.461*	*113.914*	*0.000*

Source: Authors' Own.

Researchers used multiple linear regression to test the hypothesis. A significant positive association (r = 0.679) exists between the independent and dependent variables. The independent values can explain 46.1% of the variation in the dependent variable. Taking into consideration the significance of the F-value, IA, including RPA, BPM, and DDDM, has an impact on the perceived value of the Jordanian social security system.

H0.1.2 According to Table 4.5, there is no statistical impact or significance of IA in its combined dimensions (RPA, BPM, and DDDM) on reliability/credibility in the Jordanian social security system.

Researchers used multiple linear regression to evaluate the hypothesis. The independent and dependent variables are positively correlated (r = 0.693). The independent variables may explain 48% of the variation in the dependent

Table 4.5. H01.2 Testing in Recipients Sample.

Model	Correlation	R^2	F	Sig.
1	*0.693*	*0.480*	*122.816*	*0.000*

Source: Authors' own.

variable, considering that the F-value is significant. IA, including RPA, BPM, and DDDM, significantly impacts reliability and credibility in the Jordanian social security system ($\alpha \leq 0.05$).

H0.1.3 There is no statistical impact or significance of IA with its combined dimensions (RPA, BPM, and DDDM), at the level of statistical significance ($\alpha \leq 0.05$) on the response in the Jordanian social security system (based on the findings presented in Table 4.6.

Researchers used multiple linear regression to evaluate the hypothesis. Independent and dependent variables are positively correlated ($r = 0.700$). The independent variables may explain 49% of the dependent variable's change. Note that the F-value is significant. IA, including RPA, BPM, and DDDM, has an impact on the Jordanian social security response.

Table 4.6. H01.3 Testing in the Recipients Sample.

Model	**Correlation**	**R^2**	**F**	**Sig.**
1	*0.700*	*0.490*	*127.600*	*0.000*

Source: Authors' Own.

8.2 Employees Sample

The main hypothesis:

H0.1: According to Table 4.7, there is no statistical impact or significance of IA in its combined dimensions (RPA, BPM, and DDDM) at the level of statistical significance ($\alpha \leq 0.05$) on the satisfaction of service recipients with their combined dimensions (perceived value, reliability/credibility, response) in the Jordanian social security system.

Researchers used multiple linear regression to evaluate the hypothesis. Independent and dependent variables exhibit a strong positive correlation ($r = 0.696$). The independent factors may explain 48.5% of the variation in the dependent

Table 4.7. H01 Testing in the Recipients Sample.

Model	**Correlation**	**R^2**	**F**	**Sig.**
1	*0.696*	*0.485*	*11.288*	*0.000*

Source: Authors' Own.

variable. Note that the F-value significance level is set at 0.05, which means that IA, across its various dimensions (RPA, BPM, and DDDM), has a significant impact on service recipients' satisfaction with perceived value, reliability, credibility, and response in the Jordanian social security system.

From the main hypothesis, the following sub-hypotheses branch.

H0.1.1: There is no statistical impact or significance of IA in its combined dimensions (RPA, BPM, DDDM) at the level of statistical significance ($\alpha \leq 0.05$) on the perceived value in the Jordanian social security system (as presented in Table 4.8.

Table 4.8. H01.1 Testing in Recipients Sample.

Model	Correlation	R^2	F	Sig.
1	*0.777*[a]	*0.604*	*18.341*	*0.000*

Source: Authors' Own.

Researchers used multiple linear regression to evaluate the hypothesis. A substantial positive association (r = 0.777) exists between the independent and dependent variables. The independent variables can explain 60.4% of the variation in the dependent variable. Note that the F-value significance level is set at 0.05, which means IA, including RPA, BPM, and DDDM, has an impact on the perceived value of the Jordanian social security system.

H0.1.2: There is no statistical impact or significance of IA in its combined dimensions (RPA, BPM, and DDDM) at the level of statistical significance ($\alpha \leq 0.05$) on reliability/credibility in Jordanian social security (based on the results shown in Table 4.9).

Researchers used multiple linear regression to test the hypothesis. The independent and dependent variables exhibit a medium positive correlation (r = 0.558). The independent factors may explain 31.1% more of the variation in the dependent variable. Note that the F-value significance level is set at 0.05, which means that IA,

Table 4.9. H01.2 Testing in Recipients Sample.

Model	Correlation	R^2	F	Sig.
1	*0.558*[a]	*0.311*	*5.426*	*0.003*

Source: Authors' Own.

including RPA, BPM, and DDDM, has an impact on reliability and credibility in the Jordanian social security system.

H0.1.3: There is no statistical impact or significance of IA with its combined dimensions (RPA, BPM, DDDM) on the response in Jordanian social security system (based on the results shown in Table 4.10).

Researchers used multiple linear regression to evaluate the hypothesis. Independent and dependent variables exhibit a strong positive correlation (r = 0.776). The independent factors may explain 60.3% more of the variation in the dependent variable. Note that the F-value significance level is set at 0.05, which means IA, including RPA, BPM, and DDDM, has an impact on Jordanian social security response.

Table 4.10. H01.3 Testing in Recipients Sample.

Model	**Correlation**	**R^2**	**F**	**Sig.**
1	*0.776*[a]	*0.603*	*18.212*	*0.000*

Source: Authors' Own.

9. Discussion

This study examines IA at the Jordanian Social Security Corporation and its impact on service recipient satisfaction. Here is what we found out:

- The study shows that men make up 45.2% of recipients, while women account for 54.8%. In the employee group, males represent 47.5% and females 52.5%. Recipients mostly have BA degrees, followed by those with postgraduate qualifications. The employee sample flips this, with postgraduate degree holders leading and bachelor's degree holders coming in second. Among survey participants, 7.9% are under 30, 29% are in the 30–39 age range, 45.4% fall into the 40–49 bracket, and the rest are 50 or older. For employees, 10% are younger than 30, 40% are 30–39, 45% are in their 40s, and 5% are over 50. Job roles break down as follows: 35% of employees work in IT management, 30% in IS management, and 17.5% in OM.
- There is a statistical impact or significance of IA in its combined dimensions (RPA, BPM, and DDDM) on the satisfaction of service recipients with their combined dimensions (perceived value, reliability/credibility, response) in the Jordanian social security. This result applies to both the group receiving services and the staff members we surveyed. We see this effect more in the people receiving services than in the employees. Our findings align with the

work done by Ruan & Mezei, 2022, as well as that of Gavrila and others in 2023, and with other studies.

- There is a statistical impact or significance of IA in its combined dimensions (RPA, BPM, and DDDM) on the perceived value in the Jordanian social security system. This result is consistent for both the group receiving services and the surveyed employee sample. The results align with the studies by Ruan and Mezei (2022) and Gavrila Gavrila et al. (2023), as well as other research.
- There is a statistically significant impact of IA in its combined dimensions (RPA, BPM, and DDDM) on reliability and credibility in the Jordanian social security sector. This result is consistent for both the group receiving services and the surveyed employee sample. The results align with the studies by Ruan and Mezei (2022) and Gavrila Gavrila et al. (2023), as well as with another research study.
- There is a statistical impact or significance of IA with its combined dimensions (RPA, BPM, and DDDM) on the response in the Jordanian social security system. This result is consistent for both the group receiving services and the surveyed employee sample. The results match the studies by Ruan and Mezei (2022) and Gavrila Gavrila et al. (2023), as well as another research.

10. Conclusion

The study provides compelling evidence of the role of IA in enhancing the integrity and effectiveness of public service delivery within the Jordanian Social Security Corporation (JSSC). Through empirical analysis of both service recipients and employees, it becomes clear that technologies such as RPA, BPM, and DDDM have a statistically significant positive impact on several aspects of service quality—namely perceived value, reliability/credibility, and responsiveness. The results from multiple regression models show a strong correlation between these automation dimensions and the satisfaction of service recipients, explaining a considerable portion of the variance in satisfaction levels (over 60%). Among these, DDDM emerged as the most influential factor, particularly in shaping perceptions of value and credibility. Furthermore, the absence of multicollinearity confirms the robustness of the variables involved in the model. The high Cronbach's Alpha values indicate that the study tool is reliable. These findings reinforce the argument that integrating intelligent systems can play a transformative role in combating corruption, increasing transparency, and enhancing operational efficiency in public institutions. Given the complexity and sensitivity of social security services, the deployment of intelligent systems can help mitigate risks of misconduct and ensure fair service distribution. The study ultimately highlights the potential of digital transformation as a strategic tool not only for improving performance but also for building public trust in governmental institutions. Future research is encouraged to explore the long-term impacts and broader applications across other public sectors.

11. Recommendations

The researchers suggested these steps based on the study results:

We propose that policymakers should systematically examine the challenges present at each level of implementation in order to gain a comprehensive understanding of the barriers to technology adoption, as well as the interconnected requirements of both policy formulation and system development. To validate the applicability of this framework, we encourage further studies across diverse sectors and national contexts. Additionally, local and sub-national governments may encounter unique obstacles related to the access, development, and deployment of data-driven technologies. Therefore, conducting comparative analyses across sectors, administrative levels, and countries would not only test the model's generalizability but could also contribute to the emergence of a broader theory of digital governance.

In future research, consider examining additional service areas, such as communications AI and ERP (Enterprise Resource Planning).

References

Aguiar-Costa, L. M., Cunha, C. A., Silva, W. K., & Abreu, N. R. (2022). Customer satisfaction in service delivery with artificial intelligence: A meta-analytic study. (Mackenzie, Ed.) *RAM. Revista de Administração Mackenzie*, *23*(6), 1-29. https://doi.org/10.1590/1678-6971/eRAMD220003.en

Al-Abedallat, A. Z., Jaafreh, A. B., & Alshbib, D. K. (2021). The automation of robotic processes in Jordanian banks: Obstacles and applications. *European Scientific Journal*, *17*(21), 350.

Al-Araj, R. E. E. M., Haddad, H. O. S. S. A. M., Shehadeh, M. A. H. A., Hasan, E., & Nawaiseh, M. Y. (2022). The effect of artificial intelligence on service quality and customer satisfaction in Jordanian banking sector. *WSEAS Transactions on Business and Economics*, *19*(12), 1929–1947.

Al-Hashedi, A. H., & Abkar, S. A. (2017). The impact of service quality dimensions on customer satisfaction in telecom mobile companies in Yemen. *American Journal of Economics*, *7*(4), 186–193.

AWS. (2024). *(Amazon Web Services) retrieved from what is intelligent automation?* https://aws.amazon.com/what-is/intelligent-automation/

Elragal, A., & Elgendy, N. (2024). A data-driven decision-making readiness assessment model: The case of a Swedish food manufacturer. *Decision Analytics Journal*, *10*. https://doi.org/10.1016/j.dajour.2024.100405

Feith, J. (2018). *Potential impact of automation technology in the IS/IT customer service industry*.

Fontana, A. (2021). *The AI-First company: How to compete and win with artificial intelligence*. Portfolio.

Gavrila Gavrila, S., Blanco González-Tejero, C., Gómez Gandía, J. A., & de Lucas Ancillo, A. (2023). The impact of automation and optimization on customer experience: A consumer perspective. *Humanities and Social Sciences Communications*, *10*(1), 1–10.

Kancherla, P. (2024). *The ultimate guide to customer perceived value (with examples)*. Ozonetel. https://ozonetel.com/customer-perceived-value/

Kedziora, D., & Hyrynsalmi, S. (2023). Turning robotic process automation onto intelligent automation with machine learning. In *Proceedings of the 11th international conference on communities and technologies* (pp. 1–5).

Kopp, C. M. (2020). *Investopedia, retrieved from perceived value: What it is and why it's important*. : https://www.investopedia.com/terms/p/perceivedvalue.asp#:~:text=Perceived%20value%20is%20measured%20by,design%2C%20accessibility%2C%20or%20convenienc

Loten, A. (2020). Businesses expected to lean on automation for recovery. *The Wall Street Journal*. https://www.wsj.com/articles/businesses-expected-to-lean-on-automation-for-recovery-11589967002

Parikh, S. (2021). *Why businesses need the 'Holistic automation – the change driver' Edge in 2021*. Nividous. https://nividous.com/blogs/why-businesses-need-holistic-automation

Qafesha, W., Kilani, Y. M., & Samawi, V. W. (2024). An automated system to evaluate learning outcomes for higher education programs. *Journal of System and Management Sciences*, *14*(6), 424–440. https://doi.org/10.33168/JSMS.2024.0626

Ruan, Y., & Mezei, J. (2022). When do AI chatbots lead to higher customer satisfaction than human frontline employees in online shopping assistance? Considering product attribute type. *Journal of Retailing and Consumer Services*, *68*. https://doi.org/10.1016/j.jretconser.2022.103059

Salameh, M., Balaji, K., Murugan, A., Rajesh, P., Kumar, P. H., & Alotoum, F. (2023). A novel study on customer relationship management using artificial intelligence in the retail sector. *J Pharm Negative Results*, *13*(9), 9810–9819.

Sarioguz, O., & Miser, E. (2024). Data-driven decision-making: Transforming management in the information age. *International Research Journal of Modernization in Engineering Technology and Science*, *06*(02), 1642–1652.

Sekaran, U., & Bougie, R. (2016). *Research methods for business: A skill-building approach* (7th ed.). Wiley & Sons.

Taherdoost, H., & Madanchian, M. (2023). Blockchain and business process management (BPM) synergy: A comparative analysis of modeling approaches. *Information*, *15*(1), 9.

Chapter 5

Money Laundering and Financial Systems: Mechanisms, Impacts, and Responses

Ankit Srivastava

Rajiv Gandhi National University of Law, India

Abstract

Money laundering is one of the most insidious and sophisticated threats to the integrity of worldwide financial systems. With criminals increasingly employing sophisticated methods to disguise the origin of ill-gotten gains, formal and informal financial structures are acutely exposed to abuse. This chapter discusses the underlying mechanisms and stages of the laundering process—placement, layering, and integration. It discusses the profound interlinkages between money laundering and other criminal activities, such as drug trafficking, terrorist financing, and kleptocracy, to establish its status as the fulcrum of world illicit economies. Economic consequences of illicit financial flows are carefully weighed, citing their role in undermining market integrity, facilitating capital flight, undermining tax systems, and exacerbating social inequality. Case studies, such as the FinCEN Files and the Danske Bank case, expose structural weaknesses in regulation and enforcement. An assessment of international legal mechanisms—such as the FATF Recommendations, EU AML Directives, and US PATRIOT Act—examines their efficacy, implementation, and cross-border cooperative frameworks. Key compliance tools such as know-your-customer (KYC), suspicious transaction reporting (STR), and beneficial ownership registers are evaluated in the context of the evolving role of financial intelligence units. Lastly, this chapter discusses the new challenges posed by digital finance, namely with regard to crypto-assets and decentralized finance platforms. It assesses the potential of regulatory technology, artificial intelligence, and blockchain analytics in strengthening enforcement measures. This chapter concludes with recommendations for reforms aimed at enhancing transparency, institutional coordination, and global financial resilience against laundering operations.

Corruption and Crime in Finance, 83–107

doi:10.1108/978-1-83708-170-720261013

Keywords: Illicit financial flows; anti-money laundering; financial regulation; regulatory technology; transnational crime

1. Introduction

Money laundering is likely the most pervasive and enduring threat to the international financial order, degrading economic integrity, legal order, and democratic governance across borders. In its simplest terms, money laundering is the process by which illegally accumulated money is hidden and integrated into the legitimate economy so criminals may profit from crime without detection. But underlying this seemingly simple definition is a vast and complex network of financial deception, transnational organized crime, regulatory arbitrage, and systemic weakness. Most insidious about money laundering, however, is its capacity to alter constantly in response to changing regulatory landscapes, technological advancement, and geopolitical conditions. The very forces that facilitate the free flow of legitimate capital—liberalized trade, digitized banking, and financial integration—facilitate the concealment, transfer, and reinvestment of illicit capital as well.

The history of money laundering is closely intertwined with the general evolution of the world economy since the Bretton Woods era. As the world's financial markets have become more integrated and liberalized, new channels have opened not only for legal business but also for illegal financial flows. Terrorist groups, crime syndicates, kleptocracies, and tax evaders exploited such channels ever more sophisticatedly. Money laundering of proceeds of illegal transactions—from narcotic trade and human trafficking to arms trade and grand corruption and business crime—has grown so massive in volume that it exceeds the GDP of nations. United Nations Office on Drugs and Crime estimates show that in one year the total volume of money laundered worldwide totals 2–5% of world GDP, or approximately USD 800 billion to USD 2 trillion (FATF, 2022a). Such estimates, although not very accurate due to the clandestine nature of the phenomenon, reflect its systemic size and worldwide dissemination. The impacts of money laundering extend far beyond the sphere of economic interests. Illegal financial flows destabilize governments, create conflict, undermine the rule of law, and entrench social inequalities. The entry of laundered money into property, luxury items, art, and capital markets not only distorts prices and market efficiency but also provides opportunities for further criminal opportunity and corruption. In weak institutional environments, money laundering can overwhelm governance systems, undermine law enforcement agencies, and consolidate the political power of criminal operators. Additionally, the nexus between money laundering and terrorist financing tends to appear as a duality; laundering activity is a key structural component facilitating funding of violent extremism and thus presents threats not only to financial regulation but also to national and international security.

As a response to the money laundering issue, an advanced structure of anti-money laundering (AML) systems has developed over the past three decades. Major international institutions, such as the Financial Action Task Force (FATF), the United Nations, the European Union (EU), and the International Monetary Fund, have played a major role in influencing norms, setting up regulatory norms, and promoting international cooperation. National governments have passed legislation—such as the USA PATRIOT Act in the United States and the Prevention of Money Laundering Act (PMLA) in India—that aimed to criminalize money laundering, establish financial intelligence units (FIUs), and implement due diligence through know-your-customer (KYC) norms. Despite these advances, enforcement weaknesses, jurisdictional fragmentation, and political interference remain and weaken these systems. Money launderers continue to adapt, and prefer to exploit regulatory loopholes, use tax havens, and employ impenetrable structures of ownership in their favor.

The issues are compounded by the emergence of digital financial ecosystems. Technologies such as cryptocurrencies, decentralized finance (DeFi), peer-to-peer payments, and anonymous virtual wallets have created new challenges for the tracking of AML. The technologies have real value—such as expanding financial inclusion and streamlining operational efficiency—but create opportunities for money launderers to manipulate them. The observability of the velocity and anonymity of digital payments and the absence of centralized control enable hiding and make it challenging to detect and prosecute. Conventional financial monitoring practices, based on existing paper trails and institutional gatekeeping, are ineffective in these decentralized realms. Regulators are now therefore looking to sophisticated technologies such as artificial intelligence (AI), machine learning (ML), blockchain analytics, and regulatory technology (RegTech) to enhance real-time monitoring, detect anomalies, and streamline compliance procedures.

This chapter adopts an integrated and interdisciplinary approach in examining the money laundering phenomenon, and its complex relationship to modern financial systems. It initially outlines the conventional stages of the laundering process—placement, layering, and integration—and demystifies the various mechanisms employed to facilitate these transactions. These range from legitimate financial institutions to shell companies, to newer platforms like nonfungible tokens (NFTs) and virtual gaming currency. It then examines the interrelated dynamics between money laundering and cross-border crime, demonstrating how laundering both feeds and is fed by complex networks of criminal enterprise. This chapter subsequently examines the economic effects of money laundering, i.e., its effect on market distortion, perpetuation of inequality, undermining of state capacity, and its role in macroeconomic instability. Empirical outcomes will be drawn from high-profile real-life scandals and probes—such as the FinCEN Files leak, the Danske Bank scandal, and the ongoing exploitation of offshore tax havens. These case studies demonstrate both the scale of laundering activities and the failure of institutional responses. In the examination of legal and institutional controls, attention will be given not only to international standards such as the FATF Recommendations and the EU AML Directives but also to domestic controls, such as suspicious transaction reporting (STR), beneficial ownership disclosure, and asset recovery regimes.

Briefly, this chapter examines the new issues of laundering risk in the digital age. It will discuss the double-edged role of technology—as enabling laundering and a potential ally for enforcement—and examine the innovative responses being developed by regulatory authorities and compliance practitioners around the world. The analysis concludes with predictive recommendations for reform: increasing financial transparency, enabling regulatory cooperation, strengthening institutional capacity in risk jurisdictions, and applying risk-based measures informed by empirical research. Combining insights from law, economics, criminology, and RegTech, this chapter argues that money laundering is not only essential to preventing criminality but also central to promoting equitable development, national security, and the integrity of financial governance itself. In a period marked by financial sophistication and accelerated digital innovation, fights against laundering challenges will necessitate technical solutions as much as political will, international cooperation, and recommitment to transparency and accountability.

2. Phases and Mechanisms of Money Laundering

The architecture of money laundering is deceptively intricate. Despite the common perception that it involves little more than moving cash through banks or shell companies, laundering is in fact a multi-staged, transnational operation designed to obfuscate the origin of criminal proceeds, integrate them into the legal economy, and ultimately provide their possessors with social, political, and economic legitimacy. Understanding its mechanisms requires close scrutiny of its procedural phases—**placement, layering, and integration**—as well as the increasingly sophisticated instruments and sectors exploited for laundering purposes. This section dissects these components while situating them within the broader geopolitical and technological contexts that sustain laundering operations.

2.1 The Tripartite Process: Placement, Layering, and Integration

The classical definition of money laundering separates the process into three stages, which are not necessarily sequential or mutually exclusive. Frequently, stages overlap, and the launderers sequence the stages dynamically according to jurisdictional weaknesses and operating needs. Placement is the initial and weakest stage of the laundering process. At this stage, illegal proceeds are introduced into the financial system. The goal is to strip the funds from the immediate shadow of the root criminal activity and position it beyond direct law enforcement detection. Typical techniques include structuring large amounts into small deposits to circumvent reporting thresholds, utilizing cash-intensive enterprises (e.g., casinos, restaurants, or car washes), and smuggling currency into foreign countries to deposit in more liberal jurisdictions (FATF, 2022a).

Layering transcends placement and is the phase where the criminal source of the funds is deliberately concealed through sophisticated financial manipulations. This phase is the most complicated, typically involving many foreign-to-domestic and domestic-to-foreign transactions between financial institutions, investments in offshore trusts, trade mis-invoicing, and the use of virtual currencies. The aim is to break the audit trail and hide the source of the funds. Funds can go through shell companies, trade across high-frequency trading platforms, or be transformed into anonymous crypto-assets—each has the effect of increasing volume of transactions while avoiding institution detection (Levi & Reuter, 2006). Integration, the final step, is the phase where the laundered funds become part of the legitimate economy, typically as apparently legal income or property. Having been integrated, the funds can be used to buy luxury real estate, invest in legitimate business, or shape political processes through lobbying or donations. It is here that it is practically impossible to disentangle criminal and legitimate capital without extensive forensic financial analysis (Unger, 2007).

2.2 Expanding Channels of Laundering

While the tripartite model remains conceptually useful, real-world laundering schemes have diversified far beyond their original frameworks, leveraging both traditional and emergent financial infrastructure.

2.2.1 Banking and Trade Finance

Banking institutions are still a main channel for laundering because they are globally interconnected, operate on a trust-fund basis, and have high volumes of transactions. Banks have been time and again accused of laundering scandals even after exercising due diligence, mostly for neglecting proper KYC and STR procedures (ICIJ, 2020a, 2020b). Trade finance presents other loopholes in the form of invoice manipulation, under- and over-valuation of products, and ghost shipments—all named as trade-based money laundering (TBML). These misrepresentations conceal the movement of capital under the veil of legitimate business, particularly in jurisdictions that lack strong customs monitoring (FATF & Egmont Group, 2020).

2.2.2 Real Estate and High-Value Commodities

The money laundering role of property is well-documented. Real property can absorb huge sums of capital, appreciate, and resell with minimal supervision in those states that do not require disclosure of beneficial ownership. The same can be said for art and luxury products such as jewellery, yachts, or rare collectibles, which are transportable and easily under-valued items that make laundering easy and hard to value and establish ownership (UNODC, 2021).

2.2.3 Offshore Structures and Shell Entities

Offshore financial havens offer a degree of anonymity, minimal regulatory scrutiny, and favorable tax treatment. Shell companies, legal structures with minimal assets or business activity, are a ubiquitous tool for money laundering. Those structures are go-between organizations that split up the chain of possession and obscure the identity of the money's Ultimate Beneficial Owner(s). The Panama Papers and Pandora Papers leak revealed the worldwide network of lawyers, accountants, and corporate service providers that support these laundering conduits (ICIJ, 2016).

2.2.4 Virtual Assets and Cryptocurrency Ecosystems

Digitization of the financial system has radically altered the channels available for money laundering. Cryptocurrencies, while providing transparency via blockchain technology, also enable pseudo-anonymity, speed in cross-border transactions, and decentralized transactions via DeFi platforms. Criminals employ privacy-focused currencies (such as Monero or Zcash), mixing services that blend funds from multiple sources, and peer-to-peer trading mechanisms to circumvent KYC checks and maintain anonymity (Zetzsche, Buckley, & Arner, 2021). Regulatory attempts to impose control on Virtual Asset Service Providers (VASPs) remain patchy across jurisdictions, therefore enabling laundering networks to take advantage of existing regulatory loopholes.

2.2.5 Professional Enablers

Lawyers, notaries, accountants, and estate agents—collectively referred to as gatekeepers—are most often at the forefront of enabling sophisticated schemes of laundering, most often in the shadow of client secrecy or regulatory loopholes. Notwithstanding global standards demanding increased due diligence from Designated Non-Financial Businesses and Professions (DNFBPs), compliance varies (FATF, 2018).

2.3 Money Laundering as a Systemic Risk

Aside from its criminal meaning, money laundering is also a systemic threat to financial integrity. It dissolves the line of demarcation between licit and illicit finance, allowing corrupt elites and criminal networks to infiltrate licit economies. Moreover, laundered funds can be invested strategically in political lobbying, legal counsel, or media ownership, facilitating a state capture effect that undermines democratic institutions and the rule of law (Sharman, 2011). The problem, therefore, goes beyond specific transactions and is a macro-level problem to financial governance.

3. Intersections with Transnational Crime

Money laundering is not an isolated phenomenon but is firmly embedded within a larger nexus of transnational criminal economies. It is both a cause and consequence of a range of illicit business—drug trafficking and arms smuggling, terrorist investment, human trafficking, environmental crime, and kleptocracy. These are not random but are part of the logic and viability of international organized crime. By enabling the legitimization of criminal proceeds, laundering mechanisms shelter perpetrators from legal and financial risk, thus enabling circular reinvestment of criminal capital into still more criminal enterprise (UNODC, 2023).

3.1 Drug Trafficking and Narcotic Networks

One of the most well-documented connections is that of money laundering and the international narcotics trade. The narcotics trade produces enormous amounts of liquid cash, especially in consumer economies like the United States and Western Europe. These funds need advanced laundering channels to re-enter the formal financial system. Cartels use methods like smurfing (dividing large transactions into smaller amounts), TBML, and remittance networks like hawala and fei ch'ien to layer and consolidate proceeds into seemingly legitimate businesses. For example, the 2012 HSBC case exposed how vulnerabilities in the bank's AML regulation allowed Mexican drug cartels like the Sinaloa cartel to launder hundreds of millions through its US operations (US Senate Permanent Subcommittee on Investigations, 2012a). This case highlights the key nexus of banking vulnerabilities and illicit finance. The reinvested capital from laundered proceeds not only allows for the growth of trafficking networks but also the militarization of cartels, corruption of public officials, and weakening of local governance institutions.

3.2 Human Trafficking and Smuggling Networks

Parallel laundering infrastructures underpin human trafficking and migrant smuggling businesses. These activities create vast illicit proceeds, which need to be hidden and laundered back into the financial system to finance operations and avoid detection. Money launderers serving trafficking rings typically depend on shell companies, informal value transfer systems (IVTS), and integration through hospitality, construction, and domestic labor sectors where there is weak regulation. A 2020 Europol report illustrated how North African migrant smuggling into the EU included multi-layered laundering schemes through transnational logistics companies and shadow banking intermediaries (Europol, 2020a, 2020b). The durability of such laundering infrastructures perpetuates exploitative labor economies and increases vulnerabilities among already excluded groups.

3.3 Terrorist Financing

Terrorist financing and money laundering nexus both presents conceptual as well as operating issues. While laundering is traditionally about masking the origin of funds, terrorist financing can be about clean funds being diverted to undesirable ends. However, when terrorist groups earn revenues from criminal enterprises such as extortion, kidnapping, or illicit trade (e.g., war-zone antiquities), laundering conduits are necessary to fund logistics and ideology-related activities. For example, the Islamic State of Iraq and the Levant was found to have used networks of cash couriers, gold smuggling, and Iraqi and Syrian banks to launder proceeds from oil sales and plundering to useable funds for terror activities (FATF, 2015). Despite global sanctions and financial blacklisting, loopholes in regulatory coverage—particularly in weak and postconflict jurisdictions—provided the group access to financial services indirectly. Anti-terror financing efforts have therefore needed to shift from traditional AML practices to proactive surveillance and interdiction measures with behavioral analytics and financial intelligence sharing.

3.4 Environmental and Wildlife Crimes

Money laundering is increasingly connected to green crime, such as illegal logging, wildlife trade, and unlicensed fishing. These crimes, traditionally under-emphasized in AML policy, earn billions a year and are directly connected to organized crime groups and political corruption. The illicit wildlife trade, in turn, is heavily dependent on laundering channels to move and sell endangered animals, with proceeds laundered through art markets, gem trade, and cash-intensive sectors. Environmental crime, as estimated by the FATF, is now the fourth-largest criminal business in the world, but remains under-regulated in national AML systems (FATF, 2021a). Proceeds from such crimes laundered continue to finance ecological destruction, undermine biodiversity, and support further criminal activity.

3.5 Kleptocracy and State-Capture Networks

One of the most insidious forms of transnational laundering is from kleptocratic regimes, where state officials systematically move public money into private offshore accounts. These systems rely on legal advisers, financial consultants, and enablers in global financial centers to construct opaque ownership structures and move money across borders. The "state capture" phenomenon transcends corruption—it institutionalizes laundering as a method of sustaining authoritarianism, quashing dissent, and insulating elites from the rule of law. The 1Malaysia Development Berhad (1MDB) scandal in Malaysia is a classic case. Billions of dollars intended for public development were pilfered and laundered through complex corporate vehicles, high-end property, and entertainment companies worldwide (US DOJ, 2016). Large financial institutions, including Goldman Sachs, were implicated in the scandal and highlighted weaknesses in international due diligence mechanisms and beneficial ownership disclosure. These forces highlight an important point: money laundering is not simply an artifact of criminality but also a reflection of structural violence that reinforces elite criminal impunity and erodes democratic accountability. The presence of "professional enablers" such as legal professionals, financial accountants, and notaries operating under complicit jurisdictions presents an additional complicating factor in prosecuting laundering networks.

3.6 Weaponization of Laundered Funds

More and more, laundered money is being tracked as used to destabilize democracies and finance hybrid warfare. Disinformation operations, election meddling, and foreign lobbying are typically paid for using laundered money channeled through shell companies and shadowy investment funds. The targeted deployment of such money by state and nonstate actors obscures the distinction between criminal finance and geopolitics. Investigative reporting in the FinCEN Files traces how politically exposed persons used international banks to process suspect transactions related to election meddling and foreign influence operations (ICIJ, 2020a, 2020b). The weaponization of financial secrecy subsequently became a national security issue, leading regulatory officials to push new standards for political contribution and cross-border financial transparency.

4. Economic and Regulatory Implications

The economic implications of money laundering are systemic in that they impact domains from macroeconomic stability to market distortion, tax evasion, and government failure. As the volume and velocity of illicit financial flows (IFFs) in formal financial systems and shadow banking sectors grow, their effects are not only criminal but inherently systemic. Money laundering inflicts long-term harm on the integrity of the economy by distorting investment incentives, destabilizing mature real estate and financial markets, undermining regulatory systems, and perpetuating corrupt activities. This section considers these interrelated effects in the context of analyzing the shortcomings of existing regulatory systems in addressing these issues effectively.

4.1 Distortions in Market Dynamics and Capital Allocation

One of the most harmful impacts of laundering is its interference with legitimate market competition. When criminal money is invested in legal businesses—whether as equity injections, cash businesses, or real estate ownership—the usual supply, demand, and price dynamics are disrupted. Crime-backed businesses can price below their legal counterparts because their terminal goal is not maximization of profits but legitimization of profits made illegally. This behavior distorts the competitiveness of compliant businesses, reduces productivity, and yields monopoly market structures maintained by criminal capital (Levi & Reuter, 2006). Moreover, illegal funds tend to be invested in very safe and illiquid asset classes. Real estate, luxury goods, art markets, and precious metals are generally chosen—not merely due to their economic inherent value but due to the ease with which wealth can be hidden in them. These markets thus suffer from an unjustified inflation, which attracts more speculative funds and further disconnects prices from genuine demand. This leads to asset bubbles that are inherently precarious and highly susceptible to collapse, and the implications for middle-class affordability and financial stability in general (OECD, 2021a).

In globalized capital markets, money laundering through sophisticated cross-border schemes and structured transactions causes inefficient capital allocation, particularly in emerging economies. Dirty money seeks to escape regimes with effective regulatory implementation, resulting in capital flight from emerging economies to weakly regulated offshore havens. The result is an artificial shortage of investible capital in economies most in need of developmental finance, thus exacerbating under-investment in public infrastructure and essential services (UNCTAD, 2022).

4.2 Undermining of Tax Infrastructures and Public Revenues

IFFs, such as those from money laundering, have a significant adverse effect on the tax bases of states. Launderers frequently use tax havens and shell corporations to avoid reporting, conceal ownership structures, and avoid paying taxes. Global tax losses from offshore tax avoidance and corporate profit shifting total an estimated more than USD 483 billion each year based on a report of the Tax Justice Network (2023). Less-developed nations, which depend more on indirect taxation because of narrow tax nets, can be particularly decimated by such losses, leaving the state only to provide healthcare, education, and welfare. Concurrently, the diversion of large amounts of economic activity into the illicit or informal economies causes GDP to be consistently underestimated in most countries, which distorts policymaking and causes inflationary pressures and growth potential to be overestimated (Global Financial Integrity, 2021). Whole sectors of a nation's economy can even be partially criminalized in the worst cases, as in the property economies of some of Southern Europe, Southeast Asia, and Latin America. The nexus between money laundering and tax evasion renders traditional regulatory measures ineffective—such as tax audits or customs declarations—unless supported by international information sharing agreements and political will to implement.

4.3 Corruption, Institutional Capture, and State Fragility

Money laundering into developing nations has the impact of pushing not only economic distortion but also political corrosion. Where political elites are themselves part of laundering networks—either as recipients or facilitators—the apparatus of the state can be suborned. Such "kleptocratic capture" erodes the rule of law, undermines judicial independence, and diminishes the incentive to implement effective AML reforms (Rose-Ackerman & Palifka, 2016). In these conditions, regulatory institutions can become performative rather than functional, in being able to tick international compliance checklists but without the institutional capacity—or political will—to implement them. Moreover, laundered funds routinely enter politics directly. Political campaign finance, vote-buying, and lobbying are typically terminal stages of the laundering process. Once sunk into governance systems, these funds drive policy outputs in the interests of private rather than public interests, yielding regulatory inertia, under-enforcement, and systemic impunity. Democratic institutions are compromised both as cause and consequence of continued laundering activity (Transparency International, 2020).

4.4 Real Estate, Capital Markets, and Social Inequality

Real estate is one of the most widely used vehicles for laundering the world over. Anonymity of property transactions, combined with the high dollar value of real estate assets, makes the sector highly susceptible to the integration stage of laundering. Research has indicated that in urban centers such as London, Vancouver, and Dubai, the majority of high-value real estate transactions are suspicious or involve direct IFFs (Financial Transparency Coalition, 2022). Such activity fuels prices in urban centers through inflation, rendering housing unaffordable to ordinary citizens and thus sustaining spatial inequality. The same holds for capital markets. In weakly regulated financial markets, shell corporations or special purpose vehicles (SPVs) may be used to buy stocks, bonds, or derivatives anonymously. Not only does this taint the integrity of markets but it also introduces systemic risk, particularly when such investments are financed through leverage or packaged into securitized products.

Financial crises such as the 2008 subprime meltdown illustrated the way in which operational opacity within capital flows can generate cascading failure in global systems. Although laundering was not the causative source, the presence of trace-less capital greatly amplified the crisis by obscuring the true extent of financial exposure (Acharya & Richardson, 2009). Social inequality is also augmented through laundering. As criminal capital builds untaxed riches, it operates to maintain elite economic dominance and facilitates gated economic enclaves. Wealth disparity is not merely deepened but also legitimated, since prior to illicit riches being indistinguishable from fair assets. Such moral hazard gives rise to cynicism in society regarding markets' and governments' integrity, reducing public confidence in institutions (Piketty, 2014).

4.5 Regulatory Shortfalls and Enforcement Weaknesses

Despite diffusion of global AML regimes, national-level enforcement is patchy and uneven. Most jurisdictions have enacted legal requirements of customer due diligence (CDD), beneficial ownership disclosure, and STR, but these are often weakly monitored or enforced. The Danske Bank scandal, where more than

USD 230 billion was laundered out of its Estonian branch, exposed systemic failure of cross-border oversight, flawed risk assessment, and weak internal controls (European Banking Authority, 2019). Furthermore, regulatory agencies in smaller or developing economies are usually underfunded, politically hamstrung, or technologically inferior. The emphasis on formal compliance—completing FATF checklist indicators—often substitutes for deeper structural changes addressing the political economy of laundering. Financial institutions, in contrast, rely on compliance-based rather than risk-based practices, subcontract surveillance functions to software programs without simultaneous human oversight (FATF, 2022b). Lastly, loopholes in enforcement are augmented by jurisdictional arbitrage. Offenders take advantage of differences in national enforcement to transport capital through "weak links" in the global regulatory chain. This necessitates not only greater cooperation but harmonization of legal standards, and creation of supranational AML authorities empowered to conduct investigations and prosecutions (Zoromé, 2007).

5. Legal and Institutional Responses

It is sustained by a multi-faceted matrix of legal frameworks and institutional structures such as international agreements, regional legislation, and national laws. While the fundamental frameworks have been in place since the later half of the 20th century, the evolving sophistication of laundering techniques—spurred by technological financial innovations, regulatory weaknesses, and geopolitical instability—requires continuous refinements in these tools. It presents the organizational structure, robustness, and weaknesses of prominent legal and institutional responses in the context of the international compliance environment.

5.1 International Normative Architecture

The foundation of global response to money laundering is the FATF, founded in 1989 by the G7. FATF's "40 Recommendations" are the international standard for AML and Countering the Financing of Terrorism (CFT). They include legal requirements such as criminalizing money laundering, creating FIUs, requiring CDD, and requiring reporting of suspicious transactions by financial institutions. FATF's mutual evaluation process—a peer review—is a member and nonmember state compliance scorecard and influences access to international capital markets. Criticism has, however, been raised at uneven enforcement of these standards, particularly in politically fraught or resource-constrained jurisdictions, and the prioritization of formal legal compliance over effective enforcement in practice (FATF, 2023a). Regional bodies like the EU have evolved further through the adoption of binding legal tools, including a series of Anti-Money Laundering Directives (AMLDs). From the Third Directive's focus on risk-based measures to the Fifth and Sixth Directives requiring public beneficial ownership registers and harmonizing predicate offense definitions, the EU has shown active legal development. However, intra-EU variation in enforcement capability, bureaucratic inclination, and banking control still hinders uniform implementation (European Commission, 2020). The United States, by the Banking Secrecy Act (1970) and the USA PATRIOT Act (2001), codified one of the most ambitious AML enforcement schemes, including extraterritorial reach by the "correspondent banking" doctrine. These enactments empower the Treasury's Financial Crimes Enforcement Network (FinCEN) to probe global institutions enabling laundering through dollar-clearing systems (US Department of the Treasury, 2022a). The United Nations Convention Against Transnational Organized Crime (UNTOC) and the International Monetary Fund (IMF) have also established normative and technical support infrastructures, particularly for lower-income countries. However, compliance fatigue and cross-prioritization of development goals usually water down their effectiveness in countries plagued by institutional and infrastructural deficits (UNODC, 2022).

5.2 Domestic Legal Frameworks and Enforcement Agencies

At the national level, AML legal regimes have evolved. Most countries have specialized laws criminalizing money laundering and codifying regulatory powers. In India, for example, the PMLA, 2002, is the key legal tool, managed by the Enforcement Directorate (ED). While the PMLA offers attachment of property, arrest, and adjudication by special courts, it has been criticized for procedural complexity, low rates of conviction, and political abuse (Government of India, 2019). FIUs are the working backbone of AML regimes. FIUs collect, analyze, and disseminate STRs from banks, financial intermediaries, and DNFBPs. While more than 170 countries have created FIUs, their effectiveness is highly variable. Weaknesses include lack of autonomy and technical capability, weak inter-agency coordination, and budget limitations. The Egmont Group, a global network of FIUs, attempts to harmonize cooperation and information exchange, but laws of secrecy and sovereignty concerns continue to undermine transnational cooperation (Egmont Group, 2022).

Other domestic measures are KYC regulations, Enhanced Due Diligence (EDD) for high-risk customers, and obligatory maintenance of beneficial ownership registers. Enforcement is undermined by low standards of data verification, loopholes in trust and company arrangements, and nominee shareholders concealing accurate ownership. For instance, the Panama Papers and Pandora Papers revealed the widespread use of shell companies and trusts to conceal assets and evade tracking of assets (ICIJ, 2016–2021; UNODC, 2022).

5.3 Compliance, Supervision, and Penalty Structures

Successful AML regimes should also be under regular monitoring and enforcement by independent regulatory authorities. Central banks and securities authorities police the finance sector for compliance, whereas legal and accounting professions are continually policed by self-regulatory organizations (SROs). Capture of the regulator, under-funded supervisory offices, and the threat of "de-risking"—banks removing customers from high-risk geographies to escape scrutiny—far too frequently result in unintended financial exclusion in place of genuine compliance (World Bank, 2021). The deterrent impact of AML law relies to some extent on the risk of detection and magnitude of penalty. The United States and United Kingdom, for example, have levied multi-billion dollar penalties on noncompliant institutions (e.g., HSBC, Deutsche Bank, Standard Chartered), frequently through the use of Deferred Prosecution Agreements (DPAs) (US Seate Permanent Subcommittee on US Senate Permanent Subcommittee on Investigations, 2012b). Fines, though in the billions, are, it is argued, a cost of doing business for megabanks, and do not deter systemic abuse. Individual manager criminal prosecutions are still the exception, and questions around accountability and structural incentives persist (Financial Times, 2023).

5.4 Institutional Challenges and Reform Gaps

Despite the vast legal infrastructure, AML enforcement continues to suffer from four primary deficiencies:

(1) **Fragmented coordination**: Within and between countries, the lack of integrated databases and inter-agency cooperation undermines detection and prosecution.
(2) **Asymmetrical enforcement**: Smaller states or politically exposed jurisdictions often become "soft spots" for laundering, creating safe havens even as larger economies impose tough compliance regimes.
(3) **Over-criminalization versus under-conviction**: While legal thresholds for suspicious activity reporting are low, actual prosecutorial standards are high, leading to overburdened systems with low yield in convictions.
(4) **Technological lag**: Law enforcement agencies are often ill-equipped to trace laundering involving DeFi, dark web marketplaces, and privacy-enhancing technologies.

These shortfalls need to be met not only with legislative overhaul but institutional reconfiguration as well. Cross-border coordination frameworks, real-time information sharing regimes, and linked asset recovery systems need to become core pillars of AML policy (INTERPOL, 2023).

5.5 The Compliance Burden and the Question of Balance

There is mounting controversy surrounding the compliance burden on financial institutions and its disproportionate effect on smaller operators and developing nations. The cost of compliance infrastructure—integration of RegTech, in-house legal counsel, audit procedures—can be beyond sustainable reach for fintechs and smaller banks (Deloitte, 2022a). Moreover, the "chilling effect" of overregulation can suppress innovation, deter financial inclusion, and perpetuate systemic disparities, wherein AML law is employed to over-police informal economies and marginalized groups. Achieving a balance between risk reduction and financial accessibility is a policy imperative (UN CDF, 2023).

6. Emerging Challenges in the Digital Era

The 21st century has witnessed a fundamental transformation of financial systems due to accelerated digitization, radically changing the dynamics of both legitimate and illegitimate capitals. While digitization offers unparalleled ease of use, speed, and greater financial inclusion, it also enables new laundering methods that bypass traditional gatekeeper processes. Contemporary money launderers take advantage of the anonymity, decentralization, and global nature of digital technologies to enable and conceal financial crime to an unprecedented level. The regulatory regimes designed for the analogue world are increasingly being outpaced by new digital platforms, creating formidable obstacles to the effective implementation of AML policies.

6.1 The Rise of Crypto-Assets and Decentralized Finance

Arguably the most ground-breaking of modern financial laundering phenomena is the spread of crypto-assets, such as cryptocurrencies like Bitcoin, Ethereum, and Monero. Initially designed as mechanisms of decentralized innovation and democratized finance, these instruments have proven to be alluring conduits for laundering due to their pseudonymous character and ease of cross-border transmission. The FATF has consistently identified cryptocurrencies as high-risk money laundering, terrorist financing, and sanctions evasion techniques, particularly in light of their ability to conduct business outside of the formal financial system (FATF, 2021a, 2021b). Of special note is the emergence of privacy-enhancing coins (e.g., Zcash, Monero) and technologies such as coin mixers and tumblers, which have significantly hindered the ability to trace transactions. These technologies conceal the digital footprint of crypto transactions by blending coins from various sources, effectively "cleaning" its origin (Europol, 2020a, 2020b). Blockchain-based finance's decentralized architecture also constrains enforcement capability, as there are no central intermediaries whose activities can be monitored and regulated to control flows of transactions.

Even more sophisticated is the development of DeFi, a financial system of applications running on public blockchains, allowing peer-to-peer transactions in the absence of centralized intermediaries. DeFi platforms allow for lending, borrowing, asset exchange, and even synthetic derivatives without necessarily incurring meaningful KYC and AML compliance (Zetzsche, Buckley, Arner, et al., 2021). The pseudonymity of wallet addresses, self-executing smart contracts, and interoperable protocols all serve to create an ecosystem vulnerable to abuse. Of particular note is that recent enforcement efforts such as the US Department of Treasury sanctioning of Tornado Cash, a DeFi mixing service, reflect the growing acknowledgment of such threats (US Dept. of Treasury, 2022b).

6.2 Virtual Assets, NFTs, and Online Gaming

The laundering terrain has overflowed from conventional financial assets to novel digital classes of assets like NFTs. Such tokens, originally attached to digital art, are increasingly being used in complex laundering operations because they can quickly appreciate in value, be traded anonymously, and hold high-value capital in easily transferable mediums (FATF, 2022c). NFTs can be sold to shell wallets at artificially high prices—basically a self-dealing operation—thereby facilitating value transfer without raising red flags in conventional financial systems instantly. Online gaming websites and virtual economies are also being used for money laundering. Virtual currencies in massively multiplayer online games (e.g., World of Warcraft gold or Fortnite V-bucks) can be bought using dirty money and sold to other users for clean money, acting essentially like IVTS. The regulatory uncertainty of such systems makes it difficult to enforce, and their decentralized global user base makes it difficult for jurisdictions (INTERPOL, 2021).

6.3 Regulatory Lag and Jurisdictional Fragmentation

One of the inherent difficulties of money laundering in the digital age is the chronic regulatory lag—a process by which the institutional and legal frameworks lag behind the curve of technological innovation. Although the FATF has broadened its guidance to VASPs and called for the application of the "Travel Rule" to crypto transfers, patchiness of compliance remains (FATF, 2023b). The majority of nations are still to implement robust licensing regimes for crypto exchanges or demand strong due diligence, and this creates regulatory arbitrage and forum shopping by bad actors (Basel Institute of Basel Institute on Governance, 2023). Such fragmentation is particularly challenging in cross-border scenarios. A money laundering scheme employing a DeFi protocol hosted on a decentralized server, registered by a shell company in a tax haven, and accessed via a VPN by actors from several countries easily evades the reach of the regulatory powers of any single nation-state. Law enforcement agencies, despite greater cooperation, are frequently lacking in technical capabilities or jurisdictional reach to deal with the problem. Lack of mutual legal assistance treaties (MLATs) or harmonized definitions of digital assets between jurisdictions further erodes international efforts (UNODC, 2023).

6.4 AI, Deepfakes, and Identity Laundering

Money laundering in digital form is not merely a matter of financial transactions; it is also a matter of more sophisticated identity manipulation techniques. Deepfake technologies are being utilized by criminals these days to produce forged biometric identification (e.g., video KYC), or synthetic identities composed of genuine and composite forged data. Synthetic identities are able to pass through conventional AML screening, obtain bank accounts, and access credit systems—all without revealing the real beneficiaries (Deloitte, 2022b). AI, at times regarded as a regulatory enhancement tool, can also be exploited by launderers against it. For instance, AI-generated trading bots or market manipulation algorithms can conceal legitimate financial activity, camouflaged by layers of algorithmic "plausibility." Additionally, the scalability of AI-powered operations allows for rapid money laundering of microtransactions, a technique called "smurfing 2.0," where criminal funds are broken down into thousands of small payments on digital networks (IBM, 2023).

6.5 Displacement of Risk to Vulnerable Jurisdictions

As regulation by advanced economies' governments grows, money laundering networks are moving operations to politically unstable or weakly regulated territories, where banks lack resources and weak enforcement. This migration disproportionately targets developing nations, not only subjecting them to international organizations' blacklisting (e.g., FATF gray-listing) but also eroding public trust in financial management (OECD, 2021b). The spillover of digital assets into shadow economies also undermines the potency of monetary policy, tax enforcement, and socioeconomic fairness in poor states.

6.6 The Path Forward: Technology-Enabled Regulation

While these are problems, technology also has solutions. Solutions typically involving blockchain analytics, AI-powered risk assessment, and natural language processing are starting to transform compliance processes. Chainalysis, Elliptic, and TRM Labs are some of the solutions enabling law enforcement and regulators to track crypto transactions in near-real-time, providing more insight into historically opaque systems (Chainalysis, 2024). Utilizing real-time monitoring of transactions, the creation of cross-border data sharing frameworks, and the application of digital identity verification through tamper-proof cryptography technologies can assist in reducing nascent risks. Of particular note, regulators will need to implement a risk-based approach acknowledging different vulnerabilities across financial products, institutions, and user bases. Leveraging public–private partnerships and shared data ecosystems will be critical in combating dynamic laundering techniques in the digital era (WEF, 2023).

7. Regulatory Technology and Future Trajectories

The advent of RegTech in the AML system is a revolution in regulatory compliance and financial supervision thought and practice. While traditional approaches lag behind the increasing volume and sophistication of suspicious financial flows—especially in the virtual world—technological innovation holds out new avenues to enhance transparency, identify abnormalities, and facilitate enforcement in real time. However, technological adoption is correlated with various normative, operational, and infrastructural hurdles. This section discusses both the prospects and constraints of RegTech, the increasing applications of AI and ML, and the visionary regulatory reforms needed to build an effective and fair global AML system.

7.1 RegTech as a Paradigm Shift

RegTech, in its broadest sense, is the application of technology to enhance regulatory processes through automation, data processing, and machine-driven decision-making. In the AML context, RegTech allows financial institutions and regulators to screen large volumes of transactional data with higher precision, velocity, and cost efficiency. RegTech solutions compare favorably with traditional manual compliance systems, which are typically based on retroactive audits and static rule bases, by dynamically, in real time, inspecting suspicious activity indicators, and lowering false positives as well as investigation delays. The possibility of substituting bureaucratic bulk-reporting systems with smart compliance architectures is a paradigm shift in financial regulation (Arner et al., 2017). RegTech solutions of interest include identity verification platforms, automated KYC processes, real-time risk scoring engines, AI-driven transaction monitoring, and blockchain analytics for tracing crypto-flows. Institutions like HSBC, Standard Chartered, and JPMorgan Chase have deployed RegTech platforms to identify anomalies and streamline reporting requirements (FATF, 2022d). Likewise, regulatory authorities like the UK Financial Conduct Authority and the Monetary Authority of Singapore have introduced regulatory sandboxes to experiment and validate new RegTech solutions in controlled environments (Zetzsche et al., 2020).

However, institutional adoption of RegTech is not even. While there are technology and financial means in mature markets to test RegTech, low- and middle-income countries lack the digital infrastructure and legal certainty to implement such systems on a broad scale. This digital divide undermines equity, efficiency, and the possibility for AML gaps to be widened across borders.

7.2 AI and Behavioral Surveillance

AI, most commonly in its ML form, has greatly improved the functionality of AML systems of compliance to analyze huge volumes of data and identify nonlinear patterns of suspicious activity. Supervised ML algorithms are pre-trained on past STRs to forecast future danger, and unsupervised learning techniques identify outliers and unusual clusters of transactions without upfront labeling (Sahin & Duman, 2021). Another emerging application is behavioral monitoring, which depends on AI systems to create "normal" patterns of transactions for specific customers or industries and identify deviations in real time. For example, spikes in transactions outside geographic regions or inconsistent with reported income profiles might trigger warnings or alerts (Broeders & Prenio, 2018). One of the thrilling applications is uncovering "smurfing," or structured deposits to stay below reporting thresholds. AI software can track micro-patterns of cash inflows over time and cross-match them across accounts and geographies, revealing laundering operations that human monitors might overlook (Radu, 2020). Blockchain analysis tools like Chainalysis and Elliptic now feature AI modules to track funds across thousands of wallet addresses and smart contracts, thus disrupting the anonymization of crypto-assets.

But algorithmic transparency, data bias, and due process remain a concern. AI systems, particularly ones trained on historical enforcement records, can perpetuate discriminatory profiling or mirror the biases in such legacy data (Eubanks, 2018). Second, explainability is a difficult problem: regulators and defendants need to be able to understand and challenge the reasoning behind flagged transactions in order to maintain fairness and legality (Wachter et al., 2017). Regulatory frameworks for ethical AI use in AML are in nascent stages and need to develop further to weigh efficiency against accountability.

7.3 Blockchain Analytics and DeFi Surveillance

The rise of DeFi platforms and virtual assets has essentially made AML enforcement harder. DeFi systems are middleman-free, substituting algorithmic smart contracts for traditional actors (De Filippi & Wright, 2018). Although such arrangements introduce efficiencies and democratize access to financial services, they also anonymize transactions and bypass the central chokepoints traditionally used for enforcement. Blockchain analytics bridges the gap. With graph-based tracking, clustering algorithms, and heuristic modeling, analytics companies can track the flow of funds between pseudonymous addresses and identify connections to known criminal wallets (Chainalysis, 2022). Importantly, blockchain immutability means that once illegal flows are identified, they cannot be deleted or manipulated—leaving robust evidentiary trails.

However, DeFi's permissionless nature allows actors to regularly "hop" between protocols or "wash" funds through mixers and privacy coins (e.g., Monero, Tornado Cash) (FATF, 2023c). Jurisdictional mismatches also make enforcement difficult, as DeFi platforms can be developed and deployed in one nation but controlled by actors in another, all without any discernible legal obligation. Thus, blockchain analytics need to be paired with strong cross-border cooperation and on-chain regulatory standards in order to be effective.

7.4 Toward a Future-ready AML Framework

The integration of RegTech and AI into AML architecture demands concurrent reforms in regulatory philosophy and institutional design. The following policy directions are critical:

- Risk-based supervision: Regulators need to shift from rule-based compliance tick-boxes to risk-based supervision, which directs enforcement resources in line with sectoral risks and behavior indicators (IMF, 2021).
- International interoperability standards: Technical interoperability amongst databases, registries of KYC, and FIUs is important in a bid to allow for cross-border exchange and action on AML data.
- Public–private intelligence sharing: Joint frameworks such as the UK's Joint Money Laundering Intelligence Taskforce (JMLIT) must be copied worldwide to facilitate real-time intelligence sharing between banks, regulators, and technology providers (UK Home Office, 2021).
- Vulnerability capacity building: International institutions need to facilitate AML infrastructure building in low-capacity states through technical assistance, training programs, and funding assistance (World Bank, 2020). Otherwise, illicit flows will keep taking advantage of global asymmetries in readiness to enforce.
- Ethical and legal protections of algorithmic monitoring: National AML legislation should have rights-based protections, auditability requirements, and channels for algorithmic accountability to avert misuse and overreach (Casey & Niblett, 2021).

The future of AML enforcement lies in a coordinated fusion of law, technology, and institutional design. RegTech offers an indispensable arsenal in the fight against laundering—but only when deployed with democratic oversight, international harmonization, and a firm commitment to equitable financial governance.

8. Conclusion

The battle against money laundering has come to a turning point in the 21st century. As the following chapters illustrate, money laundering is not a distinct or secondary criminal activity but an integral process by which proceeds to transnational crime are cleaned, legitimized, and reinserted into formal economies. Its persistence and proliferation testify not only to the imagination of criminal networks but to the habitual institutional vulnerabilities, fragmentation of regulation, and technology disparities that characterize the contemporary global financial system. The variety of laundering techniques—from banking and real estate markets to holdings in cryptocurrency and trade-based laundering—serves to highlight both the gravity of the challenge and the difficulty of developing effective interventions. At the nexus of the challenge lies a fundamental paradox: while the financial globalization has facilitated faster capital flows and more financial inclusion, it has also opened unprecedented opportunities for IFFs. The transnational character of laundering schemes thrives in the regulatory frontiers of nation-states, where unevenly distributed capacities for enforcement, divergent legal traditions, and disparate political will have created a patchwork landscape. The doctrine of banking secrecy, the use of tax havens, and the potential to conceal beneficial ownership continue to undermine transparency and conceal illicit capital from view. Meanwhile, jurisdictions with weak institutions or weak compliance cultures have too often become sanctuaries for criminal proceeds, undermining global anti-laundering efforts from within. But the impacts of money laundering extend far beyond mere financial opacity. Dirty money laundering undermines the very pillars of economic governance. It diminishes tax collections, promotes corruption, causes rent-seeking, and distorts the purity of markets. When illicit capital flows into real estate, luxury goods, or financial securities, it inflates asset prices, distorts supply-demand imbalances, and spreads inequality. Moreover, the reputational blow incurred by regions plagued with serial laundering scandals—illustrated by high-profile examples such as the Danske Bank scandal or revelations in the FinCEN Files—discourages legitimate investment and erodes confidence in financial institutions. Particularly for developing nations, the impacts can be even more extensive, leading to capital flight, undermined institutions, and a cycle of underdevelopment.

The symbiotic nature of money laundering with other kinds of organized crime—arms smuggling, terrorist financing, kleptocracy, and drug trafficking—substantially enhances its geopolitical and humanitarian significance. Money laundering is the economic lifeblood of criminal gangs, enabling illicit players to re-invest in their enterprise, bribe government officials, and extend their reach across borders. In countries ravaged by conflict or under the shadow of authoritarian regimes, the diversion of laundered proceeds can be used to finance repression, support violence, or co-opt public institutions. The battle against money laundering is, therefore, more than a matter of financial regulation; it is an issue of the utmost urgency to preserve democratic integrity, human rights, and international stability. To respond effectively, legal and institutional frameworks must move beyond the sterility of compliance. The international AML system—built on the guidance of the FATF and regional standards—has made significant strides toward common standards. The gap between regulatory advancements and enforcement, however, remains significant, with many jurisdictions indulging in superficial compliance to avoid blacklisting and effective enforcement trailing behind. STR systems are typically clogged with false positives, as FIUs often lack the resources or freedom of action. Additionally, beneficial ownership registries—while widely touted—tend to be plagued by data quality, missing verification processes, and access restrictions.

The digitization of the financial system has further made the landscape more complex. Cryptocurrencies, DeFi, and noncustodial wallets pose new challenges to regulators trying to reconcile the paradigms of anonymity, decentralization, and global reachability with the necessities of traceability, accountability, and enforcement. Here again, traditional AML approaches relying on institutional gatekeepers and static risk categories may increasingly prove inadequate. A paradigm shift, therefore, is needed that combines regulatory innovation, technological adaptability, and collaborative governance. Encouragingly, the emergence of RegTech, AI, and blockchain analytics holds enormous transformative power. These tools can facilitate real-time monitoring of transactions in volume, pattern recognition, and anomaly detection. Through automating compliance tasks and facilitating proactive oversight, RegTech can reduce the regulatory burden and human fallibility. But this technological potential must be matched with effective data privacy protections, algorithmic accountability, and institutional capacity building. Failing this, there is a danger of outsourcing core state functions to the private sector or hardwiring biases into the training data. In addition, there is a need to rebuild international cooperation with actual action, not symbolic action. Multilateral action—through the Egmont Group of FIUs, the OECD Global Forum on Transparency, and the initiatives of the United Nations on IFFs—needs more robust mandates, more financial resources, and more effective coordination. Law enforcement authorities, regulatory agencies, and financial institutions have to work together across borders in a timely and mutually advantageous way, transcending jurisdictional limitations and political hesitations. Of particular importance is the need to harmonize definitions, enhance MLATs, and ensure the integrity of transnational data exchange.

At a national level, governments need to invest in establishing strong institutional ecosystems. This involves not just reinvigorating judiciary systems and financial intelligence agencies but also establishing independent monitoring agencies, safeguarding whistleblowers, and involving civil society in transparency initiatives. Financial crime detection training and education need to be institutionalized across the board, and compliance cannot be left solely in the hands of outsourced consultancies or high-end actors. Similarly, the private sector needs to shift from risk mitigation to action and appreciate the fact that strong AML practices are the key to long-term reputational and operational resilience.

Finally, an effective response must face the political economy of secrecy. The global architecture underpinning money laundering cannot be effectively dismantled without challenging the incentives that underpin it—financial havens protected by powerful governments, financial elites lobbying, and the tacit complicity of professionals who facilitate complex laundering schemes. Naming individuals who facilitate such activity—accountants, lawyers, real estate agents—acting as middlemen in money laundering transactions is a necessary step. Legal accountability must be applied, not just to the criminal perpetrators but also to the wider context that makes laundering not just possible but profitable.

The struggle against money laundering is marked both by urgency and tenacity. It calls for a shift away from fragmented, palliative action to systemic, integrated change. This challenge demands the convergence of legal scholarship, technological innovation, and political will. Above all, it depends on a common ethical commitment to building transparent, fair, and accountable financial systems. Without such determination, the money laundering cycle of illegal wealth creation, concealment, and reintegration will continue to undermine our institutions, destabilize our economies, and corrode the very foundations of financial governance. The question, therefore, is not whether money laundering can be effectively confronted, but whether there exists the necessary political and institutional will to apply the measures that its resolution clearly requires.

References

Acharya, V. V., & Richardson, M. (2009). *Restoring financial stability: How to repair a failed system.* Wiley.

Arner, D. W., Barberis, J., & Buckley, R. P. (2017). FinTech, RegTech, and the reconceptualization of financial regulation. *Northwestern Journal of International Law & Business*, *37*(3), 371–413.

Basel Institute on Governance. (2023). *Basel AML index report.*

Broeders, D., & Prenio, J. (2018). *Innovative technology in financial supervision (SupTech)* (Vol. Vol. 9). BIS Financial Stability Institute Insights.

Casey, B., & Niblett, A. (2021). Self-driving laws: When artificial intelligence rules the world. *University of Toronto Law Journal*, *71*(1), 1–44.

Chainalysis. (2022). *The 2022 crypto crime report.* Available at: www.chainalysis.com

Chainalysis. (2024). *Crypto crime report.* available at www.chainalysis.com

De Filippi, P., & Wright, A. (2018). *Blockchain and the law: The rule of code.* Harvard University Press.

Deloitte. (2022a). *Global survey on the cost of compliance in financial institutions.*

Deloitte. (2022b). *Synthetic identities in financial crime.*

Egmont Group. (2022). *Best practices for the effective functioning of FIUs.*

Eubanks, V. (2018). *Automating inequality: How high-tech tools profile, police, and punish the poor.* St. Martin's Press.

European Banking Authority. (2019). *Report on the danske bank case.*

European Commission. (2020). *Action plan for a comprehensive EU policy on preventing money laundering and terrorist financing* COM (2020) 280 final.

Europol. (2020a). *Migrant smuggling in the EU: Challenges and counter-measures, strategic report.*

Europol. (2020b). *Cryptocurrencies and the future of money laundering.*

FATF. (2015). *Financing of the terrorist organisation Islamic State in Iraq and the levant (ISIL).*

FATF. (2018). *Professional money laundering.*

Financial Action Task Force (FATF) and Egmont Group. (2020). *Trade-based money laundering: Trends and developments.*

FATF. (2021a). *Money laundering and environmental crime.*

FATF. (2021b). *Virtual assets and virtual asset service providers: Updated guidance.*

FATF. (2022a). *Money laundering through the physical transportation of cash.*

FATF. (2022b). *Outcomes of the FATF plenary.*

FATF. (2022c). *Targeted update on implementation of the FATF standards on virtual assets (VAs) and virtual asset service providers (VASPs).* FATF, Paris. (Covers NFTs under Rec. 15).

FATF. (2022d). *Opportunities and challenges of new technologies for AML/CFT.* FATF-GAFI.

FATF. (2023a). *Methodology for assessing technical compliance with the FATF recommendations.*

FATF. (2023b). *Outcomes of the FATF plenary meeting*, 25–27 October 2023. (VA/NFT implementation updates).

FATF. (2023c). *Illicit finance risks of decentralised finance.* FATF-GAFI.

Financial Times. (2023). *AML failures: Why bankers still walk free.*

Financial Transparency Coalition. (2022). *Luxury real estate and illicit financial flows.*

Global Financial Integrity. (2021). *Illicit financial flows to and from developing countries: 2008–2017.*
Government of India. (2019). *Prevention of money laundering act, 2002, as amended by finance act.*
IBM. (2023). *Emerging financial crimes in the AI era.*
International Consortium of Investigative Journalists. (2016). *Pandora papers, 2021; Panama papers.*
International Consortium of Investigative Journalists (ICIJ). (2016–2021). *Panama papers and pandora papers investigations.*
International Consortium of Investigative Journalists (ICIJ). (2020a). *The FinCEN files.*
International Consortium of Investigative Journalists (ICIJ). (2020b). *The FinCEN files: Politically exposed persons and global laundering.*
International Monetary Fund (IMF). (2021). *Risk-based approach to AML/CFT supervision.* Technical Guidance Note.
INTERPOL. (2021). *Cybercrime and .virtual gaming economies.*
INTERPOL. (2023). *Cross-border financial crime coordination report.*
Levi, M., & Reuter, P. (2006). Money laundering. *Crime and Justice*, *34*(1), 289–375.
OECD. (2021a). *Money laundering through real estate.* OECD Publishing.
OECD. (2021b). *Illicit financial flows in fragile States.*
Piketty, T. (2014). *Capital in the twenty-first century.* Harvard University Press.
Radu, R. (2020). Artificial intelligence and the detection of financial crime: Emerging applications. *Journal of Financial Crime*, *27*(3), 821–837.
Rose-Ackerman, S., & Palifka, B. (2016). *Corruption and government: Causes, consequences, and reform.* Cambridge University Press.
Sahin, Y., & Duman, E. (2021). Detecting money laundering activities with supervised and unsupervised machine learning. *Expert Systems with Applications*, *173*, 114686.
Sharman, J. C. (2011). *The money laundry: Regulating criminal finance in the global economy.* Cornell University Press.
Tax Justice Network. (2023). *State of tax justice report 2023.*
Transparency International. (2020). *Money, politics and corruption: Political finance and State capture.*
UK Home Office. (2021). *The economic crime plan: Progress and reflections.*
UN Capital Development Fund. (2023). *Balancing financial integrity and inclusion.*
UNCTAD. (2022). *Trade misinvoicing and capital flight in developing countries.*
Unger, B. (2007). *The scale and impacts of money laundering.* Edward Elgar Publishing.
United Nations Office on Drugs and Crime. (2021b). *Legislative guides for the implementation of the United Nations convention against transnational organized crime.*
United Nations Office on Drugs and Crime (UNODC). (2021). *Money laundering through real estate.*
United Nations Office on Drugs and Crime (UNODC). (2022). *Strengthening legal cooperation in cyberspace.*
United Nations Office on Drugs and Crime (UNODC). (2023). *Global report on crime trends and responses.*

US Department of Justice. (2016). *United States v. Wolf of wall street" assets and others (1MDB case)* Case No. CV 16-5362.

US Department of the Treasury. (2022a). *Financial crimes enforcement network (FinCEN) guidelines.*

US Department of the Treasury. (2022b). *Press release on sanctions against tornado cash.*

US Senate Permanent Subcommittee on Investigations. (2012a). *U.S. vulnerabilities to money laundering, drugs, and terrorist financing: HSBC case study.*

US Senate Permanent Subcommittee on Investigations. (2012b). *Correspondent banking and HSBC case study.*

Wachter, S., Mittelstadt, B., & Floridi, L. (2017). Why a right to explanation of automated decision-making does not exist in the general data protection regulation. *International Data Privacy Law*, *7*(2), 76–99.

World Bank. (2020). *StAR initiative annual report: Strengthening asset recovery and AML capacities.*

World Bank. (2021). *The De-risking dilemma: Drivers and impact of bank account closures.*

World Economic Forum (WEF). (2023). *Public-private collaboration for responsible blockchain development.*

Zetzsche, D. A., Buckley, R. P., & Arner, D. W. (2020). The rise of regulatory sandboxes in financial regulation. *Journal of Banking Regulation*, *21*(2), 85–104.

Zetzsche, D., Buckley, R., & Arner, D. (2021). Decentralized finance (DeFi). *Journal of Financial Regulation*, *7*(2), 172–203.

Zetzsche, D. A., Buckley, R. P., Arner, D. W., & Barberis, J. N. (2021). Decentralized finance (DeFi). *Journal of Financial Regulation*, *7*(2), 172–203.

Zoromé, A. (2007). Concept of offshore financial centers: In search of an operational definition. *IMF Working Paper* (IMF Working Paper WP/07/87). https://www.imf.org/external/pubs/ft/wp/2007/wp0787.pdf

Chapter 6

Harnessing AI for Forensic Financial Audits: Ethical and Legal Challenges in Combating Insider Trading and Manipulation

Ashwani Panesar and Rohit Sood

Lovely Professional University, India

Abstract

The entire world has got divided into developed, developing, and under-developed categories. As economic liberalization is taking the center-stage under the preview of brittle regulatory frameworks, the risk of unethical financial practices and corporate fraud becomes more evident. The prevalence of financial crimes such as insider trading and market manipulation represents a serious threat to economic stability and investor confidence. These unethical and illegal practices are not mere regulatory infractions, but they constitute strategic crimes that distort the fundamental principles of transparency, fairness, and efficiency in capital markets. Economies under transition like BRIICS reveal how rapid globalization can breed systemic weaknesses. Data from the Association of Certified Fraud Examiners indicate that organizations in developing regions face median losses of $200,000 per fraud case, compared to $100,000 in developed economies. This chapter will explore how digital technologies like artificial intelligence, blockchain, and data analytics can be leveraged to further strengthen the audit precision and real-time fraud detection. This chapter explores the cognitive and behavioral effects on investors, particularly during periods of regulatory exposure or market uncertainty in the light of herd behavior, trust erosion, and information asymmetry are explored to explain how perceptions of crime influence investor decision-making. In conclusion, this chapter aims to contribute to the existing body of knowledge by presenting

Corruption and Crime in Finance, 109–132

doi:10.1108/978-1-83708-170-720261017

forensic auditing not merely as a financial investigative tool but as a strategic instrument in institutional reform and ethical realignment.

Keywords: Artificial intelligence; financial fraud; forensic audit; greed; insider trading

1. Introduction

The entire world has undergone paradigm shift from being a self-reliant to be competitive or comparative advantage position among its peers (Campanella, 2023). With the developed markets growth getting saturated owing to population degrowth, the entire focus has shifted to the emerging economies to pave the way for global economies in these turbulent times (Saito, 2024). The world is divided into three parts namely developed, developing, and underdeveloped. This has made emerging markets to be the focal points of global attention, offering substantial potential in terms of resources, and consumer demand (Alonge et al., n.d.). Countries like India, Brazil, Indonesia, and Nigeria are witnessing industrialization, urbanization, and technological transformation to become engines of global power. Economic indicators like foreign direct investment (FDI), liberalization, digitalization, and digitization (Kumar & Roy, 2025). This accelerated growth trajectory does not come without ethical costs (Morinière, 2023). Beneath this optimism of growth lies a complex web of greed-driven practices, systemic fraud, and institutional weaknesses, which threaten to derail sustainable development. Table 6.1 brings more deeper insights as to huge disparity in all the social and economic indicators across the economies.

Emerging economies grappling with various problems in the transition phase are spending money on the social indicators to uplift their economic activity in the manufacturing and services sectors. Also, emerging economies getting flooded with funds, the race for profit and market dominance has overshadowed the ethical boundaries. Investors or institutions either domestic or foreign, are frequently driven by the greed to have short-term profits thereby resorting to unethical practices like insider trading (SEC, 2017), market manipulation, tax evasion, and bribery. The liberalization of markets has further triggered and created various loopholes for unethical behavior to flourish (Morinière, 2023). Financial crimes such as accounting fraud, shell company misuse, and illicit capital flows have become common, which depicts the darker side of rapid economic development.

Greed too has become an unspoken currency in many emerging markets and visible in the form of inflated valuations, speculative bubbles, and overleveraged conglomerates. This unchecked pursuit of profit has often resulted in corporate scandals and financial collapses, eroding public trust in both the market and institutions. Case studies such as the Harshad Mehta, Telgi scam, and Satyam scandal in India, Petrobras in Brazil, and numerous banking failures in African nations underscore how fraudulent practices, often aided by weak regulatory

Table 6.1. Disparity in Social and Economic Indicators Among Developed, Under-developed, and Developing Economies.

Indicators	Developed Economies	Developing Economies	Underdeveloped Economies
Per capita income	High (>\$13,000, often > \$30,000)	Medium (\$1,046–\$13,000)	Low (<\$1,046)
Economic structure	Dominated by services and technology	Mixed: Industrial and agricultural sectors	Informal economy with primarily agricultural
Industrialization level	Highly industrialized	Moderately industrialized	Low; limited to small-scale or resource-based sectors
Technological advancement	Cutting-edge (AI, robotics, biotech)	Growing use of tech, digital adoption rising	Basic or limited tech use
GDP growth rate	Stable but slow (~2–3%)	Higher but volatile (~4–7%)	Unstable, often <2% or negative
Education level (literacy rate)	Very high (>95%)	Improving (70–95%)	Low (<70%)
Human development index (HDI)	Very high (>0.85)	Medium to high (0.55–0.84)	Low (<0.55)
Governance and political stability	Stable democratic institutions	Mixed; improving governance	Often unstable or authoritarian
Social protection systems	Robust (pensions, unemployment benefits, welfare)	Expanding systems	Weak or absent
Digital penetration	>85% population online	50–80%, rapid growth	<40%, digital divide

Source: Authors' Own.

enforcement, can devastate economies and livelihoods that too for the sake of amassing wealth owing to greed. India's Satyam Computers scandal in 2009 involved falsified accounts to the tune of $1.5 billion, triggering a nationwide debate on corporate accountability. Also, Harshad Mehta's scam of 1992 which involved manipulation of stock prices by exploiting the loopholes in Indian financial system amounting to over ₹4,000 crore.

With economies in transition, the governance structure of majority of companies are fragile which evoke ethical dilemmas in decision making. Regulatory bodies in these countries lack autonomy to act and control to enforce legal and ethical standards. This vacuum makes the ground ready for corruption, favoritism, and crony capitalism, allowing powerful entities to grow and expand beyond the preview of law. Economic growth in these types of economies might be robust but is socially regressive and compromised.

Moreover, the informal sector dominates a significant share of economic activity in these markets, leading to tax evasion, labor exploitation, and lack of accountability. Multinational corporations, too, are not immune to unethical conduct; many have been accused of turning a blind eye to exploitative labor conditions, environmental degradation, and unfair pricing strategies in pursuit of profit maximization. The ethical dilemma here is stark: how to reconcile the hunger for economic success with the need for transparency, justice, and long-term social welfare. Moreover, the data from the Association of Certified Fraud Examiners (ACFE) indicates that organizations in developing regions face median losses of $200,000 per fraud case, compared to $100,000 in developed economies. The table highlights the urgency of adopting forensic audits in financial investigations. Emerging markets, often plagued by institutional voids, require such audit mechanisms not just for detecting fraud but also for deterring it.

In this chapter, in-depth insight to be provided given that there exist lot of opportunities for economic transformation and global rebalancing insight of ethical pitfalls. The interplay of ambition, greed, and inadequate oversight can perpetuate cycles of inequality and instability unless checked by strong institutions and principled leadership. Also, the economic drivers alongside the ethical dilemmas particularly those rooted in fraud, greed, and systemic abuse being critical in designing policies and practices that promote inclusive, responsible, and resilient development of the economies.

2. Challenges in the Financial Environment of Emerging Nations

Fig. 6.1 brings a deeper insight to as to what type of problems these economies are facing to purse their ambition of unparallel growth to be developed economy. Moreover, for the better understanding the entire categories has been bifurcated into two namely internal and external. Corruption, crime and fraud being the center stage of the discussion, so the indicators taken are those which are largely responsible for the bottleneck of growth.

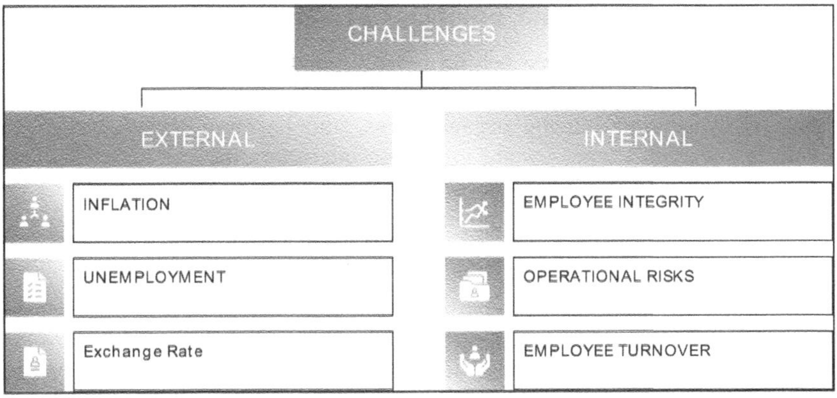

Fig. 6.1. External and Internal Challenges for Organizational Growth. *Source:* Author's Own.

Fig. 6.1 illustrates how external and internal challenges drive employees to resort to insider trading and falsifying financial statements.

A study from World Bank (2017) reported that the average income in countries with a high level of corruption is about a third of that of countries with a low level of corruption. It is quite difficult to eliminate the corruption in the form of insider trading and manipulation, but the steps need to be taken to reduce its impact on the society. The external challenges consist of inflation, unemployment and volatile exchange rates. It has been reported that corruption too leads to high inflation due to inefficiencies in public spending, misallocation of resources, and rent-seeking behavior (IMF, 2016). IMF (2016) found that corruption increases inflation as it distorts fiscal policies, leading to excessive money printing to cover deficits. Bribes and embezzlement reduce government revenue, forcing central banks to monetize debt, increasing money supply and inflation.

Like, in 2000s, corruption and greed made hyperinflation under Robert Mugabe's rule in Zimbabwe (Hanke & Kwok, 2009). The greed of some people to seize the opportunity to amass wealth led the collapse of entire fiscal system and later on forced the country to leave their own currency and adopt other currency. Similar results were witnessed in Nigeria and Venezuela (Dabla-Norris et al., 2019) whereby corruption in one of the state entities led to entire erosion of the wealth of a nation leading to wide economic devastation. External factors being just the driving force for the people who are largely driven by their internal stimuli like their integrity, turnover, and risks. Corruption and fraud undermine integrity, increase turnover, and heighten organizational risks (Transparency International, 2020).

3. Driving Forces Behind Financial Frauds

Greed being the driving force behind corruption, fraud, and tyranny, is often fueled by the pursuit of cash and power. These practices being unethical lead to erosion of trust, destabilizing organizations, and harming societies. The discussion below gives deeper insight into these interrelationships.

Fig. 6.2 illustrates the vicious cycle of accumulating wealth through the tyranny of greed, power, and corruption, driven by the urge to expand one's cash reserves through illegal means such as insider trading and market manipulation.

- Corruption to Abuse of Power for Personal Gain: Corruption occurs when individuals in their positions of authority tend to exploit their power for selfish benefits, keeping aside fairness and justice. Globally, there are numerous examples where a small instance of corruption, but it became a habit led to the downfall of entire organization. Like, the year 2001 Enron Scandal (2001) took place when some of the executives manipulated company's balance sheets to hide debt and built a business which otherwise was not of that quantum, leading to the company's collapse and the investors suffered heavy losses (Sørensen, 2025). Also, the 2014 Brazil Petrobras Scandal whereby some of the prominent Politicians and some executives embezzled billions from the state-run oil company, triggering an economic turmoil (de Melo Gomes & Branco, 2025). The seeds of corruption breeds distrust in companies and increases turnover of ethical workers amidst toxic environments. Insider Trading Element: In cases like the Martha Stewart ImClone Scandal of 2001,

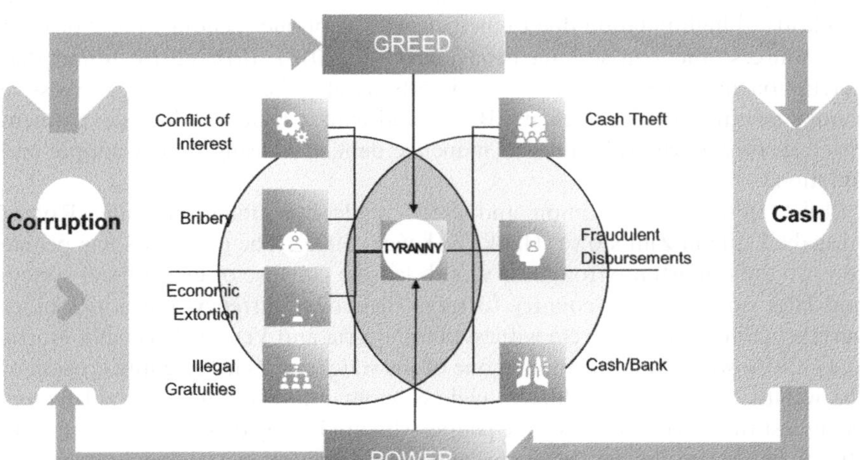

Fig. 6.2. Destructive Force With Integration of Greed, Corruption, Cash, and Power. *Source:* Author's Own.

executives used confidential information to avoid losses, demonstrating how corruption extends to securities fraud (Anthony et al., n.d.).

- Fraud for Deception for Financial Gain: Fraud involves intentional deception for personal or organizational profit, often at the expense of stakeholders. The person who is committing the fraud is aware of the scenario and its implications. Fraud involves amassing people's money on the pretext of giving them higher returns or when something unrealistic targets to be met which is otherwise not possible. For example, Bernie Madoff's Ponzi Scheme ($65B Fraud), where the investors were made to deposit their money for high returns, but the said money was used to repay the capital of the old investors, leading to collapse in 2008 (Imtiaz Mazumder & Ahmad, 2010). Ramalinga Raju (Satyam Computers) created fake employment records of thousands of employees and amassed their salaries for years leading erosion of company's wealth and finally takeover by Tech Mahindra (Raghunathan, 2010). Fraud leads to huge financial losses and in terms of reputation and most employees don't want to be part of such companies. Insider Trading Element: The Raj Rajaratnam (Galleon Group) case of 2011 showed how corporate fraud overlaps with insider trading, where confidential earnings data was illegally used for stock market gains (Henning, 2017).
- Tyranny in Leadership due to Corrupt Power: Leaders who are Tyrannical abuse their authority, suppress dissent, and create toxic workplaces which lead to thriving of unethical behavior. Emerging economies are the one who are facing this kind of abuse of power as power is concentrated in few hands and citizens face restrictions on their speech and right to representation. For example, Travis Kalanick (Uber's Toxic Culture) whereby aggressive leadership cultivated harassment and unethical practices, leading to mass employee protests and executives' resignation (Santora, 2020). Also, Vladimir Putin's Oligarch Control in Russia leading to amassing wealth through his political influence, while all those who were dissidents were liable to face imprisonment or exile (Cunningham, 2021). This form of leadership increases employee turnover, stifles innovation, and put the reputation of a country at risk. Insider Trading Element: In Russia, politically connected oligarchs like Mikhail Khodorkovsky were accused of using insider knowledge to manipulate privatization deals (Monday, 2017).
- Cash and Power Lead to Corporate Scandals: The greed and urge to acquire more money beyond the regular income in an aspiration to be wealthy and prosperous being the point for corruption and lead to corporate scandals. This chase for money leads to make unethical decisions. Like, the financial crisis of 2008 triggered by Lehman Brothers due to risky mortgage investment decisions, due to greed without taking into context the liquidity of the investment, triggered a global economic meltdown (Mason, 2020). Volkswagen Emissions Scandal in the year 2015, whereby the company showed deceived data of emission norms of their vehicles to boost the sales to be globally number one in automobile sales but ended up with fines of huge money (Tarsa, 2017). So, the greed, lust of money and being in the center stage of power whereby it is being exploited to amass the wealth at the cost of the stakeholders. Insider

Trading Element: The Goldman Sachs "Big Short" Scandal of 2010 revealed how banks profited from insider knowledge of mortgage market collapses while selling toxic assets to clients (Kane, 2008).

From the above discussion, it is evident that greed supported by the lust of executives to be wealthy promotes the instances of fraud, so the companies need to mitigate this act of corruption and fraud by promoting transparency.

4. Forensic Audit as a Future Tool

Forensic audit plays a pivotal role in ensuring the investigation, gather, compliance, and strengthen the system to ensure that rising crimes and frauds have a minimal impact on the finances of the company. The pictorial diagram and henceforth the discussion on their interrelationships has made forensic auditing an essential future tool.

Fig. 6.3 illustrates the significance of forensic audits in identifying critical cues, collecting substantial evidence to ensure compliance, and ultimately reinforcing the financial infrastructure of an organization.

- Investigation, being the key area of scope of forensic auditing, cohesively works to detect, analyze, and prevent financial fraud, misconduct, and non-compliance. Forensic auditing employs structured methodologies for in-depth examination of financial records, while investigation applies legal procedures

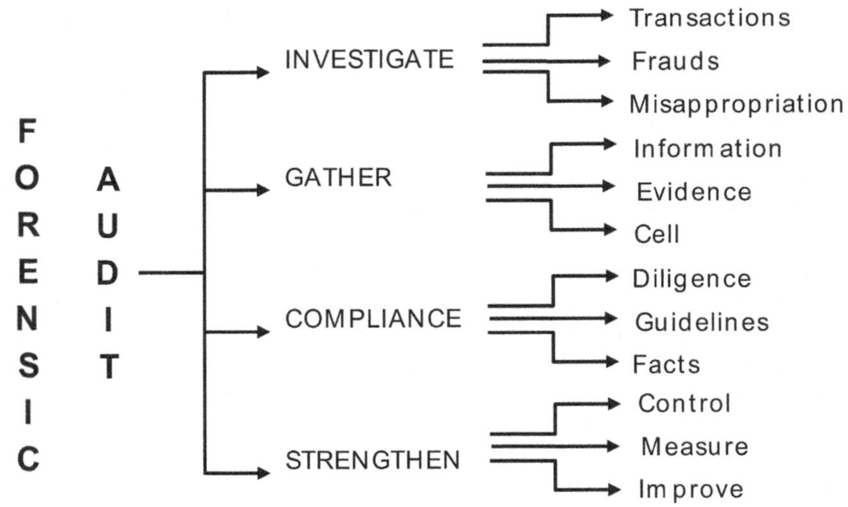

Fig. 6.3. Forensic Audit as an Investigative Tool. *Source:* Author's Own.

to gather evidence and fix accountability (Zientek, 2020). Both form powerful tools for uncovering financial crimes like insider trading, where privileged information is exploited for stock market gains (Seyhun, 1992). Forensic audits systematically analyze records to identify loopholes such as unexplained transactions, accounting discrepancies, and unauthorized fund transfers. They collect financial documents, electronic records, and transactional data to trace money trails—critical in proving insider trading cases like the Galleon Group scandal, where hedge funds traded on illegal tips (Henning, 2017). Fraud audits enhance financial expertise to detect asset misappropriation, corruption, and fraudulent statements.

- Gathering the financial and non-financial related data with the help of forensic auditing ensures that the evidence is collected for better detection and misconduct as to how the fraud took place. Without proper evidence collection, forensic audits would lack credibility and fail to support legal or disciplinary actions (Njanike et al., 2009). Evidence can be of **financial records, electronic data, physical documents, witness statements,** and **digital forensics.** They employ various techniques for gathering of evidence some of them being **data mining and analytics, subpoenas and legal requests, chain of custody documentation,** and **forensic imaging.** These various techniques applied in the evidence collection have to face various challenges like **data manipulation, privacy laws,** and **volume of information.** Techniques like data mining (to spot irregular trading patterns) and chain of custody documentation (to preserve evidence integrity) face challenges such as data manipulation—common in insider trading schemes where perpetrators destroy digital trails (Mesioye, 2025).
- For better **regulatory compliance and adherence,** forensic audits need to validate whether a company complies with **financial regulations** of (SOX, FCPA, AML, GDPR), sector **specific laws** (HIPAA for healthcare, Basel III for banking) and **internal policies** of the company related to expenses and procurement. In instances when the compliance is not there as per the standards, the questions will be asked as to how and why adherence to compliance has failed. It can be due to instances of **Intentional violations** like bribery or tax evasion; **unintentional breaches** like accounting errors and weak internal controls; **emerging risks** like cybercrime and third-party fraud. Also, when the breaches occur in the context of preset standards of compliance, forensic audits help to **gather evidence, trace the violations,** and **assist regulators. All this is being done to fix the gaps in compliance, implement fraud-resistant mechanisms,** and ensure that **training be provided to employees** for their compliance toward compliance. Noncompliance may stem from intentional violations (e.g., insider trading rings like the 1980s Ivan Boesky case), unintentional lapses, or emerging risks like cybercrime (Sharma, 2018). Audits help trace violations like undisclosed stock trades by executives—and implement fraud-resistant controls.
- Strength of forensic auditing lies in its ability of systematic, structured, evidence-based approach to reveal any type of financial irregularity. Its strength helps to detect sophisticated fraud schemes, support legal scrutiny,

provide investigative findings so as to ensure there is no future financial misconduct of any form. The strength of forensic **auditing lies in its support of four pillars, namely methodological, investigative, legal and organizational impacts strengths. *Methodological strength* consists of rigorous processes** (IIA/ ACFE guidelines); **multi-disciplinary approach** (accounting, law breaches); **data analytics (tools for** pattern recognition) and **chain of evidence** (Maintain legalized procedure). ***Investigative strength* encompasses depth of investigative examinations (reveal** hidden fraud); **interview techniques** (cognitive interview); **digital forensics** (Recover/procure evidence); and **asset tracing** (follow money trails). ***Legal strengths* are that evidence which are admissible in the court of law, have expert Testimony, regulatory alignment and protection to whistleblowers. *Organizational impact strength* lies in fraud deterrence, improvements in control mechanisms, stakeholder confidence, and how the loss in the fraud is to be recovered.**

As regulations grow more globally, forensic auditing will remain a critical tool for maintaining compliance and combating financial crime, especially in the context of emerging economies which have loopholes as they are in the state of transition.

5. Transition to Future Financial Scenario Amidst AI/ML/IoT

Internal audit must undergo a transformative evolution to address escalating threats such as fraudulent transactions, cyber-crimes, healthcare claims, and insurance fraud. The integration of artificial intelligence (AI) and machine learning (ML) enables more effective and efficient risk mitigation, providing enhanced security through real-time anomaly detection, predictive analytics, and continuous risk assessment—all of which significantly improve audit accuracy and efficiency. Further convergence with Internet of Things (IoT) technology allows for detailed physical asset monitoring and contextual data integration, strengthening forensic capabilities and helping to prevent financial crime.

These advancements are particularly critical in detecting sophisticated insider trading schemes, where AI-driven pattern recognition can identify unusual trading activities (e.g., abnormal options volumes before mergers) that traditional audits might miss (Seyhun, 1992). ML models trained on SEC Rule 10b-5 violations can flag suspicious transactions, such as executives liquidating shares before negative earnings announcements—a tactic exposed in the Martha Stewart-ImClone case (Cleveland, 2018). IoT-derived data (e.g., geolocation tracking of corporate devices) further strengthens cases by proving insider access to material non-public information, as seen in the Galleon Group prosecution (Henning, 2017).

Fig. 6 4 examines the application of AI, emphasizing the integration of AI and ML with conventional methods to address insider trading and minimize financial fraud.

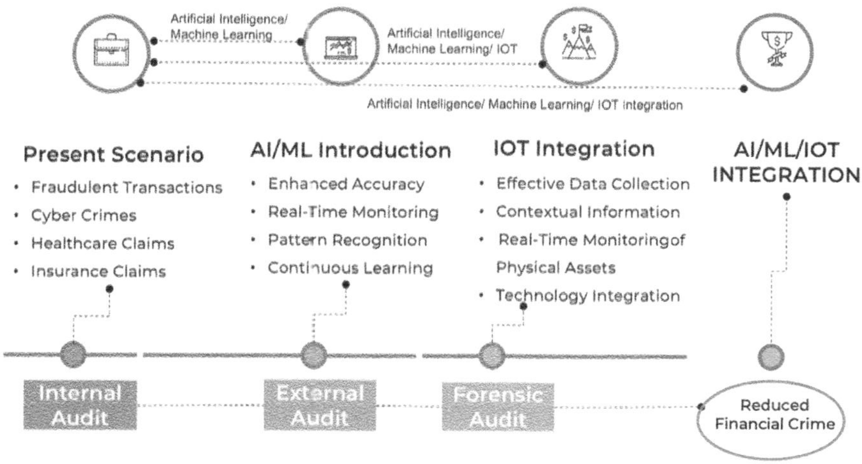

Fig. 6.4. AI/ML/IOT Integration for Modern Infrastructure to Combat Financial Frauds. *Source:* Author's Own.

6. Fraudulent Transactions and Financial Crime Prevention

The continuous data pattern is detected by the artificial chat bots to analyze the transactions on real-time basis for the smooth conduct of regular practices and to find out the different irregularities like spiked data patterns and unusual consumer spending with respect to spending with highest accuracy and precision. The algorithms designed by ML can help the organizations to adapt itself to emerging world financial frauds and dynamic predictive analysis for upcoming fraud tactics through data trends and patterns, leading to an efficient AI-enabled trend-based algorithm as compared to rule-based algorithm, reducing false positives by 40% compared to rule-based systems.

These AI systems are equally effective in detecting insider trading patterns, such as unusual trading volumes in employee stock options before earnings announcements—a red flag exposed in the SEC versus Tesla in 2018 case where Elon Musk's tweets triggered abnormal trading activity (BACK, n.d.). ML can identify such suspicious patterns by cross-referencing employee trade timestamps with corporate event calendars, as demonstrated in the Mathew Martoma insider trading case involving Alzheimer's drug trial results (Henning, 2017).

For example, the use of AI tools for analyzing the double dip in the expense can be attributed to the smooth cross cross-referencing receipts across departments, The human element is reduced to the acceptance of the logic and the procedural work is being taken care by the AI, the proactive risk mitigation is the answer to the internal auditors' queries of surreptitious fraud been happening in the organization and the strategic shift to AI can help the organizations in removal of manual bottlenecks and ultimately lead to conquer the unproductive problems at hand and in turn pave the way for effective combating of financial fraud. AI-driven surveillance systems are now capable of monitoring thousands of employee communications simultaneously to detect potential insider trading, as seen in Goldman Sachs' implementation of natural language processing to flag suspicious phrases like "confidential merger" in chats (Prentice & Spence, 2022).

Internal audit should also prioritize cyber risks to mitigate cybercrime, as AI-enabled firewalls can help organizations achieve enhanced operational efficiency. Real-time monitoring via ML applications optimizes process traffic and enables organizations to develop AI-based threat detection software for combating financial fraud at its onset. Risk reporting and risk mitigation are key areas requiring focus, and AI can support organizations with AI-driven cybersecurity frameworks to drastically reduce incident response times, ultimately leading to enhanced operational efficiency. These cybersecurity measures are equally crucial in preventing electronic evidence tampering in insider trading cases, such as the destruction of Bloomberg chat records in the SAC Capital investigation (Chapman et al., 2015), where AI-powered data preservation could have provided irrefutable evidence.

Table 6.2 provides the use of AI for internal auditors.

6.1 Healthcare and Insurance Claims Auditing

Automating compliance audits for healthcare claims through error detection in coding can help companies avoid exorbitant costs associated with unscrupulous claim acceptance or denials. Real-time monitoring and cross-verification of claim records can save both time and costs by reducing fraudulent financial crimes related to healthcare and insurance claims. ML algorithms can be developed for precise modeling of future claims and uncertainties, supporting effective internal audits for organizations. Fraud detection rates can be substantially reduced with AI/ML integration by verifying policyholder health claims, arbitration, adjudication, and claim accuracy step by step. These same AI audit principles apply to detecting insider trading in healthcare stocks, where algorithms can flag:

- Suspicious trading spikes before FDA drug approvals, as seen in the 2016 Celgene insider case where employees traded ahead of cancer drug results (SEC, 2017).
- Anomalous options activity preceding merger announcements, like the Pfizer-Wyeth deal where unusual call options predicted the acquisition (Cornell & Sirri, 2022).
- Employee trading patterns contradicting market trends, exposed in the Insys Therapeutics case where executives dumped shares before opioid lawsuit disclosures (Baldock, 2024).

Table 6.2. Technological Insinuations for combating Insider Trading.

Function	Description	Outcome
Real-time transaction analysis	Continuous monitoring through data patterns and effective monitoring	Early detection for enhanced time productivity
Dynamic anomaly detection	Identification of unusual trends and patterns to uncover the hidden bottlenecks	Enhanced precision in anomalies detection
Machine learning algorithms	Dynamic predictive modeling and analysis for future financial projections	Effective and efficient fraud detection within the processes
Artificial intelligence vs. human intelligence	AI enabled predictive forecasting	Reduction in false positives
Mechanical analysis	Inter departmental mechanical approach and analysis	Automation of similar procedural tasks
Proactive risk mitigation	Reactive approach to proactive approach of handling the problems	Discard the unwanted processes to uncover surreptitious frauds
Strategic artificial chatbots	AI-enabled fraud mitigators applications	Effective financial management

Source: Authors' Own.

6.2 IoT Integration for Forensic and Asset Audits

AI/ML integration into internal audit processes enables forensic investigations through real-time dynamic monitoring of physical assets, ultimately reducing error scope and improving operational feasibility for organizations. Barcode scanners can replace manual checks, allowing internal auditors to detect ghost assets, account manipulations, and location mismatches more quickly and precisely to save time and enhance accuracy—similar to how Walmart's blockchain-based IoT system reduced inventory shrinkage by 15% through real-time asset tracking (Forbes, 2022). Transaction timestamps via IoT integration, combined with updated infrastructure, help companies identify financial crime anomalies faster, as IoT devices enrich ML models with contextual data; continuous monitoring through AI/ML/IoT integration can reduce financial fraud losses by 30%.

6.3 AI/ML-Driven Efficiencies in External Auditing

External Audit through AI can enhance organizational efficiency with optimized time savings and innovative trend integration into organizational processes through AI-driven "ACCEPT" external auditing described below.

Fig. 6.5 presents the "ACCEPT" technology, which demonstrates the precision, accuracy, efficiency, and effectiveness of external audit-driven practices aimed at enhancing the auditing infrastructure for an efficient, error-free audit experience to combat financial crimes.

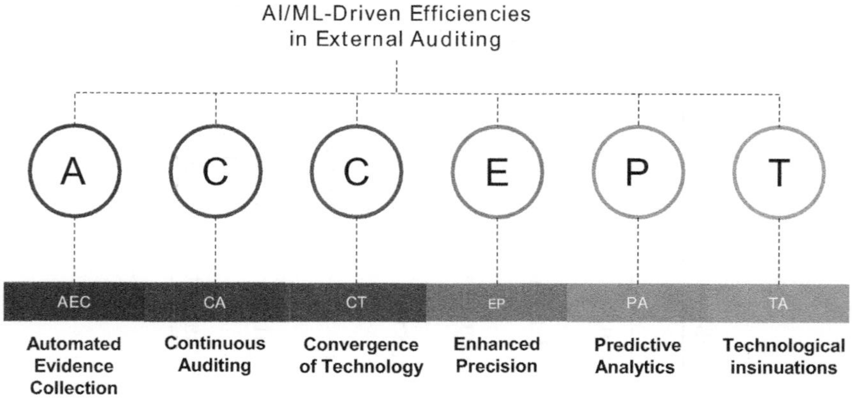

Fig. 6.5. AI/ML as an Efficient Enabler for the External Audit.
Source: Author's Own.

- **Automated evidence collection:** The use of AI-enabled cloud computing can help the organizations in aggregation of data at one place, ultimately helps in optimized reconciliation, reduced transactional errors, and enhanced operational efficiency.
- **Continuous auditing:** Continuous and periodic reviews of internal processes can pose a threat to organizational time management and have an impact on the current and future projected revenues. The use of real-time monitoring through AI can help the organizations build a response mechanism that can operate as quickly as possible in case of an exigency and replace the current manual processes to the core.
- **Convergence of technology:** The seamless adoption of technology can help the organization in making a balanced sync between internal and external audits making it feasible for the organization to attain technology insinuation at a priority level.
- **Enhanced precision:** AI/ML/IoT integration in organization current practices can help them in achieving zero error philosophy of internal and external audit process, making stringent rules and punishments for financial frauds and manipulations.
- **Predictive analytics:** ML projections through historical data analysis and future projections with putting more focus on critical variables can lead to efficient predictive analytics, allowing the auditors to focus on sensitive variables that can have huge impact on the reduction in financial frauds and financial crimes within the organization.
- **Technological insinuations:** high risk area should be the areas that need to be concentrated for effective auditing and Robotic Process Automation (RPA) can help the organization in efficient auditing practices through technological insinuations.

7. Cross-Cultural Forces Driving Economies in Context of Ethics for Holistic Forensic Audit

Emerging economies have huge diversity in their sociocultural context. These cultural factors have various factors like communication, behavior, psychology, and cultural intelligence which makes difficult for the regulators to follow a single set of regulations. These factors drive the elements of economics encompassing work ethics, consumer behavior, economic stability, and their adoption of new technology. This transition in the micro and macro-economic factors generate numerous risks of compliance, governance, systematic, and managerial ones. As the economies are in the phase of transition it generates an element of nepotism, corruption and insider trading. They together in the urge of greed lead to fraud. Weak institutions enable cases like Brazil's Petrobras, where politicians traded shares using privatization knowledge (Paz, 2015).

Fig. 6.6 highlights the economy's transition from a static phase to a dynamic phase through technology integration, aiming to reduce the consequences of nepotism, corruption, and insider trading driven by greed and fraudulent intent.

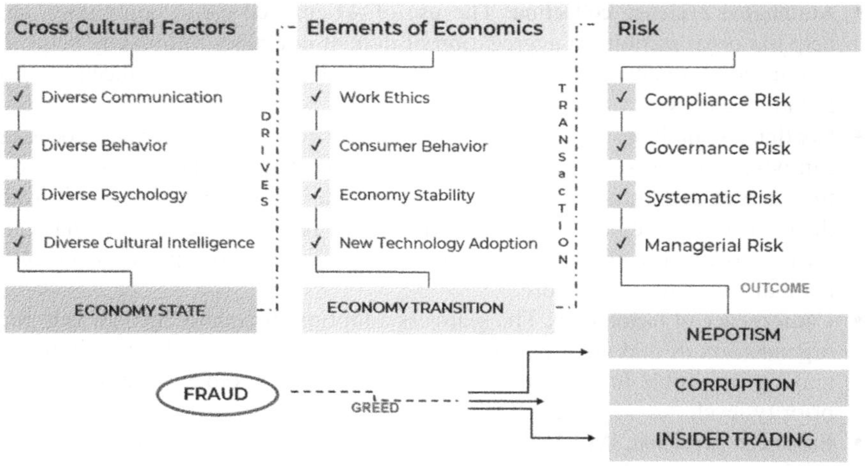

Fig. 6.6. Economy State and Transition Through Cross Cultural Factors. *Source:* Author's Own.

7.1 Cross-Cultural Factors

Cross-cultural factors play a pivotal role in shaping behavior of an organization and decision-making. Leaders have a diverse communication styles, behavioral norms, psychological perspectives, and forms of cultural intelligence which influence as to how individuals and teams interact in the era of globalized markets. Misconceptions arising due to cultural differences within the team can lead to conflicts, inefficiencies, or unethical practices. Also, people have diverse psychological approaches toward the risk and reward will impact the financial decisions, sometimes leading to exploitation. Cultural intelligence is defined as the ability of an individual to adapt toward various cultural scenarios to help mitigate the risks by building mutual understanding and ethics. Various instances have proved that if cultural differences are being ignored, they might lead to unethical outcomes such as nepotism, where favoritism is shown based on familial or ethnic ties rather than merit, or corruption, where cultural norms around gift-giving to shadow ethical boundaries. Like, A multinational company operating in Asia faces backlash when its Western managers misinterpret local gift-giving customs as bribery, damaging relationships with key stakeholders. Meanwhile, local employees perceive the foreign executives as disrespectful for refusing gifts, leading to distrust and reduced collaboration. When Walmart failed in Germany, its American-style cheerleader culture clashed with German workers' preference for formality, costing \$1B before exit (Kaelberer, 2017).

7.2 Elements of Economics

Economic factors such as work ethics, consumer behavior, economic stability, and technology adoption strongly influence corporate conduct and risk exposure—including insider trading. Strong work ethics drive productivity and integrity, whereas weak ethical standards can normalize misconduct, such as fraud or insider trading (e.g., the Martha Stewart or Raj Rajaratnam cases) (SEC, 2021). Consumer behavior dictates market trends, pressuring companies to adopt aggressive and unethical strategies to maintain competitiveness. Economic instability fuels these risks, as financial desperation may lead to insider trading or exploitative policies—such as executives trading on non-public information during mergers or earnings reports (e.g., the SAC Capital scandal) (Heitzman & Klasa, 2021). Meanwhile, rapid technology adoption, while beneficial for efficiency, can introduce vulnerabilities if governance lags innovation—such as cybersecurity gaps enabling data theft for insider trading (e.g., the 2015 hack of SEC's EDGAR system used for illegal trades) (Morinière, 2023). Economic inequality in society can fuel greed, incentivizing executives to prioritize short-term profits over long-term sustainability, increasing insider trading risks (e.g., the case of former Congressman Chris Collins) (Collins, 2009). When economic pressures align with weak regulatory oversight, unethical behaviors like insider trading or accounting fraud become more likely. Therefore, a stable, well-regulated economic environment with strong ethical foundations is essential to mitigate these risks and promote sustainable business practices. For example, during an economic recession, a struggling retail chain engages in fraudulent accounting to inflate profits and attract investors, only to face legal action when auditors uncover the deception, leading to bankruptcy and job losses.

7.3 Risk Factors

Risk factors—compliance, governance, systematic, and managerial—are critical in determining an organization's vulnerability to unethical behavior. Compliance risks arise when companies fail to adhere to laws, leading to legal penalties and reputational damage. Weak governance structures, such as lack of board oversight, enable misconduct like nepotism or corruption by allowing unchecked decision-making. Systematic risks, including economic downturns or market volatility, create environments where fraud and insider trading thrive as individuals seek illicit gains. Managerial risks, such as poor leadership or unethical executives, set a toxic tone at the top, normalizing greed and exploitation. When these risks intersect, they create a breeding ground for financial crimes and unethical practices. For instance, weak governance combined with high systematic risk may lead to insider trading (e.g., the 2020 Wirecard scandal, where lax oversight and market pressure enabled fraudulent reporting) (Jo et al., 2021). Poor compliance paired with managerial negligence can result in large-scale fraud, as seen in Theranos' collapse due to deceptive practices and weak internal controls (Vij et al., n.d.). Effective risk management—through strong policies, transparency, and accountability is essential to prevent these outcomes and maintain organizational integrity. For example: A bank collapses after its executive's bypass compliance checks to approve high-risk loans for personal gain, exposing the institution to massive defaults and regulatory fines, ultimately causing a systemic financial crisis.

8. Strategies

The below-mentioned strategies can leverage forensic audit to design the governance system, assess and mitigate risks arising from greed, power misuse, insider trading and transitions, while enhancing economic drivers through improved governance, trust, and operational integrity.

Fig. 6.7 highlights various modern strategies to combat financial crimes by leveraging technology to enhance an organization's operational feasibility.

8.1 Mindfulness

Mindfulness through integration of existing internal controls with ongoing new trends and catering to the updated innovative regulations, recommending improvements to ensure optimal bifurcation of assigned tasks with continuous monitoring and controls can aid in forensic audit applications and help in combating the greed and misuse of power. The fortification through strengthening internal controls can help in reinforcing and rejuvenation of organizational well-being and efficient as well as effective processes.

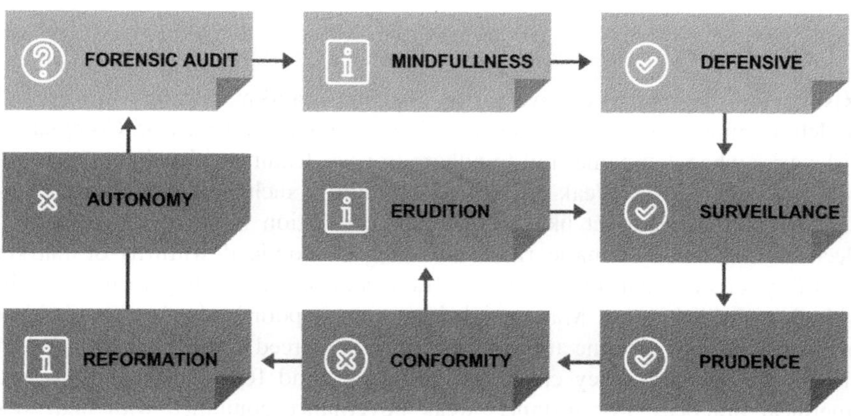

Fig. 6.7. Strategies to Combat Financial Crimes to Enhance Operational Integrity. *Source:* Author's Own.

8.2 Defensive

Regular conduct of forensic risk assessment and mitigation practices can help the organizations in identification of the forces that are more prone to power induced fraud and misappropriations. Defensive strategies can help the organizations in application of optimal preventive control measures as well as detection of unusual patterns that are creating hindrance in the smooth functioning of organizational activities.

8.3 Surveillance

Monitoring of inbound cracks in internal processes and the timely adoption of surveillance measures to detect the errors can aid in the effective application of forensic audit and raise an alert on suspicious activities like greed and power and in turn can help the organization in combating corruption and desire to increase cash and bank balance through illegal means.

8.4 Prudence

The passing of information from one channel to another channel without any coercive force can aid organizational information related to oppression, misconduct, and the forensic audit application will create an affirmative and positive environment for the anonymous whistleblower channels. The swift response to the information attained through the said channel can help the organization in strengthening of positive work culture, ensuring the timely handling of employee grievances and reduction in vulnerabilities related to greed and power.

8.5 Conformity

The use of digitized forensic tools to uncover the hidden malpractice can help the organizations in attaining the proficiency of data analysis and help them in future embezzlements related to financial frauds. The effective forensic data analytics system can analyze multiple electronic records for evidence of fraud or trace illicit funds to combat financial crimes within the organization.

8.6 Erudition

The awareness of the employees from top to bottom level through digital forensic training can help them in early detection of fraud and in turn can help the management in early detection and management of financial crimes. The staff must be made aware of the power of integrity and principles of conflict of interest, organizational ethical standards, and the consequences of greed and power abuse, fostering a culture of belongingness and loyalty to the organization.

8.7 Autonomy

The expert and dedicated forensic audit teams, comprising of different stakeholders, within organizations, must be made to ensure impartial and effective investigation and the names of such tram members should also be shown in the balance sheet, for effective accountability.

8.8 Reformation

Anti-corruption laws must be enforced within the organization, and the staff should also be trained in the existing and upcoming changes in regulations related to anti-corruption laws. The punishments for the committed financial crimes at the world level can be made available to the employees in the digitized form in different time intervals on a day for effective and efficient application of forensic audit, providing actionable evidence for legal proceedings and regulatory compliance. The investor confidence is must and should always be preserved that can help the organization in organic as well as inorganic growth. Forensic audits can drive policy reforms, strengthen internal governance standards, and promote transparency which in turn can ultimately lead to sustainable growth and help in solving the paradox of accountability and responsibility.

Table 6.3 provides the summation of above-mentioned strategies for better understanding and execution for smooth running of business operations and enhanced operational efficiency.

Table 6.3. Summary of Strategies for Combating Financial Fraud.

Strategy	Summary
Mindfulness	Integrating internal controls with evolving trends
Defensive	Regular forensic risk assessments and mitigation practices
Surveillance	Continuous monitoring and timely surveillance measures to detect suspicious activities
Prudence	Encouraging safe, anonymous whistleblowing
Conformity	Forensic tools and analytics to uncover hidden malpractices
Erudition	Comprehensive training and awareness initiatives for staff and management
Autonomy	Impartial, dedicated forensic audit teams
Reformation	Enforcing anti-corruption laws and promoting regulatory awareness

Source: Authors' Own.

9. Conclusion

The integration of AI into forensic financial audits presents transformative potential in detecting and preventing insider trading and market manipulation. By leveraging advanced algorithms, ML, and big data analytics, AI enhances the speed, accuracy, and efficiency of identifying suspicious trading patterns, anomalies, and complex fraud schemes that traditional methods may overlook. However, this technological advancement also introduces significant ethical and legal challenges that must be addressed to ensure responsible adoption.

Ethically, the use of AI in financial forensics raises concerns about transparency, accountability, and bias. Algorithmic decision-making must be explainable to maintain trust among regulators, corporations, and the public. Additionally, reliance on AI should not replace human judgment entirely, as ethical discretion remains crucial in interpreting findings and avoiding false accusations. Legal challenges include regulatory gaps in governing AI-driven audits, data privacy concerns, and jurisdictional complexities in cross-border investigations. Existing frameworks, such as securities laws and anti-fraud regulations, must evolve to keep pace with AI's capabilities while safeguarding against misuse. To harness AI effectively, stakeholders must prioritize robust governance, including stringent validation of AI models, continuous monitoring for bias, and clear protocols for human oversight. Collaboration between regulators, auditors, and technologists is essential to establish standardized guidelines that balance innovation with accountability. Ultimately, AI can revolutionize forensic audits—but only if implemented within an ethical and legally sound framework that upholds fairness, transparency, and justice in financial markets. By addressing these challenges proactively, the financial industry can leverage AI as a powerful ally in combating fraud while maintaining public confidence in market integrity.

References

Alonge, E. O., Eyo-Udo, N. L., Ubanadu, B. C., Daraojimba, A. I., Balogun, E. D., & Olusola, K. (n.d.). Innovative business development framework for capturing and sustaining growth in emerging and niche markets. *World*, *2579*, 0544.

Anthony, S. M. A., Gimbard, D. P., & Visvanathan, J. (n.d.). *Journal of Economic Crime Management*. https://library.help.edu.my/wp-content/uploads/2025/12/Volume-9-2025.pdf

BACK, A. F. (n.d.). *The Silicon Valley high-tech Black-listing antitrust litigation and big Tech's attacks on democracy*. https://yournews1.com/LIES%20AND%20SCAMS%20OF%20ELON%20MUSK/Edward%20Ring%27s%20Paid%20Gig%20Kissing%20Elon%20Musk%27s%20-%20Unknown.pdf. Accessed on January 7, 2026.

Baldock, M. G. (2024). Sharing the blame: Using market share to allocate liability in opioid public nuisance lawsuits. *Notre Dame Journal of Law, Ethics, and Public Policy*, *38*, 315.

Campanella, E. (2023). Economic self-reliance in a leaderless world. *The Washington Quarterly*, *46*(3), 103–126. https://doi.org/10.1080/0163660X.2023.2259256

Chapman, F. E., Jennings, M., & Tarasuk, L. (2015). SAC capital: Firm criminal liability, civil fines, and the insulated CEO. *American University Business Law Review*, *4*, 441.

Cleveland, S. J. (2018). Unintentional irony in landmark decisions of the Delaware Supreme Court regarding corporate law. *Michigan Business & Entrepreneurial Law Review*, *8*, 173.

Collins, M. (2009). *Financial crisis and future securities regulation*. https://openscholarship.wustl.edu/cgi/viewcontent.cgi?article=1479&context=etd

Cornell, B., & Sirri, E. (2022). Options trading before takeovers: The pfizer-wyeth case. *Journal of Financial Economics*, *144*(2), 411–429.

Cunningham, D. (2021). *Putin's Russia: The rise of a dictator*. Myriad Editions. https://books.google.com/books?hl=en&lr=&id=9hVyEAAAQBAJ&oi=fnd&pg=PA1948&dq=Vladimir+Putin%E2%80%99s+Oligarch+Control+in+Russia+leading+to+amassing+wealth+through+his+political+influence,+while+all+those+who+were+dissidents+were+liable+to+face+imprisonment+or+exile&ots=R_GBEH4nsM&sig=xXyEO6m363L0qqYzu0yau7uH9ZA

Dabla-Norris, E., Kochhar, K., Suphaphiphat, N., Ricka, F., & Tsounta, E. (2019). *Causes and consequences of income inequality: A global perspective*. International monetary fund. https://www.imf.org/en/Publications/Staff-Discussion-Notes/Issues/2016/12/31/Causes-and-Consequences-of-Income-Inequality-A-Global-Perspective-42986

de Melo Gomes, V. P., & Branco, M. C. (2025). Repairing legitimacy through sport-related corporate social responsibility disclosure in Brazil: The case of Petrobras. In *Research handbook on corporate social responsibility in sport* (pp. 252–270). Edward Elgar Publishing. https://www.elgaronline.com/edcollchap/book/9781803926476/chapter14.xml

Forbes. (2022). *How walmart's blockchain system is transforming inventory management*

Hanke, S. H., & Kwok, A. K. F. (2009). On the measurement of zimbabwe's hyperinflation. *Cato Journal*, *29*(2), 353–364. https://www.cato.org/cato-journal/fall-2009

Heitzman, S., & Klasa, S. (2021). Informed trading reactions to new private information: Evidence from nonpublic merger negotiations. *Management Science*, *67*(4), 2630–2656. https://doi.org/10.1287/mnsc.2020.3629

Henning, C. R. (2017). *Tangled governance: International regime complexity, the troika, and the euro crisis*. Oxford University Press. https://books.google.com/books?hl=en&lr=&id=NzxdDgAAQBAJ&oi=fnd&pg=PP1&dq=henning+2017&ots=asmRtfyII8&sig=qIaMy34-76t4tq7ne7FIoaP_90U

International Monetary Fund (IMF). (2016). *Corruption: Costs and mitigating strategies* Vol. 16(5). IMF staff zote. https://www.imf.org/en/Publications/Staff-Discussion-Notes/Issues/2016/12/31/Corruption-Costs-and-Mitigating-Strategies-44185

Imtiaz Mazumder, M., & Ahmad, N. (2010). Greed, financial innovation or laxity of regulation? A close look into the 2007–2009 financial crisis and stock market volatility. *Studies in Economics and Finance*, *27*(2), 110–134.

Jo, H., Hsu, A., Llanos-Popolizio, R., & Vergara-Vega, J. (2021). Corporate governance and financial fraud of Wirecard. *European Journal of Business and Management Research*, *6*(2), 96–106.

Kaelberer, M. (2017). Wal-mart goes to Germany: Culture, institutions, and the limits of globalization. *German Politics and Society*, *35*(1), 1–18.

Kane, M. (2008). Crash, burn, & learn: As lenders and borrowers pick up the pieces from the US mortgage crisis, internal auditors say heeding the warning signs may deter companies from future high-risk ventures. *Internal Auditor*, *65*(1), 34–41.

Kumar, N., & Roy, S. (2025). *FDI, MSMEs, digitalization, and green industrialization: Challenges, opportunities and policy lessons for India* (Vol. 1). Springer Verlag.

Mason, P. (2020). *Meltdown: The end of the age of greed.* Verso Books. https://books.google.com/books?hl=en&lr=&id=r1qcEAAAQBAJ&oi=fnd&pg=PA1903&dq=due+to+greed+without+taking+into+context+the+liquidity+of+the+investment,+triggered+a+global+economic+meltdown+&ots=FS_nebpDQr&sig=IkzD0CnnZHbXpPaDhQKyEJqO-10

Mesioye, O. (2025). The nexus between insider trading and organized crime: Challenges in enforcing ethical market practices. *International Journal of Research Public Review*, *6*(1), 1817–1831.

Monday, C. (2017). Privatization to putinization: The genesis of Russia's hobbled oligarchy. *Communist and Post-Communist Studies*, *50*(4), 303–317.

Morinière, A. (2023). Ethical implications of acceleration: Perspectives From health professionals. *Journal of Business Ethics*, *188*(4), 741–758. https://doi.org/10.1007/s10551-023-05499-6

Njanike, K., Dube, T., & Mashayanye, E. (2009). *The effectiveness of forensic auditing in detecting, investigating, and preventing bank frauds.* https://jsd-africa.com/Jsda/V10N4_Spring2009/PDF/Effectiveness%20of%20Forensic%20Auditing.pdf

Paz, M. J. (2015). Institutional change and state-owned enterprises: Reflections from the Petrobras case study. *Public Management Review*, *17*(6), 791–811. https://doi.org/10.1080/14719037.2013.822534

Prentice, R., & Spence, M. (2022). AI surveillance in financial markets: The new frontier of insider trading prevention. *Journal of Corporate Law Studies*, *22*(1), 45–78.

Raghunathan, V. (2010). *The corruption conundrum and other paradoxes and dilemmas.* Penguin Books India. https://books.google.com/books?hl=en&lr=&id=30jGqzhNjz8C&oi=fnd&pg=PA1&dq=Ramalinga+Raju+(Satyam+Computers)+created+fake+employment+records−of+thousands+of+employees+and+amassed+their+salaries+for+years+leading+erosion+of+company%E2%80%99s+wealth+and+finally+takeover+by+Tech+Mahindra+&ots=1kag5GjKGm&sig=OraDQTNb7RjvPYiYRbhuuGiGDak

Saito, K. (2024). *Slow Down: The degrowth manifesto.* Astra Publishing House. https://books.google.com/books?hl=en&lr=&id=J_f4EAAAQBAJ&oi=fnd&pg=PR9&dq=With+the+developed+markets+growth+getting+saturated+owing+to+population+degrowth,+the+entire+focus+has+shifted+to+the+emerging+economies+to+pave+the+way+for+global+economies+in+these+turbulent+times+&ots=LnR-qcHkND&sig=9TLEMhymiiZEc0KtCdaUGK4tKO8

Santora, J. C. (2020). *Dara Khosrowshahi: Changing the company culture at Uber.* SAGE Publications: SAGE Business Cases Originals. https://sk.sagepub.com/cases/dara-khosrowshahi-changing-the-company-culture-at-uber

SEC. (2017). SEC vs. celgene corp: Insider trading in pharmaceutical securities. Litigation Release No. 23897.

SEC. (2021). *Insider trading cases*. https://www.sec.gov/

Seyhun, H. N. (1992). The effectiveness of insider-trading sanctions. *The Journal of Law and Economics*, *35*(1), 149–182.

Sharma, N. P. (2018). A reading into insider trading: Concept, cases, consequences and countermeasures. *NJA Law Journal*, *12*, 113.

Singleton, T., & Singleton, A. (2010). *Fraud auditing and forensic accounting* (4th). Wiley.

Sørensen, J. (2025). Investigating balance sheet, income statement and earnings manipulation. In J. Sørensen (Ed.), *Shorting fraud* (pp. 235–239). Springer Nature. https://doi.org/10.1007/978-3-031-81834-9_23

Tarsa, K. (2017). Won't Get fooled again: Why VW's emissions deception is illegal in Europe and how to improve the EU's auto regulatory system. *Boston College International and Comparative Law Review*, *40*, 315.

Vij, S., Sharma, R., & Kainth, N. (n.d.). *Case studies of corporate misconduct and failures: Major learnings and Indian response*. https://www.researchgate.net/profile/Sandeep-Vij/publication/388167316_Case_Studies_of_Corporate_Misconduct_and_Failures_Major_Learnings_and_Indian_Response/links/678c9bbd1ec9f9589f4f9263/Case-Studies-of-Corporate-Misconduct-and-Failures-Major-Learnings-and-Indian-Response.pdf. Accessed on January 7, 2026.

World Bank. (2017). *The economic costs of corruption*. World Bank Policy Research Working Paper, Vol. 8069. https://documents.worldbank.org/en/publication/documents-reports/documentdetail/212371468340158724/the-economic-costs-of-corruption

Zientek, D. (2020). *Framework for accountability in criminal investigations*. https://shsu-ir.tdl.org/items/c2de5865-00f9-4e9d-9623-627b713b394c

Chapter 7

Cybercrime in the Digital Finance Ecosystem: Typologies, Terminology, and Economic Cost

Nehir Balcı

Dokuz Eylül University, Turkey

Abstract

In today's digital age, the significance of cybercrime is indisputable, as it directly undermines the interests of individuals, institutions, and even nation-states. Unauthorized access to sensitive information, assets, and systems, accompanied by acts of manipulation, theft, or extortion, has led to an increasing number of victims, particularly within digital financial systems. Such incidents erode trust in these systems and substantially threaten financial stability. As digitalization and internet-based operations expand within the financial sector, cybercriminals continuously develop new and sophisticated attack methods. This chapter categorizes cybercrimes within the digital finance ecosystem under six distinct typologies: (1) Identity Theft and Data Breach Based Cybercrimes, (2) Cybercrimes Targeting Banking Systems and Payment Infrastructure, (3) Social Engineering-Based Scams, (4) Crypto Asset and Blockchain-Based Crimes, (5) Extortion-Based Cybercrimes, and (6) Cyber-Enabled Money Laundering. By adopting a holistic perspective, this chapter aims to clarify key terms and concepts associated with cybercrime, raise awareness among stakeholders, and provide a comprehensive overview of the economic impacts of cybercrime in the digital finance domain.

Keywords: Crime; cybercrime; digital finance; cybercrime typologies and feature; economic cost

Corruption and Crime in Finance, 133–154

doi:10.1108/978-1-83708-170-720261019

1. Introduction

The rapidly growing and developing cybercrimes committed in this area pose a serious threat to individuals, institutions, countries, and economies due to the structure of cyberspace that crosses national borders, is autonomous, and facilitates the commission of crimes. Due to the nature of cybercrimes that transcend political and geographical boundaries, there is no single accepted definition of "cybercrime." In addition, considering the impact of developing technologies on the scale, speed, and scope of criminal offenses, the problem of the framework within which cybercrime should be addressed arises. In the most general sense, unauthorized access to computer networks and all devices connected to these networks and engaging in behaviors that cause material and moral damage to individuals or institutions is cybercrime (Marsh & Melville, 2019; Wall, 2004).

With advancing technology and increasing internet use, the financial sector has also undergone a significant transformation process and has become digitalized. Digital finance delivers financial services using mobile, online, blockchain, or financial technologies (FinTech) (Tanda & Schena, 2019). While the speed and dynamism of technological advances such as artificial intelligence (AI), big data analytics, and cloud solutions have brought many advantages and conveniences to the digital finance ecosystem, they have also brought some disadvantages. Among these drawbacks are cybercrimes committed in this field.

This chapter aims to summarize the infrastructure of digital finance and the historical background of the transformation, to clarify the terms and concepts related to cybercrimes in the field of digital finance that cause financial and moral losses to individuals, institutions, and countries, and to discuss future trends and predictions by examining academic studies on these concepts. This chapter first mentions the concept of digital finance and the digitalization process in the financial sector. Then, the concept of cybercrime, types of cybercrime in digital finance, and the economic dimension of cybercrime are discussed. In the conclusion, an evaluation is made on what practical and policy oriented actions can be taken to reduce cybercrime. This study will contribute to raising awareness about cybercrimes in digital finance among all financial sector stakeholders and readers. In addition, this chapter is thought to be useful for future studies by providing a reference point for new studies on cybercrime in digital finance.

2. Digital Finance

The changes that have emerged in the information and technology sector worldwide in recent years have caused digitalization to enter our lives. As a dynamic process, digitalization improves business models, creates new sources of revenue, and creates opportunities to generate higher levels of value through digital technologies (O'Leary, 2022). According to Kusters (2022), digitalization can be defined as "the transformation of processes." New technologies such as the internet, AI, robotics, and data analytics, which are the driving forces of digitalization, are transforming financial markets and companies in the same way that steam power and electricity did in the past, leading to revolutionary changes in production and consumption processes. In the financial sector, digitalization has ceased to be a voluntary process. It has become a survival necessity in the face of technological progress, leading to the emergence of digital finance.

2.1 Digital Finance: Concepts, Applications, and Technological Infrastructure

In its simplest form, digital finance is defined as conducting financial business and transactions in digital environments. Ozili (2018) defines digital finance as providing financial services through the internet, mobile phones, personal computers, and cards linked to a reliable payment system. Similarly, Durai and Stella (2019) and Manyika et al. (2016) define digital finance as delivering financial services through credit and debit cards, mobile wallets, e-wallets, mobile banking, mobile phones, personal computers, and the internet. Today, when digital finance is mentioned, words such as computer technology, software, mobile banking, FinTech, digital payment systems, and cryptocurrencies come to mind.

Since the use of digital finance applications in financial systems depends on the existence of advanced technology and the infrastructure to enable it, these applications have been implemented in developed economies before developing or undeveloped economies. Therefore, many studies in the literature have been conducted on developed countries, such as Agbeve et al. (2025), Brandl and Hornuf (2020), Cao et al. (2021), and Tang (2019). With the increasing use of the internet, the use of digital financial applications in developing countries has increased, leading to many studies in the literature on undeveloped and developing countries, such as Agur et al. (2020), Al Khub et al. (2024), Khera et al. (2022), and Kingiri and Fu (2020).

Digital finance has made many positive contributions to the financial system and economies. Its positive contribution to increasing financial inclusion (Ozili, 2018; Shofawati, 2019; Thathsarani & Jianguo, 2022) is one of them. Particularly in less developed countries with areas lacking banking infrastructure, digital finance can provide access to banks and services that are otherwise difficult to access, such as payment systems and credit. The impact of digital finance on poverty reduction (Kelikume, 2021; Risman et al., 2021; Tay et al., 2022; Wang & He, 2020) is another positive contribution to economies. Many studies in the literature indicate digital finance's contribution to sustainable development and financial stability (Daud et al., 2022; Li et al., 2022; Nguyen, 2016).

Gomber et al. (2017) examined digital finance under six main headings: digital funding, digital money, digital investment, digital payment, digital financial advisory, and digital insurance.

(1) *Digital Financing:* Digital financing is the ability of individuals and institutions to obtain resources via the internet in addition to traditional financing sources, using methods such as factoring, electronic invoicing, leasing, and crowdfunding.

(2) *Digital Investments:* Digital investments are a set of methods that enable individuals or institutions to organize the necessary investment transactions on their own by using new digital technologies in their investment decisions. For example, trading financial instruments using social media, i.e. social trading, or buying and selling financial instruments with the help of mobile devices are considered digital investments (Gomber et al., 2017).
(3) *Digital Money:* Digital money fulfills all the functions of traditional money, such as being a measure of value, a medium of exchange, and a savings instrument, but exists only digitally (Dodgson et al., 2015). The literature refers to digital currency by different names, such as e-money, crypto-currency, digital currency, and virtual currency.
(4) *Digital Payments:* In the broadest sense, digital payments are forms of payment that cover all payments made electronically (Hartmann, 2006).
(5) *Digital Insurances:* Digital insurance involves individuals and institutions carrying out insurance transactions through digital platforms instead of insurance companies. This approach aims to reduce insurance costs.
(6) *Digital Financial Advisory:* It provides advisory services for all kinds of financial transactions, such as investment, budget management, retirement planning, etc., through digital platforms. Today, robo-advisors or portfolio management services guided by AI can be examples of digital financial advisory.

FinTech is one of the most important elements of digital finance based on technological changes. This term, which emerged due to the integration of finance and technology, represents forming a new financial sector that uses technology to enhance financial activities (Schueffel, 2016). According to Mamoshina et al. (2018), FinTech refers to all organizations that have emerged from Industry 4.0 technology and use digital technologies (specialized software and algorithms) to provide innovative financial services. FinTech provide markets with various investment products in the form of digital stocks, digital gold, financial derivatives, and commodities (Risman et al., 2021). FinTech companies offering FinTech are a marketplace that organizes *peer-to-peer lending (P2P)*, *crowdfunding*, and *tokenization of assets*.

P2P is a system that allows individuals or firms to borrow and lend directly without a financial intermediary. As with any system, it has advantages and disadvantages. The prominent advantages of the system include easy access to finance, high returns to investors, and eliminating intermediary costs. The main disadvantages of the system are the lack of state guarantee and the high risk of loans.

Crowdfunding is a system where funds are raised over the internet through methods such as donations, rewards, and voting rights (Belleflamme et al., 2010). With crowdfunding, small funds collected through online platforms can accumulate and reach the capacity to fund a large project. The sale of a traded digital asset as a digital blockchain is defined as the tokenization of assets (Laurent et al., 2018). The growth of funding and transactions in FinTech companies contributes positively to share returns in financial markets (Li et al., 2017).

The most important services and technologies offered by FinTech companies and digitalizing banks are *Application Programming Interface (API)*, *Cloud Computing*, and *Mobile Banking*. An API consists of commands, functions, protocols, and objects that enable software or services to communicate with external systems to make certain functions of a software or service available to other software or services (Prinakaa et al., 2024). It plays an important role in internet applications such as mobile apps and e-commerce sites (Sun et al., 2022). The reflection of API in banking has been the "Open Banking" system.

An open banking system enables banks to share customer data with FinTech companies securely. This system allows users to manage all their account transactions with a single device. The most important advantages of the open banking system include the ability of customers to compare banks' products cost effectively, easy fund transfer, and improved customer experience (Benmoussa, 2019).

Cloud computing provides computing services for storing, processing, and managing data over the internet. The term cloud refers to a network or the internet. Cloud computing stores data online instead of on local drives and can be accessed anytime via remote servers. Thanks to cloud computing, banks can increase data security and adapt to new technological updates without changing their infrastructure through remote updates. Mobile banking provides all kinds of financial transactions, such as accessing customer account information, making money transfers, and making investments (Corporate Finance Institute, 2021).

2.2 The Evolution of Digitalization in the Finance Industry

The digitalization process, which has accelerated in the last two decades in the world, is also called digital transformation. Digital transformation is a tool for changing business processes, cultures, and organizational structures to adapt to changing market conditions due to the rapid advancement of digital technologies (Nasiri et al., 2020). According to Verhoef et al. (2019), digital transformation is the change of business processes by using new technologies to maximize profit and ensure customer satisfaction. The historical process of digitalization in the financial sector started with the introduction of the first credit card in the 1950s and the increase in its use in the 1960s, accelerated during the COVID-19 pandemic, and continues to rise with blockchain technologies today. The historical process of digital finance could be categorized into three main periods. These periods are the automation, internet, mobile payments, and blockchain technology phases (Liu & Hou, 2023).

- *Automation Phase (1960–1990):* The launch of the Diners Club Card in 1950 and the United Kingdom's first ATM by Barclays in 1967 marked early steps in financial digitalization. SWIFT was launched in 1973 to facilitate international money transfers, laying the groundwork for modern electronic funds transfer (EFT) system. Visa introduced the first POS devices in 1979, and

ATMs became globally widespread in the 1980s. This era, often termed the traditional finance phase, saw major technological advancements such as ATMs, Internet banking's early forms, international payment systems like SWIFT, and large-scale computers (Liu & Hou, 2023). Financial transactions remained largely physical despite these innovations, with services delivered through bank branches and financial institutions.
- *Internet Phase (1990–2010):* The rise of internet technology in the 1990s ushered in the "Internet phase" of finance. In 1994, Stanford Federal Credit Union introduced the first online banking service, followed by the United Kingdom's Egg Bank in 1999 as the first fully digital bank. PayPal, originating from the 2000 merger of Confinity and X.com, became one of the first global digital payment platforms. This period also saw the emergence of mobile payment systems, digital wallets (2009), and Bitcoin, the first cryptocurrency utilizing blockchain for decentralized and secure transactions. Financial institutions began offering digital solutions, promoting globalization, cost efficiency, and accessibility through customer centric online services (Liu & Hou, 2023).
- *Mobile Payment and Blockchain Technology Phase (2010–. . .):* Mobile technologies have significantly reduced the cost of financial services while expanding access, marking a major milestone in digital finance. Notable innovations include the launch of the first robo-advisor, Betterment, in 2010, and the emergence of N26 as the first fully licensed neobank in Europe in 2016. The rise of branchless digital banks reflects growing demand for fully digital financial services. Advancements in digital technology have also enabled the creation and diversification of financial products, including those by nonfinancial firms. Blockchain and crypto assets represent the latest evolution, with the launch of Ethereum in 2015 initiating the DeFi era. Since 2020, central banks worldwide have pursued blockchain enabled digital currencies. Overall, technologies like FinTech, robo-advisors, DeFi, and blockchain are foundational to the continued evolution of digital finance.

While the above mentioned developments in the digitalization of financial services have contributed to improving customer experience, reducing costs, and making financial systems more accessible, they have also led to the emergence of many threats, such as personal data security, unauthorized access, and cyber risks.

3. Cybercrime

3.1 Definition and Scope of Cybercrime

To accurately grasp the concept of cybercrime, it is essential to clarify the meanings of the terms "cyber" and "crime." According to the United Nations, the term "cyber" refers to a global system composed of internet-connected computers, communication infrastructures, users, and data systems (Andress & Winterfeld, 2013). In this context, the term "cyber" encompasses information and communication networks and internet users. "Crime," on the other hand, is a dynamic concept that denotes behaviors prohibited by law, varying across societies, periods, and geographic contexts (Sandilaç, 2022).

In the related literature, cybercrime is also referred to as "internet crime," "digital crime," or "e-crime" (McGuire, 2019). While there is no universally accepted definition, a widely acknowledged perspective considers cybercrime as illegal acts committed via computers, networks, and digital systems (Gordon & Ford, 2006; Phillips et al., 2022). Thomas and Loader (2000) defines cybercrime as unlawful activities perpetrated through global digital networks. The proliferation of emerging technologies has accelerated digital transformation, leading to a significant increase in cybercrime (Al-Khater et al., 2020). Offenders exploit cybercrime as an asymmetric tool to target states, institutions, and individuals for various purposes, including data theft, financial gain, reputational damage, espionage, and threats to national security (Nobles et al., 2023).

Technological advancements in the 21st century have given rise to new categories of crimes. Cybercrimes committed through computers and the internet are among the most rapidly evolving and adaptive forms of criminal activity (Okutan & Çebi, 2019). Özkan (2006) categorized cybercrime into seven distinct types, drawing on resources such as Interpol's "Computer Crime Manual," the United Nations' "Handbook on the Prevention and Control of Computer-Related Crime," and the Australian Federal Police's "Minimum Requirements for Investigating Computer-Based Crime." According to Özkan (2006), the types of cybercrime include:

a. *Unauthorized Access to Computer Systems and Services:* Gaining access to a computer system, server, network, or service without permission, including the technical interception of a network or computer system without authorization.
b. *Computer Sabotage:* The intentional destruction, corruption, or obstruction of computer systems, software, or data.
c. *Computer-Based Fraud:* The use of information systems to deceive individuals for the purpose of unjust enrichment.
d. *Computer-Based Forgery*: The production of counterfeit materials such as currency, bonds, or credit cards, or the manipulation of digital documents via information systems.
e. *Unauthorized Use of a Protected Program/Software:* The reproduction, sale, or use of copyrighted software without authorization.
f. *Illegal Publications:* The creation, distribution, or storage of any publication, website, email, newsgroup, or digital recording deemed illegal or criminal under the law.
g. *Other:* A broad category encompassing the theft of trade secrets, misuse of data, identity fabrication, and impersonation.

3.2 Predominant Cybercrime Typologies in the Digital Finance Ecosystem

Cybercrimes targeting individuals, institutions, governments, and financial systems manifest in various forms. In the digital finance ecosystem, the majority of cybercrimes are motivated by financial gain. Baur-Yazbeck et al. (2019) identifies the most prevalent types of cybercrime affecting African digital financial services as social engineering attacks, insider fraud, malware, ransomware, and denial-of-service (DoS) attacks. Wang et al. (2020) highlight phishing, bank verification number (BVN) scams, cyber theft/banking fraud, and theft of bank cards as the leading cyber threats in the banking sector. Similarly, Austin-Olowo et al. (2023) points to compromised data, unencrypted data, spoofing, unsecured third party systems, and malware as the most prominent threats in digital banking. It is important to distinguish between types of crime and the methods used to commit them. For example, malware is malicious software designed to compromise systems for nefarious purposes (Bhavani & Sankaradass, 2025). While not a crime in itself, it is a method used to perpetrate crimes. Accessing personal account data via malware and transferring funds without consent constitutes a criminal offense. The primary legally defined categories of cybercrime in the digital finance ecosystem are typologically organized in Fig. 7.1.

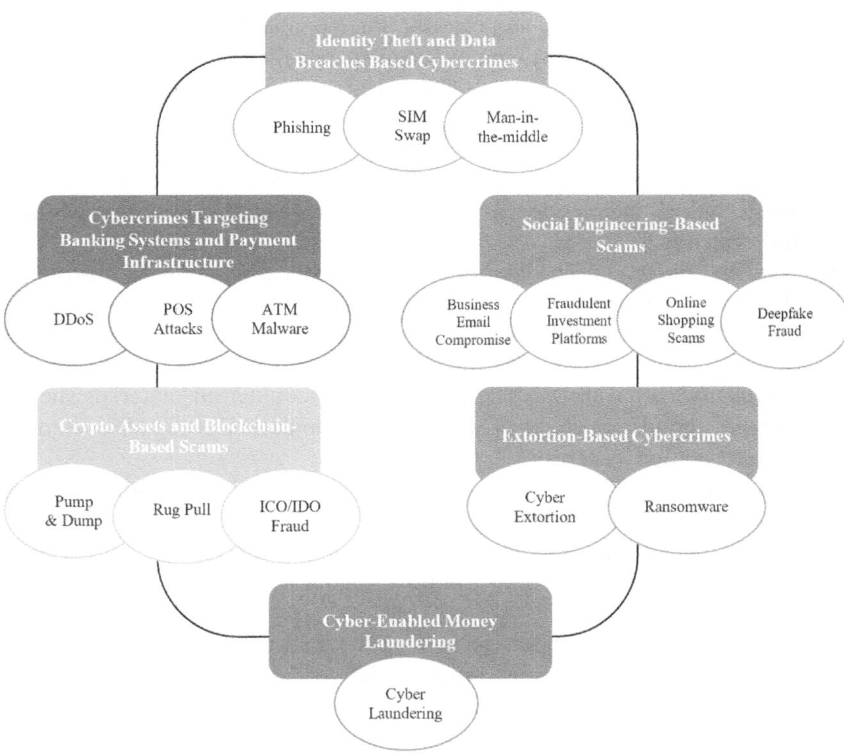

Fig. 7.1. Predominant Cybercrimes in the Digital Finance Ecosystem. *Source:* Author's own elaboration.

3.2.1 Identity Theft and Data Breaches Based Cybercrimes

Identity theft and data breach based cybercrimes involve the unauthorized acquisition and misuse of personal or financial data belonging to individuals or organizations.

- *Phishing:* Derived from the English word "fishing." Phishing refers to identity theft through social engineering tactics, where cybercriminals attempt to deceive users into divulging sensitive information (Gupta et al., 2016). Attackers typically use phone calls, emails, or malicious websites to extract personal data. Phishing is among the most critical and widespread attack vectors in digital finance. Recent studies indicate that approximately 27% of global phishing attacks specifically target the financial sector (APWG, 2022). In the digital finance ecosystem, financial transactions conducted via online platforms including mobile payments, digital banking services, and cryptocurrency operations are especially vulnerable to phishing attacks.
- *SIM Swapping:* An emerging form of cybercrime, SIM swapping involves the unauthorized use of cloned SIM cards to take control of a victim's mobile service subscription. Through this method, attackers can access the users' bank accounts, credit card numbers, and other sensitive financial data (Awale & Gupta, 2019). In the digital finance ecosystem, attackers often use this technique to drain online banking accounts, access cryptocurrency wallets, or exfiltrate corporate data.
- *Man-in-the-Middle (MITM) Attacks:* MITM attack is a form of phishing technique that occurs during digital banking transactions, via network infiltration between the bank and the customer, subsequently enabling unauthorized access to encrypted data and monitor unencrypted information (Alsayed & Bilgrami, 2017). Through this attack method, attackers can intercept the communication between the user and the bank while customers are using their online banking accounts, allowing attackers to steal the user's account information. For instance, during an online fund transfer, an attacker may see the customer transferring and change the recipient's account number or the transaction amount. Neither the bank nor the user is typically aware of the intrusion until after the unauthorized transfer is complete (Swanink et al., 2016).

3.2.2 Cybercrimes Targeting Banking Systems and Payment Infrastructure

These crimes are directed at banks, fintech companies, and financial service providers with motives ranging from monetary theft to data breaches and reputational harm.

- *Distributed Denial of Service (DDoS):* One of the most prevalent methods of cyberattack in the financial sector involves Distributed Denial of Service attacks (Somani et al., 2017). In these attacks, systems are flooded with excessive traffic, such as HTTP requests or UDP/TCP packets, intended to

system resources or disrupt normal operations. This form of attack can render online services inaccessible. Due to the need for multiple processing units or sources in DDoS attacks, they are often executed through botnets, which is a network of malware infected computers controlled remotely by cybercriminals. Attackers exploit computer vulnerabilities through botnets to access a large number of computers and to form an "army" for attacks (Zargar et al., 2013). Today, financial institutions and major corporations are frequently exposed to such attacks.
- *Point of Sale (POS) Attacks:* POS system is a combination of hardware and software that facilitates shopping with debit or credit cards (Talukder et al., 2019). These attacks target devices used in everyday retail environments, such as supermarkets or restaurants, compromising customer data including credit/debit card information and PINs, often leading to fraud.
- *ATM Malware:* The first variant of ATM-targeted malware appeared in 2009. Initially developed to facilitate unauthorized cash withdrawals (ATM jackpotting), this malware has since evolved to compromise corporate networks and capture customer transaction data (virtual skimming). In short, ATM malware is a type of crime aiming to manipulate systems, clone card information, and commit unlawful withdrawals.

3.2.3 Social Engineering Based Scams

Social engineering refers to a set of deceptive techniques used to gain the trust of individuals, via phone calls, fake customer service interactions, and other methods, in order to manipulate them into transferring money or disclosing critical account information (Kalnins et al., 2017; Krombholz et al., 2015). These frauds are manipulative and deceptive forms of cybercrime, which are committed by exploiting human psychology and vulnerabilities in trust.

- *Business Email Compromise (BEC):* BEC is a social engineering driven cybercrime, also known in the literature under different terms such as CEO attack (Atlam & Oluwatimilehin, 2022), CEO fraud (Gupta et al., 2016), email account compromise (Symantec, 2019), and email spoofing (Kruck & Kruck, 2006). BEC is an engineering attack aiming at financial fraud by compromising employees' corporate email accounts. Initially, the attacker gains access to account numbers, access credentials, or other sensitive information belonging to suppliers, senior company executives, or trusted employees (Jakobsson, 2016; Zweighaft, 2017). Subsequently, using fake emails, invoices, or payment instructions, attackers redirect company funds into their own accounts, causing significant financial damage to the business (Verizon, 2019). These emails, which are often personalized for the received and lack clearly malicious payloads are difficult for individuals to detect (Cidon et al., 2019). Causing severe financial losses, such attacks typically target companies rather than individuals (Cross & Gillett, 2020). For instance, Google and Meta (formerly Facebook) reportedly lost over $100 million due to BEC attacks between 2013 and 2015 (Gibbs, 2017). Globally, BEC attacks resulted in losses of approximately $26 billion between June 2016 and July 2019 (Cross & Gillett, 2020).

- *Fraudulent Investment Platforms:* Investment fraud involving deceptive investment in digital assets with promises of high returns and minimal risk is executed through social engineering related marketing techniques, misleading social media promotions, and fake testimonials. These scams are often facilitated through online platforms called fake or fraudulent investment platforms. Until they gain the investors' trusts, scammers initially persuade victims to invest small amounts, and then encourage them to invest larger sums. Early returns convince victims of the platform's legitimacy, leading them to invest more heavily. At the end of this process, investors do not withdraw their funds, lose them eventually (Wang et al., 2024).
- *Online Shopping Scams:* With the global digitalization, e-commerce has become an increasingly important and powerful mode of trade. With the growing volume of e-commerce, the appetite of fraudsters to commit such crimes has also intensified. In these scams, fraudsters create fake online stores or listings to sell nonexistent products or services. After receiving payment, they disappear without delivering the promised goods. Alternatively, scammers use e-commerce platforms to collect users' personal data for criminal purposes (Tripathi & Tripathi, 2024).
- *Deepfake Fraud:* Deepfake is a one of the emerging problems introduced by advancing technology. Hyper realistic videos generated by AI are referred to as "deepfakes" (Westerlund, 2019). In this type of fraud, online videos are edited or merged to create fabricated content, which can be used to manipulate and deceive individuals (Maras & Alexandrou, 2019). Through this method, highly convincing imitations of financial advisors, CEOs, or clients can be produced, which are nearly impossible to detect without advanced detection techniques/ technologies (Sharma & Tiwari, 2024). These fabricated identities can then be used to carry out fraudulent transactions, such as impersonating a company CEO to instruct the accounting department to transfer funds to a fraudster's account, manipulating stock prices, or gaining unauthorized access to others' accounts. Such incidents erode trust in financial institutions. It can also trigger sudden stock sell-offs or deposit withdrawals (IMF, 2024).

3.2.4 Crypto Assets and Blockchain Based Crimes

Crypto and blockchain based cybercrimes involve the use of digital assets and blockchain technology in cybercrime activities.

- *Pump and Dump Scams:* Originally prevalent in traditional stock markets, this form of unjust enrichment has now found its way into cryptocurrency market. In these schemes, attackers artificially inflate the price of a digital asset, a practice known as "pumping". The price rise is typically driven by coordinated buy orders or false investment advice aimed at attracting buyers. Once investors have purchased the artificially valued assets, the perpetrators exploit the market volatility by selling it at a profit, a stage referred to as “dumping”. This causes a sudden market crash, resulting in substantial losses for investors (Siregar & Nababan, 2025). These scams usually target low-volume and newly launched tokens (Asad & Shah, 2025).

- *ICO/IDO Fraud:* Initial Coin Offerings (ICOs) are a method of raising funds for new cryptocurrencies or blockchain projects, which as of yet, remain legally unregulated (Meraklı, 2021). In ICO scams, fraudsters claim to be launching a new digital asset or project and lure investors with promises of high returns during the token’s early phases. However, in many cases, these actors never generate a functional product; the primary objective is to collect substantial funds from investors and subsequently disappear (Asad & Shah, 2025). Initial DEX Offerings (IDOs) involve the first public sale of a crypto project’s token on a decentralized exchange. IDO scams are similar to ICO scams but occur within a decentralized trading environment (Agarwal et al., 2023). Basically, this type of fraud involves the misuse of investor trust to gain financial profit through fake, manipulated, or hastily constructed projects, after which the fraudsters vanish (Başbüyük, 2023).
- *Rug Pulls:* A rug pull is a type of fraud that ends in the perpetrators’ rapid exit from the market. In other words, it is a sudden scam where criminals (developers in crypto projects or malicious actors) manipulate investors, collect the funds they have deposited, and then abandon the project or withdraw the funds, causing financial losses to investors (Mazorra et al., 2022; Trozze et al., 2023). The perpetrators first create a token and provide liquidity for it on a decentralized market. Here the aim is to encourage investors to swap the new token with another existing cryptocurrency, such as Ethereum. Investors are manipulated through social media platforms or messaging applications like Telegram to manipulate the swap. The fraud concludes when investors realize that tokens they hold are worthless, resulting in financial loss (Trozze et al., 2023.

3.2.5 Extortion Based Cybercrimes

The coercion of individuals or organizations to perform actions against their will constitutes a criminal offense under the law. In the literature, these crimes are generally categorized into two main types:

- *Cyber Extortion:* Cyber extortion refers to crimes in which perpetrators target victims’ information systems and demand money or other valuables in exchange for not causing harm to their systems (Sulkoswki, 2007). Through cyber extortion, digital assets such as data, systems, or files belonging to individuals or institutions are seized, and the offenders ask for payment or other benefits in return for not disclosing or blocking access to these assets. Cyber extortion is not a new form of crime, which has evolved with technological advancements and has been exploited by criminals for approximately three decades (Hampton & Baig, 2015). This type of crime generally involves unauthorized access to victims' devices.

- *Ransomware:* Ransomware involves malicious software that infiltrates computer systems, or encrypts the files of users or institutions, and then demands a ransom for the decryption or restoration of access to the files (Begovic et al., 2023). Ransomware encrypts the files on the infected system and blocks the user's access (Kim et al., 2017). The files become unusable if the user does not know a specific decryption key. Perpetrators demand a ransom from the victim in exchange for restoring the documents or files. Criminals often ask the victims to make the payment in cryptocurrency due to the greater difficulty of tracing payments made in cryptocurrencies and the lower likelihood of identifying the perpetrators (Despotović et al., 2023). Once attacked, victims may face the loss of the targeted documents and files, whether they agree to pay the ransom or not, since there is no guarantee that the information will be recovered (Despotović et al., 2023; Everett, 2016). Financial institutions and banks are particularly targeted by ransomware attacks.

3.2.6 Cyber-Enabled Money Laundering

Cyber-enabled money laundering is a type of crime that arises from the application of traditional money laundering techniques combined with the new generation technological methods.

- *Cyber laundering:* Money laundering is the process of concealing the source, nature or ownership of proceeds obtained through illegal activities including human trafficking, arms smuggling and drug trafficking, to present these proceeds as if they were obtained from legitimate sources (Wronka, 2022). With the advanced technology, the concept of cyber-laundering has emerged as criminals have committed money laundering in cyberspace (Calafos & Dimitoglou, 2022; Handa & Ansari, 2022; Nizovtsev et al., 2022). Digital systems are more efficient for transferring large sums of money compared to cash. Remote business relationships facilitate the use of fake identities (Souto, 2022). Cyber laundering is the integration of criminal proceeds into the financial system with a legitimate appearance by obscuring their origins through digital technologies, such as cryptocurrencies, virtual wallets, mixer/tumbler services, in game money transfers, anonymous offshore systems. Although the term cyber-laundering may not be explicitly defined in each country's laws, it is a legally defined crime under terms like "money laundering," "committing crimes through information systems," and "laundering assets obtained through fraud."

3.3 Economic Costs of Cybercrimes

With the advanced technology, the shift of criminals to cyberspace has led to an increasing effect of the economic costs associated with cybercrimes. In addition, the diversity of economic costs related to cybercrimes has made it even more difficult to assess the total damage resulting from these crimes. Moreover, the difficulty of assessing the cost of security investments made to prevent cybercrimes and forecasting the net losses that may arise from these crimes has challenged decision makers in both public and private institutions (Cobos, & Cakir, 2024; Gordon et al., 2020).

Cybercrimes may pose risks that may disrupt the macroeconomic stability of countries. One of the immediate examples among these risks is the market losses that may occur in a country's stock market due to cybercrimes (Kamiya et al., 2021; Piccotti & Wang, 2022). Similarly, possible systematic disruptions in financial markets because of cybercrimes (Corbet & Gurdgiev, 2019) are included among the risks that may affect macroeconomic stability. Duffie and Younger (2019) state that cyberattacks, such as data breaches, could lead to a loss of confidence in targeted institutions, causing sudden money withdrawals or bank runs, which could increase the liquidity risk abruptly and significantly. Liquidity risks can lead to solvency issues for firms, potentially driving them into bankruptcy. This could rapidly affect other stakeholders within the financial system. For example, if a cyberattack affects a key institution or financial market structure in the financial system, risks to financial stability could suddenly emerge. Healey et al. (2018) reports that any hacking of a central bank, ransomware attacks targeting large banks, disruptions to clearinghouses or electronic trading systems, or the failure of major cloud service providers may have negative effects on financial stability. Eisenbach et al. (2022) highlights that common asset holdings are financially connected to each other through interbank markets or settlement systems and that there are technological connections across institutions using the software. The effect of a cyberattack could spread across the entire financial system through these connections. The potential financial losses for companies due to cyberattacks have risen significantly from 300 million dollars in 2017 to 2.2 billion dollars today, with an approximate increase of 633% since 2017 (IMF, 2024).

Costs associated with cybercrimes can be classified as direct costs and indirect costs. Everything related to the tangible financial costs and damages incurred by the victims are included under direct costs. For instance, ransom payment, banking or financial resource losses, investigation and forensic costs, legal expenses, and system and hardware repair/replacement costs fall under the direct costs category. In addition, the illegal financial gains obtained by cybercriminals are also considered as direct costs (Anderson et al., 2013). On the other hand, the indirect costs of cybercrimes encompass broader impacts that extend beyond the immediate financial losses related to a breach. Loss of reputation, operational disruptions and productivity loss, customer attrition, long term security investments, psychological and institutional cultural impacts are among the indirect costs. The indirect costs created by cybercrimes are as critical as their direct costs (Antonescu and Birău, 2015). An example of how indirect costs of such crimes can put firms in difficulty is the case of JPMorgan Chase, the largest bank in the United States. Recently, JPMorgan Chase has declared that it spends 15 billion dollars annually on technology to protect itself against cyberattacks and faces 45 billion cyber events daily (Walker, 2024).

Social engineering attacks are among the most common types of cybercrimes. The cost of social engineering attacks in the United States in 2016 is estimated to be $121.22 billion. US companies are highly susceptible to cyberattacks. For example, Equifax, a large credit reporting agency based in the United States, faced one of the biggest data breaches in its history in 2018. Critical information was stolen from the company's database, including Social Security numbers, birth dates, driver's license numbers, and addresses of 145.5 million users, which are essential for both identity theft and financial fraud activities. Similarly, it has been detected that US companies exposed to CEO fraud and email scams lost more than $ 2.3 billion (Salahdine & Kaabouch, 2019).

Data breaches are another frequent type of cybercrime, leading the affected firms to face both direct and indirect costs. In a study of 75 firms, Kamiya et al. (2021) reported the direct loss to shareholders due to a data breach as $104 billion, while the indirect costs that followed the breach amounted to $1.2 billion. Iyer et al. (2020) found that shareholders of companies exposed to cyberattacks experienced an average financial loss of $3.8 million compared to those of companies that were not affected.

The integration of AI technologies into the financial sector has occurred rapidly. These technologies can be used both to prevent and to execute cyber-attacks. For instance, phishing messages or deepfakes generated by AI can be used for identity theft fraud (Deep Instinct., 2023). In 2024, an employee at a multinational company in the Hong Kong Special Administrative Region who was deceived by deepfake videos and audios led to a payment of $25 million to cybercriminals (Chen & Magramo, 2024). Also, the costs associated with cryptocurrency-related crimes are expected to reach $ 30 million US dollars by 2025, and ransomware attacks will cost $265 million by 2031 (eSentire & Cybersecurity Ventures, 2023).

The diversity of costs related to cybercrimes results in varying cost estimates. Despite this, industry reports and studies in the related literature indicate that global costs across various sectors have been steadily increasing (Cobos & Cakir, 2024).

4. Conclusion and Policy Recommendations

Cybercrimes, which develop and expand with technology, are increasingly threatening financial systems. The disruption of services in the financial sector and the decline in confidence in the system pose a threat not only to institutions but also to financial stability. In order to build resilience against cyberattacks in the financial sector, it is necessary to develop cyber security strategies with effective regulatory and supervisory capacity (Wilson et al., 2019).

Evidence in the form of electronic data is needed to detect cybercrime (Shao, 2022). Although company reporting on these attacks has increased, there is still a lack of data. This makes establishing an effective regulatory framework and international legislation on cybercrime is difficult. Data gathering cyberattacks should be prioritized and systematically shared with financial system stakeholders.

Global identification of critical infrastructures related to cyberattacks and rapid updating of cybersecurity laws through data gathered on these attacks will contribute to the prevention of cyberattacks. However, the legal regulations of many countries have not yet reached a level to cover all aspects of cybercrime. Nevertheless, ultimately, a comprehensive and robust legal infrastructure on a global scale is urgently needed to lay the foundation for a stable digital society (Dutta et al., 2019).

In addition, studies in the literature indicate a significant relationship between digital financial literacy and cybercrimes (Khalid et al., 2024). Conducting country-by-country studies to increase digital financial literacy will increase individuals' resilience against such attacks.

In conclusion, to prevent financial cybercrimes, it may be possible to improve the relevant legislation and regulations globally and on a country-by-country basis, increase crime prevention measures, improve and enhance internet financial supervision, and eliminate the lack of public education and awareness.

References

Agarwal, S., Atondo-Siu, G., Ordekian, M., Hutchings, A., Mariconti, E., & Vasek, M. (2023, May). Short paper: DeFi deception—uncovering the prevalence of rugpulls in cryptocurrency projects. *International conference on financial cryptography and data security* (pp. 363–372). Springer Nature Switzerland.

Agbeve, V., Adukpo, T. K., Mensah, N., Appiah, D., & Atisu, J. C. (2025). Comparative analysis of digital banking and financial inclusion in the United states: Opportunities, challenges and policy implications. *Asian Journal of Economics, Business and Accounting*, *25*(3), 452–467.

Agur, I., Peria, S. M., & Rochon, C. (2020). Digital financial services and the pandemic: Opportunities and risks for emerging and developing economies. International monetary fund special series on COVID-19. *Transactions*, *1*, 1–2.

Al Khub, A., Saeudy, M., & Gerged, A. M. (2024). Digital financial inclusion in emerging economies: Evidence from Jordan. *Journal of Risk and Financial Management*, *17*(2), 66.

Al-Khater, W. A., Al-Maadeed, S., Ahmed, A. A., Sadiq, A. S., & Khan, M. K. (2020). Comprehensive review of cybercrime detection techniques. *IEEE Access*, *8*, 137293–137311.

Alsayed, A., & Bilgrami, A. (2017). E-banking security: Internet hacking, phishing attacks, analysis and prevention of fraudulent activities. *International Journal of Emerging Technology and Advanced Engineering*, *7*(1), 109–115.

Anderson, R., Barton, C., Böhme, R., Clayton, R., Van Eeten, M. J., Levi, M., Moore, T., & Savage, S. (2013). Measuring the cost of cybercrime. In *The economics of information security and privacy* (pp. 265–300). Springer Berlin Heidelberg.

Andress, J., & Winterfeld, S. (2013). *Cyber warfare: Techniques, tactics and tools for security practitioners*. Elsevier.

Antonescu, M., & Birău, R. (2015). Financial and non-financial implications of cybercrimes in emerging countries. *Procedia Economics and Finance*, *32*, 618–621.

APWG. (2022). Phishing activity trends report 3rd quarter 2022. https://docs.apwg.org/reports/apwg_trends_report_q3_2022.pdf. Accessed on March 17, 2025.

Asad, S., & Shah, W. (2025). *Digital asset scams and cryptocurrency fraud: Investigating the tactics of convicted fraudsters.* https://www.researchgate.net/publication/389939167_Digital_Asset_Scams_and_Cryptocurrency_Fraud_Investigating_the_Tactics_of_Convicted_Fraudsters?channel=doi&linkId=67d960237c5b5569dcc0918d&showFulltext=true. Accessed on March 17, 2025.

Atlam, H. F., & Oluwatimilehin, O. (2022). Business email compromise phishing detection based on machine learning: A systematic literature review. *Electronics*, *12*(1), 42.

Austin-Olowo, L. B. A., Anike, O. I., & Ailemen, I. O. (2023). Cybersecurity issues affecting online banking and transactions in Nigeria. *International Journal of Arts, Languages and Business Studies*, *9*, 25–35.

Awale, S. M., & Gupta, D. P. (2019). Awareness of sim swap attack. *International Journal of Trend in Scientific Research and Development*, *3*(4), 995–997.

Başbüyük, İ (2023). Blokzincir-kripto varlık bağlantılı yaygın sahtekarlık türlerinin dolandırıcılık ve ilişkili suçlar yönünden analizi. *Dokuz Eylül Üniversitesi Hukuk Fakültesi Dergisi*, *25*(2), 805–846.

Baur-Yazbeck, S., Frickenstein, J., & Medine, D. (2019). Cyber security in financial sector development. *CGAP Background Documents*, *5*(2).

Begovic, K., Al-Ali, A., & Malluhi, Q. (2023). Cryptographic ransomware encryption detection: Survey. *Computers and Security*, *132*, 103349.

Belleflamme, P., Lambert, T., & Schwienbacher, A. (2010). Crowdfunding: An industrial organization perspective. In *Prepared for the workshop digital business models: Understanding strategies*, held in Paris on June 25-26. https://www.researchgate.net/profile/Paul-Belleflamme/publication/228468454_Crowdfunding_An_Industrial_Organization_Perspective/links/02bfe5146fedab2af1000000/Crowdfunding-An-Industrial-Organization-Perspective.pdf. Accessed on March 17, 2025.

Benmoussa, M. (2019). API "Application Programming Interface" banking: A promising future for financial institutions (international experience). *Revue des Sciences Commerciales*, *18*(2), 31–43.

Bhavani, R., & Sankaradass, V. (2025). Net based malware detection in IoT devices. *International Journal of Machine Learning and Cybernetics*, 1–19.

Brandl, B., & Hornuf, L. (2020). Where did FinTechs come from, and where do they go? The transformation of the financial industry in Germany after digitalization. *Frontiers in Artificial Intelligence*, *3*, 8.

Calafos, M. W., & Dimitoglou, G. (2022). Cyber laundering: Money laundering from fiat money to cryptocurrency. In *Principles and practice of blockchains* (pp. 271–300). Springer International Publishing.

Cao, S., Nie, L., Sun, H., Sun, W., & Taghizadeh-Hesary, F. (2021). Digital finance, green technological innovation and energy-environmental performance: Evidence from China's regional economies. *Journal of Cleaner Production*, *327*, 129458.

Chen, H., & Magramo, K. (2024, February 4). *Finance worker pays out $25 million after video call with deepfake "Chief financial officer"*. CNN. https://edition.cnn.com/2024/02/04/asia/deepfake-cfo-scam-hong-kong-intl-hnk/index.html. Accessed on March 18, 2024

Cidon, A., Gavish, L., Bleier, I., Korshun, N., Schweighauser, M., & Tsitkin, A. (2019). High precision detection of business email compromise. In *28th USENIX security symposium*, August 14–16, 2019 Santa Clara, CA, USA (pp. 1291–1307).

Cobos, E. V., & Cakir, S. A. (2024). *Review of the economic costs of cyber incidents*. World Bank.

Corbet, S., & Gurdgiev, C. (2019). What the hack: Systematic risk contagion from cyber events. *International Review of Financial Analysis*, *65*, 101386.

Corporate Finance Institute. (2021). *What is mobile banking?* https://corporatefinanceinstitute.com/resources/knowledge/finance/mobile-banking/. Accessed on March 20, 2025.

Cross, C., & Gillett, R. (2020). Exploiting trust for financial gain: An overview of business email compromise (BEC) fraud. *Journal of Financial Crime*, *27*(3), 871–884.

Daud, S. N. M., Khalid, A., & Azman-Saini, W. N. W. (2022). FinTech and financial stability: Threat or opportunity?. *Finance Research Letters*, *47*, 102667.

Deep Instinct. (2023). *Generative AI and cybersecurity: Bright future or business battleground?* (4th ed.). Voice of SecOps.

Despotović, A., Parmaković, A., & Miljković, M. (2023). Cybercrime and cyber security in fintech. In *Ddgital transformation of the financial industry: Approaches and applications* (pp. 255–272). Springer International Publishing.

Dodgson, M., Gann, D., Wladawsky-Berger, I., Sultan, N., & George, G. (2015). Managing digital money. *Academy of Management Journal*, *58*(2), 325–333.

Duffie, D., & Younger, J. (2019). *Cyber runs. Hutchins center working paper 51*. Brookings Institution.

Durai, T., & Stella, G. (2019). Digital finance and its impact on financial inclusion. *Journal of Emerging Technologies and Innovative Research*, *6*(1), 122–127.

Dutta, N., Tanchak, K., & Delvadia, K. (2019). Modern methods for analyzing malware targeting control systems. In *In recent developments on industrial control systems resilience*(pp. 135–150). Springer International Publishing.

Eisenbach, T. M., Kovner, A., & Lee, M. J. (2022). Cyber risk and the US financial system: A pre-mortem analysis. *Journal of Financial Economics*, *145*(3), 802–826.

eSentire & Cybersecurity Ventures. (2023). Official annual cybercrime report. https://www.esentire.com/resources/library/2023-official-cybercrime-report. Accessed on March 6, 2025.

Everett, C. (2016). Ransomware: To pay or not to pay? *Computer Fraud & Security*, *4*, 8–12.

Gibbs, S. (2017). *Facebook and google were conned out of $100m in phishing scheme*. The Guardian. https://www.theguardian.com/technology/2017/apr/28/facebook-google-conned-100m-phishing-scheme. Accessed on March 27, 2025.

Gomber, P., Koch, J. A., & Siering, M. (2017). Digital finance and fintech: Current research and future research directions. *Journal of Business Economics*, *87*(5), 537–580.

Gordon, S., & Ford, R. (2006). On the definition and classification of cybercrime. *Journal in Computer Virology*, *2*, 13–20.

Gordon, L. A., Loeb, M. P., & Zhou, L. (2020). Integrating cost–benefit analysis into the NIST cybersecurity framework via the gordon–loeb model. *Journal of Cybersecurity*, *6*(1), tyaa005.

Gupta, S., Singhal, A., & Kapoor, A. (2016). A literature survey on social engineering attacks: Phishing attack. Proceedings of the International Conference on Computing, Communication and Automation (ICCCA), IEEE April 2016, 537–540.

Hampton, N., & Baig, Z. A. (2015). Ransomware: Emergence of the cyber-extortion menace. Proceedings of the *13th Australian Information Security Management Conference*, 30 November–2 December, 2015, Edith Cowan University Joondalup Campus, Perth, Western Australia (pp. 47–56). https://ro.ecu.edu.au/ism/180/

Handa, R. K., & Ansari, R. (2022). Cyber-laundering: An emerging challenge for law enforcement. *Journal of Victimology and Victim Justice*, *5*(1), 80–99.

Hartmann, M. (2006). E-Payments evolution. In T. Lammer (Ed.), *Handbuch EMoney, E-Payment and M-Payment*. Physica-Verlag.

Healey, J., Mosser, P., Rosen, K., & Tache, A. (2018). *The future of financial stability and cyber risk*. Brookings Institution.

IMF. (2024). *Global financial stability report*. https://www.imf.org/en/Publications/GFSR/Issues/2024/10/22/global-financial-stability-report-october-2024. Accessed on February 02, 2025.

Iyer, S. R., Simkins, B. J., & Wang, H. (2020). Cyberattacks and impact on bond valuation. *Finance Research Letters*, *33*, 101215.

Jakobsson, M. (2016). Case study: Business email compromise. In M. Jakobsson (Ed.), *Understanding social engineering based scams* (pp. 115–122). Springer.

Kalnins, R., Purin, s. J., & Alksnis, G. (2017). Security evaluation of wireless network access points. *Applied Computer Systems*, *21*, 38–45.

Kamiya, S., Kang, J. K., Kim, J., Milidonis, A., & Stulz, R. M. (2021). Risk management, firm reputation, and the impact of successful cyberattacks on target firms. *Journal of Financial Economics*, *139*(3), 719–749.

Kelikume, I. (2021). Digital financial inclusion, informal economy and poverty reduction in Africa. *Journal of Enterprising Communities: People and Places in the Global Economy*, *15*(4), 626–640.

Khalıd, W. E., Ali, M. M., Garbaa, R. A., & Mohammed, M. A. (2024). Digital financial literacy and cybercrimes: Measuring the role of Sudanese banks enhancing their users "confidence". *The Seybold Report*, *19*(03), 1008–1026.

Khera, P., Ng, S., Ogawa, S., & Sahay, R. (2022). Measuring digital financial inclusion in emerging market and developing economies: A new index. *Asian Economic Policy Review*, *17*(2), 213–230.

Kim, H., Yoo, D., Kang, J., & Yeom, Y. (2017). Dynamic ransomware protection using deterministic random bit generator. In *Proceedings of the Conference on Applications, Information and Network Security (AINS)*, IEEE, Miri, Malaysia (pp. 64–68). https://doi.org/10.1109/AINS.2017.8270426

Kingiri, A. N., & Fu, X. (2020). Understanding the diffusion and adoption of digital finance innovation in emerging economies: M-Pesa money mobile transfer service in Kenya. *Innovation and Development*, *10*(1), 67–87.

Krombholz, K., Hobel, H., Huber, M., & Weippl, E. (2015). Advanced social engineering attacks. *Journal of Information Security and Applications*, *22*, 113–122.

Kruck, G., & Kruck, S. E. (2006). Spoofing - A look at an evolving threat. *Journal of Computer Information Systems*, *47*(1), 95–100.

Kusters, A. (2022). *Relating digitization, digitalization and digital transformation: A maturity model and roadmap for Dutch logistics companies*. University of Twente. Bachelor's thesis.

Laurent, P., Chollet, T., Burke, M., & Seers, T. (2018). The tokenization of assets is disrupting the financial industry. Are you ready? *Inside. Triannual insights from Deloitte*, (19), 62–67.

Li, Y., Spigt, R., & Swinkels, L. (2017). The impact of FinTech start-ups on incumbent retail banks' share prices. *Financial Innovation*, *3*(1), 1–16.

Li, G., Zhang, R., Feng, S., & Wang, Y. (2022). Digital finance and sustainable development: Evidence from environmental inequality in China. *Business Strategy and the Environment*, *31*(7), 3574–3594.

Liu, Z., & Hou, W. (2023). Opportunities and challenges of digital financial development. In *Digital finance*. Springer. https://doi.org/10.1007/978-981-99-7305-7_1

Mamoshina, P., Ojomoko, L., Yanovich, Y., Ostrovski, A., Botezatu, A., Prikhodko, P., & Zhavoronkov, A. (2018). Converging blockchain and next-generation artificial intelligence technologies to decentralize and accelerate biomedical research and healthcare. *Impact Journals*, *9*(5), 5665–5690.

Manyika, J., Lund, S., Singer, M., White, O., & Berry, C. (2016, September). *Digital finance for all: Powering inclusive growth in emerging economies*. McKinsey Global Institute.

Maras, M. H., & Alexandrou, A. (2019). Determining authenticity of video evidence in the age of artificial intelligence and in the wake of deepfake videos. *International Journal of Evidence and Proof*, *23*(3), 255–262.

Marsh, I., & Melville, G. (2019). *Crime, justice and the media* (3rd ed.). Routledge. https://doi.org/10.4324/9780429432194

Mazorra, B., Adan, V., & Daza, V. (2022). Do not rug on me: Zero-dimensional scam detection. *Mathematics*, *10*(6), 949.

McGuire, M. (2019). It ain't what it is, it's the way that they do it? Why we still don't understand cybercrime. In *The human factor of cybercrime* (pp. 3–28). Routledge. https://doi.org/10.4324/9780429460593

Meraklı, S. (2021). Merkeziyetsiz finans (DeFi) faaliyetlerinin izinsiz bankacılık faaliyetinde bulunma suçu bakımından değerlendirilmesi. *Marmara Üniversitesi Hukuk Fakültesi Hukuk Araştırmaları Dergisi*, *27*(2), 1156–1190.

Nasiri, M., Ukko, J., Saunila, M., & Rantala, T. (2020). Managing the digital supply chain: The role of smart technologies. *Technovation*, *96–97*, 102121.

Nguyen, Q. K. (2016). Blockchain-a financial technology for future sustainable development. In *2016 3rd international conference on green technology and sustainable development* (pp. 51–54). (GTSD) IEEE. https://doi.org/10.1109/GTSD.2016.22

Nizovtsev, Y. Y., Parfylo, O. A., Barabash, O. O., Kyrenko, S. G., & Smetanina, N. V. (2022). Mechanisms of money laundering obtained from cybercrime: The legal aspect. *Journal of Money Laundering Control*, *25*(2), 297–305.

Nobles, C., Burton, S. L., & Burrell, D. N. (2023). Cybercrime as a sustained business. In F. Adedoyin & B. Christiansen (Eds.), *Handbook of research on cybersecurity risk in contemporary business systems* (pp. 98–120). IGI Global Scientific Publishing. https://doi.org/10.4018/978-1-6684-7207-1.ch005

O'Leary, D. E. (2022). Digitization, digitalization, and digital transformation in accounting, electronic commerce, and supply chains. *Intelligent Systems in Accounting, Finance and Management*, *30*(2), 101–110.

Okutan, A., & Çebi, Y. (2019). A framework for cyber crime investigation. *Procedia Computer Science*, *158*, 287–294.

Ozili, P. K. (2018). Impact of digital finance on financial inclusion and stability. *Borsa istanbul Review*, *18*(4), 329–340.

Özkan, T. (2006). Siber Terörizm Bağlamında Türkiye'ye Yönelik Faaliyet Yürüten Terör Örgütlerinin İnternet Sitelerine Yönelik Bir İçerik Analizi (Master's thesis, Anadolu University, Türkiye).

Phillips, K., Davidson, J. C., Farr, R. R., Burkhardt, C., Caneppele, S., & Aiken, M. P. (2022). Conceptualizing cybercrime: Definitions, typologies and taxonomies. *Forensic Science*, *2*(2), 379–398.

Piccotti, L. R., & Wang, H. (2022). Informed trading in the options market surrounding data breaches. *Global Finance Journal*, *56*, 100774.

Prinakaa, S., Bavanika, V., Sanjana, S., Srinivasan, S., & Sarasvathi, V. (2024). A real-time approach to detecting API abuses based on behavioral patterns. In Proceedings of the *8th International Conference on Cryptography, Security and Privacy* (pp. 24–28). (CSP) IEEE. https://doi.org/10.1109/CSP62567.2024.00012

Risman, A., Mulyana, B., Silvatika, B., & Sulaeman, A. (2021). The effect of digital finance on financial stability. *Management Science Letters*, *11*(7), 1979–1984.

Salahdine, F., & Kaabouch, N. (2019). Social engineering attacks: A survey. *Future Internet*, *11*(4), 89.

Sandilaç, N. (2022). Siber suç, siber terör ve siber savaş üçgeninde siber dünya. *Bilişim Hukuku Dergisi*, *4*(1), 81–140.

Schueffel, P. (2016). Taming the beast: A scientific definition of fintech. *Journal of Innovation Management*, *4*(4), 32–54.

Shao, Y. (2022). General rules and framework resolution about cybercrime governance in the era of globalization. In *Cybercrimes and financial crimes in the global era* (pp. 241–247). Springer Nature Singapore.

Sharma, A., & Tiwari, R. (2024). Banking in the age of deepfakes: Evaluating perceptions of deepfake fraud risks. In G. Lakhera, S. Taneja, E. Ozen, M. Kukreti, & P. Kumar (Eds.), *Navigating the World of Deepfake Technology* (pp. 454–469). IGI Global Scientific Publishing.

Shofawati, A. (2019). The role of digital finance to strengthen financial inclusion and the growth of SME in Indonesia. *KnE Social Sciences*, 389–407.

Siregar, B., & Nababan, R. (2025). Legal responsibility of digital platform companies for protecting shareholder losses in the era. *Journal of Law and Social Politics*, *3* (2), 36–43.

Somani, G., Gaur, M. S., Sanghi, D., Conti, M., & Buyya, R. (2017). DDoS attacks in cloud computing: Issues, taxonomy, and future directions. *Computer Communications*, *107*, 30–48.

Souto, M. A. (2022). Money laundering, cybercrime and criminal responsibility of legal persons. In *In cybercrimes and financial crimes in the global era* (pp. 145–164). Springer Nature Singapore.

Sulkoswki, A. J. (2007). Cyber-extortion: Duties and liabilities related to the elephant in the server room. *U. Ill. JL Tech. & Pol'y*, *19*.

Sun, R., Wang, Q., & Guo, L. (2022). Research towards key issues of API security. In W. Lu, Y. Zhang., W. Wen, H. Yan., & C. Li. (Eds.), *Cyber Security*. CNCERT 2021, Communications in Computer and Information Science, (Vol. 1506, pp. 179–192), Springer. https://doi.org/10.1007/978-981-16-9229-1_11

Swanink, R., Poll, E., & Schwabe, P. (2016). *Persistent effects of manin-the-middle attacks* (pp. 23–32). Radboud University.

Symantec. (2019). *BEC scams remain a billion-dollar enterprise, targeting 6K businesses monthly*. www.symantec.com/blogs/threat-intelligence/bec-scams-trends-and-themes-2019. Accessed on March 27, 2025

Talukder, M. A. I., Shahriar, H., & Haddad, H. (2019). Point-of-sale device attacks and mitigation approaches for cyber-physical systems. In *Cybersecurity and privacy in cyber physical systems* (pp. 367–391). CRC Press.

Tanda, A., & Schena, C. M. (2019). *FinTech, BigTech and banks: Digitalisation and its impact on banking business models*. Springer.

Tang, H. (2019). Peer-to-Peer lenders versus banks: Substitutes or complements? *Review of Financial Studies*, *32*(5), 1900–1938.

Tay, L. Y., Tai, H. T., & Tan, G. S. (2022). Digital financial inclusion: A gateway to sustainable development. *Heliyon*, *8*(6).

Thathsarani, U. S., & Jianguo, W. (2022). Do digital finance and the technology acceptance model strengthen financial inclusion and SME performance? *Information*, *13*(8), 390.

Thomas, D. & Loader, B. (2000). *Cybercrime: Law enforcement, security and surveillance in the information age* (1st ed.). Routledge Press.

Tripathi, R., & Tripathi, S. (2024). Frauds and cyber security issues in the finance sector. In G. Malik, G. Malik, & S. Aggarwal (Eds.), *Transforming the financial landscape with ICTs* (pp. 165–189). IGI Global Scientific Publishing. https://doi.org/10.4018/979-8-3693-1503-3.ch008

Trozze, A., Davies, T., & Kleinberg, B. (2023). Of degens and defrauders: Using open-source investigative tools to investigate decentralized finance frauds and money laundering. *Forensic Science International: Digital Investigation*, *46*, 301575.

Verhoef, P. C., Broekhuizen, T. L., Bart, Y., Bhattacharya, A., Qi Dong, J., Fabian, N. E., & Haenlein, M. (2019). Digital transformation: A multidisciplinary reflection and research agenda. *Journal of Business Research*, *122*, 889–901.

Verizon. (2019). *2019 data breach investigations report*. https://enterprise.verizon.com/resources/reports/dbir/. Accessed on March 27, 2025.

Walker, O. (2024). *JPMorgan suffers wave of cyber attacks as fraudsters get "more devious"*. Financial Times. https://www.ft.com/content/cd287352-cb3b-48d8-a85b-668713b80962. Accessed on January 17, 2025.

Wall, D. (2004). *What are cybercrimes? Criminal Justice Matters*, *58*(1) 20–21. https://doi.org/10.1080/09627250408553239

Wang, X., & He, G. (2020). Digital financial inclusion and farmers' vulnerability to poverty: Evidence from rural China. *Sustainability*, *12*(4), 1668.

Wang, V., Nnaji, H., & Jung, J. (2020). Internet banking in Nigeria: Cyber security breaches, practices and capability. *International Journal of Law, Crime and Justice*, *62*, 100415.

Wang, J., Zhang, L., Xu, L., & Qian, X. (2024). The dynamic emotional experience of online fraud victims during the process of being defrauded: A text-based analysis. *Journal of Criminal Justice*, *94*, 102231.

Westerlund, M. (2019). The emergence of deepfake technology: A review. *Technology Innovation Management Review*, *9*(11).

Wilson, C., Gaidosch, T., Adelmann, F., & Morozova, A. (2019). *Cybersecurity risk supervision*. International Monetary Fund. https://doi.org/10.5089/9781513507545.087. Accessed on January 22, 2025.

Wronka, C. (2022). Cyber-laundering: The change of money laundering in the digital age. *Journal of Money Laundering Control*, *25*(2), 330–344.

Zargar, S. T., Joshi, J., & Tipper, D. (2013). A survey of defense mechanisms against distributed denial of service (DDOS) flooding attacks. *IEEE Communications Surveys and Tutorials*, *15*(4), 2046–2069.

Zweighaft, D. (2017). Business email compromise and executive impersonation: Are financial institutions exposed? *The Journal of Investment Compliance*, *18*(1), 1–7.

Chapter 8

Cryptocurrency and Financial Crime: The New Frontier of Financial Crime

Enver Buçaj and Naim Baftiu

University "Ukshin Hoti" Prizren, Republic of Kosovo

Abstract

Cryptocurrencies represent a disruptive innovation within the global financial landscape, introducing decentralized, borderless systems for value exchange that challenge traditional banking structures. As digital assets such as Bitcoin and Ethereum gain widespread adoption, they offer significant advantages—promoting financial inclusion, reducing transactional costs, and empowering users with greater privacy and autonomy in their financial affairs. Yet, these same attributes—anonymity, decentralization, and ease of transfer—also make cryptocurrencies particularly vulnerable to misuse. Their capacity to operate outside regulated financial channels has enabled their use in a growing range of illicit activities, including money laundering, fraud, ransomware attacks, and the financing of terrorism. As a result, cryptocurrencies have become integrated into the toolkit of financial criminals, complicating the efforts of regulators, law enforcement, and financial institutions to mitigate associated risks. The increasing prevalence of digital currencies calls for a nuanced understanding of both the technologies underpinning them and the motivations driving their misuse. Effective regulation must strike a balance between enabling innovation and ensuring robust oversight mechanisms to prevent abuse. Recognizing the dual nature of cryptocurrencies—as tools of progress and potential platforms for crime—is essential for shaping responsible policies that support technological advancement while safeguarding economic stability. This chapter explores the complex intersection of cryptocurrency and financial crime, examining the underlying issues and proposing strategies to reduce risk, enhance transparency, and support the sustainable development of digital financial systems.

Corruption and Crime in Finance, 155–186

doi:10.1108/978-1-83708-170-720261021

Keywords: Cryptocurrency; financial crime; cybercrime; blockchain; money laundering; fraud; ransomware; terrorist financing; privacy coins

1. Introduction

Cryptocurrency is a disruptive technology that has transformed the financial landscape, enabling nonstate, decentralized, and borderless forms of digital money and value exchange that blur geographic boundaries, challenging traditional banking systems. Although cryptocurrencies provide novel paths to financial inclusion and technological innovation, they have also created avenues for licensed and unlicensed financial crime, highlighting their dual nature as financial products. The rise of bitcoin, Ethereum, and other cryptocurrencies has opened new opportunities for financial inclusion, decentralized technologies, and global commerce. By providing digital values that avoid traditional intermediary transactional costs and risks, they represent a burgeoning area of innovation for people interested in autonomy and privacy in financial transactions.

Nonetheless, this innovation paradigm is problematic. The qualities that make cryptocurrencies attractive for legitimate uses (i.e., anonymity, decentralization, price volatility in trades, and ease of transfer) also create even greater opportunities for illegitimate uses. They are a new instrument in the financial crime toolkit, with money laundering, fraud, financial ransomware crime, and even terror financing taking hold in financial crime practices, posing difficult challenges for regulators, law enforcement, and financial institutions around the world. The use of cryptocurrencies is expanding, and so too is their use by bad characters abusing these digital assets in inappropriate ways. To combat these threats, one must have a nuanced understanding of the technologies, the goals of criminals, and the regulatory loopholes that allow these acts to occur. This article discusses the relationship between cryptocurrencies and financial crime, looks at the issues, and offers recommendations to recognize opportunities and lower risk while contributing to the potential change that comes with these digital innovations.

2. Methodology

The article undertakes a multidimensional methodological approach to investigating the relationship between cryptocurrencies and financial crime. The methodology includes the following steps:

- *Literature review:* The literature on the criminal misuse of financial systems through blockchain and related digital assets is extensive and multifaceted. Researchers have examined how blockchain technology influences mechanisms associated with fraud prevention, anti-money laundering (AML), and counter-terrorist financing (CTF) guidelines imposed by international bodies like the Financial Action Task Force (FATF) and agencies such as Europol. A comprehensive literature review reveals three primary strands: academic analyses of blockchain's potential to combat criminality; regulatory guidelines and recommendations from international bodies; and industry and policy reports that critically assess emerging criminal risks and compliance strategies Goce (2024).

- *Case Studies:* Case studies of actual crypto-related crimes, such as ransomware attacks, as well as money laundering and fraud, were considered. These cases offer real-world insight into the abuse of cryptocurrencies as well as the challenges faced by law enforcement.
- *Technology Assessment:* The technologies underpinning cryptocurrencies include blockchain, privacy technologies, and how they might simultaneously empower financial crime and the fight against it.
- *Legal Framework Assessment:* The applicable legal framework was assessed to consider current regulations, for example, as informed by FATF, as well as regulations regionally such as in the European Union and the United States.
- *Stakeholder Assessment:* The possible perspectives of all stakeholders, including regulators, law enforcement agencies, foundations, and crypto users, were considered to inform regulatory policy.
- *Solutions:* Solutions have been mapped through evaluating the findings. This includes identifying regulatory issues, possible technical safeguards, and enhancing inter-agency co-operation to address threats to the economy.

This offers an even-handed and comprehensive approach to considering this process, combining normative considerations and drawing some recommendations.

2.1 Criminal Perspectives of Cryptocurrency

The criminal attraction to cryptocurrencies includes pseudonymity, global reach, and lack of intermediaries. These opportunities allow criminals:

- *Trade illegally:* Cryptocurrencies facilitate payments for illegal goods and services in dark web marketplaces (Nakamoto, 2008).
- *Money Laundering:* Criminals can hide the origins of illicit funds through layering and mixers in cryptocurrency (Europol, 2020).
- *Fraud:* Initial Coin Offerings (ICOs) and trade in securities often act as a front for fraud (FATF, 2021).
- *Boundary Responses to Sanctions:* Cryptocurrencies present sanctioned entities with an expandable means of navigating traditional financial systems to resume their business (U.S. Treasury Department, 2021).

2.2 Types of Financial Crimes in the Cryptocurrency Space

2.2.1 Money Laundering

The use of cryptocurrencies in money laundering increasingly exploits sophisticated tools such as tumblers (or mixers) and privacy coins (e.g., Zcash and Monero) to obstruct transaction trails, creating significant challenges for law enforcement agencies. The inherent design of privacy coins incorporates advanced cryptographic methods that hide transaction details such as sender, receiver, and transaction amount, thereby obscuring the conventional traceability available on standard blockchain ledgers (Ishmaev, 2017, 2024). Concurrently, mixing services combine funds from multiple users, effectively obscuring clear transactional relationships and further complicating efforts to trace illicit money flows (Shojaeinasab et al., 2023).

2.2.2 Fraud and Scams

Fraudulent schemes range from Ponzi schemes to phishing attacks that target unsuspecting investors in the cryptocurrency space. There is an even higher number of scams due to the lack of regulatory oversight (FTC, 2021).

2.2.3 Ransomware

Cybercriminals are increasingly using ransomware attacks that involve cryptocurrency payments. This has been illustrated by high-profile cases that have shown the damage or disruptions that ransomware attacks can cause to the operational, technical, and financial aspects of an organization (Coveware, 2021).

2.2.4 Terrorist Financing

The use of cryptocurrencies to fund terrorist activities is rare compared to other forms of financial crime, but there are occasions of exploitation by terrorist groups to raise funds while avoiding the detection of law enforcement. Moreover, qualitative analyses emphasize that terrorist groups have, on occasion, exploited the enhanced anonymity provided by cryptocurrencies, using techniques such as decentralized autonomous organizations (DAOs) to discreetly aggregate and transfer funds without triggering immediate law enforcement attention (Teichmann, 2018). Although these findings suggest potential threats, Bilan (2023) describes how the international regulatory community, including bodies like the FATF, has observed and addressed these emerging threats. Nonetheless, the overall risk profile of terrorist financing via cryptocurrencies remains lower than that of more pervasive financial crimes.

2.3 Law Enforcement and Regulatory Challenges

The regulatory and law enforcement challenges related to cryptocurrency financial crimes are widespread due to the decentralized nature of cryptocurrency:

- Anonymity: It is common for transactions to be only pseudonymous so that it can be difficult to identify law breakers (FATF, 2021).
- Jurisdictional Issues: Cryptocurrencies have no borders, so international cooperation and investigations are much harder (Interpol, 2020).

- Rapid Technological Advances in Blockchain: The swift speed of technological advancements in blockchain technologies far exceeds regulatory frameworks (WEF, 2020).
- Lack of Available Expertise: Even with the overwhelming interest from law enforcement to pursue cryptocurrency financial crimes, there is limited success due to the lack of technical expertise and resources (CipherTrace, 2021).

2.4 Regulatory Responses

Here are some of the methods governments and international entities are starting to implement to disrupt financial crime trends in the cryptocurrency space:

- KYC and AML: Exchanges and wallet providers enable users to have verified accounts and report suspicious activity (FATF, 2019).
- Travel Rule: The FATF endorses the sharing of information on cryptocurrency among all financial institutions (FATF, 2020).
- Public–Private Partnerships (PPP): Regulatory bodies, financial institutions, and tech companies are utilizing PPP initiatives to create better defenses against financial crime (Europol, 2021).
- Blockchain Analysis tools: New technologies are being used to trace crypto transactions and potential illicit activity (Chainalysis, 2022).

2.5 The Path Forward

The growing use of cryptocurrencies requires a more thoughtfully and carefully coordinated, multipronged approach to curtail financial crimes and misuse of cryptocurrencies:

- Engaging Cooperative Governance Across Regions: Increasing global interdependence means it is imperative to strengthen partnerships in law enforcement collaboration to deter criminals from committing cross-border crimes, as it applies to cryptocurrency (United Nations, 2021).
- Regulating Cryptocurrency Frameworks Responsively: Creatively utilizing regulatory mechanisms for effectively governing cryptocurrencies should not limit innovation (IMF, 2021).
- Prevention Education: Educating and informing investors and the public audience to recognize potential risks and red flags of cryptocurrency investments and scams will limit their victimization potential (OECD, 2020).
- Technological Capabilities: Investing in blockchain analysis tools and artificial intelligence could help disrupt advanced approaches by sophisticated criminals involved in utilizing the latest technology (MIT Technology Review, 2021).

3. Introduction

This paper is directed toward students on the "deviation from the main use" of modern communication technologies, primarily focusing on information technology. The application and use of these technologies that raise significant questions are really the use of those technologies by criminal elements, popularly referred to as cybercrime or computer-based crime.

During daily practice, there seem to exist two dominant orientations toward the phenomenon of cybercrime. First, commonplace users of technology tend to have the orientation of "bad things only happen to others." To a certain level of distinction, there are professionals in the field, trained and privileged to have created knowledge and effect, and they orient exactly in the extreme opposite direction to attain the view that "we are all equally 'vulnerable' (presumably at least statistically), if not equally likely to be a target of a 'cyber' attack." The experts are dedicating time and resources, beyond typical users, to understanding the details of how the cyber threats can be analyzed, and to mitigate their effects.

On the first point, I ask you to note the caution that should be taken in view of eliminating the risk of being subjected to cyberattacks, in any instance. Cyber threats will continue to increase as the spread of use of information technologies, and particularly internet technologies, permeates everyday life. This change is taking place not so much because of how government or private industry, for-profit or not-for-profit organizations work, but even more so because of how individuals work or participate, either personally or professionally.

With any technology that is widely available and accessible, the internet does offer a myriad of benefits and efficiencies but brings an array of new risks and dilemmas. It is not necessary to consider an extensive list of benefits, as it is relatively easy to specify and observe, because of the nature of the internet as an open and decentralized tool. These advantages can be summarized quite simply: fast, cost-effective, and distance-free communication across the globe.

Cybercrime and technology-based criminal behavior have also started to come to the fore in Kosovo. As noted by the Kosovo Police, although this type of crime has only emerged relatively late, it is now fast expanding and has been recorded in almost every region of the country. Cybercrime, which we previously thought of as something that belonged in a different time, is now an emerging and burgeoning reality within our own national context.

4. Emergence and Nature of Cybercrime

In the past year alone, the Kosovo Police have reported eight verified cases of cybercrime. They all used complicated and advanced technological tools. Most behaviors associated with information technology and ICT are now part of every aspect of human activity, regardless of the geographical point of origin. Daily operations in fields such as business, communication, and finance are now increasingly reliant on ICTs, which are accepted as part of an information revolution. There is unequivocally acceptable progress brought on by this information revolution; on the other hand, there are equally clear disadvantages.

The development of high-tech solutions has provided access to whole new formats of criminal behavior—misbehaviors that could not have been possible without some form of digitalization. Therefore, it is important that we understand this is something that each of us has to begin to proactively advocate for and that whether we are exercising corporate or individual responsibility, we must think about the ways in which we confront these new threats. It is a collective approach involving governments and citizens. Because cybercrime is everywhere, preventing it is the only—and obviously most logical—method of combating this issue—both of remedial and preventive value. It is simply "socially unacceptable" that our modern-day lives can be under threat from another form of modern-day organized criminal activity. The challenge of cybercrime is not limited to developed economies but is also pervasive in developing economies, and it is steadily becoming a global concern Buçaj and Idrizaj (2024).

Crime has always commanded interest from researchers and organizations, especially because of its negative influence on social fabric. For centuries, researchers have theorized the sources, influences and methods of crime. Similarly, various theorists have formulated theories on the prevention of various crimes and their reporting.

4.1 What Is Cybercrime?

Despite a wealth of scholarship on cybercrime, there is still no universal definition. Cybercrime presents itself as an entirely different set of crime categories, making it difficult to define. The distinction of cybercrime, making this difficulty in definition, is complex in itself because of the multitude of criminal behaviors and ongoing change in criminal methodology. These characteristics of cybercrime have led researchers to conclude that cybercrime does not yet represent a defined unified phenomenological category.

One researcher, Don Parker, described cybercrime as a diverse range of distinct criminal activities that are rapidly growing, with forms of cyber disturbance likely to be the dominant forms of crime going forward. Due to the inconsistency in forms and methods, theoretical and practical perspectives diverge readily when defining the range of crimes termed "cybercrime." Overall, two main definitions have emerged: the first definition aims to provide a concise and clear definition of cyberspace crime, and the second definition is more descriptive and indirect, which is important to remember when determining what qualifies as cyberspace crime.

4.2 Conceptualizing and Defining Cybercrime

In the following, various perspectives will be highlighted regarding definitions by academics, particularly those scholars who refer to an explicit and clear definition of cybercrime, which is the majority of scholars in this area. According to a report prepared by the Bureau of Statistics of the United States Department of Justice, along with the Stanford Research Institute (SRI), cybercrime can be defined as "any criminal action that requires the offender to have a technical knowledge of computers to interfere with or manipulate them."

Computer Crime: Criminal Justice Manual (1979), stated that cybercrime refers to: "any unlawful act that requires significant knowledge of computer technology and is prosecutable."

This definition was further defined during a seminar hosted by Interpol in France (1981) in which the definition was expanded to: "any unlawful action where a perpetrator's essential knowledge of computer systems is key to his or her performing, investigating, prosecuting or sentencing."

In 1983, a Swedish delegation at the Second Nordic Conference on Economic Crime held in Helsinki presented a related definition, "cybercrime is a crime that involves an action that is directed at or through the use of computer systems, and where the offender relies on his or her technical ability in computing to commit the offense."

The Organization for Economic Co-operation and Development (OECD), at a meeting in Paris in 1983, defined cybercrime as "any unauthorized, unethical or illegal behavior using automatic processing or electronic transmission of data."

Germany's Federal Criminal Police Office (BKA) addressed the cyberspace crime issue post-1981 and defined it as "any behavior where a data processing system is used as an instrument to commit criminal acts, or direct aim of criminal acts is the data processing systems." By the end of 1983, the definition had expanded to include other uses of the term cybercrime, such as computer fraud, cyber-espionage, and misuse of computing systems. Most of the scholars agree that cybercrime incorporates criminal offenses, which necessarily could not be committed without specialized knowledge, or it could not have been conducted regarding computer systems (Dodiya et al., 2024).

Theoretical and Legal Considerations of Cybercrime: Historically regarded as a form of conventional crime, cybercrime has been recognized as a threat to social order and has attracted the attention of lawmakers, researchers, and society at large.

Many understandings of criminal behavior have been constructed since ancient times. At any one point in time, there have been a multitude of ideas and theories about the origins and meaning of behavior considered criminal. As with anything in society, crime has evolved along with society, although the newly invented modes of crime still resemble their predecessors.

Against this backdrop, many criminology scholars have recognized that the characteristics and quality of crime are aligned with the change and development of social and economic systems. In today's world, the link between crime in society and human evolution is quite clear: new ways to commit criminal acts develop rapidly, whether locally or globally, in relation to time and place.

As noted in a literature review of different forms of organized crime, a new and unique type of criminal behavior has emerged in the digital world: cybercrime.

4.3 Traditional Crimes versus Cybercrimes

Cybercrime is inherently a transnational crime, unlike traditional crime. These crimes exist across borders and are often performed remotely through digital networks that connect people globally. A cyberattack can be initiated from almost anywhere in the world and potentially target a user or system located in a completely different jurisdiction. The increased occurrence of cyber-related offenses is part of a larger "declassification" of crime. In a number of cases, the term "cybercrime" does not involve using the internet infrastructure to commit a crime as a digital crime, but instead, uses information technology as an instrumentality to commit what has been labeled a traditional crime. Nevertheless, due to its trans-jurisdictional nature, both governments and international legal authorities cannot use traditional classifications to attempt to address and govern this new form of offense.

One example that illustrates this ambiguity is the ILOVEYOU virus. Experts could trace the origin of the virus and identify the country of origin as the Philippines relatively quickly after its inception. Using data from an internet service provider, the investigators could subsequently identify the suspects who created and circulated the ILOVEYOU malware fairly quickly with the Philippines National Bureau of Investigation and the FBI working together (Cartin-Pecson et al., 2025).

Despite this initial success, the investigation ultimately encountered significant legal barriers due to circumstances. The criminal code in the Philippines at the time contained few, if any, provisions addressing the creation or distribution of computer viruses. This meant that, even though the suspects were clearly identified by investigators, there was a lack to legally charge the suspects.

In other words, this situation illustrates one of the larger challenges facing legal systems around the world, which is the inadequacy or absence of viable legal frameworks used to address new and rapidly changing patterns of digital "wrongdoing." The failure of current criminal laws to keep pace with technological evolution and its ramifications is a continual challenge for lawmakers across the globe, as even the regulation and prosecution of cybercrime is a complicated and pressing issue.

Legal loopholes and the application of technology in possible criminal planning

Conversely, offenders have learned to use the loopholes in the law in both domestic and foreign jurisdictions to target and prey on people with no consequences. Cybercrimes are a perfect example of a truly global type of crime.

To combat the threats posed by activities without borders, many states have attempted to apply protective boundaries through managed digital filtering and electronic borders, while others have been asserting national jurisdiction over digital communication. Some states have been fast to restrict freedoms of movement and expression for the sake of regulation of online traffic. Many countries like Albania do not follow the international trend and do not have continuous comprehensive legislation on this type of crime.

The computer as a method for hiding, planning, and committing crimes

Among the most significant innovations of the modern technologically driven world is the computer. At this point in time, it serves benefits and comes with many applications, yet at the same time, it becomes a very useful method of abuse, particularly by underground networks and/or organized groups. As a result of their computing capabilities, computers increasingly allow for quantity and speed of coordinating criminal enterprise.

By strategic and deliberate planning, computers can be a major player in planning, organizing and directing criminal activity, regardless of whether it is committed by individuals or organized criminal enterprises. We can see an increased use of digital tools in organized crime, particularly in the preparation stage, observation stage, and during the commission or execution of their crimes. These computer tools are time and work consolidated useful tools, particularly in organized financial activities.

It has now become a common observation that the computer is the preferred method of planning, particularly in the criminal actors' space, because computer activity is more accurate and efficient while planning activities, making their crimes harder to catch or stop—especially when it comes to the underground financial systems and illegal banking. Computers allow for much more information to be processed rapidly and can enable crimes to be committed faster and without transparency or disclosure, all resulting in complications for the investigative and prosecutorial processes (Devi, 2017).

Some of the more common digitally enabled crimes include fictitious accounting records (double bookkeeping), illegal laundering of drug and other proceeds of crime, unauthorized banking and other related financial crimes. Despite being concealed behind elaborate digital operations, these financial offenders pose a serious threat to the economy and continue to demonstrate the critical need for reformed laws that address the "technological" misuse by organized crime. "The Internet and especially through its emails is providing a greater means to facilitate and support criminal organizations. In addition, the speed and secure communications that personal computers offer globally, is of particular importance to organized crime" (Salazar and Vargas, 2024).

4.4 Cyber Extortion and Cyber Espionage

Cyber extortion represents the convergence of criminal activity and computer technology. It is generally defined as a premeditated, politically motivated attack against computer-based information, systems, networks, or data, with the intent to commit acts of violence or disruption and is generally caused by international terrorist groups or agent provocateurs. Acts of cyber extortion can result in many horrible things including, but not limited to, death, injury, destruction of vital infrastructure, destruction of aircraft, contamination of drinking water, and disastrous economic consequences. Depending on the result of the cyber extortion, you may also classify the act as a cybercrime.

The digital domain is under perpetual threat. Cyber spies, hackers, and digital saboteurs are all using a combination of tactics and digital tools to attack secure systems to obtain sensitive information, personal or classified information, disrupt web service functionality, infect networks with unwanted malware, commit fraud, or participate in cyberbullying, and harass organizations or individuals. Cybercrime has become easier overall because many different "powerful" digital tools are at our disposal, and much of it can be directly used from many different sites and applications. Therefore, the likelihood of a cyberattack and the severity of the attack are also increasing.

One cyberattack was formally recognized in 1998 when Spanish protestors overwhelmed the Institute for Global Communication (IGC) by sending hundreds of bogus emails to the IGC. The emails were substantially intertwined and unclear to users' Internet Service Provider (ISPs), disrupting their normal communications so that it was nearly impossible for those recipients to find or use legitimate messages.

In that same year, a 12-year-old compromised the control systems of the Roosevelt Dam on the Salt River in Arizona. Had he enabled the floodgates, it may have caused extensive flooding and put nearly one million residents living downstream in jeopardy. The adversary has now demonstrated that even young people can use only a computer to launch a serious threat (Nyame et al., 2024).

For more than two decades, exceptionally proficient computer users have stunned the world by perpetrating cybercrimes that elicit admiration and fear. This duality has excited the entertainment industry to produce a nonstop string of media—books, movies, and television—exploring digital criminality with characters that, with only a keyboard, are a threat to the stability and safety of whole worlds.

Society is increasingly reliant on computer technology and has developed quickly. The digitization of the "work process" in all spheres of socioeconomic life today is both real and continuous. Global trade is increasingly aligned with developments in computer and internet technology.

As this industry continues to grow, there is a more intense awareness of abusing computers to commit various cybercrimes and cyberterrorism. There are many definitions of internet-based terrorism established from conducted research. The most general understanding of cyberterrorism relates to its etymology, originating from concepts in the computer domain and terrorism.

Cyberterrorism is an attack on the point of disruption between the physical or tangible world and the virtual world. Today, we acknowledge that the virtual and technological world and the world we live in share common tools. This trend has indeed created an avenue for the formation of many agencies and organizations that are dedicated to protection against cyberterrorism. Therefore, those were prime targets for cyberterrorist attacks.

The main reason is that they make it easier and cheaper to achieve the goal of destruction of a functioning system.

The FBI defines cyberterrorism as deliberate and politically or socially motivated attacks conducted by covert actors against computer systems, information infrastructures, software applications, military targets, and data. These attacks are intended to cause significant harm, potentially impacting national security and military operations. Unlike disruptive but limited cyber incidents, such as nuisance viruses, cyberterrorist actions are designed to produce substantial damage, including serious consequences for critical infrastructure and financial services.

The US Commission of Critical Infrastructure Protection lists the following areas as potential targets of cyberterrorism: banking industry, military bases, power plants, air traffic control centers, and water systems.

Cyberterrorism has also been defined as electronic terrorism or information warfare. Cyberterrorism essentially denotes the use of computer systems and the internet to plan and implement a terrorist attack. The reality is that individuals or groups can employ computer methods to target specific sources for a military attack or terrorist attack.

Cyberterrorism, or electronic crime, is any crime that involves a computer and computer network. Either the computer could be used to commit a crime, or the computer could be the target. Cyberterrorism is the criminal use of the internet.

These terrorist crimes can threaten a nation's health and financial security. This type of crime has risen to become a high-profile crime, particularly those relating to copyright infringement, child pornography, and human trafficking, leaving aside issues of privacy when confidentiality is lost or information is obtained illegally.

Cyberterrorism could be a real threat on par with nuclear, biological, and chemical weapons and is a crime that has not been fully explored. Detection and termination of this virtual form of terrorism is more difficult in that it has fewer physical traces being left than in the real world where evidence and traces are quite different.

Just as conventional terrorists employ explosives or small arms to achieve their objectives, cyberterrorists rely on technology, advanced information systems, computer networks, and illicit software tools to accomplish similar goals in the digital domain. These methods enable them to disrupt critical infrastructures, compromise sensitive information, and inflict significant economic, political, or security-related harm.

Many countries have already experienced episodic and severe threats from cyberterrorism, such as targeting certain aspects of the hat of a country and sponsored state actors. Whereas terrorism of the past had little opportunity to expand into a new era of theater associated with technology in terms of victimization, threatening acts, and reactive measures, terrorism today has entered into a new phase.

The most significant terrorist massacre ever recorded occurred on September 11, 2001, in the United States when 11 terrorists hijacked four passenger airliners, flying one into the Twin Towers of the World Trade Center in New York City, another into the Pentagon in Arlington, Virginia, and finally, one into a field in Shanksville, Pennsylvania, which was not the targeted objective (Güler and Demir, 2021).

The casualties, including those deceased who were passengers and crew members on the aircraft, as well as the victims who were killed in New York City and those at the Pentagon, totaled almost 3000 dead and many thousands injured. This unexpected act and its serious implications have created a whole new level of security challenges facing civilized countries.

In the next few years, there is a real fear that not only may events as disturbing as those of September 11 happen again, but that there will even be multiple actors (states, organizations, individuals) who are either loaded and/or willing to apply "super terrorism" phenomena using biological, chemical, or nuclear weapons. A prime example is Ramsi Youssef, who was responsible for the September 11, 2001 attacks, who obtained computer technology to receive his instructions and messages for organizing that event, who copied and decoded all the codes directly in notebooks.

With new technologies, terrorists may try to commit computer-based attacks against critical infrastructure systems and economic foundations. This is why you see that in a sectorial approach the international community has adopted a number of sectoral conventions against cyberterrorism for all countries to ratify. In scientific literature, two terms are often mentioned side by side "computer crime" and "cybercrime" (Shawe and McAndrew, 2023).

Are these two terms synonyms? The answer is no. Contrary to what has been said up until the present time, those two phrases do not define the same construct. Cybercrimes are crimes that are committed using computers and exist within a cyber culture. Cyberterrorism, as a legal penal phenomenon, has an international character, which can cohere to the international documents regarding international crime counts. In all the international projects and studies, there is a consistent trend indicating that cyberterrorism is increasing each year. The number of internet users continues to increase. The collection of internet communication technology is found everywhere across the world today, thanks to new technologies for mobile satellite communication devices, and can connect people from any point on the face of the earth. For this analogy, the internet is considered part of the infrastructure because it reaches at least 180 countries around the world (there are a total of 196 countries that are independent) (Grobbelaar, 2022).

With the introduction of new information technologies there has been a rise in new types of crimes associated with this, known as computer crime, cyber terror, direct and indirect means of illegal intrusion into networks and computer systems, data theft, illegal transfers, etc. According to Council of Europe experts, it is estimated that $400 million a year is being stolen through credit cards alone. Overall, viruses cost $12 billion in damage, with losses tied to intellectual property crimes averaging around $250 billion. All in all, the issues related to computer crime and cyber terror continue to hinder law enforcement from being effective in all nations and states.

Terrorist groups are actively recruiting new members in the virtual world of the internet, using email addresses. It has been noted by George Tenet the former CIA director, that terrorist organizations, including Hezbollah, Hamas, Abu Nidal, and the organization of Bin Laden known as "Al-Qaeda," are actively using computers for their operations. These regular and irregular threats to global stability create issues that require successful interventions at the national, regional, and international levels to effectively address terrorism in all its forms including progressive/new forms of terrorism such as cyberterrorism (Scanlon and Gerber, 2014).

In the event of a terrorist attack, threats to public safety and national security often arise from a variety of actors with differing motives and methods. In such contexts, technology—particularly computer-based systems—has become a powerful tool that enhances efficiency and enables perpetrators to achieve coordinated objectives. The virtual domain is increasingly integral to everyday life, as modern societies rely more heavily on technological and digital infrastructures.

While the benefits of computer technology in professional fields, commerce, and governance are substantial, its widespread use has also introduced new and unprecedented risks. Criminal activities conducted through computers and the internet now occur on a global scale, transcending traditional geographic boundaries. As a result, both governmental and non-governmental actors must cooperate internationally to mitigate and prevent cyberterrorism, counter espionage, combat financial theft, and address various forms of cross-border cybercrime.

Actions that deliberately undermine or violate a state's sovereignty and national interests through digital means are commonly referred to as cyber warfare. In response, the international legal system, including institutions such as the International Criminal Court, seeks to establish mechanisms to hold responsible actors accountable. Consequently, it is imperative to develop a clear and universally accepted definition of terrorism within international law. All international criminal treaties aimed at preventing, punishing, and prosecuting terrorist activities must therefore rely on precise and consistent legal definitions.

The international legal system is working through the International Criminal Court to hold actors accountable. It is imperative and a necessity to have a definition of terrorism in international law. Hence, all international criminal treaties intending to prevent, punish, and penalize terrorist activity need definitions that are precise.

The definition of a crime is an important aspect of international treaties and criminal law. First, and most important, it is symbolic and normative. The definition sends a message about society's disapproval of individuals who breach the prohibited act. Second, the definition creates a basis for international agreements. A definition of terrorism prevents a state from having to declare that they intend to take strict obligations in relation to domestic jurisdiction matters, and it defines the limits of those obligations, making them less costly when entering into agreements. Third, it provides a valid subjective basis for reciprocal legal duties in the courts. This will make international police cooperation easier. This is particularly important in extradition treaties, where nearly all legal systems expect the state requesting the extradition to punish terrorism (or other acts). This is also important in helping states adopt domestic laws to detect (or punish) terrorist acts defined in treaties and in accordance with human rights obligations. The principle of null crimen sine Lege (no crime without law) requires the states to define exactly what actions are prohibited before any defendant can be criminally prosecuted or punished for committing those acts in precisely the same way across all states. Ultimately, it is a moral responsibility of all states to harmonize their legislation to uniformly prevent and combat cyberterrorism (Baumer-Schuppli, 2020).

A successful legal framework to prevent or punish international terrorism cannot be predicated on a single state doing so. The international community has, likewise, adopted a sectoral policy to identify violations relevant to terrorist acts (and those acting completely outside of treaties) to categorize issues specific to both.

Overall, sectoral conventions deny the assertion that clearly defined acts of itself can constitute an international crime, notwithstanding any terrorist behavior or aims of the terrorist group. In effect, the key advantage of the sectoral conventions is that they do not define terrorism (while it includes cyberterrorist acts) because the acts are already so constituted through this type of convention. In this respect, it is simply not relevant to devise or define cyberterrorism as an act that is already defined in the sectoral convention.

A single uniform international definition and acceptance recognizably would only be required when relevant criminal acts are subject to the existence of perpetrating a specific terrorist aim; but that would unfairly target individuals. On the issue of cyberterrorism as a relevant threat, we can say it is a dangerous social phenomenon that is no longer imaginary but readily exists for both the international community and our state. The comprehensive transition toward the modernization of all available resources, together with the electronic management of technological processes, has created an environment conducive to the emergence of new forms of crime, including cyberterrorism. As societies increasingly integrate digital technologies into critical infrastructures, governance, and economic activities, opportunities for malicious exploitation have expanded accordingly. This transformation underscores the need for enhanced security measures, legal frameworks, and international cooperation to address the evolving nature of technologically driven criminal activity.

4.5 Computer Espionage

Computer espionage involves the identification of information or evidence. For instance, an industrial spy may want to find confidential information on the laptop of a project manager at Microsoft about the company's future by hacking into its operating systems. The information may vary, and ultimately become pieces of evidence, depending on it.

Besides information and evidence, there are two key components in computer espionage: the crime is generally unknown and unauthorized. The lack of consent is, in many instances, because the victim does not have actual or implied (think of a company employee) or any permission to allow a person to access their computer.

4.6 Specialized Warfare Against Modern Crime (Cybercrime)

In the beginning of 1992, hacker attacks on governments, large corporations, and businesses all over the world were becoming an exciting hobby. Cyber piracy today is a global issue with greatly alarming economic consequences. Cybercrime can no longer be considered an occasional or isolated phenomenon; it has evolved from a latent stage into a significant and persistent threat. Incidents of cyber theft, particularly involving bank accounts, credit cards, and other financial instruments, have created a favorable environment for criminal activity to flourish. Despite its growing prevalence and potential impact, cybercrime often receives insufficient attention from authorities, highlighting the need for enhanced awareness, preventive strategies, and robust institutional responses.

Modern computer networks permit new and more advanced forms of law-breakers. That is, we now have a different arena of opportunities requiring many entities of government and private distinguish how they're going to deal with law-breaking in a nontraditional way. The expansion and usage of the internet have not been met with adequate legal measures in place to provide a victim some protection from this crime. Therefore, both individuals and institutions, whether public or private, are increasingly vulnerable to cybercrime, and many remain inadequately protected against its diverse manifestations, even if some incidents are relatively infrequent. Cybercrime, including acts of piracy, often occurs anonymously, which significantly complicates investigative efforts by authorities, even when they possess the necessary expertise. Additionally, the cybercriminal (or hacker) and the victim may be located in different countries, which not only further complicates investigations but also raises complex legal challenges due to variations in national legislation and approaches to cybercrime. These factors collectively make the detection, prosecution, and prevention of such offenses particularly difficult (Amoo et al., 2024).

The intangible nature of computer crime and the high social risk it poses must be dealt with through political policies by amending laws. However, the law alone cannot resolve the issue. Complementary policies are required to deter and combat this type of crime, as new forms of computer crime continue to persist as a problem throughout society. For these reasons, every effort should be put forward to finalize or amend already existing legislation and establish law-penal regulations for certain computer abuses to be classified as criminal offenses.

A priority should be placed on establishing departments or ensuring appropriate departments are created to detect, investigate, and prosecute all forms of computer crime. The specialized section established in the Prosecutor's Office under the Economic Crime Directorate must necessarily include computer experts (Nikitina, 2017).

Further investment must be put into training and equipping officers or individuals dealing with the detection of these crimes, because these crimes are performed by highly skilled individuals who detect possible instances at a much quicker pace using their skills. Intensive monitoring should be focused on emails, interactive forums, chat rooms, instant messaging, etc. Finally, political policies that are effective in combating and preventing this type of crime should be emphasized! In the short term, these policies could help improve the efficiency of the legal changes made and greatly diminish the risk of cybercrime in Albania. While the current legal regime may be contemporary, comprehensive, and consistent with international benchmarks (albeit subject to improvement), the work now consists of implementing and defending it, with effective technological means and coercive control methods that can diminish computer-based criminal activity.

Given the extent of this phenomenon, an "action" construct at averting and combating this problem in contemporary society, certainly is not debatable. If the special section at the Prosecutor's Office cannot deal with this "onslaught of piracy," then we should focus on creating further functional and specialized sections for computer crime detection, investigation, and prosecution at the

Prosecutor's Office. One alternative response to this issue could be, as noted above, the creation of a new sector of the State Police force: the postal police (Kadir et al., 2024).

Here we could have an entity with special duties, functional and structural autonomy, which would operate in the area of telecommunication security and regulation, specializing in all inspection activities for illegal acts committed via the internet. Again we note that the laws and institutional changes made in Albanian criminal law will not deliver results if they are not accompanied by other measures of a social and cultural nature.

In relation to these crimes, there must be widespread comprehension of the tangible and effective risks and consequences that computer-based crime brings to every aspect of life, not just a mere economic aspect. It is always important to notify the relevant authorities, and this should be done in all cases. But we should stress awareness and education for constantly vigilant security measures, such as not placing cameras or scanners near ATMs (or micro-cameras on screens), same with other devices placed near ATM frames. We should give consideration and training for the security personnel, and they should notify the relevant authorities in every case. Attention should be given to ensure that people do not respond to email requests asking them to send their personal data.

At the same time, we need to encourage all individuals to inform the relevant authorities in case of computer misuse. Cybercrime is undeniably a crime of our times and should be treated accordingly in the fight against it—vigorously and with modern resources!

4.7 Protective Mechanisms against Cybercrime

There are protective mechanisms against accessing any form of computer crime, contained in both national and international legal documents. The Republic of Kosovo attends to the issues of cybercrime and intervention when needed. Protective mechanisms do exist, and a myriad of tools address, regulate, and sanction cybercrime issues, for example, in the Republic of Kosovo. The Republic of Kosovo has a comprehensive legal framework in the combat of crime which includes, but is not limited to:

- The Constitution of the Republic of Kosovo;
- The Penal Code of Kosovo;
- The Criminal Procedure Code of Kosovo;
- The Customs and Excise Code of Kosovo;
- The Law on the Police;
- The Law on the Execution of Penal Sanctions;
- The Law on the Public Prosecutor's Office;
- The Law on Prevention and Combating of Cyber Crime.

4.8 Financial Crime

Explanation of Financial Crime: Financial crime encompasses a range of unlawful behaviors, such as financial fraud, money laundering, financing illegal operations, and tax evasion. The ongoing ability for individuals to mask their identity and location during exchanges makes these unlawful behaviors especially hard to investigate and track. With ongoing questionable developments within investigative and judicial bodies, law enforcement intends to combat the increasingly more complicated styles of conducting financial crime.

4.9 Money Laundering

Money laundering is when an individual disguises the illegal source of money obtained through criminal activity (i.e., organized and/or corporate crime, drug trafficking, corruption, or fraud) and makes it appear to be derived and used legitimately. Money laundering is usually committed in a number of defined stages:

Placement: In the initial stage, funds from any illegal source are placed in the financial system. Typically, cash is placed into several bank accounts or used to buy goods of value to later sell. For example, a person who sold drugs might go to a casino to deposit money into a personal account, then make a few small bets, or claim a few small wins to create the impression of lawful gambling income.

Layering: Next, once placed, the money will be moved through transactions such as transfers between bank accounts and/or investments like property, stocks or luxury goods, all to cloud the transaction's origin. Building these layers creates a complicated trail to establish a money laundering scheme that is difficult to trace (Villányi, 2021).

Example: Profits from drug trafficking might be wired to the individual's accounts internationally, or they might buy high-end cars, apartments, and/or invest in financial instruments. These actions help the former drug dealer sever all alerts an investigator may have made to the original money source.

Integration: Finally, a money laundering scheme might involve taking the "cleaned" money and putting it back into the real economy. They could start their own legitimate business to present the money as if it has come from lawful income (Maguera, 2010).

Example: After many years of layered transfers and reinvestments, a person might decide to open a profitable restaurant or purchase real estate with the previously laundered money. These actions now provide a plausible explanation about the source of that money and include the legitimate use of the former criminal funds.

This example, while a basic illustration of money laundering schemes in practice, will be much more advanced and sophisticated. Money laundering is a serious crime with adverse implications for national economies as well as the global financial system. It involves hiding the source of illegal money to provide illegal financial activities with a false sense of legitimacy.

Money laundering is an unlawful enterprise designed to conceal money gained illegally. It is a focus of international regulation that employs various legal and institutional approaches to detect and reduce money laundering activity. Money laundering involving algorithms or technology is equally illegal as it undermines aspects of financial transparency and security, underlining organized crime as well.

Technology can be used in a positive way to combat financial crime. For instance, algorithms can be developed to alert financial institutions that can monitor financial transactions to analyze behavior and flag suspicious behavior. This is not an act of money laundering, as it aims to prevent money laundering from occurring.

These algorithms will use data analysis, model behaviors, and will most likely involve machine learning. More specifically they will leverage anomalies that are detected over time, signaling speculative behaviors of money laundering. The following is a conceptual diagram that outlines how an algorithm would work.

4.10 Algorithm for Detecting Suspicious Activity in Financial Transactions

(1) Data Collection

- Collect all transaction data, including the source and destination of funds, the amount of the transaction, date and time of the transaction, and geolocation data.
- Client-specific information, such as identity verification information, account history, and behavioral profiles, should also be collected.

(2) Classifying Financial Activity

- Different types of transactions can be classified, e.g., income that is legitimate, number of deposits that are large, and circumstances of unusual withdrawals.
- The expected behavioral patterns for each client can be established to mark out typical behavior and atypical behaviors for a client.

(3) Behavioral Analysis

- Algorithms use machine learning, which requires identifying usage behaviors for an individual client over time.
- To identify expected behaviors for each client, common statistical modeling techniques can be used to flag behaviors that stray too far away from what is considered normal behavior as possible anomalies.

(4) Detection of Suspicious Transactions

- Money laundering has identifiable characteristics or red flags that occur frequently. For example:
- High-value deposits that are inconsistent with a customer's financial behavior.
- Frequent movement of money between unrelated accounts with no clear rationale.
- Large sums are transferred in or out of jurisdictions known for favorable financial regulations, or where money laundering may take place.

- Use predictive algorithms developed toward historical transactions to provide as much information as possible about what transactions look like if illicit activity is taking place.

(5) Reporting and Escalation

- Suspicious patterns are automatically reported to financial intelligence units, or regulation and compliance teams, who may review them in accordance with regulation.
- Algorithms must be integrated into larger risk management systems to be able to intervene or identify risks related to financial crime.

(6) Continuous Learning and Calibration

- Adaptive learning mechanisms are used to improve algorithms as transactions come in, potentially even improving algorithm sophistication in response to data.
- Algorithms must be continuously calibrated to perform with current regimes and money laundering techniques.

This model serves as a conceptual framework for detecting and preventing money laundering using data analytics and machine learning. However, indicating a very simplistic model, it illustrates the possibilities that more robust technologies can achieve to strengthen financial oversight and compliance (Labanca et al., 2022).

4.11 Financial Fraud

Financial fraud refers to an illegal or unethical act designed to obtain value through misleading or dishonest means related to financial information. Financial fraud can take many forms, such as defrauding someone like an investor or creating and signing fake financial statements. The following is a basic example of financial fraud:

Example: Investment Fraud (Ponzi Scheme)

One of the more common and recognizable types of investment fraud is what is called a Ponzi scheme, where a fraudster promises a high and fast return on investor capital. The fraudster always uses the initial capital of the new investor to pay returns to the older investor, and thus creating the appearance of large sums of profits. It continues until the scheme collapses because new investor capital has slowed down to none, at which point the fraudster can't pay any returns at all, eventually leading to no returns and the start of an investigation.

How a Ponzi Scheme Works:

- Promotion of an Investment Opportunity: A person or company promotes an investment opportunity and tells the investor they will get an outlandish amount of returns, such as 20% per month. They tell the investors they will invest their actual capital in something profitable and successful, such as stocks, real estate or emerging technologies.

- Get the initial money and provide returns: The "first investors" deposit their money and, from the start, they are already earning record returns. They are also building the investors' belief that they are profiting from the enterprise.
- Paying Old Investors with New Money: The money from the new investors will be used to pay returns to the first investors. This convinces the participants that their investment is a good investment, and either makes them invest more or refers the scheme to others.
- Collapse of the Scheme: Eventually, there are not enough new investors to pay the returns to the individuals at the end of the chain who do not get new and/or earthy capitalists (invested hierarchically) to pay the returns. At the point where the payment of the returns relies solely on the new investor's funds, that is usually when the scheme collapses. At this point, there are likely to be a lot of investors who will lose their committed capital (Constantino et al., 2014).

Famous Example

One of the largest and most famous acts of financial fraud is the case of Bernie Madoff. For decades, Madoff orchestrated an enormous Ponzi scheme disguised as a legitimate operation that promised typically high returns. Madoff used deception and new investor funds to pay earlier investors until ultimately, in 2008, the scheme was uncovered, and Madoff was arrested. The total amount lost was over $65 billion.

4.12 Financial Fraud Example and Algorithms for Detecting Financial Crime

This case is a simple and not unusual one, but in certain cases, financial fraud can be far more complex and sophisticated. The consequences of financial fraud can have serious impacts on people and the economy.

Detecting financial crime requires algorithms sift through massive datasets, identify anomalies in trending patterns, and foresee possible criminal activity in possible bubbles. There are algorithms that can fulfill this role:

(1) Computers with Artificial Intelligence and Machine Learning Algorithms

- Supervised Learning: In categories such as Random Forests and Support Vector Machines (SVM), these algorithms have the capacity to classify a transaction as either suspicious or legitimate from a collection of previously labeled and known data. These algorithms are trained using transaction data and learn the patterns that identify a transaction as criminal in nature.
- Unsupervised Learning: Unsupervised learning algorithms, such as k-means clustering and DBSCAN, are powerful tools for detecting potentially anomalous or criminal patterns within large datasets. Unlike supervised learning, these algorithms do not rely on pre-labeled data; instead, they analyze the inherent structure of the data to identify hidden patterns,

clusters, and outliers. By detecting unusual groupings of transactions or behaviors, unsupervised learning can assist in the early identification of fraudulent activity, money laundering, or other illicit financial operations, providing valuable support for investigators and financial institutions in mitigating cybercrime risks.

- Deep Learning Algorithms: Deep learning algorithms are a subset of classification algorithms that can be used to identify very complicated patterns in large datasets. These models can reveal patterns that a conventional algorithm is not able to identify because it cannot distinguish minor and complex indicators of criminal activity (Babatope, 2024).

(2) Network Analysis Algorithms

- Criminal financial activity often occurs in entangled networks and connections between people and entities. There are certain network analysis algorithms, such as centrality analysis and link analysis, that can find suspicious groupings of business transactions, which may involve money laundering, fraud, or financing criminal activities. Network analysis can analyze how these entities are connected and how information flows through these connections. It can also find hidden links that are implicated in criminal activity.

(3) Anomaly Detection Algorithms

- Statistical-Based Anomaly Detection: Anomaly detection, a statistical-based approach to traditional algorithms, the information panel can include k-means clustering or Isolation Forests that identify transactions that differ from normal financial data patterns. The identified outliers implicitly weave the thread of an ongoing investigation into a possible fraudulent or criminal act.1. Algorithms for Time Series Anomaly Detection.

Time series algorithms such as Autoregressive Integrated Moving Average (ARIMA) can be used to analyze and forecast transaction levels over specified periods of time. When viewed together, the algorithms can notice anomalies in levels of financial data that may represent events of illegality, such as large unexplained payments or pattern changes (Moschini et al., 2021).

(4) Algorithms for Patterns in behavior detection

- Algorithms used to pattern a user's behavior will assist in identifying suspicious behaviors that can be identified as anomalies in the way a user acts. For instance, when the user is observed to have a history of transactions and suddenly the types of transactions vary greatly, then the records from the algorithm can indicate that potential criminal activity may now be afoot. Utilizing a user's behavior allows algorithms to discern changes not yet apparent to patrolling applicants.

Each algorithm has pros and cons; however, using a combination of these methods will lead to providing the most accurate and rapid detection of financial crime. The best algorithm depends on the type of financial data we are using and the nature of the financial offense.

4.13 Hiding Identity

The act of hiding one's identity is a method of anonymity or maintaining confidentiality. Every method of identity concealment typically involves some form of arbitrary method. Here is an example of identity concealment.

Example 1:

Imagine an individual who is knowledgeable and researching a public interest incident to report for media purposes but is unwilling to have their identity disclosed for safety or personal concerns. They would use a pseudonym and hide all identifiers that could lead to their identity.

For example:

- The name labeled in the article may read "Person X" or "Anonymous Source."
- Unless visual evidence is required, they could blur or obfuscate identifying images.
- They could hide identifying location indicators or references to personal information.

Example 2:

A person applies for a job and creates a separate email account to establish a new username to have the opportunity to "conceal or yield" where they may get identified as the relying candidate.

In The Realm of Identity Protection:

The algorithms that are best considered for use in data protection and cybersecurity technologies are often those designed to protect and hide data that can be manipulated and misused.

The identity protecting algorithms will have a variety of authentication and encryption techniques to ensure proper security of personal data and to mitigate attacks and misuse. Responsible algorithms designed for identity protection purposes may contain the following:

(1) Data Encryption

Encryption is one way to hide data and keep it secret from those who do not have the right to see it. The most popular encryption algorithms for identity protection are:

- AES (Advanced Encryption Standard): A very strong and well-understood symmetric encryption algorithm, commonly used for storage and protecting sensitive information.

- RSA (Rivest–Shamir–Adleman): An asymmetric encryption algorithm frequently used for key exchange as part of data encryption.
- ECC (Elliptic Curve Cryptography): Another asymmetric encryption algorithm that provides strong security with shorter keys (Abood and Guirguis, 2018).

(2) Authentication and Access Control
Authentication, the process of determining the identity of users in order to provide access only to authorized users, is another important approach to identity protection. Examples of algorithms used to authenticate users include:

- SHA (Secure Hash Algorithm): Algorithms that take data and create a hashed value of that data that cannot be reverse-engineered to the original data. These are often used to verify data integrity or a user.
- Two-Factor Authentication (2FA): A specific method for authenticating users by requiring two forms of identification and confirmation of a user's identity, such as a code sent via SMS and a password.

(3) Identity Hiding Algorithms
The algorithms designed to hide identity are also important for protecting personal data. These algorithms include:

- Anonymizing Algorithms (e.g., Tor): Conceal the location and activity of users, allowing them to access and browse the web anonymously through network algorithms.
- Mixnet: Involves mixing information sent by different users to maintain anonymity.

(4) Fraud Detection and Prevention Algorithms
Many systems utilize fraud detection algorithms to identify suspicious activity and fraud prevention algorithms to deter fraud in order to protect identity, including:

- Machine Learning and Artificial Intelligence Algorithms: These algorithms can be applied to assess different behaviors of users and help identify suspicious or unusual behaviors that may indicate fraudulent use of identity (Engelmann and Jukan, 2019).

The most effective algorithms for identity protection will be those that utilize strong encryption, secure authentication methods, including anonymity, and detection of suspicious activity.

4.14 Prevention of Financial Crime

Preventing financial crime is challenging and entails an array of policies, laws, oversight, and international cooperation. Here are some key measures that can be taken to prevent financial crime:

(1) Development and Assistance of Laws and Regulations

- Establishment of significant laws related to money laundering, corruption, and tax evasion is vital.
- Legislation that enforces secrecy on the ownership of assets by sanctioning suspicious reporting and monitoring suspicious transactions.

(2) Enhance Oversight and Monitoring of Financial Institutions

- Expand oversight by taxing authorities and financial institutions to ensure that banks and other companies are acting legally and avoiding suspicious behaviors.
- Enhance IT capabilities to monitor and recognize suspicious transactions.

(3) Train and Support Finance Professionals and Authorities

- Integrate further training of bankers, auditors, and prosecutors to recognize and identify the indications of potential financial crimes (Odeyemi et al., 2024).
- Improve and develop law enforcement and judicial authorities to investigate and prosecute financial crimes.

(4) International Support and Cooperation

- International efforts are important because financial crimes frequently take place across borders and often involve transfers of funds across borders. This reflects the movement of information and harmonization of laws.
- Contributing to international organizations, such as FATF, in an effort to promote international standards/regulations for the prevention of financial crime.

(5) Use of Technology and Artificial Intelligence

- Advanced data analytics systems in conjunction with artificial intelligence can be used to detect and prevent suspicious financial activities
- Enhanced cybersecurity measures can prevent online fraud and theft of financial activities.

(6) Supporting the Private Sector and Transparency

- Working to engage businesses and the private sector in promoting transparency in financial dealings and in a way, they are obliged to report suspicious activities
- Advocating for ethically responsible businesses, including clear directives on how to administer assets and investments (Adaga et al., 2024).

(7) Public Awareness

- To educate citizens about the implications of financial crime and the benefits of acting legally and ethically.
- Empowering the public with respect to the basic consumer principles of financial literacy and educating them about the risks of fraud and money laundering schemes.

If we truly come together and support one another efficiently, and if we do not disengage from taking actions in the prevention of financial crime, this concern will improve. Unfortunately, this will also require a continued cooperative effort from domestic and international, government and private sector institutions, along with citizens, if we want to engage in action.

4.15 Ban on Cryptocurrencies

An outright ban on cryptocurrency is a multilayered consideration with multiple factors that can inhibit the progression and use of cryptocurrency that need to be assessed. Cryptocurrency is decentralized and relies on blockchain technology, making transactions secure. This unique process can make it difficult for government enforcement to curtail and regulate certain actions.

However, the use of cryptocurrency, when abused for illegal purposes such as money laundering, financing criminal activity, tax evasion, etc., can be curtailed in certain ways. There are several actions that can be taken to prevent the misuse of cryptocurrency for illegal activities. Here are some:

(1) Regulation and Legislation

- National and International Legislation: Governments could pass legislation related to the use of cryptocurrencies. Governments could mandate that exchanges establish Know Your Customer (KYC) protocols, which would enhance audit trails and establish responsibilities to report transactions recognized as suspicious (AML).
- Regulate the activities of cryptocurrency service providers: As stated, there would be obligations on cryptocurrency service providers, including exchanges and digital wallets, which create expectations of compliance for relevant security measures in addition to measures to prevent illegal activity.

(2) Blocking cryptocurrency exchange platforms

- Countries may block platforms that offer cryptocurrency exchange services, or at worst restrict the use of cryptocurrencies for payments of goods and services, creating a barrier to access that specific market.

(3) Use of technology and data analysis

- Suspicious transaction identification: Many analytical tools exist that can provide monitoring mechanisms to detect suspicious cryptocurrency transactions in an attempt to prevent illegal activity. Certain companies could build software to help track cryptocurrency flows.
- Blockchain forensic services: Some companies use advanced technologies such as blockchain forensic services to analyze cryptocurrency transactions and identify risks of violating various statutes (Japinye, 2024).
- There have been attempts to prohibit currency-related payments in certain countries. Some countries may prohibit businesses and individuals from accepting cryptocurrencies as payment, creating barriers to their use.

(4) Education and Awareness

- Increasing knowledge of cryptocurrency-related risks: Providing users and businesses with education on potential risks and avenues for abusive practices can help limit the demand for its use in illegal activities.

It is necessary to remind the reader that while there are several steps that may prevent harm caused by cryptocurrencies, there may not be a complete block on their use. Particularly, cryptocurrency uses fiddles with decentralized and sophisticated technology that can be bypassed by other decentralized technology.

4.15.1 Algorithmic Applications of Deceptive Cryptocurrencies

Cryptocurrencies employ complex security and consensus algorithms to preserve their integrity, privacy, and functionality on their networks. The algorithms employed can be categorized into encryption algorithms (cryptography), proof-of-work algorithms, proof-of-stake algorithms, and communication algorithms:

(1) Encryption Algorithms (Cryptography): Cryptocurrencies employ cryptography to encode and lock transactions while maintaining data integrity and user privacy.

- Principal encryption algorithms:
- SHA-256 (Secure Hash Algorithm—256 bit): This algorithm is used by Bitcoin and many cryptocurrencies creating a hash and maintaining the function of the blockchain. This algorithm is classified as a one-way algorithm because it is easy to process input to hash but practically impossible to recover the input from the hash.
- Elliptic Curve Digital Signature Algorithm (ECDSA): This is used to create, sign and verify digital signatures by Bitcoin and other cryptocurrencies. The security provided by the ECDSA provides a way to assure that the user is the creator of the transaction, and it uses a private key.
- Ed25519: This is a faster and more secure digital signature algorithm used in alternative cryptocurrencies such as Monero, Stellar, and others (Sghaier et al, 2017).

(2) Consensus Algorithms: Consensus algorithms arrive at a collective agreement on the current state of a cryptocurrency network and for the transaction validation process. Two known consensus algorithms are:

- Proof of Work (PoW): This is the type of protocol used by Bitcoin and many other cryptocurrencies. Users, or miners, must solve complicated math problems to create a new "block" in the blockchain. The mining process uses a huge amount of energy and computer resources to find the solutions required to create the "block." Miners are rewarded with coins based on the work they have performed to verify transaction data.

- Proof of Stake (PoS): Many cryptocurrencies utilize PoS, including Ethereum, whose approach has recently changed with the rollout of Ethereum 2.0. PoS is a much more energy-efficient approach than mining. Users do not use energy to authorize a proven transaction; they "stake" the coins that they own (tokens), and transaction verification occurs based on the number of users with a specific amount of stake (or capital). PoS is more operationally sustainable, timely, etc.
- Delegated Proof of Stake (DPoS): It is an approach used by EOS and some other cryptocurrencies. Users have a vote and elect delegates to verify transactions and create new blocks on the blockchain. DPoS builds on PoS to address network speeds and performance (Buterin and Griffith, 2017).

(3) Privacy Algorithms
There are some cryptocurrencies with algorithms in the code to preserve the privacy of users and obscure any and all transaction information. For example:

- Ring Signatures: Monero is one of the more familiar privacy cryptocurrencies that use Ring Signatures to obscure the sender. Using Ring Signatures obscures a user's identity in a way that it is not possible to know which user started the transaction.
- Zero-Knowledge Proofs (ZKPs): They are used by cryptocurrencies like Zcash to allow for transactions that, at face value, appear to protect the privacy of the sender, receiver, or transaction amount. Zero-Knowledge Proofs allow for the verification of a transaction without violating security by disclosing sensitive information.

(4) Other Consensus Algorithms

- Proof of Authority (PoA): This is a consensus algorithm being used (arguably) by some cryptocurrencies. This algorithm only recognizes a limited number of trusted parties to verify transactions. It has some benefits in speed but it may be problematic by limiting the number of decentralized participants in the verification process.
- Byzantine Fault Tolerance (BFT): This algorithm can provide consensus in a decentralized setting even when some parties may not be trusted. Examples of this algorithm that have ensured consensus include Practical Byzantine Fault Tolerance, which has been adopted and implemented by some cryptocurrencies and other systems (Nijsse and Litchfield, 2020).

5. Analysis

Cryptocurrencies use various algorithms to secure and validate transactions, as well as privacy and consensus mechanisms that may be employed. Essentially the algorithms and applications utilized by cryptocurrencies matter whether carried out in a secure transaction on a blockchain or successfully carrying out a consensus algorithm, considering the different levels of security, performance, and energy efficiency.

6. Conclusion

The rapid and continuous evolution of technology has increasingly been exploited as a tool to facilitate criminal activity and cybercrime. This trend underscores the urgent need for heightened attention from policymakers, law enforcement, and the broader public. Effective responses require not only media awareness campaigns but also the development and prioritization of policies that support the adoption of appropriate regulations and their rigorous implementation. Moreover, significant investment in both legal frameworks and technological prevention measures is essential to deter cybercriminal behavior and mitigate its impact.

Current evidence and observed trends indicate that cybercrime is poised to become a central component of organized crime globally. Addressing this challenge necessitates a coordinated and multifaceted approach, including the enhancement of financial intelligence capabilities, human intelligence, and legal coordination at national, regional, and international levels. In addition, high-level cooperation among law enforcement agencies and relevant organizations through global networks is critical to effectively combat cybercrime and its associated threats.

Cryptocurrencies are both a tremendous potential opportunity in terms of advancement around financial crime and a significant threat to preventing and combating financial crime. While cryptocurrencies have the potential to disrupt global finance, any potential for disruption is countered by the indication that criminals will utilize cryptocurrency platforms to evade preventive security measures and use the anonymity offered by some of the cryptocurrencies globally. Immediate and purposeful promotive regulation, cooperation with industry, and enforcement, as well as technological advancements in security of cryptocurrencies must be carried out to address the risk of financial crime. The international community should focus on appropriately implementing a balance between innovation and economic security and exploit the benefits of cryptocurrencies while avoiding the opportunities for organized criminals to completely disregard security measures in achieving their objectives.

References

Abood, O. G., & Guirguis, S. K. (2018). A survey on cryptography algorithms. *International Journal of Scientific and Research Publications (IJSRP)*, *8*(7). https://doi.org/10.29322/ijsrp.8.7.2018.p7978

Adaga, E. M., Egieya, Z. E., Ewuga, S. K., Abdul, A. A., & Abrahams, T. O. (2024). A comprehensive review of ethical practices in banking and finance. *Finance & Accounting Research Journal*, *6*(1), 1–20. https://doi.org/10.51594/farj.v6i1.705

Amoo, O. O., Atadoga, A., Abrahams, T. O., Farayola, O. A., Osasona, F., & Ayinla, B. S. (2024). The legal landscape of cybercrime: A review of contemporary issues in the criminal justice system. *World Journal of Advanced Research and Reviews*, *21*(2), 205–217. https://doi.org/10.30574/wjarr.2024.21.2.0438

Babatope, A. (2024). *Machine learning for advanced fraud detection and content moderation*. https://doi.org/10.20944/preprints202411.0352.v1

Baumer-Schuppli, F. (2020). The proliferation of definitions of terrorism in international law. Contemporary challenges: The global crime. *Justice and Security Journal*, *1*, 23–42. https://doi.org/10.2218/ccj.v1.4941

Bilan, B. (2023). Cryptocurrency and financial crime: Emerging risks and regulatory challenges. *Journal of Financial Crime*, *30*(2), 345–360.

Buçaj, E., & Idrizaj, K. (2024). The need for cybercrime regulation on a global scale by the international law and cyber convention. *Multidisciplinary Reviews*, *8*(1), 2025024. https://doi.org/10.31893/multirev.2025024

Buterin, V., & Griffith, V. (2017). *Casper the friendly finality gadget*. https://doi.org/10.48550/arxiv.1710.09437

Cartin-Pecson, R., Karsono, B., Sulastri, L., Rony, Z. T., & Chavez, C. B. (2025). Defending the digital domain: A critical look at cybercrime legislation in Indonesia and the Philippines. *Academic Journal of Interdisciplinary Studies*, *14*(2), 198. https://doi.org/10.36941/ajis-2025-0040

Chainalysis. (2022). *Blockchain forensics in combating crime*. Chainalysis. Online. Available: The Chainalysis 2026 Crypto Crime Report. https://www.chainalysis.com/reports/crypto-crime-2026/

CipherTrace. (2021). *Cryptocurrency crime and anti-money laundering report*. CipherTrace.

Constantino, T. d. S. T., Silva, A. C. M. d., & Constantino, M. A. M. D. O. (2024). Ponzi schemes in Brazil: What leads people to still invest in this fraud?. *Journal of Financial Crime*, *31*(6), 1436–1450. https://doi.org/10.1108/jfc-10-2023-0262

Coveware. (2021). *Ransomware payments in cryptocurrency*. \n United Nations Office on Drugs and Crime (UNODC) (2020). Cryptocurrency and Terrorist.

Devi, A. (2017). Cybercrime and cyber security. *Detecting and Mitigating Robotic Cyber Security Risks*, 160–171. https://doi.org/10.4018/978-1-5225-8446-9.ch011

Dodiya, K. R., Varayogula, S. N., & Gohil, B. (2024). Rising threats, silent battles. In *Cases on forensic and criminological science for criminal detection and avoidance* (pp. 123–150). https://doi.org/10.4018/978-1-6684-9800-2.ch006

Engelmann, A., & Jukan, A. (2019). Defying censorship with multi-circuit tor and linear network coding. In *2019 12th CMI conference on cybersecurity and privacy (CMI)* (pp. 1–6). https://doi.org/10.1109/cmi48017.2019.8962147

Europol. (2020). *Internet organised crime threat assessment (IOCTA)*.

Europol. (2021). *Partnerships against cryptocurrency-enabled crime*.

FATF. (2019). *Updated guidance on digital assets*.

FATF. (2020). *The travel rule in cryptocurrency transactions*.

FATF. (2021). *Anti-money laundering measures in the cryptocurrency industry*.

Federal Trade Commission (FTC). (2021). *Consumer protection in cryptocurrency*.

Goce, A. N. R. (2024). Model investasi cryptocurrency dalam upaya pencegahan tindak pidana pencucian uang. *Mahkamah: Jurnal Riset Ilmu Hukum*, *1*(4), 181–192. https://doi.org/10.62383/mahkamah.v1i4.208

Grobbelaar, A. (2022). Cyberterrorism in Africa – Exaggerated threat or worthy foe?. *Freska*, *1*(1). https://doi.org/10.7251/znubl2201257g

Güler, A., & Demir, M. (2021). A comparison of global suicide terrorism by region before and after 9/11 terrorist attacks. *Journal of Aggression, Conflict and Peace Research*, *13*(4), 214–225. https://doi.org/10.1108/jacpr-06-2021-0604

International Monetary Fund (IMF). (2021). *Global financial stability report: Pre-empting a legacy of vulnerabilities*. IMF.

INTERPOL. (2020). *Global financial crime: Cryptocurrency and money laundering trends*. INTERPOL Global Complex for Innovation.

Ishmaev, G. (2017). Blockchain technology as an institution of property. *Metaphilosophy*, *48*(5), 666–686. https://doi.org/10.1111/meta.12277

Japinye, A. O. (2024). Integrating machine learning in anti-money laundering through crypto: A comprehensive performance review. *European Journal of Accounting, Auditing and Finance Research*, *12*(4), 54–80. https://doi.org/10.37745/ejaafr.2013/vol12n45480

Kadir, P. R. N., Darwis, D., & Nugraha, I. F. (2024). Tinjauan hukum internasional dalam menangani kasus piracy jure gentium berdasarkan yurisdiksi universal. *Konsensus: Jurnal Ilmu Pertahanan, Hukum Dan Ilmu Komunikasi*, *1*(6), 103–117. https://doi.org/10.62383/konsensus.v1i6.462

Labanca, D., Primerano, L., Markland-Montgomery, M., Polino, M., Carminati, M., & Zanero, S. (2022). Amaretto: An active learning framework for money laundering detection. *IEEE Access*, *10*, 41720–41739. https://doi.org/10.1109/access.2022.3167699

MIT Technology Review. (2021). *How cryptocurrency is reshaping illicit finance*. MIT Technology Review Insights.

Moschini, G., Houssou, R., Bovay, J., & Robert, S. (2021). Anomaly and fraud detection in credit card transactions using the arima model. In *The 7th international conference on time series and forecasting* (Vol. 56). https://doi.org/10.3390/engproc2021005056

Nakamoto, S. (2008). *Bitcoin: A peer-to-peer electronic cash system.*\n Europol (2020). Internet Organised Crime Threat Assessment (IOCTA).\n Financial.

Nijsse, J., & Litchfield, A. (2020). A taxonomy of blockchain consensus methods. *Cryptography*, *4*(4), 32. https://doi.org/10.3390/cryptography4040032

Nikitina, I. (2017). Current issues in justice and home affairs cooperation between Eu member states pertaining to forensic services and investigative operations. *Theory and Practice of Forensic Science*, *12*(3), 110–118. https://doi.org/10.30764/1819-2785-2017-12-3-110-118

Nyame, L., Marfo-Ahenkorah, E., Abrahams, A., Ashley-Osuzoka, J., Ashong, G., & Aboagye, D. (2024). *Rise in cyber threats in the United States and the need for advanced cyber risk mitigation tools and adequate skills to combat cyber threats.* https://doi.org/10.20944/preprints202409.1813.v1

Odeyemi, O., Okoye, C. C., Ofodile, O. C., Adeoye, O. B., Addy, W. A., & Ajayi-Nifise, A. O. (2024). Integrating ai with blockchain for enhanced financial services security. *Finance & Accounting Research Journal*, *6*(3), 271–287. https://doi.org/10.51594/farj.v6i3.855

OECD. (2020). *Public awareness campaigns for cryptocurrency risks.*

Salazar, J., & Vargas, M. J. S. (2024). Money laundering in the age of cybercrime and emerging technologies. *Corruption, Bribery, and Money Laundering - Global Issues*. https://doi.org/10.5772/intechopen.1004006

Scanlon, J. R., & Gerber, M. S. (2014). Automatic detection of cyber-recruitment by violent extremists. *Security Informatics*, *3*(1). https://doi.org/10.1186/s13388-014-0005-5

Sghaier, A., Zeghid, M., Massoud, C., & Mahchout, M. (2017). Design and implementation of low area/power elliptic curve digital signature hardware core. *Electronics*, *6*(2), 46. https://doi.org/10.3390/electronics6020046

Shawe, R., & McAndrew, I. (2023). Domestic cyberterrorism & strategic communications: Literature review. *Journal of Information Security*, *14*(4), Article 4027. https://doi.org/10.4236/jis.2023.144027

Shojaeinasab, A., Motamed, A. P., & Bahrak, B. (2023). Machine learning approaches for detecting illicit cryptocurrency transactions. *IEEE Access*, *11*, 1–15.

US Treasury Department. (2021). *National strategy for combating terrorism and other illicit financing*. U.S. Department of the Treasury.

United Nations. (2021). *Cryptocurrencies and money laundering: A threat to global financial stability*. United Nations Office on Drugs and Crime (UNODC).

Villányi, B. (2021). *Money laundering: History, regulations, and techniques*. Oxford Research Encyclopedia of Criminology and Criminal Justice. https://doi.org/10.1093/acrefore/9780190264079.013.708

World Economic Forum (WEF). (2020). *Blockchain's role in financial crime prevention*.

Chapter 9

Cryptocurrency and Financial Crime: Opportunities and Challenges for Regulation

Ish Kumar and Vinay Maitri

School of Planning and Architecture, India

Abstract

The rapid growth of cryptocurrencies has redefined the global financial landscape, enabling decentralized and borderless transactions. While digital assets offer efficiency, innovation, and financial inclusion, they have also introduced new avenues for financial crime. This chapter critically examines the intersection of cryptocurrency and illicit financial activity, with a focus on typologies such as money laundering, terrorist financing, ransomware payments, investment fraud, and tax evasion. Through an analysis of real-world cases and peer-reviewed research, this chapter highlights how features such as pseudonymity, decentralized finance, and privacy-enhancing technologies have complicated regulatory enforcement and forensic tracking. This chapter also provides a comparative overview of global regulatory responses, including frameworks from the United States, European Union, Singapore, India, and China, as well as guidance from international institutions such as the Financial Action Task Force and the Organization for Economic Co-operation and Development. Key challenges such as legal ambiguity, technological complexity, and institutional fragmentation are explored in depth. In response, this chapter identifies emerging opportunities to strengthen oversight, including blockchain analytics, regulatory sandboxes, supervisory colleges, and capacity-building initiatives. It concludes by recommending a coordinated, adaptive, and risk-based regulatory approach that balances innovation with accountability.

Keywords: Cryptocurrency regulation; financial crime; money laundering; blockchain governance; regulatory compliance

Corruption and Crime in Finance, 187–206

doi:10.1108/978-1-83708-170-720261024

1. Introduction

The proliferation of cryptocurrencies has emerged as a transformative development in the global financial landscape. Since the launch of Bitcoin in 2009, the cryptocurrency market has expanded exponentially, with over 25,000 unique digital assets in circulation and a combined market capitalization exceeding 2.2 trillion USD as of early 2024 (Naqbi et al., 2025a, 2025b). Cryptocurrencies offer distinct advantages over traditional financial instruments, such as decentralization, reduced transaction costs, and increased transactional speed. However, these features also create vulnerabilities that are actively exploited by individuals and networks engaged in financial crime.

The necessity to combat financial crime in the situation with cryptocurrency is explained by the fact that it becomes a normal part of economic systems. Cryptocurrencies allow anonymization or pseudonymization, which makes them friendly to the laundering of illicit earnings, terrorism funding, avoiding sanctions, and planning ransomware attacks. It is predicted that in 2022, the volume of illegal cryptocurrency operations was estimated at 20.6 billion USD (Adewuyi, 2025; Saha et al., 2024), which, in terms of absolute numbers, represented a record level of crime, but with a decrease in its relative share in the total size of transactions.

One of the most pressing issues is the regulatory vacuum that surrounds the use of digital currencies. While countries such as the United States, Singapore, and the European Union (EU) have instituted legal frameworks targeting crypto-related financial crime, many other jurisdictions lack comprehensive legislation. This regulatory fragmentation allows criminals to exploit cross-border loopholes and avoid detection. Moreover, privacy-enhancing tools such as mixers, tumblers, and privacy-focused coins like Monero and Zcash further complicate forensic investigations. These innovations, though sometimes designed to protect user privacy, are frequently repurposed for illegal activities.

Another concern is the role of unregulated or poorly regulated crypto exchanges, which act as gateways between fiat and digital assets. Weak Know Your Customer (KYC) procedures and the absence of real-time monitoring allow these platforms to become conduits for illicit financial flows. The rise of decentralized finance (DeFi, which refers to blockchain-based financial services operating without centralized intermediaries), which eliminates intermediaries altogether, has intensified these risks. Smart contracts, autonomous protocols, and anonymous token swaps have challenged the very foundation of regulatory oversight, calling for more adaptive and technologically informed policy responses.

This chapter aims to investigate the intersection between cryptocurrency and financial crime by addressing the following core questions: How are cryptocurrencies used to perpetrate financial crimes? What are the existing global regulatory frameworks, and where are the major gaps? What challenges do regulators and law enforcement agencies face? And what opportunities exist to improve oversight without undermining innovation?

To answer these questions, this chapter is organized into seven sections. Following this introduction, Section 2 traces the evolution of cryptocurrencies and their adoption across sectors. Section 3 explores typologies of financial crime enabled by digital assets. Section 4 evaluates global regulatory responses and institutional frameworks. Section 5 highlights the key challenges in regulating cryptocurrencies. Section 6 identifies technological and institutional opportunities for strengthening oversight. Finally, Section 7 concludes with policy recommendations aimed at reconciling innovation with systemic security.

2. Evolution of Cryptocurrency and Its Adoption

This section provides a structured overview of the evolution and global adoption of cryptocurrencies. The second subsection 2.1 defines the technology and ideological background of the early digital currencies, especially the genesis of blockchain and Bitcoin. In subsection 2.2, the cryptocurrency market diversification is discussed, including the appearance of the altcoins, stablecoins, and smart contract platforms. In 2.3, there is a consideration of the global adoption trends including the discrepancy among the regions and the motivators including financial exclusion and investment through institutions. Subsection 2.4 addresses technological advancements that have contributed to both innovation and risk, including the rise of DeFi and privacy tools. Finally, Subsection 2.5 underscores the regulatory urgency stemming from the rapid evolution and cross-border nature of cryptocurrency systems.

2.1 The Origins and Technological Foundations

The launch of Bitcoin in 2009 marked a watershed moment in financial innovation. Introduced through a white paper by the pseudonymous Satoshi Nakamoto, Bitcoin presented a decentralized, peer-to-peer payment system based on blockchain technology. Unlike conventional fiat currencies controlled by central banks, Bitcoin relied on a distributed ledger verified by network consensus. This eliminated the need for a trusted third party and enabled secure, tamper-resistant transactions (Adewuyi, 2025; Ibikunle et al., 2025a).

The development of Bitcoin was followed by a wave of alternative cryptocurrencies, known as altcoins, which sought to improve on scalability, privacy, and programmability. A significant turning point was the launch of Ethereum in 2015, which introduced smart contracts, self-executing code that allows decentralized applications to operate directly on the blockchain (Naqbi et al., 2025a, 2025b). This advancement broadened the scope of cryptocurrencies from payment systems to multi-functional financial ecosystems.

2.2 Diversification and Market Growth

As of 2024, the cryptocurrency market comprises more than 25,000 unique digital assets with a combined market capitalization exceeding 2.2 trillion USD.

Bitcoin continues to dominate, accounting for over 40% of total market value, followed by Ethereum, stablecoins like USD Coin and Tether, and privacy-enhancing coins such as Monero and Zcash (Ibikunle et al., 2025b; Jain et al., 2025). Ethereum-based tokens followed the ERC-20 standard (a technical specification that defines how tokens can be created and interact on the Ethereum blockchain), allowing for interoperability across decentralized applications.

Cryptocurrencies today serve a wide range of purposes, including as a store of value, medium of exchange, means of investment, and platform for decentralized services. The rise of crypto-based financial instruments, including derivatives, exchange-traded funds (ETFs), and tokenized assets, has enabled deeper institutional penetration. Concurrently, the development of crypto custody services, insurance products, and audit protocols has provided a foundation for greater integration into mainstream financial systems (Hamilton Rhiannaand Leuprecht, 2024).

Table 9.1 provides a chronological overview of the major milestones in cryptocurrency development from 2008 to 2024. It highlights key technological innovations, evolving financial use cases, and the global spread of adoption and regulation. This timeline illustrates how the cryptocurrency landscape has matured from early ideological origins and experimental use to complex decentralized ecosystems, institutional integration, and growing regulatory scrutiny.

2.3 Patterns of Global Adoption

The adoption of cryptocurrencies varies significantly across countries and regions. According to Ref (Naqbi et al., 2025a, 2025b) developing economies such as Nigeria, Vietnam, India, and Ukraine exhibit high levels of crypto use, largely due to weak domestic currencies, financial exclusion, and informal economic activity. In contrast, in North America and Western Europe, adoption is primarily driven by institutional investors, hedge funds, and fintech integration.

Retail adoption is highest in countries where traditional banking services are inaccessible or expensive. In these contexts, cryptocurrencies function as alternatives to remittances, savings accounts, and even business capital. The growing availability of mobile-based crypto wallets has further enabled financial participation among underserved populations. This duality of institutional growth and grassroots utility, has contributed to the global rise of digital currencies while simultaneously exposing regulatory weaknesses.

2.4 Technological Advancements and Emerging Risks

The development of DeFi has increased the functionality of cryptocurrencies. Through DeFi, one can lend, borrow, earn interest, and carry out asset swapping without the intermediary. These systems, while promoting financial democratization, operate with limited oversight and often lack strong identity verification protocols. Smart contract vulnerabilities, liquidity manipulation, and flash loan

Table 9.1. Timeline of Cryptocurrency Evolution and Global Adoption Patterns.

Year	Key Development	Technological Innovation	Geographic Spread
2008	Bitcoin white paper by Satoshi Nakamoto	Blockchain (Proof-of-Work)	Conceptual origin – global academic and tech interest
2009	Genesis Block mined (Bitcoin goes live)	Decentralized ledger begins	Early adoption limited to cryptography enthusiasts (US, UK)
2011	Emergence of Litecoin, Namecoin	Forked Bitcoin code with faster confirmation	Underground markets start using crypto (e.g., Silk Road)
2013	First major Bitcoin price spike (~1000 USD)	Increased mining activity and exchange platforms	China becomes largest Bitcoin miner; US IRS classifies BTC as property
2015	Ethereum launch with Smart Contracts	Introduction of programmable blockchain via Solidity	Broader global developer engagement (Europe, North America)
2016	Rise of ICOs and Ethereum-based tokens	ERC-20 standard for tokens	Singapore, Switzerland, and Estonia emerge as ICO hubs
2017	Crypto market boom; Bitcoin hits ~20,000 USD	Expansion of DeFi and dApps	South Korea, Japan adopt regulatory frameworks; India bans crypto (temporarily)
2018	Crypto crash; regulatory focus intensifies	Introduction of token compliance tools	EU introduces 5th AML Directive covering crypto assets
2019	Launch of privacy-focused coins (e.g., Zcash, Monero)	zk-SNARKs, ring signatures for anonymity	FBI and Interpol raise concerns over traceability
2020	Institutional entry: PayPal, Square, MicroStrategy enter crypto	Custodial wallets and insured crypto funds	US OCC allows banks to hold crypto; growing acceptance in Germany and Canada

(Continued)

Table 9.1. *(Continued)*

Year	**Key Development**	**Technological Innovation**	**Geographic Spread**
2021	NFT boom and DeFi growth	Tokenization, DAO protocols, Layer-2 scaling	El Salvador adopts Bitcoin as legal tender; India announces tax framework
2022	FTX collapse and stablecoin scrutiny	Focus on transparency, proof-of-reserves	Regulatory crackdowns in United States, United Kingdom, and South Korea; global DeFi concerns rise
2023	Central Bank Digital Currencies (CBDCs) pilot programs expand	Integration with existing payment infra	China expands Digital Yuan; EU moves ahead with MiCA regulation
2024	Over 25,000 crypto assets listed; Market cap > $2.2 trillion	Blockchain analytics, cross-chain bridges, real-world asset tokenization	Crypto adoption peaks in Nigeria, Vietnam, and Latin America; institutional ETFs approved in US

Source: Compiled by the authors based on various peer-reviewed journal articles.

attacks represent significant risks that remain unaddressed in most jurisdictions (Hamilton Rhiannaand Leuprecht, 2024). Cryptocurrencies like Zcash and Monero use cryptographic algorithms like zk-SNARKs (zero-knowledge interactions that enable validation of transactions without revealing underlying information), which makes it difficult to track by typical blockchain forensics.

It has an additional challenge of privacy-oriented technologies, such as mixers and anonymizing wallets. Although such tools can be used to protect the privacy of legitimate users, they are commonly used to execute illegal operations, including the concealment of funds made using ransomware or darknet markets. The presence of these dual-use technologies underscores the tension between innovation and regulatory compliance.

2.5 The Regulatory Imperative

As cryptocurrencies continue to evolve, so too does the urgency for comprehensive regulation. The lack of standardized global frameworks has enabled jurisdictional arbitrage, complicating efforts to track illicit financial flows. The introduction of Central Bank Digital Currencies (CBDCs, which are digital forms of sovereign currency issued and regulated by national central banks) in various countries signals a potential state-led response to these challenges. Yet, CBDCs are structurally and operationally different than decentralized cryptocurrencies, and this brings up new possibilities of coexistence, privacy, and surveillance.

The awareness of the history of origin and the use patterns of cryptocurrencies is also crucial to formulate proper policies. The second part talks about how these technologies are more and more being hijacked toward financial crimes and how they are used in illicit trade, frauds, money laundering, and other types of economic based crimes.

3. Nexus Between Cryptocurrency and Financial Crime

Cryptocurrency and financial crime are two issues that are growing in importance as the world of decentralized digital assets is expanding rapidly. Cryptocurrencies have a high level of transactional privacy, cross-border functionality, and minimal regulatory control by design, and these features are often used to commit illicit financial crimes. In this context, this chapter addresses the most significant categories of financial crime tied to the cryptocurrency use, including money laundering, terrorist financing, payments of ransomware, market manipulation, and fraudulent fundraising. It describes the changing typologies, tools, and institutional responses that define the riskscape.

3.1 Cryptocurrency-Enabled Money Laundering

One of the most documented forms of financial crime involving cryptocurrencies is money laundering, the process of concealing the origins of illegally obtained funds. Digital assets provide mechanisms for layering and integration that obscure the audit trail, such as chain-hopping (moving funds across different blockchains), the use of privacy coins, and engagement with unregulated exchanges.

Mixer and tumbler are special devices that are used to anonymize crypto transactions by mixing the user assets, discontinuing the traceability, and sending them to new addresses. Such services have been at the center of laundering activities associated with darknet markets and ransomware campaigns. As an example, during the BitMix and Helix probes, US law enforcement attributed thousands of Bitcoin transactions to black market drug dealers and blacklisted addresses, and prosecuted mixer operators on money laundering charges (Foley et al., 2019).

According to a Ref (Egmont Group, 2023; Fisch & Momtaz, 2020; Florysiak & Schandlbauer, 2022; Wu et al., 2021) more than 10.1 billion USD in illicit cryptocurrency was laundered in 2022 alone, with 68% of that amount moved through centralized exchanges that had weak or nonexistent KYC procedures. This highlights the urgent need for stricter compliance monitoring within major crypto platforms.

3.2 Terrorist Financing and Illicit Trade

The pseudonymous and borderless nature of cryptocurrencies makes them attractive for financing extremist and terrorist organizations. Although fiat channels remain dominant in terror funding, cryptocurrencies have increasingly featured in online fundraising efforts, especially in regions with restricted banking infrastructure or surveillance. Several cases involving the Islamic State (ISIS) and Hamas have revealed attempts to solicit Bitcoin donations via encrypted messaging platforms. In 2020, US enforcement agencies dismantled a network of more than 300 cryptocurrency accounts tied to terrorist fundraising, confiscating millions in Bitcoin, Ethereum, and other assets. These accounts were used to disguise contributions from foreign sympathizers through fragmented microtransactions (Wu et al., 2021).

Darknet marketplaces also use cryptocurrency to facilitate illegal arms and human trafficking. The Hydra Market, once the largest dark web platform in Russia, used cryptocurrency exclusively for its illicit operations, until it was taken down by international cybercrime units in 2022. Transactions through such platforms often employ privacy coins like Monero (designed to obscure sender, receiver, and amount data using ring signatures and stealth addresses), complicating law enforcement efforts.

3.3 Ransomware and Extortion Schemes

The rise in ransomware attacks has been closely linked to the use of cryptocurrencies, especially Bitcoin, as the preferred payment method. Cybercriminals deploy malicious software to encrypt victims' data and demand payment in crypto to unlock access. The anonymity of crypto wallets and the irreversible nature of transactions make enforcement difficult, while decentralized exchanges and mixers assist in obfuscating the trail.

A notable case occurred in 2021 with the Colonial Pipeline ransomware attack, where the attackers, later identified as the DarkSide group, received over 75 Bitcoin (worth 4.4 million USD at the time). Although a portion was recovered by US authorities through wallet tracking, the case underscored the vulnerabilities in critical infrastructure posed by unregulated digital payment methods (Wu et al., 2021). Ransomware-as-a-Service platforms have further democratized cyber extortion by providing kits for would-be attackers, who collect ransoms via crypto wallets. These wallets are often linked to distributed addresses, making attribution difficult and raising systemic risk concerns for financial institutions.

3.4 Market Manipulation and Fraudulent Offerings

Initial Coin Offerings (ICOs), token launches, and crypto investment schemes have created opportunities for fraud, Ponzi schemes, and pump-and-dump operations. In many instances, the lack of legal classification for crypto assets has allowed issuers to evade regulatory oversight.

BitConnect fraud was one of the biggest Ponzi schemes in the history of crypto that collected more than 2.4 billion USD all over the world on the basis of providing a trading bot service. After regulatory advises and lawsuits against it, the token lost its value as the investors suffered massive losses. Lax regulation gave the platform ample opportunity to cross regulators with little or no oversight before its downfall. Besides using outright fraud, social media and organizing investor action have been employed to move token values especially in low liquidity markets. Pump-and-dump schemes are based on artificially increasing the price of a given cryptocurrency and then engaging in a wide sell-off; this usually targets naive investors. Such manipulation has created a demand to regulate some of the tokens in the same way as securities (de Andrés et al., 2022; Kushelevitch, 2025).

3.5 Regulatory Evasion and Tax Fraud

Cryptocurrencies are also used to evade capital controls, sanctions, and taxation. People living in nations that have strict financial regulation like Venezuela, Iran and North Korea-utilize cryptocurrencies to circumvent the official banking system. In 2023, the Financial Crimes Enforcement Network (FinCEN) flagged over 17,000 suspicious transactions involving wallets in sanctioned jurisdictions, many linked to ransomware and state-sponsored cybercrime.

In the context of tax fraud, undeclared crypto holdings and capital gains have become a growing concern. Many jurisdictions lack the infrastructure to track wallet ownership or enforce tax disclosures. The Organization for Economic Co-operation and Development's (OECD's) Crypto-Asset Reporting

Framework (CARF), introduced in 2022, seeks to standardize the automatic exchange of tax information related to digital assets across countries, but implementation remains inconsistent. To synthesize the above discussion, Table 9.2 presents the primary types of financial crime enabled by cryptocurrencies, along with typical tools and enforcement challenges.

4. Regulatory Frameworks and Global Responses

The proliferation of cryptocurrencies has prompted a wide array of regulatory responses across the globe. Policymakers and enforcement bodies face the dual challenge of enabling innovation while mitigating the financial risks posed by crypto-enabled crime. The decentralized and borderless nature of cryptocurrencies complicates traditional regulatory paradigms, necessitating both national reforms and international coordination. This section analyzes global regulatory efforts, highlighting country-specific frameworks and international initiatives that seek to govern cryptocurrency markets and limit financial crime.

4.1 The United States: Fragmented Oversight with Aggressive Enforcement

The United States has one of the most liberal but divided regulatory conditions of cryptocurrency. Several branches of the government, most prominently the Securities and Exchange Commission (SEC), Commodity Futures Trading Commission (CFTC), Internal Revenue Service (IRS) and Financial Crimes Enforcement Network (FinCEN), perform services with overlapping jurisdiction.

The SEC has asserted that many crypto-assets constitute securities under the Howey Test and are therefore subject to securities regulation. It has brought enforcement actions against fraudulent ICOs and unregistered exchanges. The CFTC, in contrast, classifies Bitcoin and Ethereum as commodities and oversees derivatives markets. FinCEN requires crypto service providers to register as money services businesses and comply with KYC and Anti-Money Laundering (AML) rules. However, no comprehensive national legislation exists, leading to regulatory uncertainty (Zetzsche et al., 2019).

Nevertheless, the US enforcement efforts have been heeded. The IRS and the Department of Justice managed to retrieve in 2021 $2.3 million worth of Bitcoin in the ransom attack on the Colonial pipeline, proving the increasing ability to perform blockchain forensics (Paquet-Clouston et al., 2019).

4.2 EU: Toward Harmonized Legislation

The EU has made considerable progress toward harmonizing crypto regulation. The Fifth Anti-Money Laundering Directive (5AMLD), implemented in 2020, extended AML obligations to crypto exchanges and wallet providers, mandating registration and customer verification.

Table 9.2. Typologies of Cryptocurrency-Enabled Financial Crime.

Type of crime	Mechanisms	Key challenges	Sources
Money laundering	Mixers, chain-hopping, privacy coins	Traceability, cross-jurisdiction enforcement	(FATF, 2020; Kushelevitch, 2025)
Terrorist financing	Anonymous donations, darknet wallets	Fragmented transactions, lack of KYC	(DIOP, 2025; Egmont Group, 2023; Teichmann, 2018)
Ransomware payments	Crypto wallets, decentralized exchanges	Victim compliance, lack of recovery tools	(Baig, 2015; Wu et al., 2021)
ICO and investment fraud	Fake tokens, unregistered offerings	Legal ambiguity, social media manipulation	(Almeida & Gonçalves, 2023; Fisch & Momtaz, 2020; Kotiloglu & Ometto, 2024; Momtaz, 2021)
Market manipulation	Pump-and-dump schemes, insider trading	Lack of disclosure laws	(Charfeddine & Mahrous, 2024; Gandal et al., 2018; Pennec et al., 2021)
Sanctions/tax evasion	Offshore wallets, peer-to-peer transfers	Identity masking, absence of audit mechanisms	(Anomah et al., 2024; Burgess, 2024; de Vries et al., 2021; Ibikunle et al., 2025b)

Source: Compiled by the authors based on various peer-reviewed journal articles.

The markets in crypto-assets regulation (MiCA) is a wide-ranging regulatory framework implemented in 2023 by the EU that controls the issuance, trading, and custody of the crypto-assets. MiCA establishes licensing, capital reserves, and consumer protection. It also enables national overseers to track the systemic risk of crypto markets (Houben & Snyers, 2018). The EU has been at the forefront of progressive legal change in its attempt to harmonize crypto regulation with the goal of financial stability.

Moreover, the European Banking Authority and the European Securities and Markets Authority are developing technical standards for the implementation of MiCA, addressing areas such as stablecoin reserve management and audit trails. These developments reflect the EU's commitment to both innovation and risk mitigation.

4.3 Singapore: Innovation-Driven Compliance

There is no doubt that Singapore has become an example of how to find the optimal balance between the transparency of the regulation and fintech innovation. The Monetary Authority of Singapore (MAS) regulates digital payment token services under the Payment Services Act (2019). Service providers must obtain licenses and comply with AML, counter-terrorism financing (CFT), and cybersecurity obligations. In 2022, MAS released guidelines prohibiting crypto advertisements to the general public and imposed strict due diligence requirements on crypto firms. The country's approach emphasizes regulatory technology (RegTech) and public–private collaboration. Singapore is also exploring Project Orchid, which investigates the design and issuance of a CBDC for retail use.

Singapore's success stems from its principle-based regulation and early recognition of blockchain's potential. Its sandbox model allows firms to test products under supervisory oversight, providing flexibility while maintaining institutional integrity.

4.4 India: Gradual Policy Shift Under Fiscal and Legal Scrutiny

India's regulatory stance has evolved from blanket bans to cautious integration. In 2018, the Reserve Bank of India (RBI) prohibited banks from facilitating crypto-related transactions, citing systemic risk. This ban was overturned by the Supreme Court in 2020, which ruled the restriction unconstitutional. Since then, India has adopted a taxation-led strategy. In 2022, the government introduced a 30% capital gains tax on crypto transactions and a 1% Tax Deducted at Source (TDS) on each trade. The move formalized crypto activities without establishing a regulatory framework. As of 2024, a draft bill on crypto regulation remains under parliamentary consideration. In the interim, the Ministry of Finance has emphasized alignment with the Financial Action Task Force (FATF) standards and participation in global AML cooperation efforts. Despite its fiscal approach,

India remains cautious due to concerns over capital flight, investor protection, and national security.

4.5 China: Prohibition and State-Led Alternatives

China has taken a restrictive approach, banning all crypto transactions and mining activities. In 2021, the People's Bank of China declared all crypto-related activities illegal, citing financial instability, energy consumption, and fraud concerns. At the same time, China has pioneered its own digital currency, the Digital Yuan, under the Digital Currency Electronic Payment system. Unlike decentralized cryptocurrencies, the Digital Yuan is fully controlled by the central bank and integrated with the country's surveillance and fiscal tools. China's ban on private crypto and simultaneous development of a state-backed CBDC reflects its strategy of asserting monetary sovereignty while preventing capital outflows and illicit finance (Naqbi et al., 2025a, 2025b).

4.6 FATF and International Coordination

At the global level, the FATF has played a central role in shaping crypto governance. In 2019, FATF issued updated recommendations extending AML/CFT obligations to virtual asset service providers (VASPs). The most significant guideline is the "Travel Rule," which requires VASPs to share sender and receiver information for transactions exceeding a threshold. Although FATF's recommendations are nonbinding, over 100 jurisdictions have committed to implementing them. However, disparities in domestic law, enforcement capacity, and technological readiness hinder uniform adoption. Other international bodies, including the International Monetary Fund, World Bank, and Basel Committee, have issued guidance on crypto risk assessment and prudential regulation. Yet, coordination remains limited, particularly in cross-border enforcement and data sharing.

4.7 Systemic Weaknesses and the Road ahead

Despite global efforts, several unresolved challenges hinder effective cryptocurrency regulation:

- Inconsistent Legal Classification: Crypto-assets are defined differently across jurisdictions (e.g., as securities, commodities, or property), creating fragmented compliance requirements and complicating enforcement.
- Unregulated DeFi and Privacy Tools: DeFi platforms and privacy-enhancing technologies (e.g., mixers, zk-proofs) operate outside traditional regulatory frameworks, making it difficult to apply KYC/AML norms.
- Technological Capacity Pits: Most countries do not have the machinery, qualified workers, and infrastructure to support blockchain analysis and enforcement mainly within the developing economies.

- Regulatory Arbitrage: Criminal actors take advantage of varying national regulations by shifting operations to jurisdictions, which are less controlled.
- Innovation versus Control Dilemma: Excessive regulation leads to reduction in innovation and pushing the activities underground whereas insufficient regulation poses greater risks to financial crimes and adversely affects its credibility.

Way Forward

- Regulatory Sandboxes: Crypto Sandboxes should facilitate a sensible mid-way regulation by providing safe facilities to conduct regulatory supervised experiments.
- Blockchain Analytics Partnership Proposal: Working or collaboration with the private companies can allow increasing the monitoring capabilities of the law enforcement.
- Joint Cross-Border Information Sharing and Coordinated Action Platforms: International enforcement can be enhanced by the creation of shared platforms with supervising colleges.
- Standardized Frameworks: Initiatives like the OECD's CARF can promote global tax transparency and reduce evasion.

Effective governance will depend on a globally coordinated, adaptive approach that balances risk mitigation with innovation.

5. Challenges in Regulating Cryptocurrency

Cryptocurrency regulation is hampered by a mix of legal obscurity, jurisdiction restrictions and lack of capacity closely related to the technological and institutional fragmentation and volatility of cryptocurrency market. Jurisdictional inconsistency of a category of crypto-assets is one of the challenges and the highlights have been beyond excellent. This also puts them in a gray zone between securities and commodities or digital property and a part of that creates confusion which law to apply and the ability to create regulatory arbitrage where countries may choose to regulate as securities and others as commodities or digital property (Silfversten et al., 2020).

Enforcement is further complicated by the decentralized and borderless structure of blockchain systems. It is likely that the transaction is made without an intermediary, so the activities cannot be traced, monitored, or controlled by authorities, especially on DeFi financial systems (Nartey, 2024). Privacy-enhancing technologies such as mixers, ring signatures, and zero-knowledge proofs further reduce traceability, creating blind spots for regulators and forensic auditors (Gandal et al., 2018).

Institutionally, oversight is fragmented across multiple agencies, including tax authorities, financial regulators, law enforcement, and central banks, often resulting in conflicting guidance and limited coordination. This incoherence deteriorates the pace of enforcement and undermines structures of accountability. Also, the extreme instability of crypto markets and repeated collapse of exchanges and token projects put retail investors at great financial risk. The collapse of high-profile platforms such as FTX and Terra-LUNA revealed major gaps in platform governance, risk disclosure, and audit standards (Jain et al., 2025). A combination of these factors shows how necessary the more integrated, technologically equipped and internationally harmonized system of regulation is. The second section contains a brief description of the potential solutions and choices that would enhance tracking and security among the crypto community.

6. Opportunities for Strengthening Oversight

As the cryptocurrency landscape matures, opportunities have emerged to strengthen regulatory oversight through a combination of technological innovation, institutional reform, and international cooperation. Addressing the risks posed by crypto-enabled financial crime requires an adaptive approach that leverages emerging tools while preserving the core benefits of decentralization and innovation.

The use of blockchain analytics is one of the most optimistic ways forward. Software provided by companies like Chainalysis, Elliptic and CipherTrace can map transactions, detect groups of wallets, and attribute on-chain transactions to real-world entities. These tools have helped to a great extent in increasing the ability of law enforcement agencies to track money used in illicit activities, uncover case manipulation of the market and the recovery of stolen funds. Regular action due to the intersections of the regulators and crypto exchanges, with the analytics providers, has now become more prevalent in significant jurisdictions. Nonetheless, these tools are associated with competent analysists and strong legal infrastructure to realize deployment (de Vries et al., 2021).

Regulatory sandboxes also present a structured mechanism for oversight. These controlled environments allow crypto firms to test new products and services under the supervision of regulators without immediately triggering the full suite of compliance obligations. Other countries include Singapore, the United Kingdom, and the United Arab Emirates that have developed regulatory sandboxes to facilitate innovation but also to discover policy gap and areas of exposure in real time. Another role of the sandboxes plays in the regulation context, allowing regulators to develop an institutional feel with emerging technologies, which can help to make more informed regulations (Gandal et al., 2018; Pennec et al., 2021). There is a global trend to convergence of reporting and tax compliance regimes. In 2022, OECD released the CARF that was supposed to facilitate cross-jurisdictional automatic exchange of information on holdings and transactions in crypto assets. CARF, in this respect, supplements the adopted Common Reporting Standard (CRS) and its application is expected to result in minimizing the misuse of digital assets in a tax evasion context and cross-border fraud. Should be adopted on a large scale, this framework would be able to enhance transparency at the same time reducing the extent of regulatory arbitrage (Almeida & Gonçalves, 2023).

The other significant course of action is the growth of supervisory colleges and mutual task forces. The mechanisms allow different country regulators to share intelligence, harmonize enforcement, and share a common risk analysis of national platforms across borders. Similar models already exist in traditional banking supervision and are being considered for application in the digital asset space. Cross-border information exchange will be essential in tackling crimes that exploit the pseudonymous and transnational features of blockchain networks.

Additionally, the establishment of crypto-specific self-regulatory organizations (SROs) offers a complementary approach to formal regulation. These industry-led bodies can develop technical standards, certification schemes, and compliance best practices. In Japan, the Japan Virtual Currency Exchange Association functions as a licensed SRO with the authority to monitor registered exchanges and report suspicious activity. Such models could be adapted in other jurisdictions to create hybrid frameworks that combine state oversight with industry accountability (Fisch & Momtaz, 2020).

Lastly, it is important to reinforce institutional capacity. Regulatory authorities and governments should focus on investing on talent emerging, technical infrastructure and inter agency coordination. In such jurisdictions as the United States, South Korea, and the European Union, capacity-building initiatives that involve creating blockchain forensic labs and special training programs are already in place. These types of initiatives will contribute to the reduction of the existing gap relating to expertise and possibly can contribute to the reaction to the newly appeared risks in a more prompt and appropriate fashion.

In other words, control anchored on multidimensionality comprising, modern technology, legislative reform, global action, and institutional novelty is the remedy to speed up the process of regulation in cryptocurrency ecosystem. The integration of these tools held in a single way has created an opportunity of having more secure, transparent, and accountable digital asset markets.

7. Conclusion and Policy Recommendations

7.1 Summary of Key Insights

Cryptocurrencies have significantly altered the global financial landscape by enabling decentralized, borderless, and programmable transactions. While these innovations offer benefits such as financial inclusion and transaction efficiency, they have also introduced vulnerabilities. As outlined in this chapter, cryptocurrencies are increasingly being misused for financial crimes including money laundering, ransomware payments, terrorist financing, and fraud.

This chapter highlights that conventional regulatory mechanisms, designed for centralized and jurisdiction-bound financial systems, are insufficient for managing the complexity of digital asset ecosystems. Regulatory ambiguity, fragmented institutional responsibilities, and technological barriers continue to impede effective oversight.

7.2 Strategic Policy Directions

To respond to these challenges, a multi-level strategy is essential, one that integrates legal reform, technological capacity, and institutional innovation:

- Binding definitions of crypto-assets across jurisdiction should be established to minimize regulatory arbitrage and ease domestic enforcement. The defined approach of classification would allow closer interaction between national and global agencies.
- Regulators will have to deploy combinations of blockchain analysis, automated compliance tools, and identity verification systems to raise monitoring and enforcement. That consists of the cooperation with blockchain forensics vendors and building technical ability in-house.
- More vigilance is needed between financial regulators, law enforcements and the taxing authorities. Supervisory colleges, multi-agency task forces and platforms of cross-border information-sharing can enhance systemic oversight.

7.3 Public–Private Collaboration and Capacity Building

Public–private partnerships are essential in promoting industry accountability. Crypto exchanges, wallet providers, and decentralized platforms should be integrated into compliance networks. Mandated reporting of suspicious transactions and active collaboration with regulators can support early detection of illicit activity. Capacity-building remains a foundational element. In particular, developing economies must invest in technical training, policy development, and institutional readiness. Equipping enforcement and regulatory bodies with blockchain expertise will be crucial for implementing effective oversight strategies.

7.4 Concluding Reflections: Toward a Flexible, Future-Ready Framework

As the cryptocurrency ecosystem evolves, regulatory approaches must remain flexible, proportionate, and technologically informed. Differentiated model may be implemented depending on the amount of risks and type of platforms, without overregulating but focusing on high-risk actors. The future of crypto governance should be based on such principles as accountability, interoperability, and innovation-enabling oversight. Ultimately, building a secure and accountable digital financial ecosystem depends on sustained global cooperation, adaptive policy design, and a shared commitment to financial integrity. The enhanced supervision is not only the demand of the law but also the core of its trust security, transparency, and the sustainability of the digital asset market.

References

Adewuyi, O. (2025). The double-edged ledger: Cryptocurrency, financial crime, and the potential of blockchain forensics. *International Journal of Research and Innovation in Social Science, IX*, 5739–5742. https://doi.org/10.47772/IJRISS.2025.905000442

Almeida, J., & Gonçalves, T. C. (2023). A systematic literature review of investor behavior in the cryptocurrency markets. *Journal of Behavioral and Experimental Finance, 37*, 100785. https://doi.org/10.1016/J.JBEF.2022.100785

Anomah, S., Ayeboafo, B., Aduamoah, M., & Agyabeng, O. (2024). Blockchain technology integration in tax policy: Navigating challenges and unlocking opportunities for improving the taxation of Ghana's digital economy. *Scientific African, 24*, e02210. https://doi.org/10.1016/J.SCIAF.2024.E02210

Baig, Z. (2015). *Ransomware: Emergence of the cyber-extortion menace*. https://doi.org/10.13140/RG.2.1.2529.1602

Burgess, T. (2024). A multi-jurisdictional perspective: To what extent can cryptocurrency be regulated? and if so, who should regulate cryptocurrency?. *Journal of Economic Criminology, 5*, 100086. https://doi.org/10.1016/J.JECONC.2024.100086

Charfeddine, L., & Mahrous, A. (2024). What drives cryptocurrency pump and dump schemes: Coin versus market factors? *Finance Research Letters, 67*, 105861. https://doi.org/10.1016/J.FRL.2024.105861

de Andres, P., Arroyo, D., Correia, R., & Rezola, A. (2022). Challenges of the market for initial coin offerings. *International Review of Financial Analysis, 79*, 101966. https://doi.org/10.1016/J.IRFA.2021.101966

de Vries, A., Gallersdörfer, U., Klaaßen, L., & Stoll, C. (2021). The true costs of digital currencies: Exploring impact beyond energy use. *One Earth, 4*(6), 786–789. https://doi.org/10.1016/J.ONEEAR.2021.05.009

DIOP, M. B. (2025). Combating money laundering in the age of digital transformation: A comparative study between Türkiye and Nigeria. *Journal of Economic Criminology, 9*, 100165. https://doi.org/10.1016/J.JECONC.2025.100165

Egmont Group. (2023). *Report on abuse of virtual assets for terrorist financing purposes: Public summary*. https://egmontgroup.org

FATF. (2020). *Money laundering and terrorist financing red flag indicators associated with virtual assets*. https://www.fatf-gafi.org/publications/fatfrecommendations/documents/Virtual-Assets-Red-Flag-Indicators.html

Fisch, C., & Momtaz, P. P. (2020). Institutional investors and post-ICO performance: An empirical analysis of investor returns in initial coin offerings (ICOs). *Journal of Corporate Finance, 64*, 101679. https://doi.org/10.1016/J.JCORPFIN.2020.101679

Foley, S., Karlsen, J. R., & Putniņš, T. J. (2019). Sex, drugs, and bitcoin: How much illegal activity is financed through cryptocurrencies? *Review of Financial Studies, 32*(5), 1798–1853. https://doi.org/10.1093/rfs/hhz015

Florysiak, D., & Schandlbauer, A. (2022). Experts or charlatans? ICO analysts and white paper informativeness. *Journal of Banking & Finance, 139*, 106476. https://doi.org/10.1016/J.JBANKFIN.2022.106476

Gandal, N., Hamrick, J. T., Moore, T., & Oberman, T. (2018). Price manipulation in the bitcoin ecosystem. *Journal of Monetary Economics, 95*, 86–96. https://doi.org/10.1016/J.JMONECO.2017.12.004

Hamilton, R., & Leuprecht, C. (2024). The crime-crypto nexus: Nuancing risk across crypto-crime transactions. In L. Goldbarsht Doron & de Koker (Eds.), *Financial crime and the law: Identifying and mitigating risks* (pp. 15–42). Springer Nature. https://doi.org/10.1007/978-3-031-59543-1_2

Houben, R., & Snyers, A. (2018). *Cryptocurrencies and blockchain: Legal context and implications for financial crime, money laundering and tax evasion*. European Parliament, Policy Department for Economic, Scientific and Quality of Life Policies, PE 619.024. http://www.europarl.europa.eu/supporting-analyses

Ibikunle, G., Mollica, V., & Sun, Q. (2025a). Why so many coins? Examining the demand for privacy-preserving cryptocurrencies. *The British Accounting Review*, 101637. https://doi.org/10.1016/J.BAR.2025.101637

Ibikunle, G., Mollica, V., & Sun, Q. (2025b). Why so many coins? Examining the demand for privacy-preserving cryptocurrencies. *The British Accounting Review*, 101637. https://doi.org/10.1016/J.BAR.2025.101637

Jain, S., Sarkar, T., & Subbaiyan, R. (2025). Cryptocurrency's dark side: Uncovering its role in money laundering and illicit transactions. *The Empirical Economics Letters*, *1*, 174–198. https://doi.org/10.5281/zenodo.13620284

Kotiloglu, S., & Ometto, M. P. (2024). An exploratory look at the role of ownership in initial coin offerings (ICO): Different audiences and ICO success. *Journal of Business Venturing Insights*, *21*, e00438. https://doi.org/10.1016/J.JBVI.2023.E00438

Kushelevitch, M. (2025). Unveiling the crypto-terror nexus: Law enforcement intelligence challenges against terrorist financing. *Journal of Financial Crime*, *32*(2), 403–415. https://doi.org/10.1108/JFC-12-2023-0330

Momtaz, P. P. (2021). Entrepreneurial finance and moral hazard: Evidence from token offerings. *Journal of Business Venturing*, *36*(5), 106001. https://doi.org/10.1016/J.JBUSVENT.2020.106001

Naqbi, S. A. Al, Nobanee, H., & Ellili, N. O. D. (2025a). Global trends and insights into cryptocurrency-related financial crime. *Research in International Business and Finance*, *75*, 102756. https://doi.org/10.1016/J.RIBAF.2025.102756

Naqbi, S. A. Al, Nobanee, H., & Ellili, N. O. D. (2025b). Global trends and insights into cryptocurrency-related financial crime. *Research in International Business and Finance*, *75*, 102756. https://doi.org/10.1016/J.RIBAF.2025.102756

Nartey, J. (2024). *Decentralized finance (DeFi) and AI: Innovations at the intersection of blockchain and artificial intelligence*. https://ssrn.com/abstract=4781328

Paquet-Clouston, M., Haslhofer, B., & Dupont, B. (2019). Ransomware payments in the bitcoin ecosystem. *Journal of Cybersecurity*, *5*(1). https://doi.org/10.1093/cybsec/tyz003

Pennec, G. Le, Fiedler, I., & Ante, L. (2021). Wash trading at cryptocurrency exchanges. *Finance Research Letters*, *43*, 101982. https://doi.org/10.1016/J.FRL.2021.101982

Saha, S., Hasan, A., Mahmud, A., Ahmed, N., Parvin, N., & Karmakar, H. (2024). Cryptocurrency and financial crimes: A bibliometric analysis and future research agenda. *Multidisciplinary Reviews*, *7*, 2024168. https://doi.org/10.31893/multirev.2024168

Silfversten, E., Favaro, M., Slapakova, L., Ishikawa, S., Liu, J., & Salas, A. (2020). *Exploring the use of zcash cryptocurrency for illicit or criminal purposes*. RAND, https://doi.org/10.7249/RR4418

Teichmann, F. (2018). Financing terrorism through cryptocurrencies – a danger for Europe? *Journal of Money Laundering Control*, *21*, 513–519. https://doi.org/10.1108/JMLC-06-2017-0024

Wu, L., Hu, Y., Zhou, Y., Wang, H., Luo, X., Wang, Z., Zhang, F., & Ren, K. (2021). *Towards understanding and demystifying bitcoin mixing services*. https://doi.org/10.1145/3442381.3449880

Zetzsche, D. A., Arner, D. W., Buckley, R. P., & Weber, R. H. (2019). *The future of data-driven finance and RegTech: Lessons from EU Big Bang II*. European Banking Institute Working Paper Series 2019/35. https://doi.org/10.2139/ssrn.3359399

Chapter 10

Whistleblowing and Transparency: Tools for Preventing Financial Crime

Hakan Özkaya and Şebnem Yaşar

Dokuz Eylül University, Türkiye

Abstract

This chapter explores the critical roles of transparency and whistleblowing in the prevention of financial crime, emphasizing their significance in strengthening institutional integrity and public accountability. It begins by examining how transparency mechanisms—such as robust financial reporting, internal audits, and international regulatory standards—mitigate information asymmetry and deter financial misconduct. The chapter then delves into whistleblowing as a complementary safeguard, analyzing its definitions, classifications, and behavioral determinants. Drawing on theoretical frameworks and empirical studies, it highlights the challenges whistleblowers face, including retaliation, legal loopholes, and cultural barriers. The analysis further incorporates cross-jurisdictional comparisons and high-profile case studies—including the Panama Papers, Danske Bank, and major Ponzi schemes—to demonstrate the practical implications of whistleblowing and transparency failures. The chapter concludes by advocating for an integrated approach that combines legal reform, ethical organizational culture, and global cooperation to foster more resilient financial systems.

Keywords: Financial crime; transparency; whistleblowing; corporate governance; ethics

1. Introduction

Corruption is a phenomenon that significantly impacts both countries and the global economy. In addition to its economic effects, corruption also harms the security and welfare of society in general. Furthermore, corruption discourages

Corruption and Crime in Finance, 207–233

Published under exclusive licence by Emerald Publishing Limited
doi:10.1108/978-1-83708-170-720261026

investment decisions, increases income inequality, raises the cost of public services, and undermines trust in government, fueling political instability and negatively affecting national, regional, and global development. The scale of the global corruption problem that governments face has reached enormous proportions. According to United Nations data, the amount stolen from rightful owners through corruption worldwide has reached 2.6 trillion U.S. dollars, equivalent to 5% of the annual global GDP. The scale of bribes alone is approximately one trillion U.S. dollars annually. Funds stolen through bribery and corruption occupy a much larger share of the global economy than those that could be transferred to developing countries (World Bank, 2020, pp. 7, 13). Being one of the least corrupt regions in the world, the European Union suffers from the cost of corruption estimated to be up to 256 billion Euros per year (Meenakshi & Lenka, 2023, p. 3). Defined as "the abuse of entrusted power for private gain" (Transparency International, 2025), corruption exists in various forms like paying and receiving bribes, gaining privileged access to goods, contracts, and public services (Meenakshi & Lenka, 2023, p. 1). Various intentional or unintentional wrongdoings disrupt the proper functioning of institutions and organizations.

Based on their survey, Near et al. (2004) grouped wrongdoings in organizations into seven broad categories. The categories of wrongdoing are stealing, waste, mismanagement, safety problems, sexual harassment, unfair discrimination, and violation of the law. Waste, which includes funds being received by people other than those who should have received it, waste resulting from mismanagement of aid programs, and waste of organizational resources, was the most frequently observed wrongdoing (almost 44% of all wrongdoings). Discrimination, which accounted for 13% of all reported wrongdoings, refers to situations where people are mistreated based on characteristics such as their race, gender, or religious beliefs. Mismanagement, which accounts for 11% of all wrongdoings, includes covering up poor performance rather than correcting it and management misconduct in determining performance. Theft, which comes to mind first regarding misconduct, has a share of almost 10% in all wrongdoings. The theft misconduct class includes theft of public funds, theft of public property, bribery, use of official positions for personal gain rather than public interest, unfair advantages to contractors for various services outside the contract, and employee misconduct. Safety misconduct and sexual harassment are two classes of misconduct that account for about 8% of all wrongdoings. Safety misconduct can be caused by inappropriate products or services or working conditions. Sexual harassment, on the other hand, includes sexual advances, sexually explicit remarks, or physical contact that is considered unwanted by individuals. The final class is legal violations, which have the smallest share of all wrongdoings (around 7%) but potentially have the most impactful consequences (Near et al., 2004, pp. 226-227).

2. Transparency as a Tool for Financial Crime Prevention

2.1 Transparency in Financial Systems

Transparency lies at the intersection between the public's right to know and the company's right to privacy (Borgia, 2005). The public's right to know refers to stakeholders' interest in information about the company's managerial practices and strategy. The company's right to privacy refers to its entitlement to control over the collection, use, and disclosure of all information about the company and its management strategies.

The sustainability and stability of modern economies largely depend on the effective functioning of financial systems. Transparency is fundamental for these systems to have a reliable, equitable, and inclusive structure. Transparency means not only the disclosure of information but also the timely, accurate, complete, and comparable presentation of this information (Bushman et al., 2004; Fung et al., 2007). Transparency in financial systems allows market participants to make rational decisions, while establishing trust in markets, mitigating systemic risks, and playing a role in preventing crises.

2.2 The Role of Transparency in Financial Crime Prevention

The complexity of globalized financial systems has made financial crimes more sophisticated. Crimes such as money laundering, corruption, tax evasion, insider trading, and accounting fraud are associated with internal auditing weaknesses, weak corporate governance, and inadequate disclosure practices. In this context, transparency is considered not only an element of good governance but also a preventive mechanism that makes it harder for financial crimes to occur and continue (Bushman et al., 2004). Transparency requires allowing stakeholders to see into systems and understand the rationale behind decisions made. More transparent working methods will reduce the opportunities for corrupt behavior and the reasons for others to suspect corruption (Osborne, 2004, p. 292). In this sense, increased transparency and accountability are seen as essential antidotes to corruption, which undermines governance and organizational integrity.

Brandeis (1913) expressed his approach to transparency with his famous quote: "*If the broad light of day could be let in upon men's actions, it would purify them as the sun disinfects.*" This approach, which frames transparency as a remedy for illegal or unethical actions, has significantly influenced contemporary anti-corruption strategies (Kaufmann & Weber, 2010). Empirical research consistently shows that organizations with high levels of transparency are less likely to engage in financial misconduct such as money laundering, corruption, and accounting fraud (e.g., Borgia, 2005; Bushman et al., 2004). In addition, countries that adopt international transparency norms are more capable of detecting, deterring, and prosecuting financial crimes. Cross-country analyses using data from Transparency International (2024) show that countries with higher transparency index scores tend to experience lower incidences of crimes such as money laundering and financial fraud.

2.3 Transparency Mechanisms for Reducing Financial Crime

Financial crimes often flourish in environments where information asymmetry is high, reporting systems are inadequate, and accountability is lacking. Transparency establishes mechanisms that address these vulnerabilities and serves as a counter-strategy by reducing information asymmetry on the one hand and improving accountability and the quality of financial reporting on the other.

2.3.1 Reducing Information Asymmetry

Information asymmetry, which refers to the situation where market participants cannot access information equally and fairly, has a direct and inverse relationship with transparency. Enhanced transparency reduces information asymmetry, allowing investors, shareholders, and regulatory bodies to make better-informed decisions. Financial reporting standards and public disclosure obligations play a crucial role in reducing information gaps and narrowing down areas open to abuse (Healy & Palepu, 2001). Reducing information asymmetry also increases investors' trust in companies, facilitating their access to legitimate financial resources, thus reducing the incentive or necessity for companies to resort to illicit means of funding.

2.3.2 Improving Accountability

Transparency plays a critical role in enabling accountability by making managerial and organizational actions visible and traceable. Internal audit processes are central to reinforcing accountability. By continuously monitoring and assessing the effectiveness of an organization's risk management, control, and governance processes, internal audit not only enhances transparency but also strengthens the mechanisms of accountability. Organizations with low levels of transparency often exhibit weak internal audit and internal control systems, which are vulnerable to manipulation and inefficiency (Hutton et al., 2009). Although these mechanisms exist on paper in such organizations, they frequently fail in practice due to insufficient independence, ineffective monitoring, or inadequate reporting procedures. In organizations where transparency and accountability are supported by internal audit and internal control processes, the ethical culture usually tends to be strong. Such a holistic structure reduces the risk of corruption and enhances confidence in the integrity and reliability of the organization.

2.3.3 Improving the Quality of Financial Reporting

Transparency contributes to the development of discipline mechanisms within markets. Market surveillance driven by publicly available information exerts indirect pressure on organizations even in the absence of formal regulatory intervention. Transparent financial reports prepared in accordance with frameworks such as the International Financial Reporting Standards (IFRS) enhance the efficiency of capital markets and also serve as a preventive measure against financial abuses. Therefore, financial reporting quality is not only a technical requirement but also one of the main determinants of corporate transparency. Cuijpers and Buijink (2005) have shown that firms adopting IFRS in Europe are associated with lower levels of corruption risk. Moreover, the relationship between financial reporting quality and transparency is further reinforced through external audit mechanisms. The external audit ensures that financial statements are examined by independent auditors in terms of accuracy, integrity, and compliance with legislation. Thus, external audits not only increase the quality of financial reporting but also deepen corporate transparency.

2.4 Legal and Regulatory Frameworks

International regulations promoting transparency in financial systems are essential for facilitating comparability and cooperation between countries. IFRS, International Auditing Standards (IAS), Financial Action Task Force (FATF) recommendations, OECD Corporate Governance Principles, OECD Common Reporting Standard (CRS), EU Fifth Money Laundering Directive (5AMLD), and the United Nations Convention Against Corruption (UNCAC) are the main global norms focused on transparency. These instruments collectively aim to harmonize disclosure practices, improve oversight mechanisms, and prevent financial misconduct on a global scale.

3. Whistleblowing in the Context of Financial Crime

Since what goes on inside organizations is not easily leaked out, whistleblowing is extremely important in learning about problems within organizations and preventing future problems. For this reason, the behaviors of people with knowledge from inside organizations to report organizational problems should be well understood, and appropriate whistleblowing mechanisms should be developed (Miceli et al., 2008, p. 2).

3.1 Defining Whistleblowing

Zimmermann (2025: 1) attributes the introduction of whistleblowing as a concept and research subject to the conference on professional responsibility organized by Ralph Nader and his colleagues in 1971 and the conference's final report published in 1972 (Nader et al., 1972). Whistleblowers can generally be defined as individuals who disclose negligence or misconduct within their organizations that threaten the public interest, often at significant risk of losing their jobs, damaging their careers, or being subjected to retaliation (Bok, 1980, pp. 277-278).

One of the most cited definitions of whistleblowing was provided by Near and Miceli (1985). They define whistleblowing as a rational decision-making process and define whistleblowing in terms of four elements: the whistleblower, the whistleblowing act or complaint, the authority to which the complaint is conveyed, and the organization where the complaint arises, and in four successive stages: detecting wrongdoing, deciding to blow the whistle, monitoring organizational reactions, and resolving the issue. The final definition they come up with is "the disclosure by organization members (former or current) of illegal, immoral or illegitimate practices under the control of their employers, to persons or organizations that may be able to effect action" (Near and Miceli (1985: 4). Fasterling (2014: 334) argues that there are some problems with this definition because whistleblowers do not actually disclose situations that are objectively illegal, immoral, or illegitimate but rather disclose information that they believe provides concrete evidence of practices that are illegal, immoral, or illegitimate according to their own subjective judgment.

Jubb (1999:78, 83) developed a definition of whistleblowing with six elements:

> Whistleblowing is a deliberate non-obligatory act of disclosure (Element 1, the action), which gets onto public record (Element 2, the outcome) and is made by a person (Element 3, the actor) who has or had privileged access to data or information within an organization, concerning non-trivial illegality or other wrongdoing (Element 4, the subject), whether actual, suspected or anticipated which implicates and is under the control of that organization (Element 5, the target), to an external entity (Element 6, the recipient) having potential to rectify the wrongdoing *Source*: Jubb (1999).

Similarly, Ceva and Bocchiola (2020: 2-3) define whistleblowing by six elements. Whistleblowing is the initiation of purposeful corrective action (the aim) by someone within an organization (the agent) in the form of an open or confidential report (the action) which discloses wrongdoings (the object) in an organization where the reported wrongdoing allegedly occurs (the locus) submitted to internal or external interlocutors (the addressee).

3.2 Classifying Whistleblowing

Park et al. (2008) classify whistleblowing into three types: formal versus informal, identified versus anonymous, and internal versus external. The formal versus informal classification is based on whether or not the communication channels or planned reporting procedures used by whistleblowers to report violations are already in place within an organization. Formal whistleblowing is a corporate form that uses standard communication channels or follows official protocols designed for reporting. On the other hand, informal whistleblowing is when a whistleblower personally tells close friends or someone they trust about the wrongdoing they have witnessed. Identified whistleblowing refers to the whistleblower reporting misconduct in a way that reveals their true identity. In contrast, anonymous whistleblowing refers to the employee reporting information in a way that prevents a direct link between the report and their true identity (e.g., by using a pseudonym or fake identification). The third and most commonly distinguished classification in the literature is internal versus external whistleblowing. This classification is based on whether the party to whom the employee reports the information is part of the organization's formal structure.

Internal whistleblowing means that the employee reports the wrongdoing they have witnessed to someone else within the organization. The person to whom the report is made may be a supervisor with the authority to correct the wrongdoing or a party with no official responsibility or authority to correct the wrongdoing. External whistleblowing, on the other hand, refers to reporting the wrongdoing to parties outside the organization who are believed to have the necessary authority to correct it (Park et al., 2008, p. 930).

Being one of the elements in the systematic definitions of whistleblowing, the party to whom the wrongdoing is reported matters. Near and Miceli (1987) in Dworkin and Baucus (1998: 1282) argue that the distinction of the authority to which a complaint is addressed is a legal distinction. From a social science perspective, there is no such distinction. Which channel and/or authority, internal or external, to which misconduct detected under the law should be reported can have important consequences for whistleblowers. In some cases, employees who choose a recipient not designated by law will not receive legal protection from punishment. The choice of recipient may also affect whether judges and arbitrators will protect the whistleblower. Whether internal or external, whistleblowing can affect the organization's response to the whistleblower and the effectiveness of whistleblowing and retaliation processes. Appropriate whistleblowing for social scientists involves internal and external recipients, while internal whistleblowing is seen as better for the organization (Dworkin & Baucus, 1998, pp. 1281-1283). When organizations adopt a sound code of ethics and ethical infrastructure that would enhance the moral values of the organization, the need for employees to choose external whistleblowing would decrease. Eliminating the negative consequences associated with internal whistleblowing will be made possible by the relational ethics approach (Ray, 2006, p. 444). Other factors that enhance employees' internal whistleblowing intentions are ethical leadership mediated by psychological safety (El-Gazar et al., 2025, p. 847) and decent work mediated by felt obligation and self-identification (El-Gazar & Zoromba, 2025, p. 2462).

Individual, organizational, or situational factors significantly influence employees' choice between internal and external channels when reporting wrongdoings. For example, public sector employees with higher public service motivation (PSM) tend to engage in external whistleblowing despite higher personal risks. They believe that external parties will be more effective in resolving wrongdoing. Additionally, fear of retaliation discourages employees from making internal reports and directs them toward external channels. Organizational factors also play an important role in employees' choices between internal and external whistleblowing. Employees who believe they are treated fairly at work and have received organizational training on whistleblowing procedures prefer internal reporting because they believe that their concerns about the future of their organization will be addressed appropriately within the organization. The characteristics of the abuse, a situational factor, also influence whistleblowing decisions. For example, employees are more likely to engage in external whistleblowing, especially when internal resolution is unlikely or ineffective (Jeon, 2017, p. 167).

The choice of external or internal whistleblowing channels may influence the decision of the organization regarding the wrongdoing that occurred and how to respond to the whistleblower. In the case of internal whistleblowing, the organization has a significant say in determining the rightness of the wrongdoing and the response to it, whereas in the case of external whistleblowing, both the rightness of the whistleblower and what to do afterward will be out of the initiative of the organization. For organizations, the option of doing nothing in the face of wrongdoing will be off the table. Whether the complaint is justified or unjustified, the employee's risk of retaliation will be higher in the case of external whistleblowing, as it is a challenge to the organization's authority in any case. In the case of external whistleblowing, the risk of potential reputational damage for all concerned will be greater (Near & Jensen, 1983, p. 6).

3.3 Factors that Shape Whistleblowing Behavior

One of the most influential factors that play a role in shaping whistleblowers is the international and national level legal framework supporting whistleblowers. Scandals such as Ahold, Parmalat, Enron and WorldCom led to the rapid enactment of corporate governance laws in the United States and Europe (e.g., the Sarbanes-Oxley Act (SOX) in 2002 in the United States, the Corporate Governance Code by the Cromme Committee in 2002 in Germany, the Combined Code on Corporate Governance in 2003 in the United Kingdom, the "Tabaksblat Code" in 2003 in the Netherlands, the Code on Corporate Governance by the Lippens Committee in 2004 in Belgium). Financial scandals and corporate governance laws have also increased companies' awareness of whistleblowing and led them to include it in their business regulations and guidelines (Hassink et al., 2007, p. 26). With the introduction of supportive programs and legal regulations, whistleblowing has become more common. One source of observational data on the factors that motivate whistleblowers and lead them to whistleblowing is the SEC Office of the Whistleblower annual reports on the progress of the Dodd-Frank Whistleblower Program. The report, which includes data from 2023, shows that the number of whistleblowing cases, which was 3,001 in 2012, increased significantly to 18,354 by 2023 (Schmolke & Utikal, 2025, p. 6).

Legal regulations at the organizational level also play a crucial role in shaping whistleblowing behavior. It is argued that companies' own whistleblowing policies, aimed at protecting and supporting whistleblowers, are even more effective than national-level regulations in influencing whistleblowing behavior. The internal whistleblowing policies implemented by major companies in Europe allow employees to report unethical behavior, but the scope and implementation of these policies vary significantly between companies. While most companies allow confidential and anonymous reporting, some do not encourage anonymous reporting. Additionally, procedures for retaliation protection and good-faith reporting are not sufficiently detailed. It has been suggested that strengthening whistleblower protection mechanisms by establishing clear procedures for good-faith complaints, offering anonymous reporting options while considering the risks of abuse, standardizing internal whistleblowing processes to enhance the reliability of whistleblowing mechanisms, and increasing employee awareness of whistleblowing systems through training programs are suggested to contribute to improving companies' corporate governance and ethical policies (Hassink et al., 2007, pp. 26, 40-43).

The mechanism explaining whistleblowing has often been characterized as a black box. In their theoretical model, Keil et al. (2010:804) explained how the determinants of whistleblowing identified in the literature affect whistleblowing intention. It was revealed that the driving forces behind whistleblowing affect whistleblowing intention by changing the holistic cost-benefit balance perceived by a potential whistleblower. Unlike what is usually modeled and tested, it is argued that individuals faced with a whistleblowing decision do not consider a direct effect between the determinants of whistleblowing and whistleblowing intention but rather consider a range of factors and make a holistic assessment of the perceived costs and benefits, consciously or unconsciously. In making this assessment, individuals include the effects of various factors in their decision mechanisms with different weights. Factors in order of the magnitude of the impact on whistleblowing intention are trust in the supervisor, management responsiveness, organizational climate, responsibility to report, reporting anonymity, and senior management attachment (Keil et al., 2010, pp. 804, 805)

When an employee decides to speak up about wrongdoing in his/her organization and takes action, he/she may face different reactions within the organization. The first possible reaction is to try to determine whether the employee is right or not. Once the rightness of the employee to raise the negativity has been determined, the organization should decide how to act afterward. Some organizations may choose not to take any steps against the negativity expressed in some cases. In some cases, the organization may choose to change the allegedly negative situation, or it may choose to retaliate against the employee who raised the wrongdoing, regardless of whether the employee was right or not. How the organization responds may depend on the channels through which the whistleblower discloses the wrongdoing. In the case of external whistleblowing, it will not be up to the organization to determine whether the complaint is justified. The rightness will be determined by public opinion, third parties, or institutions (courts, regulatory authorities, etc.), in which case the organization is more likely to react in a retaliatory manner (Near & Jensen, 1983, p. 6).

Kenny (2019: 14) categorized whistleblowing research into three broad categories. The first category is legal analyses that reveal whistleblowing laws and policies and examine their relationship with organizations. The second category is descriptive studies that examine whistleblowing practices in organizations and the results of whistleblowers' disclosures, and the third category is theoretical studies that examine the conceptual foundations of whistleblowing. Zimmermann (2025: 4) considers this classification as an important configuration that provides a basis for understanding how whistleblowing is handled in the literature of different disciplines that examine whistleblowing from different perspectives and for different purposes.

Whistleblowing studies also focus on the conditions under which the intention to whistleblowing arises and is turned into action. Figuring out the conditions under which retaliation happens following whistleblowing is another area of research. Studies focusing on the determinants of the decision to report corporate misconduct, the level of correlation between these determinants, the reporting process, and the modeling of the outcomes of reporting generally use variables related to the whistleblower, such as the characteristics of the whistleblower, variables related to the context in which the whistleblowing occurred and variables related to the nature of the misconduct and the characteristics of the perpetrator. Studies examining these variables in the whistleblowing process typically collect data through surveys with actual whistleblowers or through scenarios and interviews (Mesmer-Magnus & Viswesvaran, 2005, p. 278).

The more seriously the nature or consequences of misconduct observed in an organization are perceived, the more likely individuals are to be willing to blow the whistle. However, the potential for retaliation due to whistleblowing negatively affects employees' willingness to blow the whistle and increases their tendency to remain silent. There are other factors that amplify the effects of these direct factors. One factor that supports whistleblowing behavior is the rationalization that whistleblowers are legally protected, can report anonymously, and are supported by their peers and superiors. The expected feeling of regret is a factor that negatively affects the willingness to report. Whistleblowers may anticipate future regret if they feel that their decision to report is not necessarily superior to their decision to remain silent and may, therefore, avoid reporting (Khan et al., 2022, p. 14).

3.4 Challenges to Effective Whistleblowing and Transparency

In a sense, whistleblowing can be considered a corporate governance mechanism that enables employees to supervise their superiors by increasing transparency in organizations. Even when employees witness wrongdoing that threatens the organization's future or value, high 'whistleblowing costs' often prevent them from reporting these issues through official internal or external channels (Heese & Pérez-Cavazos, 2021, p. 1).

In many ways, it is not easy for an employee to become a whistleblower. Various conflicts require whistleblowers to not only make an ethical decision but also to act in anticipation of the possible consequences of the disclosure. Whistleblowers may experience various internal and external conflicts when disclosing negligence or misconduct within their organization. Bok (1980) categorized these conflicts into three main headings. First, before making a disclosure, the whistleblower must evaluate whether the identified violation and malpractice actually harm the public interest. The materiality of the detected negativity, its potential impact, and whether the disclosure will lead to a positive change should be analyzed. This is a difficult decision for the whistleblower to make. The second conflict arises when whistleblowers are torn between their responsibility to protect the public interest and their loyalty to their colleagues and organizations. On the one hand, ethical values emphasize the need to protect the public interest; on the other hand, professional ethics and corporate culture emphasize loyalty to colleagues and the organization. Whistleblowers are obliged to strike a balance in their minds between these high values. The third and perhaps the most challenging conflict for whistleblowers is the personal risks they face due to the disclosure. Whistleblowers may be subjected to practices threatening their careers, financial and personal security, and reputations, such as dismissal, exile, and forced psychiatric evaluation (Bok, 1980, pp. 277-279).

Dungan et al. (2015) define whistleblowing in general terms as a person reporting another person's unethical behavior to a third party, evaluating this behavior from a psychological perspective, and identifying the determinants that influence individuals' decisions to engage in whistleblowing. First, feelings of justice and loyalty play a significant role in people's decisions to engage in whistleblowing. As the importance of justice increases, the likelihood of whistleblowing rises, while the value of loyalty increases, this likelihood decreases. Second, individuals who have worked at the same company for a more extended period, have a higher level of education, and hold a strong position at work may be more willing to engage in whistleblowing. Although whistleblowers often face adverse reactions and may be ostracized or retaliated against, whistleblowing can lead to more collaborative and justice-oriented groups. Supporting an organizational culture that aligns people's sense of justice with loyalty and establishing appropriate organizational structures can create a healthier whistleblowing culture. This makes individuals feel comfortable reporting unethical behavior while maintaining group loyalty (Dungan et al., 2015, pp. 129-133).

3.4.1 Fear of Retaliation

Retaliation is an unwelcome response directed at a whistleblower as a consequence of their disclosure. The actions that the whistleblower would not wish to face include, on the one hand, active negative actions such as demotion and, on the other hand, the withholding of an action that would have been taken had the whistleblower not been involved in the whistleblowing activity, such as promotion. When we talk about retaliation, an action against a current employee of the organization usually comes to mind. In fact, the person subjected to retaliation for whistleblowing may be a current employee of the organization or a former employee. Although this is not the first situation that will come to mind, it is not impossible. An example of such a situation is when a former employee is accused of misconduct against the organization, such as embezzlement, by the former workplace where he or she informed. While the dismissal of the former employee is already a form of retaliation in itself, it is possible that the former employee may be subjected to a second retaliation for concealing the reason for the dismissal (Miceli et al., 2008, p. 11).

Miceli et al. (2008) explained why whistleblowers experience retaliation and the individual and organizational consequences of this process within the framework of power theories. Factors influencing the retaliation outcome include whistleblower characteristics (gender, rank, position in the organization), job characteristics (job security, level of organizational support, and relationships with managers), and the nature of the whistleblowing (the seriousness of the wrongdoing, to whom it is reported and the organization's response). For example, there is empirical evidence that the risk of retaliation is higher for external whistleblowers, and that female whistleblowers are more likely to be retaliated against. Whistleblowers exposed to retaliation may experience psychosocial consequences such as anxiety, stress, and loneliness, as well as negative emotions such as distrust and anger toward managers. In addition, whistleblowers may be stigmatized within the organization after whistleblowing, and individuals who face adverse consequences due to internal whistleblowing may resort to external channels. Retaliation is not only a phenomenon shaped by the individual circumstances of whistleblowers but is also closely related to organizational culture. Therefore, creating an environment of transparency and trust in organizations is critical in preventing retaliation (Miceli et al., 2008, pp. 101-130).

When the cases of whistleblowers who have been subjected to retaliation are examined, it is seen that the discourses of the individuals focus on exclusion and stigmatization, which is performed via mental illness. Those subjected to retaliation feel that they are outside the norms, are not trustworthy employees for the organization, and that this situation is painful and a source of stress. These thoughts and feelings that arise as a result of organizational retaliation can lead to damage to the self and deterioration of mental health. This can be used to weaken and devalue the complaints and allegations that have been the subject of whistleblowing. On the one hand, those who have been subjected to retaliation try to accept that their mental health was not impaired at the time they complained; on the other hand, they emphasize the effect of the punitive actions of wrongdoers against them and express that their mental health deteriorated after the retaliation (Kenny et al., 2019, p. 810).

3.4.2 Legal Loopholes and Insufficient Protections

The importance of legal regulations in supporting whistleblowing and increasing its effectiveness is indisputable. No matter how many regulations are put in place, legal loopholes that may exist within all legal regulations or insufficient levels of protection are some of the significant obstacles to effective whistleblowing and transparency. Despite existing legal regulations, whistleblowers may be subject to retaliation. They may refrain from reporting, and efforts to ensure that legal regulations serve transparency, accountability, and good governance may fall short.

It is crucial for legislators to establish an effective legal and regulatory framework that promotes coordination and synergy among different laws and institutions related to whistleblowing behavior. Clarity and certainty in legal regulations concerning whistleblowing behavior will encourage whistleblowers to report and make whistleblowing more effective. However, in most countries, whistleblowing is regulated by different laws and is subject to limited protection regarding the type of employees or information covered. When evaluated from the perspective of most countries, legislative activities aimed at combating corruption and abuse are generally fragmented and limited in scope (Gibbs, 2020, p. 591).

National laws and policies are designed to ensure that whistleblowers' identities and other personal information remain confidential and are not subject to retaliation. When the implementation and results of laws that appear sufficient on paper for combating corruption and increasing transparency are examined through various observations, oral statements, and case analyses, it is seen that the provisions of laws, policies, and agreements are being violated. It is necessary not only to enact laws but also to carefully exercise judicial oversight to close loopholes that reduce whistleblowers' protection in the laws. Legal loopholes may arise from a single regulation or failure to harmonize multiple regulations. Legal regulations at different levels regarding the protection of whistleblowers should be harmonized and incorporated into organizations' internal procedures. Employees and managers should be trained on official procedures for reporting and ways to protect such reports (Alshoubaki & Harris, 2022: 5).

Just as the insufficient protection of whistleblowers can be an impediment, in some cases, the overprotection of employees and managers can challenge effective whistleblowing. A good example of this situation can be seen in public sector organizations. Public sector organizations are generally much more reluctant than private sector organizations to encourage whistleblowing and protect whistleblowers through their internal regulations. This situation, inherent in the structure of public bureaucracies in developed countries, poses a greater challenge for developing countries. Public administrations may also adopt a protective or even clientelistic stance toward their employees, as they can be an extension of politics. The effects of bureaucratic secrecy and networks formed by certain interest groups that have been entrenched within organizations for a long time can be observed in public administrations. Public employees are generally subject to numerous laws and complex hierarchical processes, making dismissing them less straightforward than dismissing them as private sector employees. Under these conditions, conflicts of interest among employees are less clear-cut, existing wrongdoings are less noticeable and less likely to be punished, whistleblowers are often discredited, and whistleblower protection legislation may not be effectively enforced (Onyango, 2021, p. 169).

3.4.3 Cultural and Organizational Issues

Cultural issues significantly impact the implementation of effective whistleblowing policies and their applications. Establishing legal and institutional regulations, promoting whistleblowing, and increasing transparency do not occur at the same pace and with the same effectiveness in every culture and organizational environment. Especially in the absence of sound national legislation on whistleblowing, cultural factors and institutional arrangements can significantly impact employees' reporting behavior (Gibbs, 2020, p. 591).

4. Whistleblowing in Different Jurisdictions

Regulations regarding whistleblowing vary significantly depending on the legal, political, and cultural structures of countries. Below, regulations in various countries are discussed together with important events that took place in these countries.

4.1 United States

In the United States, whistleblowing is considered an important tool in revealing corruption, misconduct, and illegal activities, especially those concerning the public interest, and it is secured by various federal laws. These regulations are supported not only within the framework of ethical and legal responsibility but also through financial incentives and strong protection mechanisms. The US framework serves as a prominent example of how robust legal and institutional infrastructure can be mobilized to promote transparency and accountability:

- **Sarbanes-Oxley Act (2002):** The accounting and auditing scandal of Enron, which emerged in 2001, caused a major shock in the US capital markets. Enron misled investors by concealing substantial debt through off-balance sheet partnerships, ultimately resulting in the sudden collapse of the company (Swartz & Watkins, 2004). Sherron Watkins, who served as the vice president at Enron, alerted the company's CEO to these irregularities in an internal letter and later became an important figure in the public eye. Her actions significantly shaped the discourse around corporate whistleblowing. This incident was a turning point in the formal institutionalization of whistleblower protections. The Sarbanes-Oxley Act (SOX), passed by the US Congress in 2002, strengthened corporate internal control systems and provided legal protection for whistleblowers. Specifically, Section 806 of SOX encourages employees of publicly traded companies to report financial fraud while protecting them from retaliation, such as termination or harassment (US Congress, 2002).
- **Dodd-Frank Act (2010):** The Dodd-Frank Act, which came into effect after the 2008 global financial crisis, introduced reforms to enhance oversight and accountability within the financial markets, including the establishment of a formal whistleblower program under the authority of the US Securities and Exchange Commission (SEC) (US Congress, 2010). The Act incentivizes individuals to report violations of securities laws by offering monetary rewards along with robust protection against retaliation. The SEC awarded over $255 million in whistleblower rewards in 2024, bringing the total amount distributed under the program to over $2.2 billion (SEC, 2024).
- **Bank Secrecy Act (1970):** The Bank Secrecy Act (BSA) serves as the cornerstone of the United States' anti-money laundering (AML) regulatory framework. Under the BSA, banks are required to report Currency Transaction Reports (CTRs) and Suspicious Activity Reports (SARs) to the Financial Crimes Enforcement Network (FinCEN). In this context, the BSA ensures the

confidentiality of whistleblowers and, under certain circumstances, provides financial rewards (FinCEN, 2016).

- **False Claims Act (1863, revised 1986):** The main purpose of the False Claims Act (FCA) is to deter and penalize fraudulent claims against government institutions. It is particularly applied in areas where public funds are heavily used, such as healthcare, defense, education, and infrastructure. The most striking aspect of the FCA is the "qui tam" provision, which aims to increase whistleblowers through financial incentives. According to this provision, individuals (whistleblowers) can file a lawsuit on behalf of the federal government against entities suspected of committing fraud, and depending on the outcome of the case, the whistleblower can receive a portion of the financial recovery obtained by the government (US Congress, 1986).
- **Whistleblower Protection Act (1989):** The Whistleblower Protection Act (WPA) protects reporting illegal, unethical, or public policy-threatening practices against retaliatory actions such as termination, expulsion, transfer, or demotion (US Congress, 1989). The Whistleblower Protection Enhancement Act (WPEA), enacted in 2012, was designed to address the deficiencies of the WPA and provide more effective protection for whistleblowers (US Congress, 2012).

4.2 European Union (EU)

The European Union imposed extensive whistleblower protection obligations on member states with the Whistleblower Protection Directive (EU) 2019/1937 (European Parliament, 2019). This directive sets minimum whistleblower protection standards for all 27 EU Member States, thereby replacing regulations that vary from country to country with a single, common standard. The directive includes protection provisions for a wide range of potential whistleblowers, including employees in the public and private sectors. These nonemployees serve as consultants, contractors, board members, and former employees. According to this directive, member states are required to establish internal reporting channels and ensure the anonymity of whistleblowers. It also provides legal protection against reprisals such as discrimination, mobbing, and dismissal directed at whistleblowers. All EU member states have transposed the directive into their legal systems, but Germany and France will be given special mention.

4.2.1 Germany

Until 2023, there was no direct and comprehensive regulation in Germany regarding the protection of whistleblowers. Limited protection was provided through scattered legal provisions and case law decisions. Despite this, Germany was among the last countries to adopt the Whistleblower Protection Directive of the European Union into its domestic law, a delay rectified by the enactment of the Hinweisgeberschutzgesetz (HinSchG) in 2023 (Bundesgesetzblatt, 2023).

The Wirecard scandal that broke out in 2020 played a significant role in the enactment of the HinSchG. The Germany-based fintech company Wirecard declared bankruptcy after it was revealed that approximately €1.9 billion in assets were fictitious. Pav Gill, one of the company's legal advisors, initially reported the corruption through internal channels. When his efforts failed, he leaked the information to the media and drew public attention. The scandal exposed the gross negligence of not only the company's executives but also the auditing firm Ernst & Young and the German financial supervisory authority BaFin (Heese et al., 2021). This incident triggered the reform of financial oversight structures in the country, demonstrating the need for significant legal changes regarding whistleblower protection and transparency.

4.2.2 France

France aimed to strengthen ethical conduct and transparency standards in the private sector with the Sapin II Law, which came into force in 2017. This law offers protection to employees who report corruption, conflict of interest, or serious public threats to public health (AFA, 2016). According to the law, companies are legally obliged to establish internal reporting mechanisms and safeguard the identity of the whistleblower. However, in practice, the effectiveness of the regulation remained limited due to social exclusion, psychological pressure, and lack of institutional support for whistleblowers (Brimbeuf & Fabre, 2020). The UBS Bank scandal illustrates these challenges. In France, UBS was fined for providing illicit advisory services to clients engaged in tax evasion (Reuters, 2019). Stéphanie Gibaud, who exposed the scandal, discovered irregularities while working in the marketing department of UBS and reported them to the authorities. As a result, she lost her job and was subjected to economic and social exclusion for a long time (Gibaud, 2014). Gibaud's experience reveals that the Sapin II Law, which provides protection at a theoretical level, does not provide sufficient safeguards for whistleblowers in practice.

France incorporated the EU Directive into its national law in 2022. The new regulation, also known as Sapin III, abolished employees' internal reporting obligation and allowed them to contact external authorities directly. In addition, a punitive framework aimed at sanctioning individuals or entities that retaliate against whistleblowers was introduced (Légifrance, 2022).

4.3 United Kingdom

The United Kingdom was among the first European countries to legally recognize whistleblowing through the Public Interest Disclosure Act (PIDA), which came into force in 1998. PIDA aims to protect employees who report workplace misconduct that affects the public interest (UK Legislation, 1998). However, to apply this regulation, the individual must prove that he/she is acting in "good faith" and "in the public interest". Due to the uncertainties encountered in practice and the narrow scope of protection, the need for legal reform has frequently been on the agenda in recent years.

The Barclays Bank London Inter Bank Offered Rate (LIBOR) scandal that broke out in 2012 constitutes an important example of whistleblowing. The scandal revealed that the bank violated market integrity by manipulating LIBOR, the global reference interest rate. Both employees who leaked insider information and secret applications made to regulatory authorities played a significant role in uncovering the misconduct. Particularly during the 2007–2009 period, several Barclays employees noticed that the bank was manipulating LIBOR rates and reported their concerns to senior management and internal audit departments. However, these internal reports were not taken seriously for a long time, and some whistleblowers were even tried to be silenced covertly. During the subsequent investigation, the United Kingdom's Financial Services Authority (FSA) uncovered systemic manipulation, with whistleblower testimonies playing a crucial role in deepening the inquiry (Rose & Sesia, 2013).

This scandal showed deficiencies in the United Kingdom's whistleblower protection system within the financial sector and highlighted the vulnerability of employees to retaliation. In response, regulatory reforms were introduced regarding both transparency and whistleblowing. The Financial Conduct Authority (FCA) and the Prudential Regulation Authority (PRA) have made it mandatory for financial institutions to establish independent and accessible internal whistleblowing mechanisms and to appoint a "Whistleblowing Champion" responsible for the effective implementation of these mechanisms (FCA, 2015). Although the United Kingdom is among the leading countries that recognize and legally protect whistleblowing, ongoing criticisms suggest that the existing framework is not sufficient and needs to be strengthened.

4.4 Australia

Australia has one of the most comprehensive whistleblower protection systems in the world with its highly effective whistleblowing regulations regarding financial corruption. The Corporations Act, which came into force in 2001 and comprises rules on the protection of whistleblowers in the private sector, was further strengthened by amendments in 2019 (Australian Government, 2019). In addition, the Public Interest Disclosure Act, which came into force in 2013 and was updated in 2024, provides legal safeguards for whistleblowers in the public sector (Australian Government, 2024). Together, these laws provide extensive protection for employees (and, under certain circumstances, former employees, interns, and relatives of whistleblowers) who report serious financial crimes, such as accounting irregularities, corruption, fraud, and money laundering. The legislation guarantees anonymity and protects whistleblowers from retaliation, such as dismissal, demotion, threats, or reputational harm.

4.5 Canada

Canada provides protection to public servants at the federal level through the Public Servants Disclosure Protection Act (PSDPA), which came into effect in 2007 (Government of Canada, 2005). However, the law has been criticized for not covering the private sector. In addition, the protections are limited, and the application procedures are complex.

4.6 Japan

Japan provides legal protection to public and private sector employees with the Whistleblower Protection Act of 2004. However, as it applies only to reporting certain crimes, the law's scope has been considered limited. The legal protection provided to whistleblowers was strengthened with the reforms made in 2022.

The biggest obstacle to whistleblowing in Japan is the traditional corporate culture. Traditional Japanese companies are generally characterized as stable, homogeneous organizations with meticulously structured internal systems, providing lifetime employment to their employees through internal promotion systems (Asaoka, 2020). Since loyalty to the institution is at the forefront, reporting behavior that will harm the image and interests of the institution is considered a betrayal. Consequently, whistleblowers may face social and professional difficulties. As a result, although legal frameworks regarding whistleblowing exist in Japan, cultural dynamics make it difficult to implement.

4.7 Developing Countries

In many developing countries, whistleblowing regulations either do not exist at all, or the existing regulations are not effectively implemented. Existing legal frameworks are often inadequate in protecting the confidentiality of whistleblowers, accepting anonymous reporting, and providing effective judicial remedies for those subjected to retaliation after whistleblowing. Furthermore, when judicial bodies and law enforcement agencies do not act impartially, these regulations lose effectiveness and credibility. Therefore, the effectiveness of whistleblowing regulations in these countries is generally limited due to reasons such as a lack of legal infrastructure, institutional weaknesses, cultural pressures, and weak protection mechanisms against retaliation (Onyango, 2021).

Nevertheless, progress is being observed in some countries. For example, India, Brazil, South Africa, and Indonesia have tried to strengthen their whistleblowing laws in recent years as part of their anti-corruption strategies, established independent monitoring mechanisms, and aligned their frameworks with international standards. In Indonesia, anonymous whistleblowing mechanisms have been established through the Corruption Eradication Commission (KPK). In South Africa, whistleblowing is encouraged through the safeguards provided by the Protected Disclosures Act (South African Government, 2000). Similarly, in India, the Whistle Blowers Protection Act provides protection for whistleblowers (Government of India, 2014).

However, despite all these legal frameworks, the protection mechanisms for whistleblowers in developing countries remain largely ineffective in practice. Culturally, in many developing countries, whistleblowing is often stigmatized and associated with negative notions such as "spying" or "betrayal," which pushes potential whistleblowers to remain silent (Banisar, 2011). The confidentiality of whistleblowers' identities is not always protected, leaving them vulnerable to retaliation such as job termination, social exclusion, and even physical harm. In this context, political will, judicial independence and pressure from civil society continue to be the main factors determining the real effectiveness of whistleblower systems in these countries.

5. Case Studies

5.1 The Panama Papers

The Panama Papers refer to nearly 40 years of leaked data from the Panama-based law firm Mossack Fonseca. Consisting of 11.5 million documents, this leak represents the largest whistleblower case in history. It shows how a global network of law firms and major banks facilitates financial secrecy for politicians, fraudsters, drug dealers, billionaires, celebrities, and sports figures (Trautman, 2017). Reviewed by more than 400 journalists from across the globe, the documents unveiled the offshore holdings of hundreds of public officials and political leaders from over 200 countries.

They include allegations that secret offshore vehicles were used by a wide range of companies, politicians, and others around the world for tax evasion, corruption financing, and money laundering. These individuals include Icelandic Prime Minister Sigmundur David Gunnlaugsson, former British Prime Minister David Cameron, Argentine President Mauricio Macri, Saudi Arabian King Salman, Russian President Vladimir V. Putin, and senior Chinese government officials.

The affair began in early 2015 when an anonymous whistleblower contacted the Süddeutsche Zeitung, a German newspaper known for its investigative work on financial crime. Given the sheer volume of data, the newspaper enlisted the help of the International Consortium of Investigative Journalists (ICIJ). The Panama Papers, the first of which was released in April 2016, have triggered global political fallout and numerous investigations.

All banks operating in the world offer a certain level of confidentiality to their customers. The difference with offshore tax havens, most of which are former British colonies, is that they never compromise confidentiality, even in the face of clear legal violations in other jurisdictions. While there are incentives and protections for whistleblowing in many countries, in most offshore havens, whistleblowing is an act that must be prevented and is subject to criminal sanctions. The anonymous whistleblower who initiated the incident and did not gain any monetary reward but rather risked his business security and reputation stated that his actions were driven by a desire to expose a system that he believed was detrimental to society (Deng, 2016).

The Panama Papers thus not only exposed the widespread use of offshore structures to hide wealth and evade taxes but also sparked a global reckoning with the limitations of financial transparency, the systemic weaknesses of regulatory frameworks, and the deep ethical responsibilities of both those who facilitate financial abuse and those who expose financial misconduct.

5.2 The Danske Bank Scandal

The Danske Bank scandal, one of the most significant money laundering cases in European financial history, involved the illicit flow of approximately €200 billion through the bank's Estonian branch between 2007 and 2015 (Bruun & Hjejle, 2018). These transactions originated primarily from Russia and other former Soviet states and went undetected for a long time due to inadequate internal controls, gaps in cross-border monitoring, and a general lack of transparency. The efforts of whistleblower Howard Wilkinson were decisive in exposing this secret structure (BBC News, 2018).

In 2014, a mid-level manager, Howard Wilkinson, submitted a comprehensive report on suspicious nonresident accounts at the Estonian branch. These accounts were the source of transfers of large sums of money, often from rubles to dollars. One example in Wilkinson's report, Lantana Trade LLC, appeared dormant on UK financial records while making transfers of up to $20 million per day (Logan, 2019). Many of these companies were registered in jurisdictions associated with financial secrecy, such as the Seychelles and Marshall Islands, and many accounts were linked to criminal figures.

Although Wilkinson's internal report reached the bank's senior executives, no serious institutional reflex was developed; on the contrary, the problem was covered up (Jensen, 2018). This inaction reveals both the lack of ethical governance and the lack of coordination between regulatory institutions. Prior to the scandal, the bank's home country, Denmark, was ranked high in world transparency rankings and was among the countries with low levels of corruption. The scandal prompted calls to strengthen international financial regulatory frameworks.

An independent legal report published in 2018 confirmed Wilkinson's concerns. Wilkinson resigned from Danske Bank in 2014 on ethical grounds and was later honored with the Cliff Robertson Sentinel Award "For Choosing Truth Over Self" by the Association of Certified Fraud Examiners in 2020 for his courageous whistleblowing (Carozza, 2020).

This case underscores that financial transparency is a fundamental prerequisite for the effective implementation of accountability, ethical governance, and AML regulations. It also clearly demonstrates that transparency depends not only on internal audit processes but also on effective whistleblowing mechanisms, public scrutiny, and international cooperation. The absence of transparency poses a serious threat not only to the integrity of the financial system but also to public trust in the financial system itself.

5.3 Ponzi Schemes

Ponzi schemes are fraudulent financial operations that are structured around paying old investors from funds provided by new investors and promising investors unsustainably high returns. The secretive and manipulative nature of these schemes makes it difficult to detect the internal dynamics of these systems from the outside. Therefore, the prolonged failure to uncover Ponzi schemes is due not only to the inadequacy of regulatory institutions but also to the limited flow of insider information. At this point, the role of whistleblowers is of critical importance.

5.3.1 The Bernard Madoff Case

The earnings of Ponzi businesses are less than the payments made to investors, and the liabilities to investors are greater than the assets of the scheme. From an accounting perspective, this situation technically indicates bankruptcy (Lewis, 2012). Although the collapse of such schemes is inevitable, the system continues to operate as long as new investors continue to enter the pool. However, it is unusual for a Ponzi scheme, such as the Bernard Madoff case, to last for decades rather than years.

Bernard L. Madoff, considered the biggest financial fraudster in US history, was the former Executive Chairman of the NASDAQ stock exchange. He founded the Wall Street firm Bernard L. Madoff Investment Securities LLC in 1960 and served as its chairman until his arrest in 2008. The Madoff case, known as the biggest Ponzi scheme in financial history, involved an estimated fraud of approximately $65 billion. One of the most important actors who played a role in the collapse of this system was portfolio manager Harry Markopolos. Markopolos identified that Madoff's claims of constant returns of over 10% per year were mathematically impossible. He alerted the SEC five times between 1999 and 2008 and, at one point, wrote a letter to *The Washington Post* stating that there were up to 30 "red flags" that caused concern (Markopolos, 2011). However, these attempts were ignored for a long time due to Madoff being a Wall Street legend with enormous power and influence and a charismatic and persuasive character. The system collapsed only after investors tried to withdraw their money during the 2008 financial crisis. On December 10, 2008, Madoff's sons confessed that the company was a large Ponzi scheme, and Madoff was arrested. Although Madoff said that the scheme started in the early 1990s, federal investigators revealed that the fraud has been going on since the 1970s.

The Madoff case highlights the consequences of regulatory indifference despite the early intervention of whistleblowers and shows the importance of authorities both recognizing and responding to whistleblowers' reports.

5.3.2 Tom Petters Case

The Tom Petters case is one of the largest corporate Ponzi schemes in US history, highlighted by the decisive role of whistleblowing in the collapse of the system.

Tom Petters, chairman and CEO of Petters Group Worldwide, claimed to generate high profits by purchasing electronic products at discounted prices and selling them to major retailers. However, these transactions were never actually carried out. Petters fabricated activities and transactions using falsified documents to deceive investors (Cross, 2017). The system was based on making payments to old investors with the funds from new investors in a classic Ponzi structure. In this way, Petters established a fraud network valued at approximately $3.65 billion.

The key figure who uncovered the scandal was Deanna Coleman, the company's vice president. After noticing inconsistencies in the company's financial records, Coleman reported directly to the FBI in 2008. She cooperated with the FBI and secretly recorded conversations in which Petters confessed to his illegal activities, and these recordings formed the basis of the case (FBI, 2010). Tom Petters was sentenced to prison in 2009 for fraud, money laundering, and forgery. Petters Group Worldwide went bankrupt, and thousands of investors suffered significant financial losses.

6. Concluding Remarks

Transparency and whistleblowing can be considered two important pillars that uphold financial integrity. Transparency should not be viewed merely as a one-sided and passive sharing of information with stakeholders. Transparency should be seen as an important factor in the development of a culture of governance within institutions and in the prevention of financial crime, supporting accountability, visibility, and trust. With mechanisms such as robust financial reporting, audit practices, and disclosure requirements, transparency helps prevent fraud that has existed and will continue to exist in every organization and prevents such fraud from escalating into a systemic collapse.

Whistleblowing, an important mechanism that supports transparency and prevents financial crimes, is a courageous and often costly action. It can fill the gaps where transparency mechanisms fail or are deliberately circumvented by malicious parties. Whistleblowers, motivated by various factors, have played important roles in exposing a wide range of abuses, from small-scale abuses at the corporate level to global financial crime networks. Of course, the effectiveness of whistleblowing depends on rights guaranteed by legal regulations, organizational regulations that support whistleblowing and protect employees from adverse consequences, and the cultural environment at both the societal and organizational levels.

Academic studies and cases clearly show that even the most advanced legal frameworks are only effective if they are implemented and culturally accepted. While countries may differ significantly in terms of legal development and institutional maturity, there is one common point: where ethics, public oversight, and legal support intersect, the likelihood of financial crime decreases. To build resilient financial systems, organizations, and policymakers must go beyond compliance. They must foster relational trust, support internal reporting, and create environments where transparency and whistleblowing are seen not as risks but as necessary tools for maintaining legitimacy, justice, and long-term stability.

References

AFA. (2016). *The French anti-corruption agency guidelines*. https://www.agence-francaise-anticorruption.gouv.fr/files/files/French%20AC%20Agency%20Guidelines%20.pdf

Alshoubaki, W. E., & Harris, M. (2022). Striving for protection: Whistleblowers in Jordan. *Sage Open*, *12*(2), 1–7.

Asaoka, D. (2020). A behavioral analysis of whistleblowing at Japanese firms. *Humanities and Social Sciences Communications*, *7*(95). https://doi.org/10.1057/s41599-020-00588-7

Australian Government. (2019). *Corporations act 2001*. https://www.legislation.gov.au/C2004A00818/2019-07-01/text

Australian Government. (2024). *Public interest disclosure act 2013*. https://www.legislation.gov.au/C2013A00133/latest/text

Banisar, D. (2011). Whistleblowing: International standards and developments. In I. Sandoval (Ed.), *Corruption and transparency: Debating the frontiers between state, market and society*. World Bank-Institute for Social Research, UNAM. https://ssrn.com/abstract=1753180

BBC News. (2018). *Danske bank boss quits over. €200bn money-laundering scandal*. https://www.bbc.com/news/business-45571744

Bok, S. (1980). Whistleblowing and professional responsibilities. In *Ethics teaching in higher education* (pp. 277–295). Springer US.

Borgia, F. (2005). *Corporate governance & transparency role of disclosure: How prevent new financial scandals and crimes*. American University Transnational Crime and Corruption Center, School of International Service. https://citeseerx.ist.psu.edu/document?repid=rep1&type=pdf&doi=8a42579c24f5324fd9ab10adc91d0577b7d926a1

Brandeis, L. D. (1913). What publicity can do?. *Harper's Weekly*. https://archive.org/details/sim_harpers-weekly_1913-12-20_58_2974/page/10/mode/2up

Brimbeuf, S., & Fabre, L. (2020). From compliance to commitment: A major challenge for anti-corruption actors in France. *Transparency International*. https://www.transparency.org/en/blog/from-compliance-to-commitment

Bruun, H., & Hjejle, J.S. (2018). *Report on the non-resident portfolio at danske Bank's Estonian branch*. https://danskebank.com/-/media/danske-bank-com/file-cloud/2018/9/report-on-the-non-resident-portfolio-at-danske-banks-estonian-branch.pdf

Bundesgesetzblatt. (2023). *Gesetz für einen besseren Schutz hinweisgebender Personen sowie zur Umsetzung der Richtlinie zum Schutz von Personen, die Verstöße gegen das Unionsrecht melden*. https://www.recht.bund.de/bgbl/1/2023/140/VO

Bushman, R. M., Piotroski, J. D., & Smith, A. J. (2004). What determines corporate transparency?. *Journal of Accounting Research*, *42*(2), 207–252. https://doi.org/10.1111/j.1475-679X.2004.00136.x

Carozza, D. (2020, March 1). The smoke detector. *Fraud Magazine*. https://www.acfe.com/fraud-magazine/all-issues/issue/article?s=2020-marchapril-howard-wilkinson-cover

Ceva, E., & Bocchiola, M. (2020). Theories of whistleblowing. *Philosophy Compass*, *15*(1), 1–10.

Cross, C. (2017). *Anatomy of a ponzi: Scams past and present*. Slice Publishing.

Cuijpers, R., & Buijink, W. (2005). Voluntary adoption of non-local GAAP in the European Union: A study of determinants and consequences. *European Accounting Review*, *14*(3), 487–524. https://doi.org/10.1080/0963818042000337132

Deng, B. (2016). Panama tax whistleblower steps forward. *The Times*. https://www.thetimes.com/uk/law/article/panama-tax-whistleblower-steps-forward-v2xhv0kjw

Dungan, J., Waytz, A., & Young, L. (2015). The psychology of whistleblowing. *Current Opinion in Psychology*, *6*, 129–133.

Dworkin, T. M., & Baucus, M. S. (1998). Internal vs. external whistleblowers: A comparison of whistleblowering processes. *Journal of Business Ethics*, *17*(12), 1281–1298.

El-Gazar, H. E., Baghdadi, N. A., Abdelaliem, S. M. F., & Zoromba, M. A. (2025). Linking ethical leadership to nurses' internal whistleblowing through psychological safety. *Nursing Ethics*, *32*(3), 837–850.

El-Gazar, H. E., & Zoromba, M. A. (2025). How decent work influences internal whistleblowing intentions in nurses: The parallel mediating roles of felt obligation and organisational identification—A cross-sectional survey. *Journal of Advanced Nursing*, *81*(5), 2454–2464.

European Parliament. (2019). *Directive (EU) 2019/1937 of the European Parliament and of the Council of 23 October 2019 on the protection of persons who report breaches of Union law*. https://eur-lex.europa.eu/legal-content/en/TXT/?uri=CELEX%3A32019L1937

Fasterling, B. (2014). Whistleblower protection: A comparative law perspective. In *International handbook on whistleblowing research* (pp. 331–349). Edward Elgar Publishing.

FBI. (2010). *Deanna coleman sentenced for her role in the Tom Petters Ponzi scheme*. U.S. Attorney's Office. https://archives.fbi.gov/archives/minneapolis/press-releases/2010/mp090210a.htm

FCA. (2015). *Accountability and whistleblowing instrument 2015*. https://www.handbook.fca.org.uk/instrument/2015/FCA_2015_46.pdf

FinCEN. (2016). *The bank secrecy act*. www.fincen.gov/resources/statutes-and-regulations/bank-secrecy-act

Fung, A., Graham, M., & Weil, D. (2007). *Full disclosure: The perils and promise of transparency*. Cambridge University Press.

Gibaud, S. (2014). La femme qui en savait vraiment trop. *Le Cherche Midi*.

Gibbs, T. (2020). Whistleblowing: Protection or discouragement. *Journal of Money Laundering Control*, *23*(3), 591–600.

Government of Canada. (2005). *Public servants disclosure protection act*. https://laws-lois.justice.gc.ca/PDF/P-31.9.pdf

Government of India. (2014). *The whistle blowers protection act*. https://lddashboard.legislative.gov.in/actsofparliamentfromtheyear/whistle-blowers-protection-act-2014

Hassink, H., De Vries, M., & Bollen, L. (2007). A content analysis of whistleblowing policies of leading European companies. *Journal of Business Ethics*, *75*, 25–44.

Healy, P. M., & Palepu, K. G. (2001). Information asymmetry, corporate disclosure, and the capital markets: A review of the empirical disclosure literature. *Journal of Accounting and Economics*, *31*(1–3), 405–440. https://doi.org/10.1016/S0165-4101(01)00018-0

Heese, J., & Pérez-Cavazos, G. (2021). The effect of retaliation costs on employee whistleblowing. *Journal of Accounting and Economics*, *71*(2–3), 101385.

Heese, J., Wang, C. C. Y., & Labruyere, T. (2021). *Wirecard: The downfall of a German Fintech star*. Harvard Business School Case 121-058. https://www.hbs.edu/faculty/Pages/item.aspx?num=59971

Hutton, A. P., Marcus, A. J., & Tehranian, H. (2009). Opaque financial reports, R2, and crash risk. *Journal of Financial Economics*, *94*(1), 67–86. https://doi.org/10.1016/j.jfineco.2008.10.003

Jensen, T. (2018, November 19). *Danske Bank's 200 billion euro money laundering scandal*. Reuters. https://www.reuters.com/article/business/danske-banks-200-billion-euro-money-laundering-scandal-idUSKCN1NO10D/

Jeon, S. H. (2017). Where to report wrongdoings? Exploring the determinants of internal versus external whistleblowing. *International Review of Public Administration*, *22*(2), 153–171.

Jubb, P. B. (1999). Whistleblowing: A restrictive definition and interpretation. *Journal of Business Ethics*, *21*, 77–94.

Kaufmann, C., & Weber, R. H. (2010). The role of transparency in financial regulation. *Journal of International Economic Law*, *13*(3), 779–797. https://doi.org/10.1093/jiel/jgq037

Keil, M., Tiwana, A., Sainsbury, R., & Sneha, S. (2010). Toward a theory of whistleblowing intentions: A benefit-to-cost differential perspective. *Decision Sciences*, *41*(4), 787–812.

Kenny, K. (2019). *Whistleblowing: Toward a new theory*. Harvard University Press.

Kenny, K., Fotaki, M., & Scriver, S. (2019). Mental heath as a weapon: Whistleblower retaliation and normative violence. *Journal of Business Ethics*, *160*, 801–815.

Khan, J., Saeed, I., Zada, M., Ali, A., Contreras-Barraza, N., Salazar-Sepúlveda, G., & Vega-Muñoz, A. (2022). Examining whistleblowing intention: The influence of rationalization on wrongdoing and threat of retaliation. *International Journal of Environmental Research and Public Health*, *19*(3), 1752.

Légifrance. (2022). *LOI n° 2022-401 du 21 mars 2022 visant à améliorer la protection des lanceurs d'alerte*. https://www.legifrance.gouv.fr/jorf/id/JORFTEXT000045388745

Lewis, K. L. (2012). New dogs, old tricks. Why do ponzi schemes succeed?. *Accounting Forum*, *36*(4), 294–309. https://doi.org/10.1016/j.accfor.2011.11.002

Logan, B. (2019). *The case of danske Bank and money laundering*. Seven Pillars Institute for Finance and Ethics. https://sevenpillarsinstitute.org/the-case-of-danske-bank-and-money-laundering/

Markopolos, H., & Fisher, D. (2011). *No one would listen: A true financial thriller*. John Wiley.

Meenakshi, F., & Lenka, J. (2023). *Stepping up the EU's efforts to tackle corruption–Cost of non-Europe report*. European Parliamentary Research Service.

Mesmer-Magnus, J. R., & Viswesvaran, C. (2005). Whistleblowing in organizations: An examination of correlates of whistleblowing intentions, actions, and retaliation. *Journal of Business Ethics*, *62*, 277–297.

Miceli, M. P., Near, J. P., & Dworkin, T. M. (2008). *Whistle-blowing in organizations*. Psychology Press.

Nader, R., Petkas, P. J., & Blackwell, K. (1972). *Whistle blowing: The report of the conference on professional responsibility*. Grossman Publishers.

Near, J. P., & Jensen, T. C. (1983). The whistleblowing process: Retaliation and perceived effectiveness. *Work and Occupations*, *10*(1), 3–28.

Near, J. P., & Miceli, M. P. (1985). Organizational dissidence: The case of whistle-blowing. *Journal of Business Ethics*, *4*(1), 1–16.

Near, J. P., Rehg, M. T., Van Scotter, J. R., & Miceli, M. P. (2004). Does type of wrongdoing affect the whistle-blowing process?. *Business Ethics Quarterly*, *14*(2), 219–242.

Onyango, G. (2021). Whistleblower protection in developing countries: A review of challenges and prospects. *SN Business & Economics*, *1*, 169. https://doi.org/10.1007/s43546-021-00169-z

Osborne, D. (2004). Transparency and accountability reconsidered. *Journal of Financial Crime*, *11*(3), 292–300. https://doi.org/10.1108/13590790410809239

Park, H., Blenkinsopp, J., Oktem, M. K., & Omurgonulsen, U. (2008). Cultural orientation and attitudes toward different forms of whistleblowing: A comparison of South Korea, Turkey, and the UK. *Journal of Business Ethics*, *82*, 929–939.

Ray, S. L. (2006). Whistleblowing and organizational ethics. *Nursing Ethics*, *13*(4), 438–445.

Reuters. (2019, December 20). French court slashes UBS tax evasion fine to 1.8 billion Euros. https://www.reuters.com/article/business/french-court-slashes-ubs-tax-evasion-fine-to-1-8-billion-euros-idUSNIKBN2IS0FP

Rose, C. S., & Sesia, A. (2013). *Barclays and the LIBOR scandal*. Harvard Business School Case 313–075. https://www.hbs.edu/faculty/Pages/item.aspx?num=43888

Schmolke, K. U., & Utikal, V. (2025). Whistleblowing: Incentives and situational determinants. *Journal of Business Economics*, 1–24.

SEC. (2024). *Securities and exchange commission office of the whistleblower annual report to congress for fiscal year 2024*. https://www.sec.gov/files/fy24-annual-whistleblower-report.pdf

South African Government. (2000). *Protected disclosures act 26 of 2000*. https://www.gov.za/documents/acts/protected-disclosures-act-26-2000-07-aug-2000

Swartz, M., & Watkins, S. (2004). *Power failure: The inside story of the collapse of enron*. Doubleday.

Transparency International. (2024). *Corruption perceptions index*. https://www.transparency.org/en/publications/corruption-perceptions-index-2024

Transparency International. (2025). *What is corruption?*. https://www.transparency.org/en/what-is-corruption. Accessed 06 21, 2025.

Trautman, L. J. (2017). Following the money: Lessons from the Panama Papers: Part 1: Tip of the iceberg. *Penn State Law Review*, *121*(3), 807–873.

UK Legislation. (1998). *Public interest disclosure act 1998*. https://www.legislation.gov.uk/ukpga/1998/23/contents

U.S. Congress. (1986). *False claims amendments act of 1986*. https://www.congress.gov/bill/99th-congress/senate-bill/1562/text

U.S. Congress. (1989). *Whistleblower protection act of 1989*. https://www.congress.gov/bill/101st-congress/senate-bill/20/text

U.S. Congress. (2002). *Sarbanes-Oxley act of 2002*. https://www.congress.gov/bill/107th-congress/house-bill/3763/text

U.S. Congress. (2010). *Dodd-frank wall street reform and consumer protection act*. https://www.congress.gov/bill/111th-congress/house-bill/4173/text

U.S. Congress. (2012). *Whistleblower protection enhancement act of 2012*. https://www.congress.gov/bill/112th-congress/senate-bill/743/text

World Bank. (2020). *Finding fraud: GovTech and fraud detection in the public administration*. Report No: AUS0001581.

Zimmermann, P. (2025). Staging debates in whistleblowing research: A problematizing literature review. *Journal of Business Ethics*, 1–13.

Chapter 11

Cryptocurrency and Financial Crimes Financial Accounting Implications

Dafina Abdullahu

University "Ukshin Hoti" Prizren, Republic of Kosovo

Abstract

Nowadays, increasing attention is being paid to issues related to the challenges and opportunities of handling cryptocurrencies in financial statements by financial professionals, including accountants, internal auditors, external auditors, managers, and financial analysts. To provide information on this topic, the study aims to identify the relationship between cryptocurrencies as a subject of increasing financial crimes (accounting fraud) on the one hand and the role of financial professionals in preventing fraud on the other. An analytical–statistical approach is used to analyze how the growth of the cryptocurrency market and their use has an effect on the growth of financial crimes and accounting fraud. The sample consists of 200 observations from financial professionals. The analysis of the collected data was carried out through the SPSS v.26 statistical program, where two variables were tested: the independent variable (X) the use of cryptocurrencies and the dependent variable (Y) financial crimes (accounting fraud). The findings show that financial crimes stemming from the use of cryptocurrencies are positively correlated.

This positive correlation is shown by countries characterized by weak judicial processes, low transparency due to the greater possibility of fraud, lack of knowledge in implementing and adapting to cryptocurrency standards, and lack of interest on the part of financial professionals in examining cryptocurrency issues, which remain issues of concern.

Keywords: Financial crimes; cryptocurrencies; challenges; advantages; accounting implications

Corruption and Crime in Finance, 235–247

doi:10.1108/978-1-83708-170-720261028

1. Introduction

The approach to these phenomena of financial crimes does not exclude any society, this form has become a pandemic and an opportunity in some cases selective and corrupt for society and the state to camouflage misuse. For the moment, an identifying relationship between cryptocurrencies and the possibilities of using these channels to enable financial crimes remains an enigma for both the state and the institutions that fight such financial crimes.

Today, cryptocurrencies and their implications for financial accounting are being used as an opportunity for cryptocurrencies as digital assets, although they do not yet have a unified treatment according to international accounting standards IFRS or GAAP (Fernando, 2025). Since we do not know their origin, we do not know the risk of using them. Although they do not currently have a guarantee, while at the same time they are creating uncertainty for the valuation, measurement and presentation in national and international financial statements, this line is due to the volatility of market value, they are currently posing a risk of inaccurate financial reporting. Also, the lack of fiscal and tax guidelines, and in some countries even a legal basis on how to handle and manage them, makes reporting challenging. While cryptocurrencies are often used for money laundering, the exploitation of anonymity and the lack of central and state banking control is something that is already addressable in many countries, both in terms of law and infrastructure, they do not have an approach to these dangerous phenomena for society. Addressing the numerous fraud schemes using digital currencies.

The lack of clear legal regulations and supervision makes it difficult to punish fraudsters and protect investors, but the high level of anonymity and lack of regulation that encourages illegal activities in such cases is increasingly endangering the developing and commercial market. Concrete cases and analysis of legal consequences today do not have enough expertise to prevent such a phenomenon. In many countries, they are trying to create legal frameworks to regulate the cryptocurrency market, but the pace is slower than technological development. International institutions, such as FATF, (Financial Action Task Force, 2025) have proposed rules for transparency and reporting of transactions.

Knowing that the penalties for fraud and money laundering are also severe, I think that the number of completed cases tried in these cases leaves much to be desired in terms of the damage that these groups are causing to societies and the state, this is hampered by the human resources and camouflage used by these groups, while prosecution is also very challenging, as they also operate in dark web markets for illegal purchases and manipulations, due to differences in tracking and response across jurisdictions in different countries without a standardized regulated or unregulated platform. There are cases where unsuspecting users fall prey to fake investment platforms or fraudulent "wallets."

2. Literature Review

Cryptocurrencies are virtual currencies supported by decentralized systems that are not issued by any central authority, without the presence of a third party or institution (Ramassa & Leoni, 2022). Most individuals who invest in cryptocurrencies have no security for their profits due to the low transparency they offer and weak controls. New trends in the emergence of financial crimes are also affecting Kosovo, a phenomenon that is growing with the development of the rule of law (LIGJI NR. 05/L-096, 2016), which has been reviewed for the first time since the declaration of Independence of the country where there is still a high risk of such negative phenomena, highlighting the high levels of corruption, tax evasion, unfair economy. Cryptocurrency fraud has become a growing global concern, this is due to the fact that the development of cryptocurrencies is very rapid (Trozze et al., 2022), despite the increase in financial crimes, technological advances, including new financial instruments and tools brought by cryptocurrencies built on blockchain technology, have offered new opportunities for businesses and individuals (Naqbi et al., 2025). Cryptocurrencies offer promising opportunities for innovation, but they also pose significant risks, particularly in terms of financial crime (Aidoo, 2025).

This chapter contrasts financial crimes and the development of cryptocurrencies, namely the accounting implications they may have on financial statements which then increase the possibility of fraud. Given that there are no GAAP or IFRS accounting standards specifically for cryptocurrencies, discretionary judgment is used to calculate them. (Luo & Yu, 2022), while maintaining integrity, transparency, sustainability, and effective management to reduce the risk of cryptocurrency fraud to the most acceptable level (Pravdiuk, et al., 2024).

2.1 Blockchain Technology (Bitcoin, Ethereum)

In less than a decade, bitcoin and other virtual currencies have had a significant impact on society and have become a unique payment system problem for law enforcement agencies and financial regulators around the world. The rapid introduction and spread of technological changes, such as blockchain, which serves as the cryptographic basis of bitcoin, continues to outpace the ability of law and regulation (Bokovnya et al., 2020). All of this then contributes to the growth of the cryptocurrency market by criminals who finance terrorism, money laundering, and other economic abuses, so cryptocurrencies are under constant threat of attack (Kutera, 2022). Like Bitcoin, Ethereum is a decentralized digital currency platform whose currency, known as Ether, has no intrinsic value, no centralized issuer, and uses blockchain technology to record transaction history. However, unlike Bitcoin, Ethereum goes further by allowing transactions not only through cryptocurrency, but also through "smart contracts" that allow parties to exchange anything of value without the need for the services of a lawyer or notary, thus becoming the second most widely used digital cryptocurrency platform (Kerr et al., 2023). From this it can be seen that we continue to see an increase in the entry into the market of new cryptocurrencies, which most individuals see as a good opportunity to invest and profit quickly and easily. But on the other hand there is a risk that the more we use these cryptocurrencies, the greater the risks of manipulation, misuse, which will lead to an increase in forms of financial crimes.

Table 11.1. Cryptocurrencies With Largest Market Capitalization Values.

Name	Market	Cap Price	Volume (24 h)	Change (24 h) (%)
BTCBitcoin	$2,131,419,471,698	$107,182.35	$42,123,243,422	−0.44
ETHEtereum	$97,675,152,197	$2,465.88	$16,553,055,538	−0.62
USDt Tether	$157,759,577,865	$1.00	$62,263,986,030	0.02
XRR	$131,236,404,443	$2.22	$4,096,373,298	1.68
BNB	$92,182,184,468	$654,30	$1,480,412,796	−0.04
Solana	$80,371,777,734	$150,33	$4,975,762,134	−1.71
USDC	$61,482,513,581	$0.9999	$8,420,597,504	0.02

Source: https://coinmarketcap.com/all/views/all/ (last visited July 1, 2025).

Table 11.1 shows the cryptocurrencies with the largest market capitalization values, as determined by multiplying the price by the circulating supply in 2025. Coin Market Cap is one of several websites for "checking prices" for cryptocurrencies. Currently, as can be seen, Bitcoin and ETHEtereum are the two most widely used cryptocurrencies with the largest market share.

2.2 The Role of Accounting Implication

According to the authors (Owolabi & Osanyinbi, 2023), the International Federation of Certified Public Accountants (IFAC) should issue an accounting standard that focuses on dealing with issues related to cryptocurrencies, because the forms of fraud that can occur have major implications for the development of financial crimes. Both standard setters and financial statement preparers should be well informed about the fraud that can be committed through the use of cryptocurrencies (Hubbard, 2023). According to the authors (Lazea et al., 2024), the ideal approach to valuation treatment for cryptocurrencies depends on a company's specific use case for cryptocurrencies. Careful consideration of this factor and a commitment to transparency and consistency in financial reporting are essential for companies navigating this evolving landscape. This means that companies still do not have a clear way to treat cryptocurrencies due to the lack of laws and regulations that properly address this asset. New standards for measuring cryptocurrencies are needed because existing standards do not fairly treat their value. Recently, a group of 20 of the world's largest economies, including China, the United States and Japan, met to discuss regulating cryptocurrencies, among other things. The commitment was to regulate, but not ban, the cryptocurrency market (Wilson & Beltrand, 2018). Therefore, a specific regulation/standard related to the holding of cryptocurrencies and the determination of value would greatly assist accountants and auditors in easily and timely identifying accounting fraud that may occur as a result of the use of this asset.

2.3 Hypothesis Development

Most researchers have examined the connection between the use of cryptocurrencies and financial crimes, namely accounting fraud, where the author (Cassella, 2024) reported that the use of cryptocurrencies has a significant relationship with financial crimes and that there is a positive relationship. His study finds that the use of cryptocurrencies affects the level of financial crimes. Other authors and researchers also reported similar findings of a positive relationship between cryptocurrencies and the increase in financial crimes (accounting fraud). Focusing on the dynamic environment, the rapid growth of cryptocurrencies and their anonymity for users have created challenges in the criteria for defining financial crimes (Saidalavi et al., n.d.), where they observed a significant and positive relationship between the adoption of cryptocurrencies and the risk of increased financial crimes. Therefore, focusing on the researchers' findings, the hypotheses built for this research are as follows:

H0. The use of cryptocurrencies has no impact on the level of financial crimes (accounting fraud)

H1. The use of cryptocurrencies has a positive impact on the level of financial crimes (accounting fraud)

Research Questions

(1) Is there a relationship between the number of financial crimes cases and the use of cryptocurrencies?
(2) Does the use of cryptocurrencies affect the increase in financial crimes (accounting fraud)?

2.4 Variables

The study is based on two variables, where we have an independent variable and a dependent variable. The independent variable is the use of cryptocurrencies and the dependent variable is financial crime (accounting fraud). This study will highlight the relationship between them (See Fig. 11.1).

Research model

Fig. 11.1. Hypothesis Model.

3. Study Methodology

3.1 Sample and Data Collection Procedures

To test the above hypotheses, a survey was conducted with financial professionals in Kosovo. It consists of two parts, where the first part contains demographic questions, while the second part consists of 15 statements that are measured with a Likert scale. Financial professionals from different cities in Kosovo were asked to complete the questionnaire through a link distributed on social networks. In total, data were collected from 200 respondents. The data were collected during the period February 01, 2025–April 30, 2025.

3.2 Data Analysis

The model claims that the use of cryptocurrencies affects financial crimes, so that with the increase in the use of cryptocurrencies, the level of financial crimes increases. First, descriptive data were analyzed and then with the analysis of validity (anova), regression, correlation analysis to test the linear relationship between the variables. SPSS v.26 was used to perform these analyses.4.

4. Results

The study aims to investigate the impact of cryptocurrency use on the development of financial crimes among Kosovar financial professionals. The data were analyzed using descriptive statistics, regression, correlation, etc. Regression was used to find the impact of cryptocurrency use on financial crimes (accounting fraud). Correlation was used to test the relationship between the independent variable (the use of cryptocurrency) and the dependent variable (financial crimes).

4.1 Data Analysis

4.1.1 Descriptive Statistics

Table 11.2 shows that 133 (66.5%) participants are male, while 67 (33.5%) participants are female.

Table 11.2. Distribution of Research Participants by Gender.

Gender					
		Frequency	**Percent**	**Valid Percent**	**Cumulative Percent**
Valid	Female	67	33.5	33.5	33.5
	Male	133	66.5	66.5	100.0
	Total	200	100.0	100.0	

Source: Author.

Table 11.3. Distribution of Research Participants, by Age.

Age					
		Frequency	**Percent**	**Valid Percent**	**Cumulative Percent**
Valid	25–30 years old	15	7.5	7.5	7.5
	30–35 years old	30	15.0	15.0	22.5
	35–40 years old	68	34.0	34.0	56.5
	Over 40 years old	87	43.5	43.5	100.0
	Total	200	100.0	100.0	

Source: Author.

Table 11.4. Distribution of Research Participants, According to Years of Work Experience.

Work Experience					
		Frequency	**Percent**	**Valid Percent**	**Cumulative Percent**
Valid	0–5 years	51	25.5	25.5	25.5
	5–10 years	67	33.5	33.5	59.0
	Over 10 years	82	41.0	41.0	100.0
	Total	200	100.0	100.0	

Source: Author.

Table 11.3 regarding the age variable shows that 15 people (7.5%) are aged 25–30 years, 30 people (15%) are aged 30–35 years, 68 people (34%) are aged 35–40 years, and 87 (43.5%) people are over 40 years old.

From Table 11.4 regarding the work experience of the participants, we can see that 51 participants (25.5%) have 0–5 years of experience, 67 participants (33.5%) have 5–10 years of experience and 82 participants (41%) have over 10 years of experience.

From Table 11.5 we can see that the majority of participants work in the audit and accounting department with a total of 103 people (51.5%), this is due to the major role that auditors play in identifying accounting fraud that may arise from cryptocurrencies. Followed by those working in microfinance institutions with 50 people (25%).

Table 11.5. Distribution of Research Participants, by Department of Work.

Department					
		Frequency	**Percent**	**Valid Percent**	**Cumulative Percent**
Valid	Bank	34	17.0	17.0	17.0
	Audit and accounting	103	51.5	51.5	68.5
	Microfinance institution	50	25.0	25.0	93.5
	Insurance company	13	6.5	6.5	100.0
	Total	200	100.0	100.0	

Source: Author.

4.2 Correlation Analysis

4.2.1 Research Questions

(1) Is there a relationship between the number of financial crime (accounting fraud) cases and the use of cryptocurrencies?
(2) Does the use of cryptocurrencies affect the increase in financial crimes (accounting fraud)?

The results of the correlation analysis (see Table 11.6) show that there is a positive and significant correlation (statistically significant) between the use of cryptocurrencies and financial crimes ($r = 0.391$). This correlation is significant at the $p = 0.01$ level.

4.3 Regression Analysis

H0. The use of cryptocurrencies has no impact on the level of financial crimes (accounting fraud)
H1. The use of cryptocurrencies has a positive impact on the level of financial crimes

$R^2 = 0.153$ (15.3%) shows that 15.3% of the variation in the dependent variable (financial crimes) is explained by the independent variable (use of cryptocurrencies) (see Table 11.7).

From the ANOVA Table 11.8 we see the *F* value and the Sig. value which test the significance of the regression model. If the sig. value (p) is less than 0.05 (5%),

Table 11.6. Results of Correlation Analysis.

Correlations			
		The Use of Cryptocurrency	**Financial Crimes (Accounting Fraud)**
The use of cryptocurrency	Pearson correlation	1	0.391**
	Sig. (2-tailed)		0.000
	N	200	200
Financial crimes (accounting fraud)	Pearson correlation	0.391**	1
	Sig. (2-tailed)	0.000	
	N	200	200

Source: Author.

Note: ** Correlation is significant at the 0.01 level (2-tailed).

Table 11.7. Results of Regression Analysis.

Model Summary

Model	***R***	***R* Square**	**Adjusted *R* Square**	**Std. Error of the Estimate**
1	0.391[a]	0.153	0.148	0.43549

Source: Author.

[a]Predictors: (Constant), FINANCIAL CRIMES (accounting fraud).

Table 11.8. Anova Test Results.

ANOVA[a]

Model		**Sum of Squares**	**df**	**Mean Square**	***F***	**Sig.**
1	Regression	6.766	1	6.766	35.679	0.000[b]
	Residual	37.551	198	0.190		
	Total	44.317	199			

Source: Author.

[a]Dependent variable: Use of cryptocurrency.

[b]Predictors: (Constant), financial crimes (accounting fraud).

then we say that the regression model is significant. In our case the sig. value $0.000 < 0.005$.

The Coefficients Table 11.9 summarizes the final result of the regression analysis. The constant shows how much financial crimes (the dependent variable) would be if the use of cryptocurrencies were zero (the independent variable). In this case, the value of the constant is $\beta = 1.843$, $p = 0.000 < 0.005$, which indicates that when the use of cryptocurrencies was zero, financial crimes would be 1.843 units.

Table 11.9. Coefficients Results.

Coefficients[a]						
		Unstandardized Coefficients		**Standardized Coefficients**	***t***	**Sig.**
Model		***B***	**Std. Error**	**Beta**		
1	(Constant)	1.843	0.316		5.830	0.000
	Financial crimes (accounting fraud)	0.521	0.087	0.391	5.973	0.000

Source: Author.

[a]Dependent variable: Use of cryptocurrency.

While the coefficient M shows that the use of cryptocurrencies has an impact of $\beta = 0.521$, $p = 0.000 < 0.005$ on financial crimes. So, the use of cryptocurrencies has an impact of 52.1% on the development of financial crimes and this impact is significant.

$$y = \beta_0 + \beta_1 X + u$$

Financial crimes (accounting fraud) = 1.843 + 0.521 The use of cryptocurrencies.

According to the analysis done, we can say that the use of cryptocurrencies has an impact on the increase in financial crimes and this impact is significant. Since the hypothesis is significant, then the hypothesis is accepted.

So, based on these results, the hypothesis *H1* is successfully accepted. Hypothesis *H0* falls.

5. Conclusion

Cryptocurrencies have emerged as pivotal elements exerting a profound influence on accounting systems. These technological advancements present novel challenges to accounting professionals, necessitating an adjustment to evolving conditions and the formulation of innovative standards (Pravdiuk et al., 2024). Therefore, the lack of a clear standardization framework regarding the treatment of cryptocurrencies in financial accounting may create a gap for financial professionals who do not have the necessary knowledge and acceptable level to handle such situations in companies that may be exposed to cryptocurrencies. They should use their professional judgment in the application of the standards. The purpose of this chapter was to investigate the impact of the use of cryptocurrencies on the increase in financial crimes, namely accounting fraud. The results of the research show that the use of cryptocurrencies and their growth has a positive effect on financial crimes. As expected, the results showed that the use of cryptocurrencies has a significant impact on financial crimes. A positive relationship between them was confirmed, which supported and accepted the hypothesis *H1*. Therefore, the null hypothesis *H0* is rejected, since it is clear that the use of cryptocurrencies has an impact on the increase in financial crimes.

In the regression analysis it was found that 15.3% of the variation in the dependent variable (financial crimes) is explained by the independent variable (use of cryptocurrencies). In the correlation analysis the results show that the correlation coefficient is 0.391 and it is seen that there is a positive linear relationship between the two variables, in which an increase in the level of cryptocurrency use is associated with an increase in the level of financial crimes. The biggest challenge for identifying financial crimes remains on the part of auditors and accountants.

6. Recommendations

In line with the findings of this study, financial professionals, including financial officers in banks and microfinance institutions, accountants, auditors, should consider the impact that the use of cryptocurrencies may have on the increase in financial crimes with special emphasis on the area of accounting fraud they face. They should attend training as from the results of the questionnaire we saw that the majority of respondents had no knowledge about cryptocurrencies and how they work, although this would be an additional cost for the organizations they work with by providing assistance programs, advice, and training on the proper management of the use of cryptocurrencies and avoiding fraud. The country's institutions should also raise the awareness of the individuals involved about the consequences that fraud (financial crimes) can have. Regardless of the legislation that needs to be reviewed, efforts should be necessary in order to reduce the incidence of financial crimes which can then have a major impact on the political and economic aspects of the country. Lack of transparency, weak judicial institutions, long time to handle cases, lack of experience of competent persons to identify such negative phenomena may be the key factors leading to the increase in cases of financial crimes. On the other hand, accounting fraud, which also constitutes a financial crime related to intentional actions, presents a considerable challenge because the use of cryptocurrencies is developing at a very rapid pace, especially recently, and most financial professionals still do not have any clear information on the treatment of cryptocurrencies in financial statements, but this depends on their professional judgment due to the lack of professional standards, which poses a high risk to stakeholders, a decline in credibility and accountability. Some of the recommendations arising from the study are:

- The need for global standardization in the accounting treatment of cryptocurrencies.
- Recommendations for improving financial control and transparency.
- The role of financial education in preventing fraud.
- To increase auditor's awareness in identifying accounting fraud arising from cryptocurrencies.
- Enhancing transparency and consistency for the implementation of an accounting standard tailored to cryptocurrencies.
- Training for all financial professionals regarding the treatment of cryptocurrencies in financial statements.

References

Aidoo, S. (2025). *Cryptocurrency and financial crime: Emerging risks and regulatory responses*. https://www.researchgate.net/publication/391630261_Cryptocurrency_and_Financial_Crime_Emerging_Risks_and_Regulatory_Responses

Bokovnya, A. Y., Shutova, A. A., Zhukova, T. G., & Ryabova, L. V. (2020, Septiembre). Legal measures for crimes in the field of cryptocurrency billing. *Utopía y Praxis Latinoamericana*, *25*(Esp. 7), 270–275. https://doi.org/10.5281/zenodo.4009713

Cassella, S. (2024). Editorial: Cryptocurrency and crime: Old crimes committed in new ways, or a new order of challenges for law enforcement? *Journal of Financial Crime*, *31*(5). https://papers.ssrn.com/sol3/papers.cfm?abstract_id=4998740

FATF, Financial Action Task Force. (2025). *FATF urges stronger global action to address illicit finance risks in virtual assets*. https://www.fatf-gafi.org/en/home.html

Fernando, J. (2025, May 30). GAAP vs. IFRS Investopedia: https://www.investopedia.com/terms/g/gaap.asp#toc-gaap-vs-ifrs

Hubbard, B. (2023). Decrypting crypto: Implications of potential financial accounting treatments of cryptocurrency. *Accounting Research Journal Emerald*, 369–383. https://doi.org/10.1108/ARJ-10-2022-0279

Kerr, D. S., Loveland, K. A., Smith, K. T., & Smith, L. M. (2023). Ryptocurrency risks, fraud cases, and financial performance. *Risks*. (Cryptocurrencies and Risk Management). https://doi.org/10.3390/risks11030051

Kutera, M. (2022). Cryptocurrency as a subject of financial fraud. *Journal of Entrepreneurship, Management, and Innovation*, 45–77. https://doi.org/10.7341/20221842

Lazea, G. I., Bunget, O. C., & Lungu, C. (2024). Cryptocurrencies' impact on accounting: Bibliometric review. *Journal of Risks*. https://doi.org/10.3390/risks12060094

LIGJI NR. 05/L-096. (2016, June 15). *Gazeta Zyrtare e Republikes se Kosoves, Prishtine*. Ligji Nr. 05/L -096 PËR PARANDALIMIN E PASTRIMIT TË PARAVE DHE LUFTIMIN E FINANCIMIT TË TERRORIZMIT: https://gzk.rks gov.net/ActDocumentDetail.aspx?ActID=12540

Luo, M., & Yu, S. (2022). *Financial reporting for cryptocurrency* (pp. 1707–1740). Springer. https://link.springer.com/article/10.1007/s11142-022-09741-w

Naqbi, S. A., Nobanee, H., & Ellili, N. O. (2025). Global trends and insights into cryptocurrency-related financial crime. *Research in International Business and Finance*. https://doi.org/10 1016/j.ribaf.2025.102756

Owolabi, S., & Osanyinbi, T. (2023). The historical evolution, developments and accounting implications of cryptocurrency operations. *European Journal of Accounting, Auditing and Finance Research*, *11*(10), 55–72. https://doi.org/10.37745/ejaafr.2013/vol11n105572

Pravdiuk, N., Motorniuk, U., Tkal, Y., Lukanovska, I., & Miroshnichenko, M. (2024). The impact of cryptocurrencies and blockchain technologies on the accounting and audit systems. *Economic Affairs (New Delhi)*, *69*, 107–115. https://doi.org/10.46852/0424-2513.1.2024.13

Ramassa, P., & Leoni, G. (2022). Standard setting in times of technological change: Accounting for cryptocurrency holdings. *Accounting, Auditing & Accountability Journal*, *37*(5), 1598–1624. https://doi.org/10.1108/AAAJ-10-2020-4968

Saidalavi, S., Luong, H., & Suleman, M. T. (n.d.). *Financial crime risk and cryptocurrency: International evidence* (pp. 1–16). https://nzfc.ac.nz/papers/phd/58.pdf

Trozze, A., Kamps, J., Akartuna, E. A., Hetzel, F. J., Kleinberg, B., Davies, T., & Johnson, S. D. (2022). *Cryptocurrencies and future financial crime* (pp. 19–35). https://link.springer.com/article/10.1186/s40163-021-00163-8

Wilson, M., & Beltrand, B. A. (2018). *Cryptocurrencies: Implications for the future of accounting* (pp. 24–30). https://www.tx.cpa/docs/default-source/communications/2018-today's-cpa/septemberoctober/crytocurrencies.pdf?sfvrsn=3074f6b1_4

Chapter 12

Role of International Organizations in Combatting Financial Crimes

Chirag Balyan

Maharashtra National Law University Mumbai, India

Abstract

Financial crime drains trillions from the global economy, as criminals exploit legal and regulatory gaps across borders. This chapter examines how international organizations respond through coordinated action and adopts a broad view of their role in combating money laundering, terrorist financing, fraud, and corruption. It reviews not only treaty-based and intergovernmental bodies but also standard-setting institutions, operational networks, technical assistance providers, private compliance forums, and civil society actors. These institutions shape the global response at legal, institutional, and practical levels. The chapter begins with treaty-based frameworks that create binding obligations for states, including the UN Convention against Transnational Organized Crime, the UN Convention against Corruption, and the OECD Convention on Combating Bribery. It then analyzes standard-setting bodies such as the Financial Action Task Force, MENAFATF, the Basel Committee on Banking Supervision, and the IMF, which influence national systems through peer review and compliance assessment. It examines operational networks like INTERPOL and the Egmont Group that support intelligence sharing and enforcement. It also explores technical support platforms like the UNODC, Stolen Asset Recovery Initiative and IMoLIN, which assist states with legal tools, training, and asset recovery. The chapter includes soft-law regulators like the Wolfsberg Group and the Joint Money Laundering Steering Group, professional bodies like CAMS and ACFCS, which promote global compliance standards, civil society groups, and *Shari'a* Supervisory Boards. It argues that combating financial crime requires stronger links between legal norms, enforcement, compliance practices, and public accountability across global systems.

Corruption and Crime in Finance, 249–278

Published under exclusive licence by Emerald Publishing Limited
doi:10.1108/978-1-83708-170-720261031

Keywords: Compliance; corruption; enforcement; financial crime; international organizations; money laundering

1. Introduction

Criminals exploit the global financial system through increasingly complex and borderless operations. Financial crime, a subset of economic crime, has deeply affected global economies and continues to erode public trust and socioeconomic stability (Akinbowale et al., 2020). As Bhasin (2013) notes, its reach now endangers financial institutions, governance systems, and investment climates. The internet—while revolutionizing commerce—has become a key platform for executing and concealing fraud (Arachchilage & Love, 2014; Izedonmi & Okoeguale, 2012). Technological innovation has reshaped business practices, but it has also allowed criminals to falsify records, act in collusion with insiders, and adapt rapidly to new enforcement techniques (Amjad et al., 2022). Weak legal implementation, poor litigation support, and the perception of impunity further embolden offenders, leading to low conviction rates and persistent fraud.

As Gilmore (1995) observed, the money laundering (ML) landscape has evolved with global economic integration. The elimination of capital controls and the expansion of digital finance provide tools for criminals to move funds across borders within seconds (Kent, 1992). They use shell companies and complex legal structures to obscure beneficial ownership (Smith, 1992). Smith (1992, p. 104) described this transnational manipulation as "a smorgasbord of obfuscation techniques." Such activities span multiple jurisdictions, making them difficult to trace and prosecute.

Contemporary financial crime no longer centers on drug trafficking alone. It now includes proceeds from cybercrime, corruption, insider trading, and terrorism financing (Magliveras, 1992). The United Nations (1993) warned that these illicit flows distort economic indicators, fuel inequality, and destabilize state institutions. Criminal economies increasingly mimic legitimate ones, operating in parallel and exploiting deregulated markets, offshore finance, and legal opacity (Vasciuc & Radu, 2024, p. 91; Walker & Unger, 2009).

Solomon (1994) rightly argued that effective countermeasures must match the transnational nature of these threats. The problem transcends borders, but law enforcement remains bound by national systems. States must therefore harmonize legal frameworks, share intelligence, and coordinate enforcement to ensure financial crimes do not go unpunished.

To address this challenge, states have asserted extraterritorial jurisdiction. They exercise prescriptive, enforcement, and adjudicative powers over offenses that cross borders (Nguyen, 2019). Instruments such as the Vienna Convention, Palermo Convention, and UNCAC permit jurisdiction based on territoriality, nationality, or substantial effects. However, doctrines like passive personality and universality offer limited application to crimes such as bribery and ML, which rarely involve individually identifiable victims or fall within jus cogens norms (Bassiouni, 2002). Sovereignty and international law continue to constrain extraterritorial enforcement.

Globalization has weakened traditional crime control models. While some countries have adapted regulatory systems to cope with rapid market changes, others lag behind. Criminal organizations exploit cross-border trade, cyber-markets, and deregulated financial services to grow and embed illicit proceeds. Shelley (1998) notes that global trade mechanisms now enable criminal networks to operate behind legitimate business fronts. Regional blocs like the European Union and SADC, while advancing integration, have also created openings for illicit capital flows, as porous borders blur the line between domestic and international crime (McDonald, 1995; Wiener, 1997). In South Africa, drug money has reportedly been invested in real estate, securities, and currency trading (Goredema, 2003).

Criminal groups now manipulate investment vehicles, offshore structures, and banking secrecy to insert illicit wealth into legal economies (Shelley, 1998). Global media, improved transportation, and technological advancement have further eroded the state's monopoly on enforcement. As Mugarura (2014) warns, globalization has rendered state-centric crime control strategies increasingly obsolete.

National enforcement agencies cannot combat these crimes alone. Criminal law remains a central pillar of state sovereignty, but the scale and complexity of transnational financial crime necessitate cooperative international action (Zagaris & McDonald, 1992). States must collaborate through legal instruments, shared institutions, and mutual accountability to overcome structural limitations (Maingot, 1995; Van Sickle, 2009).

The international anti-financial crime regime reflects this evolution. It combines binding legal instruments with nonbinding but influential soft law mechanisms to promote compliance, encourage norm diffusion, and enable reputational leverage (Alexander, 2001). Hard law frameworks such as the UN Conventions on transnational organized crime and corruption, and the OECD Anti-Bribery Convention establish clear state obligations. Soft law, in contrast, works through mutual evaluation, peer pressure, and adaptive guidance rather than legal compulsion.

A broad constellation of actors underpins this regime. Standard-setting bodies such as the Financial Action Task Force (FATF), MENAFATF, the Basel Committee, and the IMF coordinate national systems through shared principles and peer review. Operational networks like INTERPOL, the Egmont Group, and the Agreement for Mutual Enforcement of Debarment Decisions facilitate enforcement and intelligence-sharing across jurisdictions. Then there are technical assistance and policy support initiatives such as UNODC, the Stolen Asset Recovery (StAR) Initiative, and the International Money Laundering Information Network (IMoLIN) which help countries strengthen laws, build institutional capacity, and improve cooperation in combating financial crime.

Soft law plays a vital role in shaping the global anti-financial crime framework through nonbinding but influential standards, guidance, and practices. Several actors contribute to this ecosystem. The Wolfsberg Group, a consortium of global banks, issues voluntary principles on AML, counter-terrorism financing, and customer due diligence (Wolfsberg Group, n.d.-b). The Joint Money

Laundering Steering Group (JMLSG) provides industry-specific guidance in the United Kingdom to support firms' compliance with legal obligations. Professional certification bodies such as Certified Anti-Money Laundering Specialist (CAMS) and Association of Certified Financial Crime Specialists (ACFCS) standardize training, ethics, and professional benchmarks across jurisdictions, creating a globally consistent compliance culture. Civil society organizations, including NGOs and investigative journalism networks, operate as norm entrepreneurs by exposing financial misconduct, lobbying for reforms, and strengthening transparency. In jurisdictions governed by Islamic finance principles, Shari'a Supervisory Boards (SSBs) offer normative guidance on financial practices by ensuring that institutions operate within ethical boundaries rooted in *Shari'a*, particularly through analogical reasoning (*qiyas*) on issues like fraud and ML. While these actors lack formal enforcement powers, their collective influence on institutional behavior, regulatory expectations, and reputational accountability makes them central pillars of the soft law framework in financial crime compliance.

These institutions advance regulatory coherence and strengthen enforcement across the global financial system by operating through mandates, expertise, peer accountability, and transnational cooperation.

2. Treaty-based Legal Frameworks

International treaties provide essential tools for fighting financial crimes by establishing clear rules for cross-border cooperation (Kriz, 1992, p. 725). These agreements enable countries to work together in tracing illegal funds, freezing criminal assets, and prosecuting offenders. They create shared standards that help overcome jurisdictional challenges and close loopholes that criminals exploit.

This section examines five critical treaties that shape global efforts against financial crimes: The 1988 Vienna Convention targets drug-related ML; the 1997 OECD Anti-Bribery Convention criminalizes foreign bribery; the 2000 Palermo Convention addresses organized crime proceeds; the 2003 UNCAC establishes comprehensive anti-corruption measures; and the 2005 Warsaw Convention sets European AML standards.

By requiring information sharing and mutual legal assistance, these treaties pressure uncooperative jurisdictions to reform their banking systems. They bridge domestic laws with international enforcement, creating a unified front against financial criminals. The treaty framework transforms isolated national efforts into an interconnected global system for asset recovery and prosecution.

2.1 Vienna Convention

The United Nations Convention Against Illicit Traffic in Narcotic Drugs and Psychotropic Substances (1988), commonly known as the Vienna Convention, established the first international legal framework to combat ML by requiring

States Parties to criminalize the "conversion or transfer of property, knowing that such property is derived from [drug trafficking] offences" as well as "the concealment or disguise of the true nature, source, location, disposition, movement or ownership of such property" (United Nations, 1988, Art. 3(1)-(b)). The Convention broke new ground by mandating asset confiscation measures, requiring States to adopt laws enabling the seizure of "proceeds derived from offences established in accordance with article 3" or property of equivalent value (United Nations, 1988, Art. 5(1)). It also pioneered international cooperation mechanisms, obligating States to provide "the widest measure of mutual legal assistance in investigations, prosecutions and judicial proceedings" related to drug trafficking and associated ML (United Nations, 1988, Art. 7). While limited to drug-related proceeds, the Convention's definition of ML and its provisions for cross-border cooperation laid the foundation for modern AML regimes. Its requirement that States establish ML as an extraditable offense (United Nations, 1988, Art. 6(2)) created an early framework for international law enforcement collaboration against financial crime. The Vienna Convention's innovative approach of attacking criminal enterprises through their finances fundamentally transformed global efforts against organized crime networks.

2.2 OECD Anti-bribery Convention

The OECD Convention on Combating Bribery of Foreign Public Officials, adopted in 1997 and effective from 1999, is a core international instrument against active bribery in cross-border business. It requires states to criminalize the offering, promising, or giving of undue advantage to foreign public officials to gain improper business benefits (OECD, 2024, Art. 1). The Convention follows the principle of functional equivalence, allowing legal diversity while maintaining uniform deterrence (OECD, 2024, Commentary para. 2).

States must impose liability on legal persons (Art. 2) and apply effective, proportionate, and dissuasive sanctions, including criminal, administrative, and confiscatory measures (Art. 3). The Convention mandates jurisdiction over offenses committed within the territory or by nationals abroad and promotes consultation where jurisdictions overlap (Art. 4). It prohibits political or economic considerations from influencing enforcement, ensuring prosecutorial independence (Art. 5).

The Convention links bribery to ML frameworks (Art. 7), mandates accurate accounting to prevent concealment (Art. 8), and removes bank secrecy as a ground to deny mutual legal assistance (Art. 9). It encourages extradition and broad international cooperation (Art. 10). The Convention with its focus on legal clarity, enforceable standards, and institutional flexibility, forms the basis of the global anti-bribery regime. It operates alongside FATF Recommendations, UNCAC, and national systems to promote integrity and fair competition. Over 500 individuals and entities have faced sanctions under this regime, driving lasting reform in business practices (OECD, n.d.).

The 2021 Recommendation (OECD/LEGAL/0378) strengthens this regime. It calls for enhanced awareness, training, criminalization, international cooperation, sanctions, asset recovery, nontrial resolutions, tax denial for bribes, and whistleblower protections (OECD, 2021).

2.3 Palermo Convention

The United Nations Convention Against Transnational Organized Crime (Palermo Convention, 2000) represents a landmark achievement in international efforts to combat ML and financial crimes associated with organized criminal networks. Adopted by the UN General Assembly and entering into force in 2003, the Convention has been ratified by 190 states as of 2023, making it one of the most widely accepted international instruments against organized crime. The Palermo Convention's significance lies in its comprehensive approach to ML, which expands substantially upon previous frameworks like the Vienna Convention (1988). While the Vienna Convention limited ML provisions to drug-related offenses, Article 6 of the Palermo Convention requires states to criminalize ML derived from all serious crimes, representing a major advancement in the global AML regime. This provision specifically targets the conversion or transfer of criminal proceeds to conceal their illicit origin, the concealment or disguise of property's true nature or source, and the acquisition or use of tainted property (United Nations, 2000, Art. 6). The Convention complements these criminal provisions with robust preventive measures in Article 7, mandating that states establish comprehensive domestic regulatory systems for financial institutions, including customer due diligence requirements, record-keeping obligations, and suspicious transaction reporting mechanisms (United Nations, 2000, Art. 7). A key innovation is the requirement for states to consider establishing Financial Intelligence Units (FIUs) as national centers for collecting and analyzing financial information related to potential ML activities. The Convention also addresses emerging challenges through provisions for monitoring cross-border cash movements, while maintaining appropriate safeguards for legitimate financial flows (United Nations, 2000, Art. 7(2)). Beyond its specific AML provisions, the Palermo Convention creates a synergistic framework for combating financial crime through its asset confiscation regime (Article 12), anti-corruption measures (Articles 8–9), and mechanisms for international cooperation, including mutual legal assistance and joint investigations (Articles 18, 27). By aligning with FATF standards while providing binding treaty obligations, the Palermo Convention is the cornerstone of international efforts to disrupt the financial infrastructure of transnational criminal organizations.

2.4 UNCAC

The UNCAC, adopted in 2003 and in force since 2005, is the only globally binding instrument dedicated to combating corruption through a four-pillar framework: prevention, criminalization and law enforcement, international cooperation, and asset recovery (UNODC, 2017). The Convention underscores corruption's severe consequences—undermining democratic institutions, distorting markets, and eroding public trust—and mandates States Parties to adopt comprehensive preventive strategies, ensure the criminalization of public and private sector corruption (including foreign bribery and illicit enrichment), and strengthen anti-corruption institutions (UNODC, 2017; United Nations, 2011). Implementation reviews reveal that since 2010, 156 States have aligned their domestic legislation with UNCAC provisions, with many enhancing enforcement powers, extending definitions of public officials, and removing legal barriers to mutual legal assistance (UNODC, 2017). However, challenges persist—such as limited capacity to prosecute corruption, lack of effective whistleblower protections, and difficulties in removing immunities from high-ranking officials (UNODC, 2017, pp. 81–90). UNCAC also emphasizes the importance of asset recovery as a fundamental principle, especially for developing countries, and fosters frameworks for tracing, freezing, and repatriating stolen assets with provisions under Chapters IV and V, including requirements for verifying beneficial ownership and enhanced scrutiny of accounts held by politically exposed persons (UNODC, 2017, pp. 191–198). Mutual legal assistance provisions have been notably successful, with many states easing dual criminality requirements and expanding cooperation beyond criminal matters to civil and administrative cases, despite technical and procedural hurdles (UNODC, 2017, pp. 164–169). UNCAC encourages interagency and cross-border cooperation among law enforcement, judiciary, and FIUs. It recognizes the complexity of transnational financial crime and the need for integrated solutions (UNODC, 2017).

2.5 Warsaw Convention

The Council of Europe Convention on Laundering, Search, Seizure and Confiscation of the Proceeds from Crime and on the Financing of Terrorism (CETS No. 198, 2005) is an international legal framework to curb the financial infrastructure of criminal and terrorist operations. It provides an integrated framework for asset forfeiture, corporate accountability, cross-border cooperation, and financial intelligence coordination. Building upon the 1990 Convention (ETS No. 141), it explicitly expands its mandate to include the financing of terrorism alongside ML and asset recovery mechanisms (Council of Europe, 2005, Ch. II–III).

Its key provisions include a mandate for member states to establish legislative measures for the identification, tracing, freezing, seizure, and confiscation of criminal proceeds, even when assets are mingled with legitimate property (Articles 3–5). The Convention requires the establishment of FIUs with full access to financial, administrative, and law enforcement information to detect and act upon suspicious financial activity (Article 12). Moreover, FIUs must be empowered to suspend suspicious transactions and ensure prompt responses to international cooperation requests (Articles 12, 47).

A particularly notable feature of the Convention is its rejection of bank secrecy as a barrier to cooperation, requiring that mutual legal assistance or domestic investigations are not impeded by confidentiality laws (Article 7; Article 28(7)). It also places strong obligations on states to hold legal persons liable, both criminally and administratively, for offenses related to ML and terrorist financing, especially where internal controls or due diligence mechanisms fail (Article 10).

The Convention also lays out a comprehensive international cooperation framework, mandating mutual legal assistance for confiscation orders (Article 23). It facilitates investigative and provisional measures (Articles 16, 21) and encourages spontaneous financial intelligence sharing among states (Article 20). The Convention enables cross-border recognition and enforcement of judicial orders concerning proceeds of crime (Article 32) and offers legal guarantees for third-party rights and due process (Article 8).

The Convention is aligned with the FATF Recommendations. It incorporates international standards by reference and strengthens their implementation through a monitoring mechanism administered by the Conference of the Parties (Articles 13, 48). The Convention thus fosters harmonization of legal approaches across member jurisdictions and reinforces operational cooperation to effectively combat transnational financial crimes.

3. Standard-setters and Monitors

3.1 Financial Action Task Force

The FATF, also known by its French acronym *Groupe d'action financière* (GAFI), was established in 1989 as an intergovernmental body to set global standards and promote the effective implementation of measures to combat ML (AML), terrorist financing (CFT), and the financing of the proliferation of weapons of mass destruction (CFP) (Financial Action Task Force FATF, 2022a). Its primary objective is to protect the integrity of the international financial system, thereby enhancing broader economic safety and security (FATF, 2022a). FATF operated under a temporary mandate until 2019 when it was made permanent to ensure continued global action against financial crime (FATF, 2022a).

The FATF's central role is to develop and refine the international standards known as the FATF Recommendations (FATF, 2012). This work is spearheaded by its Policy Development Group, which is responsible for enhancing the standards and producing guidance for their effective implementation (FATF, 2022a). These 40 Recommendations, along with their interpretive notes, provide a comprehensive framework for countries to implement (FATF, 2012). The standards are continuously updated to address emerging threats (FATF, 2021a). For instance, in response to the misuse of cryptocurrencies, the FATF updated its recommendations in 2018-2019 and issued further guidance in October 2021 for virtual asset service providers (FATF, 2021a).

A significant aspect of the FATF's work is ensuring transparency (FATF, 2022b). To this end, Recommendation 24 on beneficial ownership was significantly strengthened in March 2022 (FATF, 2022b). This revision mandates that countries ensure adequate, accurate, and up-to-date information on the beneficial ownership of legal persons is available so that misuse of corporate structures for illicit activities can be prevented (FATF, 2022b).

To ensure the effective implementation of its standards, the FATF conducts peer reviews, or "mutual evaluations," of its member jurisdictions (FATF, 2022c). This process creates a system of accountability among member-states (FATF, 2022c). The fifth round of mutual evaluations, which commenced in 2024, is based on formally documented procedures, including the "2023 Methodology" and "Universal Procedures" (FATF, 2022c).

Based on these evaluations, the International Co-operation Review Group (ICRG) identifies and works with jurisdictions that have strategic deficiencies (FATF, 2022a). The ICRG is considered one of the FATF's "most effective tools" for generating positive reforms by publicly listing high-risk jurisdictions (the "grey list"), which creates strong incentives for countries to improve their AML/CFT/CPF regimes (FATF, 2022c). The new evaluation process operates on a shorter six-year cycle and gives countries a three-year window to address deficiencies before facing potential public identification (FATF, 2022c).

A 2022 FATF report noted that 76% of countries had satisfactorily implemented the FATF Recommendations, a substantial increase from 36% in 2012, proving the effectiveness of the mutual evaluation process (FATF, 2022d).

The FATF is proactive in identifying and analyzing new threats to the financial system, developing guidance and typologies to help both public and private sectors (FATF, 2023a). Recent work includes analysis of ransomware financing (FATF, 2023a), ethnically or racially motivated violent extremism financing (FATF, 2021b), trade-based money laundering (FATF and Egmont Group, 2021), COVID-19-related financial crimes (FATF, 2020a), illegal wildlife trade (FATF, 2020b), and virtual assets red flags (FATF, 2020c).

The FATF works with a global network of FATF-Style Regional Bodies (FSRBs) and maintains strong partnerships with international organizations (FATF, 2022a). For example, the Middle East and North Africa Financial Action Task Force (MENAFATF) began in 2004 as an FSRB to counter ML and terrorist financing (TF) in the region (MENAFATF, n.d.). It brings together 14 member states and operates from Bahrain as a voluntary, nontreaty body (MENAFATF, n.d.). MENAFATF aligns regional AML/CFT systems with FATF's 40 Recommendations and UN Security Council resolutions while respecting national legal and cultural frameworks (MENAFATF, n.d.). Apart from assessments, it fosters regional capacity through annual expert trainings, typology workshops to analyze emerging ML/TF trends, and peer-learning platforms that adapt global standards to regional challenges, such as informal financial systems or cross-border cash smuggling.

The International Monetary Fund (IMF) and the World Bank play a "special role" by contributing to standards development, providing technical assistance, and helping to promote the effective implementation of the standards through country assessments conducted in the context of the Financial Sector Assessment Program (FSAP) (FATF, 2022a). Furthermore, the FATF engages with the private sector and civil society to foster a dialogue that leads to more effective implementation of its standards (FATF, 2022a).

3.2 Basel Committee on Banking Supervision

The Basel Committee on Banking Supervision (BCBS) functions as the primary global standard-setter for prudential banking regulation, with its standards shaping national and regional legal frameworks despite lacking formal treaty-based authority. Its decisions, though nonbinding, produce legal and regulatory effects through widespread adoption, reflecting socially embedded commitments within the global financial architecture. The BCBS operates through institutional specialization and interdependence with other regulatory actors, reinforcing its influence in multilevel governance.

However, this role raises concerns about legitimacy and accountability. As a quasi-rulemaking body, the BCBS engages public interests and exercises normative authority without direct democratic oversight. Critics argue that its institutional design should incorporate more transparent and inclusive procedures and consider additional regulatory controls—whether soft, hard, or self-regulatory—to enhance input legitimacy (Ortino, 2019). These concerns are amplified by its interaction with bodies like the International Accounting Standards Board and the limited involvement of elected institutions such as the European Parliament. Despite this, the Committee continues to derive its authority from technical expertise, consensus-based decision-making, and its central role in maintaining global financial stability (Ortino, 2019).

It brings together central banks and supervisory authorities from 28 jurisdictions, with 45 members in total. The Core Principles for Effective Banking Supervision provide the foundation for banking oversight. These principles outline minimum standards that all banks and banking systems must follow, regardless of their structure or size.

Principle 29 embeds AML, counter-terrorist financing (CFT), and counter-proliferation financing (CPF) requirements into banking supervision. The BCBS recognizes that criminals can exploit banks, whether intentionally or not, for financial crime. It therefore directs supervisors to ensure that banks apply strong, risk-based customer due diligence (CDD), compliance systems, and governance structures (BCBS, 2024, p. 65).

The BCBS defines 14 essential criteria under Principle 29. These include transaction monitoring, enhanced due diligence for politically exposed persons (PEPs), controls over correspondent banking, group-wide AML/CFT programs, internal audits, whistleblower protection, and training and reporting systems (BCBS, 2024, pp. 66–68).

Principle 29 aligns with the FATF 40 Recommendations, including updates made in November 2023. BCBS does not duplicate FATF's mutual evaluations. Instead, it evaluates how well supervisors address any weaknesses that FATF identifies. If no recent FATF review exists, full assessments are carried out under the FSAP (BCBS, 2024, p. 15).

The Core Principles do not explain all operational aspects of Principle 29. The BCBS issued its 2017 Guidelines on the Sound Management of Risks Related to Money Laundering and Financing of Terrorism to provide banks with detailed, risk-based guidance.

These 2017 Guidelines start with the need for banks to assess and understand ML/FT risks. They require banks to build governance structures based on three lines of defense: business units, compliance functions, and internal audit (BCBS, 2017, pp. 4–6). Banks must also integrate ML/FT risks into their broader risk management systems.

The Guidelines call for strong customer acceptance policies, accurate identification of customers and beneficial owners, and detailed CDD procedures (BCBS, 2017, pp. 7–10). Banks must monitor accounts regularly, report suspicious activity, and freeze assets as required by national laws and international obligations (BCBS, 2017, pp. 10–12).

In cross-border operations, the Guidelines require banks to implement group-wide AML/CFT policies. They must share information internally and understand that responsibilities may be divided between supervisors and FIUs (BCBS, 2017, pp. 12–15).

Supervisors must ensure that banks follow these rules and apply them effectively. They use tools like risk-based inspections, account sampling, data requests, and enforcement actions (BCBS, 2017, pp. 16–17). These tools support the essential criteria under Principle 29 and complement FATF Recommendations 10, 17, and 26.

The BCBS makes clear that its 2017 Guidelines are designed to help implement FATF standards. They do not replace or alter those standards. This dual-track approach treats AML/CFT as a core responsibility in banking supervision, not as an add-on (BCBS, 2017, p. 1).

Principle 29 and the 2017 Guidelines form a complete framework. Principle 29 sets supervisory expectations, and the Guidelines show how banks should implement them. This framework links prudential regulation with financial crime prevention and strengthens cross-border supervisory cooperation.

In 2023, the Bank for International Settlements (BIS) launched Project Aurora. This project explores how advanced data analytics can improve AML efforts. It uses realistic simulations with embedded financial crime patterns. Machine learning, especially graph-based models, detect complex money laundering networks that traditional rules often miss (BIS, 2023, pp. 10–15).

Aurora shows that banks cannot succeed by working alone. Instead, they must collaborate across borders using privacy-enhancing technologies (PETs) that protect sensitive data while enabling joint analysis (BIS, 2023, pp. 16–21). The project emphasizes that "it takes a network to defeat a network" (BIS, 2023, p. 3). This model offers a powerful response to the challenge of organized and networked financial crime.

3.3 International Monetary Fund

The IMF plays a central role in combating financial crime. Over the past two decades, it has integrated AML, CFT, and CPF into its core functions—surveillance, program design, capacity development (CD), and standard-setting (IMF, 2023a). This shift reflects the recognition that illicit finance destabilizes economies, weakens financial systems, and erodes public governance.

By 2023, over 90% of Article IV consultations and 34 Financial Sector Stability Assessments (FSSAs) had incorporated AML/CFT risk diagnostics (IMF, 2023b, p. 13; IMF, 2023c). These assessments now use cross-border flow analytics and sectoral risk scores to detect vulnerabilities, especially in fragile states where money laundering often links to corruption and poor governance.

The IMF has also made AML/CFT a condition in fund-supported programs. During the 2020–2023 pandemic response, the IMF tied financial support to transparency in beneficial ownership and procurement processes to reduce fraud risks (IMF, 2023d, pp. 21–22). Implementation rates for these conditionalities reached 54%, nearing the fund's average of 65% (IMF, 2023, p. 25). Pakistan's compliance with 14 of 27 FATF action items under IMF conditions led to its removal from the FATF grey list in 2022. Similarly, Ecuador improved fiscal transparency by integrating beneficial ownership data into public procurement (IMF, 2023, p. 44). However, delisting from FATF grey lists takes an average of five years, often extending beyond IMF program cycles (IMF, 2023, p. 24).

The IMF's CD program delivers over 100 technical assistance missions annually. It now addresses emerging threats like virtual assets, environmental crime, and crypto-related risks. The IMF implements multi-year CD compacts aligned with FSAP results (IMF, 2023e, p. 29). Regional CD efforts have tackled correspondent banking loss in the Caribbean and TF risks in the Middle East. The IMF trains global AML/CFT assessors and contributes to FATF evaluations. It conducts one to two assessments annually, with plans to raise that number to three by FY2028 (IMF, 2023f, p. 27). Unlike FATF, the IMF includes macroeconomic impact analysis in its evaluations, measuring how illicit flows affect GDP, exchange rates, and capital flows (IMF, 2023g). It uses FATF standards as a reference but focuses on actual outcomes rather than formal compliance (IMF, 2023, pp. 24–25).

In 2023, the IMF set new priorities. It aims to assess the fiscal costs of illicit flows more rigorously, explore the links between financial integrity and digital assets, climate finance, and cybersecurity, and improve risk prioritization to distinguish systemic from localized threats. These efforts show the IMF's commitment to connecting financial integrity with macroeconomic stability. Citing research by Kida and Paetzold, the IMF notes that FATF grey-listing can reduce capital inflows by 7.6% of GDP, proving the economic urgency of AML/CFT compliance (Kida & Paetzold, 2021, as cited in IMF, 2023, p. 24).

The IMF plans to use artificial intelligence and cross-border analytics to track and mitigate the economic impact of financial crime. Through these measures, the IMF acts as a standard implementer, policy advisor, and integrator of financial integrity in the global financial system.

3.4 OECD Working Group on Bribery

The OECD Working Group on Bribery, established in 1994, is responsible for monitoring the implementation and enforcement of the OECD Anti-Bribery Convention and the 2021 Recommendation (OECD, 2024, Art. 12). It operates through a rigorous peer-review mechanism that includes self-evaluation, mutual evaluation, and public reporting. Transparency International describes this system as the "gold standard" of international monitoring (OECD, n.d.).

The monitoring process assesses both legal frameworks and actual enforcement, ensuring accountability and pressure for reform. The Working Group also examines compliance with obligations related to corporate liability, sanctions, jurisdiction, and international cooperation (OECD, 2024, Commentary para. 34).

The Convention, as interpreted through the Working Group, applies broadly. It extends to bribery involving officials of public international organizations, public enterprises, and autonomous territories (OECD, 2024, Commentary paras. 12–18). It offers a clear definition of "improper advantage" and adopts a restrictive view on facilitation payments, allowing them only when explicitly permitted under local law (OECD, 2024, Commentary paras. 5, 9). These provisions reflect the Convention's zero-tolerance approach while maintaining respect for domestic legal systems.

The Working Group's follow-up and review system ensures that states translate anti-bribery commitments into concrete legal, institutional, and enforcement measures.

3.4.1 International Organization of Securities Commissions

The International Organization of Securities Commissions (IOSCO) sets global standards for securities market regulation. It brings together regulators from over 130 jurisdictions who oversee more than 95% of the world's securities markets (IOSCO, n.d.). IOSCO builds its regulatory framework around three objectives: protecting investors, ensuring fair, efficient, and transparent markets, and reducing systemic risk (IOSCO, 2017). Its Objectives and Principles of Securities Regulation include 38 principles across ten categories. These principles guide the IMF–World Bank FSAPs and have G20 and FSB endorsement.

To respond to the growing financial interconnectivity, IOSCO has adopted key resolutions on cross-border cooperation, enforcement, and harmonization of standards. In 1992, IOSCO adopted the Resolution on Money Laundering, urging jurisdictions to strengthen customer due diligence, maintain detailed records, and prevent the abuse of securities markets by money launderers (IOSCO, 1992). This resolution anticipated FATF's global role and helped shape the AML/CFT framework.

IOSCO addressed cross-border fraud through its 1993 Resolution on Transnational Securities and Futures Fraud. It urged members to enhance investigative cooperation, raise public awareness, and adopt legal tools to freeze assets (IOSCO, 1993a). In 2006, IOSCO adopted the Resolution on Cross-Border Cooperation to Freeze Assets. It called on regulators to reform domestic laws to allow foreign authorities to freeze proceeds of securities law violations (IOSCO, 2006). IOSCO made clear that cross-border enforcement is essential to prevent wrongdoers from profiting and to strengthen deterrence.

IOSCO also advanced international surveillance and market integrity. Its 1987 Resolution on Cooperation in Matters of Surveillance and Enforcement supported international agreements for information exchange and action against market abuses like manipulation (IOSCO, 1987). The 1990 and 1991 Resolutions on Information Sharing and Memoranda of Understanding (MOUs) helped institutionalize enforcement cooperation. These efforts led to the Multilateral Memorandum of Understanding (MMoU), now a global benchmark for cross-border regulation.

IOSCO has addressed evolving market structures. The 1990 Resolution on Principles for Screen-Based Trading Systems and the 1993 Resolution on Coordination Between Cash and Derivatives Markets highlighted the regulatory risks of fragmented oversight and technological change (IOSCO, 1990a, 1993b). IOSCO's 1992 Resolutions on financial conglomerates and auditing standards emphasized integrated supervision and financial transparency (IOSCO, 1992a; 1992b).

After the global financial crisis, IOSCO issued a strategic plan for 2010–2015. It prioritized systemic risk identification, stronger regulatory capacity, better enforcement tools, and broader membership engagement through training and capacity building (IOSCO, 2010). IOSCO's Resolution on Mission, Goals and Priorities reaffirmed its leadership in global securities regulation. It committed to cooperation with other standard setters like the FSB and supported consistent, high-quality implementation of international rules (IOSCO, 2010).

IOSCO's resolutions reflect more than policy. They shape national laws, improve surveillance tools, and strengthen enforcement across borders. Through these efforts, IOSCO promotes a transparent, investor-focused, and globally coordinated financial system.

4. Enforcement and Intelligence Coordination Networks

4.1 INTERPOL

INTERPOL, the world's largest international police organization with 196 member countries, plays a key role in tackling transnational financial crime through coordinated global efforts (INTERPOL, n.d.-a, n.d.-b). Its International Financial Crime and Anti-Corruption Center (IFCACC) serves as the hub for cross-border investigations and intelligence exchange. Recognizing the link between money laundering and predicate offenses, INTERPOL uses financial investigations to trace illicit proceeds, dismantle criminal networks, and recover assets (INTERPOL, n.d.-a, n.d.-b). It works closely with FATF and the Egmont Group to develop targeted responses to complex laundering operations (INTERPOL, 2022).

INTERPOL's operational tools include global notices, criminal databases, and specialized response teams that support complex investigations (INTERPOL, 2022). Projects like LEAP target money laundering tied to environmental crime through Environmental Crime Task Forces (NESTs) in Latin America and Asia-Pacific. Project FLYWAY combines human trafficking and financial crime intelligence in Africa. In Southeast Asia, Project TORAID builds capacity to counter illicit financial flows (INTERPOL, n.d.-a, n.d.-b). These initiatives bridge operational gaps between law enforcement, financial institutions, and international bodies to disrupt the financial infrastructure of organized crime (INTERPOL, 2022).

Since 2020, INTERPOL's Operation HAECHI has targeted cyber-enabled financial crimes and money laundering. In HAECHI III (2022), 30 jurisdictions collaborated, resulting in nearly 1,000 arrests and the freezing of 2,800 bank and virtual asset accounts linked to $130 million in illicit funds (INTERPOL, 2022). This operation supports INTERPOL's Financial Crime Analysis File (FIN-CAF), which connects cross-border investigations and enhances the tactical response to financial crime (INTERPOL, 2022). INTERPOL also contributes to EMMA, a joint initiative with Europol and financial institutions. In 2022, EMMA identified 8,755 money mules and 222 recruiters across 25 jurisdictions, preventing €17.5 million in fraud (Europol, 2023). In another case, INTERPOL supported a 2020 cyber-trading fraud investigation where Serbian, Austrian, Bulgarian, and German authorities made nine arrests and froze €2.5 million in assets (Serbia & Council of Europe, 2020).

According to INTERPOL's Global Financial Fraud Assessment 2024, financial fraud has become more pervasive and sophisticated. Common threats include investment fraud, business email compromise (BEC), romance scams, and advance-fee fraud (INTERPOL, 2024, p. 11). Criminals increasingly use AI-generated deepfakes, crypto-based schemes like "rug pulls," and hybrid scams like "pig butchering"—a combination of romance and crypto fraud (INTERPOL, 2024, p. 11). INTERPOL's IFCACC supported investigations involving $1.2 billion in losses in 2023 alone (INTERPOL, 2024, p. 10).

A growing concern is the link between financial fraud and human trafficking. INTERPOL's Operations STORM MAKERS I and II exposed syndicates in Asia forcing trafficked individuals to operate scam centers across Southeast Asia, Africa, and Latin America (INTERPOL, 2024, p. 12). West African groups dominate BEC and crypto fraud (INTERPOL, 2024, p. 14), Latin American cartels have moved into cyber scams (INTERPOL, 2024, p. 15), and Asia faces telecom and "pig-butchering" fraud at scale (INTERPOL, 2024, p. 16). In Europe, investment fraud and AI impersonation are rising (INTERPOL, 2024, p. 17).

To counter these threats, INTERPOL launched I-GRIP (Global Rapid Intervention of Payments) to freeze suspicious funds. Since 2022, it has blocked over $500 million in illicit proceeds (INTERPOL, 2024, p. 19). HAECHI-IV in 2023 led to 3,500 arrests worldwide (INTERPOL, 2024, pp. 16, 19). INTERPOL also trains law enforcement on emerging fraud trends and runs joint cybercrime operations such as Jackal (INTERPOL, 2024, pp. 14, 20). Despite challenges like underreporting and legal gaps, INTERPOL's public-private partnerships and real-time data sharing strengthen global enforcement (INTERPOL, 2024, p. 20).

The 2024 assessment warns about Crime-as-a-Service (CaaS) platforms that lower the entry barrier for cybercrime (INTERPOL, 2024, pp. 11, 18). It also highlights the convergence of financial fraud with drug trafficking, human trafficking, and money laundering through virtual assets. INTERPOL identifies AI-driven fraud and emerging financial technologies as top threats. It calls for stronger international cooperation, improved fraud data, and better cross-border asset recovery systems (INTERPOL, 2024, p. 20).

4.2 Egmont Group of FIUs

The Egmont Group is a global network of FIUs committed to combating money laundering, terrorist financing, and related crimes (FinCEN, n.d.). It began in 1995 as an informal forum for "financial disclosure units" aiming to improve cross-border cooperation. It now includes 177 member FIUs, with recent additions such as Lao PDR, Lesotho, Iraq, and Zimbabwe (Egmont Group, 2023a, p. 6; Egmont Group, n.d.-a; FinCEN, n.d.).

The Group defines an FIU in line with FATF Recommendation 29. An FIU serves as the national center for receiving and analyzing suspicious transaction reports and disseminating the results to relevant authorities (Egmont Group, 2023b). It must access data from reporting entities and other financial, administrative, and law enforcement sources. The Egmont Group stresses that FIUs must operate independently to ensure objectivity, especially in cross-border cases. It supports this independence by promoting institutional autonomy, adequate resourcing, and technological capacity (Egmont Group, 2023a, p. 8).

FIUs play a central role in National Risk Assessments (NRAs), contributing expert analysis of STRs/SARs and other data (Egmont Group, 2024a, pp. 2–3; Egmont Group, 2024b). Currently, 96% of FIUs participate in NRA processes, often leading or coordinating the drafting (Egmont Group, 2024b). Their work includes stakeholder engagement, data collection, and strategic coordination, which varies by jurisdiction and methodology (Egmont Group, 2024a, pp. 2–3; Egmont Group, 2024b).

Collaboration is key to effective NRAs. About 89% of FIUs engage private sector actors, and 70% work with neighboring countries or regional bodies (Egmont Group, 2024b). FIUs combine quantitative data (e.g., STRs, enforcement data) and qualitative inputs (e.g., OSINT, expert opinion) (Egmont Group, 2024a, p. 4; Egmont Group, 2024b). The use of OSINT is increasing: 92% of FIUs actively use it, with 82% drawing from social media (Egmont Group, 2023a, p. 20). Most FIUs use the World Bank's NRA tool, FATF guidance, and risk scoring models. Many also tailor their methodologies to national contexts while incorporating international trends (94%) and emerging technologies (86%) (Egmont Group, 2024b).

The Information Exchange Working Group (IEWG) has led major thematic projects on terrorism financing through virtual assets, trade-based money laundering, and deeper OSINT integration (Egmont Group, 2023a, p. 5). Approximately 84% of FIUs identified virtual asset misuse in illicit markets, with 29% linking it to terrorism financing (Egmont Group, 2023a, p. 36).

FIUs face constraints. Thirty-one reported challenges with budget, staffing, or technology. Another 29 highlighted problems with data collection and coordination (Egmont Group, 2024b). Still, 35 FIUs saw operational improvements after their NRA, including better efficiency and risk targeting. Benefits included improved inter-agency relationships (52%) and stronger strategic analysis (43%) (Egmont Group, 2024b).

Effective FIUs invest in technology, train personnel, maintain trust-based communication, and adopt flexible, risk-based frameworks (Egmont Group, 2024a, pp. 6–7). Best practices include proactive communication (83% issue regular updates) and public reporting (95% publish findings). About 99% align with international standards like those from FATF (Egmont Group, 2024b).

Globally, 86% of FIUs assess risks tied to technologies such as crypto assets, though 14% do not (Egmont Group, 2024b). Leading FIUs score higher on FATF's Recommendation 1, with 89% rated partially or largely compliant (Egmont Group, 2024b). FIUs also help draft national AML/CFT strategies by applying NRA insights (Egmont Group, 2024a, p. 6; Egmont Group, 2024b). Southern FIUs show leadership, with Guatemala co-leading an OSINT project, Saudi Arabia hosting AML training, and Nigeria driving cross-border knowledge exchange (Egmont Group, 2023a, pp. 11–12).

The Egmont Center of Excellence and Leadership (ECOFEL) at FIU supports training through e-learning on ransomware, virtual assets, and SAR quality. It is also developing a certification curriculum (Egmont Group, 2023a, p. 14).

The Egmont Group facilitates secure FIU-to-FIU information sharing via the Egmont Secure Web (ESW) platform (Egmont Group, 2023a, p. 4; FinCEN, n.d.). Though the Group does not conduct investigations, it supports member FIUs by enhancing secure communication, skills, and cross-border coordination (Egmont Group, n.d.-b; FinCEN, n.d.). It encourages operational independence and offers training, technical support, and personnel exchanges.

Its Charter and Principles for Information Exchange bind all members and establish mutual trust obligations. Noncompliance triggers the Support and Compliance Process (Egmont Group, 2023b). The ESW Board governs the platform, and the Heads of FIU (HoFIU) make strategic decisions with advice from the Egmont Committee (Egmont Group, n.d.-a; Egmont Group, 2023b).

The Egmont Group strengthens global AML/CFT cooperation by deepening partnerships with FATF, INTERPOL, and UNODC. These collaborations have produced joint guidance on beneficial ownership, cyber-enabled fraud, and sanctions evasion (Egmont Group, 2023a, pp. 25–26, 31–33). Through its secure infrastructure and proactive agenda, the Egmont Group is consolidating its role as the operational backbone of the international AML/CFT regime (Egmont Group, 2023a).

4.3 Mutual Enforcement Agreement

Multilateral Development Banks (MDBs) play a key role in promoting integrity in development finance. On April 9, 2010, five major MDBs—the World Bank

Group (WBG), African Development Bank (AfDB), Asian Development Bank (ADB), European Bank for Reconstruction and Development (EBRD), and Inter-American Development Bank (IDB) signed the *Agreement for Mutual Enforcement of Debarment Decisions* (EBRD, 2010). This agreement allows each MDB to enforce the debarment decisions of the others against entities involved in corrupt, fraudulent, collusive, or coercive practices. As a result, a single debarment can have global consequences.

The agreement rests on six core principles: common definitions of misconduct, fair and consistent investigative procedures, independent decision-making bodies, due process for accused parties, a "more probable than not" evidentiary standard, and proportionate sanctions that consider the seriousness of the offense. If an MDB chooses not to enforce a peer's debarment due to legal or policy reasons, it must notify the others.

Each MDB follows its own sanctions process. The World Bank uses a two-tier system: an Evaluation and Suspension Officer reviews the case, and the Sanctions Board issues a final decision if the respondent contests the allegations. The ADB relies on its Office of Anticorruption and Integrity, which conducts investigations under administrative procedures (Leigh & Fariello, 2012).

Sanctions may include formal reprimands, conditional nondebarment, restitution, or temporary/permanent debarment. Both the WBG and ADB typically start with a three-year debarment, subject to adjustment.

This framework strengthens global anti-corruption efforts and extends MDB standards beyond national laws like the US Foreign Corrupt Practices Act or UK Bribery Act. It also urges companies to improve compliance systems, knowing that misconduct in one MDB-financed project can lead to sanctions across multiple institutions (Coogan et al., 2015).

5. Technical Assistance and Policy Support Initiatives

5.1 UN Office on Drugs and Crime (UNODC)

The UNODC is the UN's lead agency addressing drugs, transnational crime, and terrorism (UNODC, n.d.). Established in 1997 through the merger of the UN Drug Control Programme and the Centre for International Crime Prevention, it operates through a global network of field offices to assist Member States in addressing complex threats to peace and development. Its three-pillar mandate combines technical assistance, research and policy analysis, and normative support for treaty implementation and legislative reform (Achim & Borlea, 2020, p. 256).

UNODC's Global Programme against Money Laundering, Proceeds of Crime and the Financing of Terrorism (GPML) is central to its efforts against illicit financial flows (IFFs). As custodian of SDG Indicator 16.4, the GPML provides tailored capacity-building support to legal, financial, enforcement, and judicial institutions, helping countries build and implement effective AML/CFT frameworks aligned with international standards. It delivers in-depth training for both public and private sector actors, develops tools and typology reports, and supports peer-learning and knowledge-sharing platforms (UNODC, n.d.-a, n.d.-b).

The program also strengthens institutional resilience to interconnected threats such as corruption, organized crime, and terrorism financing (UNODC et al., 2009). GPML's technical assistance directly supports states in meeting SDG Target 16.4 by enhancing detection, investigation, prosecution, and asset recovery mechanisms. The UN General Assembly has consistently reaffirmed this role through resolutions such as 74/177 and 73/186, mandating GPML to align its support with FATF standards and regional AML/CFT initiatives.

A cornerstone of UNODC's normative work is its Model Legislative Provisions on money laundering and terrorist financing, developed in collaboration with the Commonwealth Secretariat and the IMF. First released in 2003 and updated in 2009, these provisions integrate FATF Recommendations and UN treaty obligations while allowing adaptation to national legal systems (United Nations Office on Drugs and Crime Commonwealth Secretariat & International Monetary Fund, 2009). Through its global reach, technical depth, and legal expertise, UNODC has become a key partner in the international fight against financial crime and its destabilizing effects on governance and development.

5.2 Stolen Asset Recovery (StAR) Initiative

The StAR Initiative is a partnership between the World Bank and UNODC that helps countries find and return stolen public assets. In 2024, StAR supported 13 countries, helped draft laws in 4, trained over 250 professionals, and joined 28 policy forums (StAR, n.d.). It works on six areas, including beneficial ownership, domestic laws, and international cooperation.

5.3 International Money Laundering Information Network

The IMoLIN helps governments share laws, typologies, and contact information. It operates under the UNODC and supports global cooperation in AML/CFT (IMoLIN, n.d.).

6. Soft-law Regulation

6.1 Wolfsberg Group

The Wolfsberg Group is a leading private sector initiative against financial crime, shaping AML and CTF standards since its founding in 2000 (Aiolfi & Bauer, 2012). It began with 11 (now 12) major international banks at Château Wolfsberg, Switzerland, responding to regulatory fragmentation and high-profile ML cases involving PEPs and corrupt officials (Pieth & Aiolfi, 2003). Founding members like UBS, Credit Suisse, and Citigroup sought unified standards in private banking, where complex transactions and HNWI clients raised serious risks (Wolfsberg Group, 2000).

The Group publishes practitioner-driven guidance to improve compliance effectiveness (Wolfsberg Group, n.d.-a). Its Working Groups develop and revise publications by pooling member expertise. Its first major output is the 2000 AML Principles for Private Banking, which set new benchmarks in CDD and beneficial ownership identification (Pieth & Aiolfi, 2003). It also introduced key innovations like enhanced scrutiny for PEPs and a risk-based onboarding approach (Aiolfi & Bauer, 2012). Importantly, it applied equally to offshore operations, addressing a key regulatory gap (Wolfsberg Group, 2000).

The Group advanced practical, risk-sensitive standards. Its 2006 Risk-Based Approach Guidance transformed resource allocation by prioritizing controls based on actual risk rather than blanket rules (Wolfsberg Group, 2006). The FATF later adopted this approach in its revised Recommendations (FATF, 2012).

The Wolfsberg Group also fosters collaboration with regulators, FIUs, law enforcement, and supervisors to enhance global financial integrity (Wolfsberg Group, n.d.-a). After 9/11, it quickly issued its 2002 Statement on Terrorist Financing, one of the first private sector responses linking banks to counter-terrorism efforts while acknowledging detection challenges in small, atypical transactions (Aiolfi & Bauer, 2012; Wolfsberg Group, 2002).

Notable outputs include the Correspondent Banking Due Diligence Questionnaire (CBDDQ) and Financial Crime Compliance Questionnaire (FCCQ) (Wolfsberg Group, n.d.-c; Wolfsberg Group, 2023b). Its 2022 Correspondent Banking Principles outline detailed requirements for risk-based due diligence, strong governance, continuous monitoring, and SAR filings (Wolfsberg Group, 2022). They prohibit relationships with shell banks and require EDD for PEPs, downstream banking, and high-risk payable-through accounts. Due diligence must assess geographic risks, PEPs, SOEs, MSBs, VASPs, regulatory history, and FCC controls. Governance structures must include defined first and second lines of defense, clear policies, independent reviews, and a risk appetite framework. Institutions must link due diligence with transaction monitoring and treat high-risk branches or affiliates as distinct respondents when appropriate.

In 2023, the Group updated its Anti-Bribery and Corruption (ABC) Compliance Programme Guidance, replacing the 2017 version (Wolfsberg Group, 2023a). The guidance defines bribery and corruption, emphasizes a firm-wide zero-tolerance policy, and advocates a risk-based approach. It requires oversight by senior management, periodic risk assessments, and independent evaluation. It also mandates controls over gifts, hospitality, third-party providers, and principal investments. Training must target high-risk employees and intermediaries. Institutions must test compliance mechanisms and investigate red flags like shell companies, flawed backgrounds, or irregular payments (Wolfsberg Group, 2023a).

Despite its achievements, critics note the Group's voluntary nature and limited membership (Aiolfi & Bauer, 2012; Pieth & Aiolfi, 2003). Its lack of enforcement power and dominance by major banks raise concerns about representativeness. To address this, the Group now hosts annual forums for broader stakeholder engagement (Wolfsberg Group, 2004–present).

The Group became a legal entity in 2021, headquartered at the Basel Institute on Governance, marking its evolution from ad hoc collaboration to a permanent institution (Wolfsberg Group, 2021). Led by Executive Secretary Ned Conway, it now tackles emerging risks like crypto-related crimes and fintech vulnerabilities (Wolfsberg Group, 2021–present).

The Wolfsberg Group shows how private actors can complement regulators. By aligning global standards with real-world banking practices, it continues to influence AML/CTF frameworks (Aiolfi & Bauer, 2012; Pieth & Aiolfi, 2003).

6.2 Joint Money Laundering Steering Group

The JMLSG represents a unique private sector collaboration comprising the UK's leading financial services trade associations, established to develop industry-wide guidance for AML and CTF compliance (Joint Money Laundering Steering Group [JMLSG], 2023). As a nongovernmental body, JMLSG produces guidance that, while not legally binding, carries substantial regulatory significance through its HM Treasury approval status, serving as a critical reference point for UK financial institutions implementing their AML/CTF obligations (JMLSG, 2023). The guidance operates as a flexible framework rather than prescriptive rules, enabling firms to develop tailored policies appropriate for their specific business models while maintaining a risk-based approach to compliance decisions (JMLSG, 2023). Its four primary objectives are to (1) outline the United Kingdom's AML/CTF legal and regulatory framework, (2) provide practical interpretation of statutory requirements, (3) demonstrate proportionate industry best practices, and (4) assist firms in designing effective risk mitigation systems (JMLSG, 2023). The 2023 revised edition's Part I establishes eight core components for financial crime prevention: senior management oversight, control frameworks, MLRO responsibilities, risk-based customer due diligence, transaction monitoring, suspicious activity reporting, staff training, and record-keeping standards (JMLSG, 2023). Notably, UK courts must consider this Treasury-approved guidance when assessing compliance failures under the Proceeds of Crime Act 2002 and the Terrorism Act 2000, while the Financial Conduct Authority references it in regulatory enforcement decisions (JMLSG, 2023). This creates a distinctive public-private partnership model where industry-developed standards inform both judicial and regulatory interpretations of AML/CTF obligations, despite the guidance's technically nonbinding status (JMLSG, 2023). The framework intentionally allows discretion in application across different products, services, and customer relationships, requiring firms to document any deviations from recommended practices (JMLSG, 2023).

6.3 Professional Certification Bodies in Financial Crime Compliance

Certification and training bodies such as ACAMS, ACFCS, and the AMLFC Institute operate as part of the soft law landscape in the transnational anti-financial crime regime. While they lack formal regulatory authority, these institutions shape compliance norms by setting professional standards, promoting technical proficiency, and diffusing best practices through education and credentialing. Their influence supports the operationalization of hard law instruments and complements standard-setting by intergovernmental bodies such as the FATF and the BCBS.

The Association of Certified Anti-Money Laundering Specialists (ACAMS), the largest professional body in this domain, certifies over 115,000 members globally through its CAMS program and advances AML/CFT implementation via 60 national chapters (ACAMS, n.d.).

The Association of Certified Financial Crime Specialists (ACFCS) offers the CFCS credential, which provides cross-disciplinary training in AML, sanctions, cybercrime, and asset recovery (ACFCS, n.d.). Similarly, the Anti-Money Laundering and Financial Crime (AMLFC) Institute trains regulators, enforcement officers, and students, offering certifications in fraud prevention, terrorist financing, cybercrime, and financial technology (AMLFC Institute, n.d.).

The Association of Certified Fraud Examiners (ACFE) trains over 95,000 members. It offers the CFE certification, teaches fraud investigation and forensic accounting, and supports law enforcement and auditors (ACFE, n.d.).

These bodies foster normative alignment and implementation readiness, making them integral actors in the soft infrastructure of financial crime control.

6.4 Civil Society

NGOs play a growing role in fighting ML and corruption. Their cooperation with public authorities helps strengthen financial transparency, especially in developing countries. For example, in 2012, UNODC partnered with the UNCAC Coalition, a global network of over 350 NGOs, to train civil society groups in Africa to work with governments against ML (UNODC, 2012). Similarly, the Devex Impact initiative, supported by USAID, promotes collaboration among NGOs, professionals, and institutions to improve anti-corruption strategies in developing economies (Devex, 2012).

NGOs also shape global AML norms. Transparency International has created tools like the *Gateway* corruption measurement index and has advocated for laws on beneficial ownership and stricter AML rules in real estate (Transparency International, n.d.-a, n.d.-b). The Financial Transparency Coalition campaigns for ownership transparency in the EU (FTC, 2014). The International Consortium of Investigative Journalists (ICIJ) has exposed financial crimes through investigations like the *Panama Papers* and *FinCEN Files*, which led to asset recovery and reforms such as the US Corporate Transparency Act (ICIJ, n.d.).

The European Parliament has recognized NGOs' role in investigating misuse of EU funds and called for more support to civil society in its 2013 resolution on organized crime and corruption (European Parliament, 2013). NGOs often help draft and implement AML rules, such as the *Global Anti-Money Laundering Guidelines for Private Banking*.

However, NGOs also face risks. Some may be misused as fronts for terrorism financing or may unknowingly support such activities (van der Does de Willebois, 2010). Oversight remains weak, and there is no uniform way to assess NGO financial transparency. The EU has raised concerns about the abuse of nonprofit status for criminal purposes (Matrix Insight, 2008).

NGOs are both key partners in AML efforts and subjects of regulatory concern. Strengthening transparency standards while preserving their civic role is essential.

6.5 Shari'a Supervisory Boards

As a form of soft law, the SSB influences financial conduct through normative guidance rather than enforceable authority—unless domestic law grants it statutory recognition. In most jurisdictions, its role remains persuasive, shaping internal governance without binding legal force.

Islam prohibits financial crimes such as insider trading, fraud, and money laundering. Although the Qur'an and Sunna do not explicitly name these crimes, scholars derive their prohibition through *qiyas* (analogy) from foundational principles of trust (*amana*), honesty (*sidq*), and justice (*adl*) (Agha, 2007). These acts constitute *khiyana* (breach of trust) and fall under *ta'zir*—offenses not specified in divine texts but punishable at the state's discretion to protect public interest and uphold Shari'a (Agha, 2007).

Because these crimes are *haram* (impermissible) (Al-Qaradawi, 2003), the SSB must treat their prevention as part of its core mandate to ensure Shari'a compliance. It reviews transactions, advises management, and monitors institutional practices. However, many SSBs struggle to fulfill this role effectively. Members often hold multiple positions across institutions and juggle diverse responsibilities—as religious advisers, legal consultants, and product reviewers—which limits focused oversight (Jabbar, 2010).

The SSB also lacks technical expertise in detecting financial crimes. Traditional Shari'a training does not equip its members to identify sophisticated misconduct like money laundering or fraud (Jabbar, 2010). In addition, many jurisdictions do not regulate SSBs formally, creating accountability gaps and exposing them to reputational risks (Jabbar, 2008).

To enhance the Board's preventive role, regulators must strengthen its institutional capacity, introduce oversight mechanisms, and promote interdisciplinary training. Without these reforms, the SSB's influence as a soft law body will remain limited, and Islamic finance will remain vulnerable to financial crime.

7. Conclusion

States alone cannot effectively combat the growing challenge of financial crime. In a globalized and digitized financial system, illicit actors exploit jurisdictional gaps, regulatory asymmetries, and enforcement constraints. While treaty-based instruments such as the UN Conventions on Transnational Organized Crime and

Corruption and the OECD Anti-Bribery Convention provide essential legal foundations, they remain insufficient in addressing the structural and operational sophistication of transnational financial crimes. Criminal operations frequently operate beyond the reach of traditional enforcement, while legal responses remain confined within national boundaries.

In this context, international organizations have emerged as critical actors in shaping a multi-layered global anti-financial crime regime. Standard-setting bodies like the FATF, the Basel Committee, and the IMF exert normative influence through peer review, technical guidance, and benchmarking. Operational networks such as INTERPOL and the Egmont Group facilitate cross-border intelligence-sharing and enforcement cooperation. Technical assistance providers—including the UNODC, the StAR Initiative, and the IMoLIN—strengthen institutional capacity, promote legislative reforms, and support the recovery of illicit assets.

Equally vital are soft law actors that influence compliance behavior through norms rather than binding obligations. The Wolfsberg Group and the JMLSG issue widely adopted guidelines that shape internal governance within financial institutions. Certification bodies such as CAMS and ACFCS professionalize the compliance workforce and promote ethical standards. Civil society organizations and investigative journalism networks function as norm entrepreneurs by exposing wrongdoing, mobilizing reform, and expanding transparency. In jurisdictions governed by Islamic finance, SSBs play a parallel normative role, interpreting principles of trust, honesty, and public interest to prohibit financial crimes such as fraud and money laundering.

Categorizing these institutions into rigid typologies often overlooks the dynamic and overlapping roles they play. Many combine functions of norm-setting, training, enforcement support, and reputational governance. This convergence reflects the evolving nature of global financial crime control, which no longer rests solely on legal obligations or coercive power. Rather, the international anti-financial crime framework operates through a hybrid model that blends binding law with voluntary compliance, peer accountability, and transnational cooperation. This integrated and multi-actor approach is essential for maintaining global financial integrity in an increasingly complex and interconnected world.

References

ACAMS. (n.d.). *Certified anti-money laundering specialist (CAMS)*. https://www.acams.org/en

ACFCS. (n.d.). *Certified financial crime specialist (CFCS)*. https://www.acfcs.org

ACFE. (n.d.). *About the association of certified fraud examiners*. https://www.acfe.com

Achim, M. V., & Borlea, N. S. (2020). *Economic and financial crime: Corruption, shadow economy, and money laundering*. Springer Nature Switzerland AG.

Agha, S. A. (2007). Money laundering from Islamic perspective. *Journal of Money Laundering Control*, *10*(4), 406–411. https://doi.org/10.1108/13685200710830899

Aiolfi, G., & Bauer, H.-P. (2012). The Wolfsberg Group. In M. Pieth (Ed.), *Collective action: Innovative strategies to prevent corruption*. Dike.

Akinbowale, O. E., Klingelhöfer, H. E., & Zerihun, M. F. (2020). An innovative approach in combating economic crime using forensic accounting techniques. *Journal of Financial Crime*. https://doi.org/10.1108/JFC-04-2020-0053

Al-Qaradawi, Y. (2003). *The lawful and the prohibited in Islam*. Al-Birr Foundation.

Alexander, K. (2001). The international anti-money-laundering regime: The role of the financial action task force. *Journal of Money Laundering Control*, *4*(3), 231–248.

Amjad, R. M., Rafay, A., Arshed, N., Munir, M., & Amjad, M. M. (2022). Non-linear impact of globalization on financial crimes: A case of developing economies. *Journal of Money Laundering Control*, *25*(2), 358–375. https://doi.org/10.1108/JMLC-03-2021-0023

AMLFC Institute. (n.d.). *About AMLFC institute*. https://amlfc.institute/

Arachchilage, N. A. G., & Love, S. (2014). Security awareness of computer users: A phishing threat avoidance perspective. *Computers in Human Behavior*, *38*, 304–312.

Bank for International Settlements. (2023). *Project Aurora: The power of data, technology and collaboration to combat money laundering across institutions and borders*. https://www.bis.org/publ/othp66.htm

Basel Committee on Banking Supervision. (2017). *Sound management of risks related to money laundering and financing of terrorism*. https://www.bis.org/bcbs/publ/d405.pdf

Basel Committee on Banking Supervision. (2024). *Core principles for effective banking supervision*. https://www.bis.org/bcbs/publ/d573.htm

Bassiouni, M. C. (2002). *International criminal law: Sources, subjects and contents* (Vol. 1, pp. 3–120). Martinus Nijhoff Publishers.

Bhasin, M. L. (2013). An empirical investigation of the relevant skills of forensic accountants: Experience of a developing economy. *European Journal of Accounting Auditing and Finance Research*, *1*(2), 11–52.

Coogan, J., Forder, E. L., Madir, J., Seiler, N., & Wee, C. (2015). Combatting fraud and corruption in international development. *Journal of Financial Crime*, *22*(2), 228–241. https://doi.org/10.1108/JFC-10-2014-0045

Council of Europe. (2005). *Council of Europe convention on laundering, search, seizure and confiscation of the proceeds from crime and on the financing of terrorism (CETS no. 198)*. https://www.coe.int/en/web/conventions/full-list/-/conventions/treaty/198

Devex. (2012). *Devex impact initiative*. https://www.devex.com

Egmont Group. (2023a). *2022/2023 annual report: Egmont group of financial intelligence units*. https://egmontgroup.org/wp-content/uploads/2024/07/2022-2023-Egmont-Group-Annual-Report.pdf

Egmont Group. (2023b). *Egmont group of financial intelligence units charter*. Revised July 2023. https://egmontgroup.org/wp-content/uploads/2021/09/Egmont-Group-Charter-Revised-July-2023-Abu-Dhabi-UAE.pdf

Egmont Group. (2024a). *The role of FIUs in the national risk assessment process*. https://egmontgroup.org/wp-content/uploads/2024/09/The-Role-of-FIUs-in-the-National-Risk-Assessment-Process.pdf

Egmont Group. (2024b). *The role of FIUs in the national risk assessment process: Information exchange working group*. https://egmontgroup.org/wp-content/uploads/2024/11/Egmont_Group_NRA_Brochure.pdf

Egmont Group. (n.d.-a). *About - Egmont group*. https://egmontgroup.org/about/

Egmont Group. (n.d.-b). *FAQs - Egmont group*. https://egmontgroup.org/faqs/

European Bank for Reconstruction and Development (EBRD). (2010). *Agreement for mutual enforcement of debarment decisions*. https://www.ebrd.com/content/dam/ebrd_dxp/assets/pdfs/sanctions-system/Agreement-for-Mutual-Enforcement-and-Debarment-Decisions-2010.pdf

European Parliament. (2013). European Parliament resolution of 23 October 2013 on organized crime, corruption and money laundering: Recommendations on action and initiatives to be taken (2013/2107(INI)). *Official Journal of the European Union, C 208*, 89–101.

Europol. (2023). *Consolidated annual activity report 2022*. Europol. https://www.europol.europa.eu/cms/sites/default/files/documents/Consolidated%20Annual%20Activity%20Report%202022.PDF

FATF, I. N. T. E. R. P. O. L., & Egmont Group. (2023). *Illicit financial flows from cyber-enabled fraud*. https://www.fatf-gafi.org/content/dam/fatf-gafi/reports/Illicit-Financial-Flows-Cyber-Enabled-Fraud.pdf

Financial Action Task Force. (2012). *International standards on combating money laundering and the financing of terrorism & proliferation: The FATF recommendations*. https://www.fatf-gafi.org/publications/fatfrecommendations/

Financial Action Task Force. (2020a). *COVID-19-related money laundering and terrorist financing risks*. https://www.fatf-gafi.org/publications/covid-19.html

Financial Action Task Force. (2020b). *Money laundering and the illegal wildlife trade*. https://www.fatf-gafi.org/publications/environmentalcrime/

Financial Action Task Force. (2020c). *Virtual assets red flag indicators of money laundering and terrorist financing*. https://www.fatf-gafi.org/publications/virtualassets/

Financial Action Task Force. (2021a). *Updated guidance on risk-based approach to virtual assets and virtual asset service providers*. https://www.fatf-gafi.org/publications/virtualassets/

Financial Action Task Force. (2021b). *Ethnically or racially motivated violent extremism*. https://www.fatf-gafi.org/publications/terroristfinancing/

Financial Action Task Force. (2022a). *Mandate of the FATF*. https://www.fatf-gafi.org/en/the-fatf/mandate-of-the-fatf.html

Financial Action Task Force. (2022b). *Public statement on revisions to recommendation 24*. https://www.fatf-gafi.org/publications/fatfrecommendations/

Financial Action Task Force. (2022c). *Procedures for the FATF AML/CFT/CPF mutual evaluations, follow-up and ICRG*. https://www.fatf-gafi.org/publications/mutualevaluations/

Financial Action Task Force. (2022d). *Report on the state of effectiveness and compliance with the FATF standards*. https://www.fatf-gafi.org/publications/fatfgeneral/

Financial Action Task Force. (2023a). *Countering ransomware financing*. https://www.fatf-gafi.org/publications/moneylaundering/

Financial Transparency Coalition (FTC). (2014). *Ownership transparency campaign*. https://financialtransparency.org

FinCEN. (n.d.). *The Egmont group of financial intelligence units*. https://www.fincen.gov/resources/international/egmont-group-financial-intelligence-units

Gilmore, W. (1995). *Dirty money: The evolution of money laundering countermeasures*. Council of Europe Press.

Goredema, C. (2003). Money laundering in East and Southern Africa: An overview of the threat. *Institute for Security Studies Papers*, *2003*(69), 20.

IMoLIN. (n.d.). *International money laundering information network*. https://www.imolin.org

International Consortium of Investigative Journalists (ICIJ). (n.d.-a). *About us*. https://www.icij.org/about/

International Consortium of Investigative Journalists (ICIJ). (n.d.-b). *Investigations*. https://www.icij.org

International Monetary Fund. (2023). *2023 review of the fund's anti-money laundering and combating the financing of terrorism strategy (Policy paper no. PPEA2023052)*. https://www.imf.org/en/Publications/Policy-Papers/Issues/2023/09/05/2023-Review-of-the-Funds-AML-CFT-Strategy-537775

International Organization of Securities Commissions. (1987). *Resolution on cooperation in matters of surveillance and enforcement*. https://www.iosco.org/library/resolutions/pdf/IOSCORES44.pdf

International Organization of Securities Commissions. (1990a). *Resolution on principles for the oversight of screen-based trading systems for derivative products*. https://www.iosco.org/library/resolutions/pdf/IOSCORES2.pdf

International Organization of Securities Commissions. (1992a). *Resolution on money laundering*. https://www.iosco.org/library/resolutions/pdf/IOSCORES5.pdf

International Organization of Securities Commissions. (1992b). *Resolution on supervision of financial conglomerates*. https://www.iosco.org/library/resolutions/pdf/IOSCORES13.pdf

International Organization of Securities Commissions. (1993a). *Resolution concerning transnational securities and futures fraud*. https://www.iosco.org/library/resolutions/pdf/IOSCORES8.pdf

International Organization of Securities Commissions. (1993b). *Resolution on coordination between cash and derivative markets*. https://www.iosco.org/library/resolutions/pdf/IOSCORES11.pdf

International Organization of Securities Commissions. (2006). *Resolution on cross-border cooperation to freeze assets derived from securities and derivatives violations*. https://www.iosco.org/library/resolutions/pdf/IOSCORES25.pdf

International Organization of Securities Commissions. (2010). *Resolution on IOSCO's mission, goals and priorities*. https://www.iosco.org/library/resolutions/pdf/IOSCORES26.pdf

International Organization of Securities Commissions. (2017). *Objectives and principles of securities regulation*. https://www.iosco.org/library/pubdocs/pdf/IOSCOPD561.pdf

International Organization of Securities Commissions. (n.d.). *About IOSCO*. https://www.iosco.org/v2/about/?subsection=about_iosco

INTERPOL. (2022). *Financial crime*. https://www.interpol.int/en/Crimes/Financial-crime

INTERPOL. (2024). *Global financial fraud assessment*. INTERPOL General Secretariat. https://www.interpol.int/content/download/21096/file/24COM005563-01%

20-%20CAS_Global%20Financial%20Fraud%20Assessment_Public%20version_2024-03_EN_v3.pdf
INTERPOL. (n.d.-a). *About INTERPOL*. https://www.interpol.int/en/Who-we-are/About-INTERPOL
INTERPOL. (n.d.-b). *Money laundering*. https://www.interpol.int/en/Crimes/Financial-crime/Money-laundering
Izedonmi, F., & Okoeguale, I. P. (2012). Forensic accounting and financial crimes—Adopting the inference, relevance and logic solution approach. *African Research Review*, *6*(4), 125–139.
Jabbar, H. S. F. A. (2008). The Shari'a supervisory board: A potential problem in Islamic finance?. *The Company Lawyer*, *29*, 29–32.
Jabbar, S. F. A. (2010). Financial crimes prohibition in Islam and prevention by the Shari'a supervisory board of Islamic financial institutions. *Journal of Financial Crime*, *17*(3), 287–294. https://doi.org/10.1108/13590791011056255
Joint Money Laundering Steering Group. (2023). *Prevention of money laundering/combating terrorist financing: Guidance for the UK financial sector - Part I (revised version)*. https://www.jmlsg.org.uk/
Kent, C. (1992). The Canadian and international war against money laundering: Legal perspectives. *Criminal Law Quarterly*, *35*, 21–45.
Kida, M., & Paetzold, S. (2021). *The impact of gray-listing on capital flows: An analysis using machine learning (IMF working paper No. WP/21/153)*. https://www.imf.org/en/Publications/WP/Issues/2021/06/30/The-Impact-of-Grey-Listing-on-Capital-Flows-An-Analysis-Using-Machine-Learning-462092
Kriz, G. J. (1992). International co-operation to combat money laundering: The nature and role of mutual legal assistance treaties. *Commonwealth Law Bulletin*, *18*(2), 723–734.
Leigh, A.-M., & Fariello, F. (2012). *The world bank group sanctions process and its recent reforms*. World Bank. http://siteresources.worldbank.org/INTLAWJUSTICE/Resources/SanctionsProcess.pdf
Magliveras, K. (1992). Defeating the money launderer—The international and European framework. *Journal of Business Law*, 161–178.
Maingot, A. P. (1995). Money laundering schemes. *Journal of Interamerican Studies and World Affairs*, *37*(4), 1–24.
Matrix Insight. (2008). *Study to assess the extent of abuse of non-profit organisations for financial criminal purposes at EU level*. European Commission, Directorate-General Justice, Freedom and Security.
McDonald, M. F. (1995). Globalisation of criminology: The new frontier in the frontier. *Journal of Transnational Crime*, *1*(1), 1–22.
Middle East and North Africa Financial Action Task Force. (n.d.). *About MENA-FATF*. https://www.menafatf.org/en
Mugarura, N. (2014). Has globalisation rendered the state paradigm in controlling crimes, anachronistic?. *Journal of Financial Crime*, *21*(4), 381–399. https://doi.org/10.1108/JFC-04-2013-0026
Nguyen, C. L. (2019). National criminal jurisdiction over transnational financial crimes. *Journal of Financial Crime*. https://doi.org/10.1108/JFC-09-2019-0117
OECD. (2021). *Recommendation of the council for further combating bribery of foreign public officials in international business transactions (OECD/LEGAL/0378)*. https://legalinstruments.oecd.org/en/instruments/OECD-LEGAL-0378

OECD. (2024). *Convention on combating bribery of foreign public officials in international business transactions and commentaries*. https://www.oecd.org/corruption/oecdantibriberyconvention.htm

OECD. (n.d.). *Fighting foreign bribery*. https://www.oecd.org/en/topics/sub-issues/fighting-foreign-bribery.html

Ortino, M. (2019). Thirty years after the Basel Accord and ten after the financial crisis: The Basel Committee on Banking Supervision and its place in international economic law. *Journal of International Economic Law*, *22*(2), 159–161.

Pieth, M., & Aiolfi, G. (2003). The private sector becomes active: The wolfsberg process. *Journal of Financial Crime*, *10*(3), 359–365.

Serbia & Council of Europe. (2020). *The Budapest convention on cybercrime: Benefits and impact in practice*. T-CY(2020)16. Council of Europe. https://rm.coe.int/t-cy-2020-16-bc-benefits-rep-provisional/16809ef6ac

Shelley, L. (1998). Transnational organised crimes: A new authoritarianism. In R. Friman & P. Andreas (Eds.), *Illicit global economy & state power* (pp. 25–40). Rowman & Littlefield.

Smith, G. (1992). Competition in the European financial services industry: The free movement of capital versus the regulation of money laundering. *University of Pennsylvania Journal of International Business Law*, *13*(1), 101–120.

Solomon, P. (1994). Are money launderers all washed up in the Western Hemisphere? The OAS model regulations. *Hastings International and Comparative Law Review*, *17*, 433–437.

StAR Initiative. (n.d.). *Stolen asset recovery initiative*. https://star.worldbank.org

Transparency International. (n.d.-a). *About transparency international*. https://www.transparency.org/en/about

Transparency International. (n.d.-b). *Global corruption barometer and related tools*. https://www.transparency.org

United Nations. (1988). *United nations convention against illicit traffic in narcotic drugs and psychotropic substances*. https://www.incb.org/documents/PRECURSORS/1988_CONVENTION/1988Convention_E.pdf

United Nations. (2000). *United nations convention against transnational organized crime*. https://www.unodc.org/unodc/en/organized-crime/intro/UNTOC.html

United Nations Office on Drugs and Crime. (2011). *Technical guide to the United Nations convention against corruption*. http://www.unodc.org/documents/corruption/Technical_Guide_UNCAC.pdf

United Nations Office on Drugs and Crime. (2017). *State of implementation of the United Nations convention against corruption: Criminalization, law enforcement and international cooperation* (2nd ed.). https://www.unodc.org/documents/treaties/UNCAC/COSP/session7/V.17-04679_E-book.pdf

United Nations Office on Drugs and Crime. (n.d.-a). *Economic & financial crime*. UNODC West and Central Africa. https://www.unodc.org/westandcentralafrica/en/economic-and-financial-crime.html

United Nations Office on Drugs and Crime. (n.d.-b). *Global programme against money laundering*. https://www.unodc.org/unodc/en/money-laundering/global-programme-against-money-laundering/.html

United Nations Office on Drugs and Crime, Commonwealth Secretariat, and International Monetary Fund. (2009). *Model provisions on money laundering, terrorist financing, preventive measures and proceeds of crime (for common law legal systems)*. https://www.unodc.org/documents/money-laundering/Model_Provisions_Final.pdf

UNODC. (2012). *Partnership with UNCAC Coalition to fight corruption*. https://www.unodc.org

van der Does de Willebois, E. (2010). *Nonprofit organisations and the combating of terrorism financing: A proportionate response*. World Bank working paper no. 208. The World Bank.

Van Sickle, A. (2009). Should there be a European criminal code? London. *Progressive Journal*, *73*, 2.

Vasciuc (Săndulescu), C. G., & Radu, F. (2024). The consequences of economic-financial crime on the economy. *Hyperion Economic Journal*, *11*(1), 90–102. https://hej.hyperion.ro/articles/HEJ%20nr1(11)_2024.pdf#page=91

Walker, J., & Unger, B. (2009). Measuring global money laundering: "The Walker Gravity Model". *Review of Law & Economics*, *5*(2), 821–853.

Wiener, J. M. (1997). International crime in the new geopolitics: A core threat to democracy. In W. F. McDonald (Ed.), *Crime and law enforcement in the global village* (pp. 41–64). Anderson Publishing Co.

Wolfsberg Group. (2000). *Wolfsberg anti-money laundering principles for private banking*. https://ms.hmb.gov.tr/uploads/sites/2/2019/04/wolfsberg_private_banking.pdf

Wolfsberg Group. (2002). *Statement on the suppression of the financing of terrorism*. https://ms.hmb.gov.tr/uploads/sites/2/2019/04/wolfsberg_on_terrorism.pdf

Wolfsberg Group. (2006). *Guidance on a risk-based approach for managing money laundering risks*. https://www.cbr.ru/Content/Document/File/124095/rba.pdf

Wolfsberg Group. (2022). *Wolfsberg financial crime principles for correspondent banking*. https://db.wolfsberg-group.org/assets/431f9f38-d56d-426d-b929-620371131654

Wolfsberg Group. (2023a). *Wolfsberg anti-bribery and corruption compliance programme guidance*. https://db.wolfsberg-group.org/assets/8cbe37e5-9286-4315-81f7-21e9ac70d8d2

Wolfsberg Group. (2023b). *Wolfsberg group financial crime compliance questionnaire 2023 (FCCQ V1.2)*. https://db.wolfsberg-group.org/assets/8f28b4be-5808-485f-aba0-ff79ebce8294

Wolfsberg Group. (n.d.-a). *About*. https://wolfsberg-group.org/about/

Wolfsberg Group. (n.d.-b). *About – Working groups*. https://wolfsberg-group.org/about/#working-groups

Wolfsberg Group. (n.d.-c). *Wolfsberg group correspondent banking due diligence questionnaire (CBDDQ) V1.4*. https://db.wolfsberg-group.org/assets/3964cedf-a462-4e55-a1e7-ca7c70dfa7ec

Zagaris, B., & McDonald, S. (1992). Money laundering, financial fraud, and technology: The perils of an instantaneous economy. *The George Washington Journal of International Law & Economics*, *26*(1), 61–85.

Chapter 13

The Development of Effective Anti-Corruption Policies: Reforms and the Legal Framework

Arsim Thaçi[a], *Enver Buçaj*[a], *Dardan Vuniqi*[a], *Fidan Haliti*[b] *and Ismail Zejneli*[c]

[a]University "Ukshin Hoti" Prizren, Republic of Kosovo
[b]University "HASAN PRISHTINA" Pristina, Republic of Kosovo
[c]South East European University, North Macedonia

Abstract

Following the declaration of independence in 2008, the Republic of Kosovo undertook significant reforms in its justice system, particularly in the area of criminal justice. Despite institutional efforts and an expanded mandate in the administration of justice, the response to corruption remained weak, with frequent instances of case dismissal due to the statute of limitations and light sentencing. In response to international criticism, particularly from the European Union, Kosovo initiated a comprehensive legal reform process and a vetting of its justice institutions. Between 2010 and 2013, key laws were adopted or amended, including the Criminal Code, the Code of Criminal Procedure, and legislation governing judicial and prosecutorial bodies. These reforms laid the foundation for a new, functional system of courts and prosecution offices, operational as of January 2013. This chapter examines whether these reforms and legal frameworks effectively combat corruption within the criminal justice system. Using a scientific methodology that includes analysis, synthesis, and historical and normative methods, the study explores the impact of legal reforms on corruption-related offenses. Findings indicate that while challenges persist, the restructuring of judicial institutions and legislative updates have contributed to improved handling of corruption cases and a measurable decline in such offenses. The research confirms that the reforms represent effective

Corruption and Crime in Finance, 279–304

Published under exclusive licence by Emerald Publishing Limited
doi:10.1108/978-1-83708-170-720261034

policy instruments in the fight against and prevention of corruption, marking progress in Kosovo's journey toward a more accountable and transparent justice system.

Keywords: Corruption; criminal offenses; criminal code; criminal justice; criminal justice reforms

1. Introduction

Corruption poses a serious obstacle to the political, economic, and social development of a state. Inefficiency in investigating, prosecuting, and adjudicating corruption cases not only facilitates its spread but also contributes to state capture for private interests, undermining democratic development, equality before the law, and increasing undue influence over public institutions. In this context, an independent judiciary plays a crucial role in preventing and combating corruption (European Commission, 2024).

In practice, the majority of corruption cases remain at the stage of investigation or prosecution and do not reach trial. Even when such cases result in convictions, the sentences imposed are often lenient and not proportional to the harm caused. This situation negatively affects public perception of justice and the effectiveness of institutions (Anti-Corruption Fund, 2023; Balkan Investigative Reporting Network, 2023; Indonesia Corruption Watch, 2023).

To improve this perception and advance in international rankings, such as the Corruption Perceptions Index (CPI) by Transparency International, it is in the interest of the Republic of Kosovo to strengthen its efforts in preventing and combating corruption. Mechanisms such as asset declaration, prevention of conflicts of interest, whistleblower protection, and strengthening law enforcement institutions are legal obligations stemming from both domestic legislation and Kosovo's international commitments in the fight against corruption (Council of Europe, 2023; GAN Integrity, 2023; Kosovo Anti-Corruption Agency, 2023).

Furthermore, international reports including the European Commission's Progress Reports and national anti-corruption strategies provide important guidance for enhancing the efficiency of institutions such as the police, prosecution, and judiciary. Only through close inter-institutional cooperation can a sustainable and effective system be built to combat corruption, one that earns the trust of the public (European Commission, 2024; Kosovo Law Institute, 2024; United Nations Development Program [UNDP], 2024).

In conclusion, despite the progress achieved, the fight against corruption remains a continuous challenge and a strategic priority for the institutions of the Republic of Kosovo. The development and implementation of sustainable anti-corruption policies, improvements in criminal legislation, and strengthening institutional integrity are essential steps toward building a society free from the influence of corruption (European Commission, 2023; Kosovo Law Institute, 2024; United Nations Development Program [UNDP], 2024).

2. Research Methodology

To achieve a scientific understanding and treatment of this social phenomenon corruption this research employs a range of methods designed to objectively present the reality of the issue. These methods include the method of analysis and synthesis, the historical method, the logical method, and the normative method.

2.1 Method of Analysis and Synthesis

Based on the principle that there can be no synthesis without analysis, and no meaningful analysis without synthesis, this method is used to examine in detail the chapter or group of criminal offenses related to corruption and abuse of official duty. Specifically, the analysis focuses on 17 criminal offenses categorized within the 44 chapters of the Criminal Code of the Republic of Kosovo. These offenses are studied starting from the Provisional Criminal Code of Kosovo, followed by the 2013 Criminal Code, and continuing with the most recent amendments and supplements to the Criminal Code.

Through the method of synthesis, a comprehensive consolidation of the elements of the research object is carried out namely, the integration of criminal provisions from the Criminal Code with those specified in special laws (so-called "blanket" offenses) related to corruption.

2.2 Historical Method

The historical method is employed to chronologically explain the development of criminal provisions against official corruption, beginning with the entry into force of the Provisional Criminal Code on April 6, 2004, followed by the 2013 Criminal Code, and the subsequent amendments and supplements introduced in the following years. This method helps to understand the evolution of legal approaches toward these offenses.

2.3 Logical Method

This method serves to analyze the conceptual development and interrelation of these criminal offenses, and to draw conclusions about trends in criminalization and the significance that criminal legislation attributes to institutional corruption at various levels.

2.4 Normative Method

The normative method is applied to identify, interpret, and assess statistical data concerning these criminal offenses in judicial practice. This includes the analysis of statistical data for the period 2020–2025, covering the number of initiated, adjudicated, and concluded cases, as well as the types of sanctions imposed for offenses related to corruption and abuse of official position.

The combination of these methods creates a solid scientific foundation for a comprehensive understanding of the phenomenon of corruption in Kosovo, with a particular focus on the analysis of the legal framework, judicial practice, and institutional developments during the studied period.

3. Literature Review

After the heroic war of the people of Kosovo and NATO's military intervention, on June 12, 1999, Kosovo was liberated from occupation and came under the temporary administration of the United Nations, based on UN Security Council Resolution 1244. Until its political status was determined, Kosovo was governed by the United Nations Mission in Kosovo (UNMIK, 1999).

Due to the lack of independent status, the Legal Office within UNMIK drafted and approved the Provisional Criminal Code of Kosovo, which was adopted by the Special Representative of the UN Secretary-General, Mr. Michael Steiner, on July 6, 2003, and entered into force on April 6, 2004, through UNMIK Regulation No. 2003/25 (UNMIK, 2003). The Criminal Code holds special political and legal significance, as it is a direct expression of the sovereignty of a people. It symbolizes the functioning of state institutions the police, prosecution, and judiciary and the state's ability to govern through a legal order (Human Rights Watch, 2006; UNMIK, 2003).

After Kosovo declared independence on February 17, 2008, through Law No. 03/L-002 dated December 22, 2008, the term "provisional" was removed from this code, affirming it as part of the independent legal system of the Republic of Kosovo (Assembly of the Republic of Kosovo, 2008a, 2008b, 2008c).

Between 2010 and 2012, domestic and international experts worked on drafting a new criminal code. Consequently, the Criminal Code of the Republic of Kosovo No. 04/L-082 was adopted on July 13, 2012, and entered into force on January 1, 2013 (Assembly of the Republic of Kosovo, 2012a, 2012b, 2012c, 2012d). This code has been reformed several times:

- On November 9, 2012, through Law No. 04/L-129 and May 15, 2014, through Law No. 04/L-273 (Assembly of the Republic of Kosovo, 2012a, 2012b, 2012c, 2012d; Assembly of the Republic of Kosovo, 2014).
- With Criminal Code No. 06/L-074, adopted on January 14, 2019, which entered into force on April 14, 2019 (Assembly of the Republic of Kosovo, 2019a, 2019b).
- Most recently, with Criminal Code No. 08/L-188, adopted on November 23, 2023 (Assembly of the Republic of Kosovo, 2023a, 2023b, 2023c).

The Criminal Procedure Code has undergone similar reforms. Initially, it was promulgated as the Provisional Criminal Procedure Code through UNMIK Regulation No. 2003/26 on July 6, 2003, entering into force on April 6, 2004. Later, by Law No. 03/L-003 on December 22, 2008, the "provisional" attribute was removed. The current Criminal Procedure Code of the Republic of Kosovo

No. 04/L-123, adopted on December 28, 2012, was amended on August 17, 2022, and November 23, 2023 (Assembly of the Republic of Kosovo, 2008a, 2008b, 2008c; Assembly of the Republic of Kosovo, 2012a, 2012b, 2012c, 2012d; Assembly of the Republic of Kosovo, 2022; Assembly of the Republic of Kosovo, 2023a, 2023b, 2023c).

3.1 Additional Laws Strengthening the Legal Framework Against Corruption

Besides reforms in the Criminal Code and Criminal Procedure Code, the fight against corruption has been reinforced through a series of special laws that constitute important parts of Kosovo's penal and institutional legislation:

- Law on the Kosovo Judicial Council No. 03/L-223 (November 3, 2010), reformed on: September 7, 2012; June 30, 2015; April 6, 2016; December 26, 2018; and January 5, 2023 (Assembly of the Republic of Kosovo, 2010a, 2010b, 2010c, 2010d, 2010e).
- Law on the Kosovo Prosecutorial Council No. 03/L-224 (October 29, 2010), amended on: September 7, 2012; June 30, 2015; and April 30, 2019 (Assembly of the Republic of Kosovo, 2010a, 2010b, 2010c, 2010d, 2010e).
- Law on the State Prosecutor No. 03/L-225 (October 29, 2010), amended on: June 30, 2015; April 19, 2018; and May 17, 2023 (Assembly of the Republic of Kosovo, 2010a, 2010b, 2010c, 2010d, 2010e).
- Law on the Special Prosecutor's Office of the Republic of Kosovo No. 03/L-052 (June 3, 2008), amended on: June 29, 2016; and November 23, 2023 (Assembly of the Republic of Kosovo, 2008a, 2008b, 2008c).
- Law on Courts No. 03/L-199 (August 24, 2010), reformed on: September 7, 2012; December 28, 2012; June 30, 2015; December 18, 2018; February 10, 2022 (regarding the Commercial Court); and January 5, 2023 (Assembly of the Republic of Kosovo, 2010a, 2010b, 2010c, 2010d, 2010e).
- Law on Prevention of Conflict of Interest in the Exercise of Public Functions No. 04/L-051 (September 14, 2011), reformed on April 27, 2018 (Assembly of the Republic of Kosovo, 2011a, 2011b).
- Law on the Anti-Corruption Agency No. 03/L-159 (February 5, 2010), amended by the Law on the Agency for the Prevention of Corruption (July 21, 2022) (Assembly of the Republic of Kosovo, 2010a, 2010b, 2010c, 2010d, 2010e).
- Law on Declaration, Origin, and Control of Property of Senior Public Officials and Declaration of Gifts, No. 04/L-050 (September 14, 2011), amended on April 28, 2014, and followed by a new law with the same purpose on August 10, 2022 (Assembly of the Republic of Kosovo, 2011a, 2011b).

3.2 Conclusion

These developments in criminal legislation demonstrate the Republic of Kosovo's continuous institutional commitment to building a strong legal system and serious efforts to prevent and combat corruption. The successive amendments to the Criminal Code and other special laws create a stable legal and institutional framework, consistent with international standards and the requirements of European integration.

4. Structure of the Research

This research is structured into three main parts, each addressing different aspects of the fight against corruption in the Republic of Kosovo, with a specific focus on criminal legislation reform, judicial implementation, and international perception. Each part analyzes a distinct segment of this social and institutional phenomenon:

Part One—Legal Reforms in the Criminal Code of the Republic of Kosovo (2004–2024)

This part focuses on analyzing the legal changes and amendments made to the group or chapter of criminal offenses related to corruption and abuse of official duty, starting from the entry into force of the Provisional Criminal Code of Kosovo in 2004 to the latest version of the Criminal Code in force (see Tables 13.1-13.4). The content of the relevant chapters is compared, and the progressive increase of incriminations and alignment with international standards is highlighted.

Part Two—Results from the Annual Reports of Kosovo Courts (2020–2024)

This part addresses the empirical results derived from the annual reports of the courts of the Republic of Kosovo regarding corruption-related cases during the period 2020–2024. The objective is to analyze whether legal reforms have influenced the efficiency of the judicial system, the number of cases handled, the conviction rate, and the types of sanctions imposed for corruption offenses.

Part Three—International Perception of Corruption in Kosovo (2020–2024)

This part presents the results of the analysis concerning Kosovo's ranking in the global CPI published by *Transparency International*. It includes a comparison of Kosovo's position with other countries in Europe and the Western Balkans and assesses the impact of legal and institutional reforms on improving the country's international image in the fight against corruption.

Part One—Amendments and Supplements to the Chapter on Criminal Offenses Related to Corruption in the Criminal Code of the Republic of Kosovo during the Period 2004–2024

Presentation of Research Data and Summary Tables on the Chapter on Corruption-Related Criminal Offenses or Abuse of Official Duty in the Criminal Code of the Republic of Kosovo.

Table 13.1. Criminal Offenses Related to Corruption Under the Provisional Criminal Code of Kosovo (2004).

Criminal Offenses related to corruption under the Provisional Criminal Code of Kosovo, UNMIK/REG/2003/25 dated 06.07.2003, entered into force on 06.04.2004		
No.	**Chapter XXIX—Criminal Offenses Against Official Duty**	**Article**
1	Abuse of official position or authority	Article 339
2	Misappropriation during duty	Article 340
3	Fraud in office	Article 341
4	Unauthorized use of property	Article 342
5	Accepting bribes	Article 343
6	Giving bribes	Article 344
7	Trading in influence	Article 345
8	Unlawful issuance of judicial decisions	Article 346
9	Disclosure of official secrets	Article 347
10	Forgery of official documents	Article 348
11	Illegal collection and payment	Article 349
12	Unlawful release of a person deprived of liberty	Article 350
13	Unlawful misappropriation of property during searches or execution of judicial decisions	Article 351

Source: Provisional Criminal Code of Kosovo, UNMIK/REG/2003/25 dated 06.07.2003.

Table 13.2. Criminal Offenses Related to Corruption Under the Criminal Code of the Republic of Kosovo No. 04/L-082 (2013).

Criminal Offenses related to corruption under the Criminal Code of the Republic of Kosovo, Code No. 04/L-082 dated July 13, 2012, entered into force on January 01, 2013		
No.	**Chapter XXXIV—Official Corruption and Criminal Offenses Against Official Duty**	**Article**
1	Abuse of official position or authority	Article 422
2	Misuse of official information	Article 423
3	Conflict of interest	Article 424
4	Misappropriation in office	Article 425
5	Fraud in office	Article 426
6	Unauthorized use of property	Article 427

(Continued)

Table 13.2. *(Continued)*

Criminal Offenses related to corruption under the Criminal Code of the Republic of Kosovo, Code No. 04/L-082 dated July 13, 2012, entered into force on January 01, 2013		
No.	**Chapter XXXIV—Official Corruption and Criminal Offenses Against Official Duty**	**Article**
7	Accepting bribes	Article 428
8	Giving bribes	Article 429
9	Bribing a foreign public official	Article 430
10	Trading in influence	Article 431
11	Unlawful issuance of judicial decisions	Article 432
12	Disclosure of official secrets	Article 433
13	Forgery of official documents	Article 434
14	Illegal collection and payment	Article 435
15	Unlawful misappropriation of property during searches or execution of judicial decision	Article 436
16	Failure to report or false reporting of property, income, other material benefits, or financial obligation	Article 437

Source: Criminal Code of the Republic of Kosovo, Code No. 04/L-082 dated July 13, 2012.

Table 13.3. Criminal Offenses Related to Corruption Under the Criminal Code of the Republic of Kosovo No. 06/L-074 (2019).

Criminal Offenses related to corruption under the Criminal Code of the Republic of Kosovo, Code No. 06/L-074 dated January 14, 2019, entered into force on April 14, 2019		
No.	**Criminal Offenses related to corruption under the Criminal Code of the Republic of Kosovo, Code No. 06/L-074 dated January 14, 2019, entered into force on April 14, 2019**	**Article**
1	Abuse of official position or authority	Article 414
2	Abuse and fraud in public procurement	Article 415
3	Misuse of official information	Article 416
4	Conflict of interest	Article 417
5	Misappropriation in office	Article 418
6	Fraud in office	Article 419
7	Unauthorized use of property	Article 420
8	Accepting bribes	Article 421

Table 13.3. *(Continued)*

Criminal Offenses related to corruption under the Criminal Code of the Republic of Kosovo, Code No. 06/L-074 dated January 14, 2019, entered into force on April 14, 2019

No.	Criminal Offenses related to corruption under the Criminal Code of the Republic of Kosovo, Code No. 06/L-074 dated January 14, 2019, entered into force on April 14, 2019	Article
9	Giving bribes	Article 422
10	Bribing foreign public officials or foreign officials	Article 423
11	Trading in influence	Article 424
12	Unlawful issuance of judicial decisions	Article 425
13	Disclosure of official secrets	Article 426
14	Forgery of official documents	Article 427
15	Illegal collection and payment	Article 428
16	Unlawful misappropriation of property during searches or execution of judicial decisions	Article 429
17	Failure to report or false reporting of property, income, other material benefits, or financial obligations	Article 430

Source: Criminal Code of the Republic of Kosovo, Code No. 06/L-074 dated January 14, 2019.

Table 13.4. Comparative Overview of Corruption-Related Criminal Offenses in the Criminal Codes of Kosovo (2004–2024).

Legal Reforms in the Chapter on Criminal Offenses Against Corruption in the Criminal Code of the Republic of Kosovo (2004–2024)

Period	Criminal Code	Chapter	Number of Offenses	Comments
2004	UNMIK/REG/2003/25	XXIX	13	Initial provisions under international administration
2013	Code No. 04/L-082	XXXIV	16	Addition of 3 new offenses including asset declaration
2019	Code No. 06/L-074	XXXIII	17	Introduction of "Abuse and fraud in public procurement"

The criminal offenses in this chapter have undergone significant reforms and legal updates through the following milestones:

- **06.04.2004**—Entry into force of the *Provisional Criminal Code of Kosovo*
- **01.01.2013**—Entry into force of *Criminal Code of the Republic of Kosovo* No. 04/L-082
- **14.04.2019**—Entry into force of *Criminal Code of the Republic of Kosovo* No. 06/L-074

Over this 20-year period, the number of criminal offenses related to corruption increased from *13* (in 2004) to *16* (in 2013), and finally to *17* (in 2019). These increases reflect both changes in nomenclature and the introduction of new offenses, driven by the evolving socioeconomic and political landscape in Kosovo.

Assessment for the Period 2004–2024:

- *Progressive increase* in the number of criminal offenses related to corruption.
- *Legal adaptation* to EU standards and evolving sociopolitical conditions in Kosovo.
- *Broader inclusion* of potentially corrupt practices across public sector, judiciary, and public procurement.
- These reforms reflect Kosovo's commitment to building a transparent, accountable, and corruption-resistant criminal justice system.

Part Two—Research Findings from the Annual Reports of the Courts of the Republic of Kosovo on Corruption Cases as a Result of Criminal Legislation Reform for the Period 2020–2024

This part of the research is based on official data published in the annual reports of the Kosovo Judicial Council (KJC) for the period 2020–2024 and aims to analyze the impact of criminal legal reforms on the handling of corruption cases within the judicial system of the Republic of Kosovo (see Tables 13.5–13.10).

Purpose of the Research:

- To examine how the amendments and additions to the Criminal Code have influenced the increased efficiency in addressing corruption cases.
- To analyze the number of cases received, processed, and concluded, including final decisions and the types of penalties imposed.

4.1 Institutional and Procedural Framework

According to the Criminal Procedure Code of the Republic of Kosovo, corruption is classified as a serious criminal offense. The institutions responsible for the investigation and prosecution of such offenses are:

Table 13.5. Guilty Verdicts for Corruption-Related Offenses in Kosovo Courts in 2020.

Kosovo Judicial Council Official Corruption and Criminal Offenses Against Official Duty Period: January 01, 2020—December 31, 2020						
No.	**Prosecution**	**Individuals**	**Verdict**	**Date Announced**	**Sentence**	**Court**
1	Gjilan	1	Guilty	November 09, 2020	Fine	Gjilan
2	Gjilan	1	Guilty	January 20, 2020	Sentence	Gjilan
3	Prizren	1	Guilty	February 03, 2020	Sentence	Prizren
4	Mitrovica	1	Guilty	January 13, 2020	Fine	Mitrovica
5	Gjakova	1	Guilty	January 20, 2020	Fine	Gjakova
6	Prishtina	1	Guilty	September 21, 2020	Sentence	Prishtina
7	Gjilan	1	Guilty	September 14, 2020	Fine	Gjilan
8	Gjilan	1	Guilty	October 23, 2020	Fine	Gjilan
9	Prizren	1	Guilty	September 11, 2020	Fine	Prizren
10	Mitrovica	2	Guilty	June 26, 2020	Sentence	Mitrovica
11	Prizren	2	Guilty	June 29, 2020	Sentence	Prizren
12	Gjakova	1	Guilty	December 21, 2020	Fine	Gjakova
13	Ferizaj	7	Guilty	October 20, 2020	Sentence	Ferizaj
14	Ferizaj	1	Guilty	September 29, 2020	Fine	Ferizaj
15	Mitrovica	1	Guilty	April 03, 2020	Sentence	Mitrovica
16	Gjilan	1	Guilty	December 12, 2020	Fine	Gjilan
17	Prizren	1	Guilty	October 22, 2020	Fine	Prizren
18	Prishtina	1	Guilty	January 08, 2020	Fine	Gjilan*
19	Gjilan	1	Guilty	November 13, 2020	Fine	Gjilan
20	Prizren	1	Guilty	December 08, 2020	Sentence	Prizren
21	Gjilan	1	Guilty	September 30, 2020	Fine	Gjilan
22	Prizren	1	Guilty	September 02, 2020	Fine	Prizren
23	Gjakova	1	Guilty	September 07, 2020	Sentence	Gjakova
24	Peja	1	Guilty	January 29, 2020	Sentence	Peja
25	Gjakova	1	Guilty	September 07, 2020	Sentence	Gjakova
26	Ferizaj	1	Guilty	July 27, 2020	Sentence	Ferizaj
27	Gjilan	1	Guilty	September 18, 2020	Fine	Gjilan
28	Prishtina	1	Guilty	October 30, 2020	Sentence	Prishtina

Source: Annual Reports of the Courts of the Republic of Kosovo on Corruption Cases.

Table 13.6. Guilty Verdicts for Corruption-Related Offenses in Kosovo Courts in 2021.

Kosovo Judicial Council Official Corruption and Criminal Offenses Against Official Duty Period: January 01, 2021—December 31, 2021						
No.	**Prosecution**	**Individuals**	**Verdict**	**Date Announced**	**Sentence**	**Court**
1	Prishtina	2	Guilty	April 14, 2021	Sentence	Prishtina
2	Prishtina	1	Guilty	June 24, 2021	Fine	Prishtina
3	Prizren	1	Guilty	January 15, 2021	Sentence	Prizren
4	Mitrovica	2	Guilty	May 27, 2021	Sentence	Mitrovica
5	Gjakova	4	Guilty	June 01, 2021	Sentence	Gjakova
6	Ferizaj	1	Guilty	February 22, 2021	Sentence	Ferizaj
7	Prishtina	1	Guilty	October 18, 2021	Sentence	Prishtina
8	Mitrovica	1	Guilty	September 17, 2021	Sentence	Mitrovica
9	Peja	2	Guilty	December 20, 2021	Sentence	Peja
10	Ferizaj	1	Guilty	May 26, 2021	Sentence	Ferizaj
11	Mitrovica	1	Guilty	May 27, 2021	Sentence	Mitrovica
12	Gjilan	5	Guilty	July 29, 2021	Fine	Gjilan
13	Ferizaj	2	Guilty	November 12, 2021	Sentence	Ferizaj
14	Gjilan	1	Guilty	July 21, 2021	Fine	Gjilan
15	Gjakova	1	Guilty	November 11, 2021	Fine	Gjakova
16	Ferizaj	1	Guilty	May 17, 2021	Fine	Ferizaj
17	Mitrovica	1	Guilty	November 09, 2021	Sentence	Mitrovica
18	Gjilan	1	Guilty	June 01, 2021	Fine	Gjilan
19	Gjilan	1	Guilty	April 28, 2021	Sentence	Gjilan
20	Gjilan	1	Guilty	April 28, 2021	Sentence	Gjilan
21	Prishtina	1	Guilty	July 30, 2021	Sentence	Gjilan
22	Gjakova	1	Guilty	January 08, 2021	Sentence	Gjakova
23	Gjakova	1	Guilty	April 27, 2021	Sentence	Gjakova
24	Prishtina	1	Guilty	06.04.2021	Sentence	Prishtina
25	Peja	1	Guilty	October 29, 2021	Fine	Peja
26	Prishtina	2	Guilty	June 17, 2021	Sentence	Prishtina
27	Prishtina	1	Guilty	May 14, 2021	Sentence	Prishtina
28	Prizren	1	Guilty	February 10, 2021	Fine	Prizren
29	Prizren	1	Guilty	February 16, 2021	Sentence	Prizren
30	Prizren	1	Guilty	March 29, 2021	Fine	Prizren
31	Prizren	1	Guilty	April 21, 2021	Sentence	Prizren
32	Prizren	1	Guilty	July 19, 2021	Fine	Prizren
33	Prizren	1	Guilty	October 06, 2021	Fine	Prizren

Table 13.6. *(Continued)*

Kosovo Judicial Council Official Corruption and Criminal Offenses Against Official Duty Period: January 01, 2021—December 31, 2021						
No.	**Prosecution**	**Individuals**	**Verdict**	**Date Announced**	**Sentence**	**Court**
34	Prizren	1	Guilty	December 23, 2021	Fine	Prizren
35	Prizren	1	Guilty	December 24, 2021	Sentence	Prizren
36	Mitrovica	1	Guilty	November 04, 2021	Sentence	Mitrovica
37	Gjakova	1	Guilty	September 28, 2021	Sentence	Gjakova
38	Ferizaj	1	Guilty	December 17, 2021	Sentence	Ferizaj
39	Ferizaj	1	Guilty	October 15, 2021	Fine	Ferizaj
40	Prizren	1	Guilty	April 21, 2021	Sentence	Prizren

Source: Annual Reports of the Courts of the Republic of Kosovo on Corruption Cases.

Table 13.7. Guilty Verdicts for Corruption-Related Offenses in Kosovo Courts in 2022.

Kosovo Judicial Council Official Corruption and Criminal Offenses Against Official Duty Period: January 01, 2022—December 31, 2022						
No.	**Prosecution**	**Individuals**	**Verdict**	**Date Announced**	**Sentence**	**Court**
1	Prishtina	2	Guilty	September 30, 2022	Sentence	Prishtina
2	Prishtina	2	Guilty	June 21, 2022	Sentence	Prishtina
3	Prishtina	2	Guilty	April 15, 2022	Sentence	Prishtina
4	Prishtina	2	Guilty	May 30, 2022	Sentence	Prishtina
5	Gjilan	2	Guilty	November 10, 2022	Fine	Gjilan
6	Prizren	1	Guilty	August 02, 2022	Sentence	Prizren
7	Prizren	1	Guilty	October 25, 2022	Sentence	Prizren
8	Prishtina	1	Guilty	June 28, 2022	Fine	Prishtina
9	Gjilan	1	Guilty	June 07, 2022	Sentence	Gjilan
10	Prizren	1	Guilty	May 31, 2022	Fine	Prizren
11	Mitrovica	1	Guilty	June 24, 2022	Fine	Mitrovica
12	Peja	1	Guilty	April 01, 2022	Sentence	Peja
13	Ferizaj	5	Guilty	August 01, 2022	Sentence	Ferizaj
14	Gjilan	1	Guilty	June 30, 2022	Sentence	Gjilan
15	Special	2	Guilty	July 21, 2022	Sentence	Prishtina
16	Prishtina	1	Guilty	February 28, 2022	Sentence	Prishtina

(Continued)

Table 13.7. *(Continued)*

Kosovo Judicial Council Official Corruption and Criminal Offenses Against Official Duty Period: January 01, 2022—December 31, 2022						
No.	**Prosecution**	**Individuals**	**Verdict**	**Date Announced**	**Sentence**	**Court**
17	Prishtina	1	Guilty	September 20, 2022	Sentence	Prishtina
18	Prishtina	1	Guilty	July 28, 2022	Sentence	Prishtina
19	Mitrovica	4	Guilty	August 04, 2022	Sentence	Mitrovica
20	Prishtina	1	Guilty	August 16, 2022	Sentence	Prishtina
21	Prizren	1	Guilty	January 27, 2022	Sentence	Prizren
22	Prizren	1	Guilty	February 08, 2022	Sentence	Prizren
23	Prizren	1	Guilty	May 12, 2022	Sentence	Prizren
24	Prizren	1	Guilty	July 14, 2022	Sentence	Prizren
25	Prizren	1	Guilty	June 21, 2022	Sentence	Prizren
26	Prizren	1	Guilty	October 06, 2022	Sentence	Prizren
27	Gjakova	1	Guilty	February 11, 2022	Sentence	Gjakova
28	Ferizaj	1	Guilty	April 27, 2022	Fine	Ferizaj
29	Mitrovica	4	Guilty	February 18, 2022	Sentence	Mitrovica
30	Prishtina	1	Guilty	October 03, 2022	Fine	Prishtina
31	Peja	1	Guilty	August 22, 2022	Fine	Peja
32	Ferizaj	1	Guilty	April 12, 2022	Fine	Ferizaj
33	Prishtina	1	Guilty	January 14, 2022	Sentence	Prishtina
34	Gjilan	2	Guilty	March 09, 2022	Sentence	Gjilan

Source: Annual Reports of the Courts of the Republic of Kosovo on Corruption Cases.

Table 13.8. Guilty Verdicts for Corruption-Related Offenses in Kosovo Courts in 2023.

Kosovo Judicial Council Official Corruption and Criminal Offenses Against Official Duty Period: January 01, 2023—December 31, 2023						
No.	**Prosecution Office**	**Persons**	**Verdict**	**Date Announced**	**Sentence**	**Court**
1	Prishtina	1	Guilty	September 26, 2023	Sentence	Prishtina
2	Prishtina	1	Guilty	March 27, 2023	Fine	Prishtina
3	Gjilan	5	Guilty	December 21, 2023	Sentence	Gjilan
4	Gjilan	1	Guilty	March 23, 2023	Sentence	Gjilan
5	Prizren	2	Guilty	January 26, 2023	Sentence	Prizren
6	Prishtina	1	Guilty	April 17, 2023	Fine	Prishtina

Table 13.8. *(Continued)*

Kosovo Judicial Council Official Corruption and Criminal Offenses Against Official Duty Period: January 01, 2023—December 31, 2023

No.	Prosecution Office	Persons	Verdict	Date Announced	Sentence	Court
7	Gjilan	1	Guilty	May 31, 2023	Sentence	Gjilan
8	Gjilan	3	Guilty	February 22, 2023	Sentence	Gjilan
9	Gjilan	1	Guilty	February 09, 2023	Fine	Gjilan
10	Mitrovica	1	Guilty	September 22, 2023	Fine	Mitrovica
11	Mitrovica	1	Guilty	April 04, 2023	Sentence	Mitrovica
12	Peja	1	Guilty	May 31, 2023	Fine	Peja
13	Peja	1	Guilty	February 16, 2023	Fine	Peja
14	Prishtina	5	Guilty	January 23, 2023	Sentence	Ferizaj
15	Prishtina	1	Guilty	May 08, 2023	Sentence	Prishtina
16	Prishtina	1	Guilty	April 19, 2023	Sentence	Prishtina
17	Prishtina	1	Guilty	December 26, 2023	Sentence	Prishtina
18	Gjilan	1	Guilty	June 09, 2023	Sentence	Gjilan
19	Gjilan	1	Guilty	December 15, 2023	Fine	Gjilan
20	Prishtina	1	Guilty	May 12, 2023	Fine	Prishtina
21	Peja	1	Guilty	November 30, 2023	Sentence	Peja
22	Ferizaj	1	Guilty	October 27, 2023	Fine	Ferizaj
23	Prishtina	1	Guilty	January 19, 2023	Sentence	Prishtina
24	Gjilan	1	Guilty	December 18, 2023	Fine	Prishtina*
25	Prizren	3	Guilty	July 05, 2023	Sentence	Prizren
26	Mitrovica	1	Guilty	July 13, 2023	Sentence	Mitrovica
27	Gjakova	2	Guilty	February 27, 2023	Sentence	Gjakova
28	Ferizaj	1	Guilty	July 13, 2023	Sentence	Ferizaj
29	Prishtina	1	Guilty	March 03, 2023	Sentence	Prishtina
30	Prizren	1	Guilty	January 30, 2023	Sentence	Prizren
31	Gjakova	1	Guilty	May 22, 2023	Imprisonment	Gjakova
32	Peja	1	Guilty	October 18, 2023	Sentence	Peja
33	Peja	1	Guilty	December 31, 2023	Fine	Peja
34	Prishtina	1	Guilty	June 14, 2023	Fine	Gjilan*
35	Prishtina	1	Guilty	September 06, 2023	Sentence	Prishtina
36	Gjilan	1	Guilty	December 18, 2023	Sentence	Gjilan

Source: Annual Reports of the Courts of the Republic of Kosovo on Corruption Cases.

Table 13.9. Guilty Verdicts for Corruption-Related Offenses in Kosovo Courts in 2024.

Kosovo Judicial Council Official Corruption and Criminal Offenses Against Official Duty Period: January 01, 2024—December 31, 2024

No.	Prosecution Office	Persons	Verdict	Date Announced	Sentence	Court
1	Mitrovica	1	Guilty	January 21, 2024	Sentence	Mitrovica
2	Mitrovica	4	Guilty	October 10, 2024	Sentence	Mitrovica
3	Peja	1	Guilty	November 19, 2024	Fine	Peja
4	Prishtina	2	Guilty	March 05, 2024	Sentence	Prishtina
5	Gjilan	1	Guilty	May 13, 2024	Sentence	Gjilan
6	Prizren	2	Guilty	October 22, 2024	Sentence	Prizren
7	Mitrovica	1	Guilty	April 24, 2024	Sentence	Mitrovica
8	Gjakova	1	Guilty	July 30, 2024	Fine	Gjakova
9	Peja	1	Guilty	December 11, 2024	Sentence	Peja
10	Ferizaj	1	Guilty	October 25, 2024	Fine	Ferizaj
11	Ferizaj	5	Guilty	March 04, 2024	Fine	Ferizaj
12	Prishtina	1	Guilty	November 25, 2024	Sentence	Prishtina
13	Gjilan	1	Guilty	April 08, 2024	Fine	Gjilan
14	Prishtina	1	Guilty	January 22, 2024	Fine	Prishtina
15	Mitrovica	2	Guilty	September 05, 2024	Sentence	Mitrovica
16	Special	1	Guilty	January 15, 2024	Sentence	Prishtina
17	Prishtina	1	Guilty	March 18, 2024	Sentence	Prishtina
18	Mitrovica	1	Guilty	November 19, 2024	Sentence	Mitrovica
19	Prishtina	1	Guilty	March 14, 2024	Sentence	Prishtina
20	Prishtina	1	Guilty	April 24, 2024	Sentence	Prishtina
21	Prishtina	1	Guilty	September 20, 2024	Fine	Prishtina
22	Gjilan	1	Guilty	January 11, 2024	Fine	Gjilan
23	Gjilan	1	Guilty	December 02, 2024	Sentence	Gjilan
24	Prizren	1	Guilty	February 05, 2024	Sentence	Prizren
25	Prizren	1	Guilty	February 05, 2024	Fine	Prizren
26	Prizren	1	Guilty	June 21, 2024	Fine	Prizren
27	Prizren	1	Guilty	July 05, 2024	Sentence	Prizren
28	Prizren	1	Guilty	November 15, 2024	Fine	Prizren
29	Prizren	1	Guilty	December 30, 2024	Sentence	Prizren
30	Mitrovica	1	Guilty	January 29, 2024	Fine	Mitrovica

Table 13.9. *(Continued)*

Kosovo Judicial Council Official Corruption and Criminal Offenses Against Official Duty Period: January 01, 2024—December 31, 2024						
No.	**Prosecution Office**	**Persons**	**Verdict**	**Date Announced**	**Sentence**	**Court**
31	Mitrovica	1	Guilty	May 13, 2024	Fine	Mitrovica
32	Mitrovica	1	Guilty	July 09, 2024	Sentence	Mitrovica
33	Gjakova	1	Guilty	July 17, 2024	Fine	Gjakova
34	Gjakova	1	Guilty	December 19, 2024	Fine	Gjakova
35	Ferizaj	1	Guilty	March 15, 2024	Sentence	Ferizaj
36	Ferizaj	1	Guilty	August 30, 2024	Fine	Ferizaj
37	Prishtina	1	Guilty	April 26, 2024	Sentence	Prishtina
38	Gjakova	1	Guilty	December 18, 2024	Sentence	Gjakova

Source: Annual Reports of the Courts of the Republic of Kosovo on Corruption Cases.

Table 13.10. Annual Summary of Guilty Verdicts and Sentencing Outcomes for Corruption Offenses in Kosovo (2020–2024).

Annual Statistics on Corruption Cases (2020–2024)			
Year	**Guilty Verdicts**	**Individuals Sentenced to Imprisonment or Other Sanctions**	**Individuals Fined**
2020	28	13	15
2021	40	28	12
2022	34	25	9
2023	36	26	10
2024	38	27	11
Total	**176**	**119**	**57**

- The Directorate for Investigation of Economic Crimes and Corruption and its regional units in: Prishtina, Prizren, Gjilan, Peja, Mitrovica, Gjakova, and Ferizaj.
- The Serious Crimes Departments within the respective Basic Prosecution Offices, responsible for criminal prosecution.
- The Basic Courts through their Serious Crimes Departments, responsible for adjudicating these cases.

4.2 Key Observations

- *Consistency and Gradual Increase*: The number of guilty verdicts has remained relatively consistent with a slight increase after 2021, which may be linked to the effects of legal reforms.
- *Prevalence of Severe Sentences*: Around 67% of convicted individuals received imprisonment or other nonfine punitive measures, indicating a stricter judicial approach toward corruption.
- *Most Active Courts*: The majority of cases were handled by the courts in Prishtina, Gjilan, Prizren, and Mitrovica, suggesting either a higher caseload or greater efficiency in these jurisdictions.

4.3 Role of the Prosecution and Police

- *Case Detection*: Primarily based on criminal reports submitted by the Kosovo Police through the Directorate for Investigation of Economic Crimes and Corruption.
- *Support from Prosecutors*: Regional investigative units work closely with specialized prosecutors for serious crimes, enhancing the quality of investigations and the efficiency of prosecutions.

4.4 Conclusion

The criminal law reforms have had a significant impact on improving the efficiency of handling corruption cases. Data from the 2020–2024 period reflect a more determined institutional approach to penalizing offenses that undermine public officials' integrity and citizens' trust in the justice system.

In this context, strong cooperation between the police, prosecution, and judiciary remains essential to the success of anti-corruption efforts in Kosovo.

Part Three—Research on the Global Ranking of the Republic of Kosovo in the CPI by Transparency International (2012–2024)

This part presents a detailed analysis of the Republic of Kosovo's global and regional ranking in the *CPI*, published annually by *Transparency International*, focusing on the period from *2012 to 2024*. The research aims to assess how Kosovo's position in this index has evolved over time, especially in comparison with other countries in *Europe* and the *Western Balkans*.

The CPI measures the perceived levels of public sector corruption, as assessed by experts and businesspeople. A higher score indicates lower perceived corruption, while a lower score reflects higher levels of perceived corruption.

This part of the research addresses the following core elements:

- *Year-by-year analysis* of Kosovo's CPI score and ranking globally.
- *Regional comparison* with other countries in the Western Balkans and Europe to contextualize Kosovo's progress.

- *Correlation* between the implementation of legal and institutional reforms and any notable improvements or stagnation in the CPI score.
- *Impact of judicial efficiency, transparency measures, and anti-corruption policies* on the international perception of corruption in Kosovo.

Through this analysis, the research aims to evaluate whether the reforms in Kosovo's criminal justice system and broader anti-corruption efforts have contributed to a *more favorable international image* and improved *CPI performance* over the 12-year period.

Presentation and Analysis of Data on the Global Ranking of the Republic of Kosovo in the CPI by Transparency International (2012–2024)

The data presented in this section are obtained from the CPI, published annually by Transparency International, covering the period from 2012 to 2024. This index measures the perceived level of public sector corruption, where higher scores indicate lower levels of perceived corruption, and lower scores indicate higher levels of perceived corruption (see Table 13.11).

Table 13.11. Kosovo's Global Ranking in the Corruption Perceptions Index by Transparency International (2012–2024).

Kosovo's Global Ranking According to the CPI (2012–2024)		
Year	**Global Ranking**	**CPI Score**
2012	105	34
2013	111	33
2014	101	33
2015	102	33
2016	95	36
2017	85	39
2018	93	37
2019	101	36
2020	104	36
2021	87	39
2022	84	41
2023	83	41
2024	73	44

Source: Global Ranking of the Republic of Kosovo in the Corruption Perceptions Index by Transparency International.

4.5 Observationsand Analysis

(1) Trend of Improvement in Corruption Perception (2012–2024):

- In 2012, Kosovo ranked 105th with a CPI score of 34.
- By 2024, Kosovo had improved to 73rd place with a score of 44.
- This represents a *10-point increase in score* and a *32-position improvement in global ranking* over a 12-year period.

(2) Significant Progress After 2020:

- Between 2020 and 2024, Kosovo demonstrated notable improvement:
    - The CPI score increased from 36 to 44.
    - The global ranking improved from 104th to 73rd.
- This progress coincides with intensified *institutional and legal reforms*, particularly in the justice system, including:
    - enhancements to the criminal legal framework;
    - increased activity by prosecutors and courts in handling corruption cases;
    - strengthened inter-institutional cooperation in combating corruption.

(3) Improvement Within the Western Balkans Context:

- With a score of 44 in 2024, Kosovo is approaching the regional average, alongside countries like North Macedonia, Montenegro, and Albania.
- However, Kosovo *remains within the category of countries with a moderately high level of corruption*, based on Transparency International's methodology (0 = highly corrupt, 100 = very clean).

4.6 Key Research Findings

- *Increased trust in judicial institutions:* The improvement in CPI reflects a growing perception both domestically and internationally of more effective functioning of Kosovo's judicial and prosecutorial institutions.
- *Implementation of legal reforms:* Stricter enforcement of anti-corruption criminal provisions, more frequent prison sentences, and active operations by Serious Crimes Units have contributed directly to improved results.
- *Institutional commitment:* A focused institutional approach to preventing and punishing corruption has yielded measurable outcomes at the international level.
- *Remaining challenges:* Despite the progress, there is still a significant need to consolidate *institutional integrity*, strengthen *judicial independence*, and increase *efficiency at all levels* of public administration in fighting corruption.

This evident improvement over the past decade is a *positive signal for Kosovo's European integration path* and a clear indicator that legal and institutional reforms can have a *direct impact on both the perception and the reality of good governance.*

5. Conclusion

The development of effective anti-corruption policies is a complex process that requires an integrated and coordinated approach among state institutions, civil society, the media, and international partners.

Legally, the *Criminal Code of Kosovo has undergone substantial developments*, which have improved the definition, prosecution, and punishment of corruption-related offenses.

Practical implementation shows that the *number of adjudicated cases has increased*, along with the *greater use of harsher punitive measures*, particularly after 2020. Justice institutions are demonstrating a *more active and coordinated approach* in combating corruption, although the presence of fines as penalties still implies a more lenient approach in some cases.

Based on a *comparative analysis* of the three Criminal Codes implemented in the Republic of Kosovo during the period 2004–2024 including the Provisional Criminal Code (2004), the Criminal Code of 2012, and the Criminal Code of 2019 the following key conclusion emerges:

(1) Continuous and Systematic Progress in Anti-Corruption Criminal Legislation
From 13 criminal offenses in 2004, the number of corruption and abuse of official duty offenses increased to 16 in 2013 and to 17 in 2019. This progress includes:

- The introduction of new criminal offenses such as:
  - misuse and fraud in public procurement;
  - nondeclaration or false declaration of assets, income, or financial obligations.
- Expansion and clearer articulation of existing criminal offenses.
- Modernization of legal terminology to align with *international standards* and *Kosovo's evolving context.*

(2) Increased Transparency and Accountability in Line with the Needs of a New State
The entry into force of the *2013 Criminal Code*, following Kosovo's declaration of independence in 2008, and the subsequent significant update in 2019, demonstrate a *deliberate effort to strengthen the fight against corruption through legal means.*

This reflects a *commitment to increase the credibility of the criminal justice system*, to address the abusive practices of public officials, and to meet the standards of the *European Union and international organizations* in the anti-corruption field.

(3) Legal Reforms as a Reflection of Political, Economic, and Social Developments
The increase in criminal offenses reflects:

- the new *statehood context* and the growing responsibilities of institutions;
- developments in public administration and public procurement;
- the need to control the wealth and influence of public officials.

This legislative evolution indicates a growing *state awareness of the consequences of corruption* and the need for *more advanced legal and penal mechanisms* to prevent and punish it.

5.1 Overall Conclusion (2004–2024)

Over the 20-year period, Kosovo has demonstrated clear and structured commitment to building a strong legal framework for combating corruption. The increase in the number of offenses, the modernization of legal definitions, and the inclusion of new criminal practices reflect the state's progressive ability to respond to the challenges of governance and accountability.

5.2 Performance of the Justice System (2020–2024)

Based on annual court reports and statistics from the Kosovo Prosecutorial and Judicial Councils for the 2020–2024 period, the following key findings emerge:

(1) Gradual Improvement in Justice System Efficiency

- The number of convictions and individuals sentenced has seen steady growth.
- From 28 verdicts in 2020, the number increased to 38 in 2024.
- A total of *176 individuals were convicted*, of whom *119 received prison sentences or other penalties*, and *57 were fined*.

(2) A Harsher Judicial Stance Toward Corruption

- Over 67% of convictions involved harsher penalties than fines, such as imprisonment or alternative sentencing.
- This reflects a more serious and stricter judicial approach, driven by legal reforms and increased public pressure to punish corruption.

(3) Most Active Courts and Prosecutors are in Major Regional Centers

- Pristina, Gjilan, Prizren, and Mitrovica handled the majority of cases.
- This indicates:
- a broader scope of public official activity in these areas;
- better-developed institutional capacities for prosecuting and adjudicating corruption cases.

(4) Investigation and Prosecution Structures Are Functional but Require Strengthening

- The *Directorate for the Investigation of Economic Crimes and Corruption*, along with its regional units, conducted key investigations leading to indictments and convictions.
- However, the *overall number of cases handled remains relatively low* for a widespread phenomenon like corruption in the public sector.

(5) Legal Reforms Have Had a Positive Impact but Require Additional Measures

- The reform of the Criminal Code and the increase in competencies of prosecutors and serious crime courts have boosted prosecution and trial effectiveness.

Still, it is necessary to:

- improve *inter-institutional cooperation*;
- provide *greater technical and logistical support* for investigations;
- increase *transparency and public access* to case progress.

5.3 Anti-Corruption Perception and International Rankings

Kosovo's global ranking in the CPI by *Transparency International* from 2012 to 2024 shows *measurable and consistent improvement* in the international perception of the country's fight against corruption.

- Kosovo progressed from *105th place in 2012* to *73rd place in 2024*, gaining *10 points in CPI score.*
- This demonstrates that institutional efforts and legal reforms have *positively impacted Kosovo's global image* in this area.

This improvement especially after 2020 signals:

- stronger *institutional commitment*;
- a *more serious judicial engagement*;
- stronger *implementation of anti-corruption measures*, including *harsher punishments* and *deeper investigations.*

5.4 Remaining Challenges

Despite progress, Kosovo still ranks among countries with a *medium-high level of corruption*, and the main ongoing challenges include:

- *consolidating the rule of law*;
- *increasing transparency and accountability*;
- *reducing political influence* in public institutions.

5.5 Final Remarks and Recommendations

The development of effective anti-corruption policies in Kosovo is a story of *slow but steady progress*. If institutions continue with the same pace of reforms supported by *strong international cooperation* and *pressure from civil society* Kosovo can build a *more just and transparent system*.

Recommendations for the future:

- *enhance judicial independence*;
- *invest in training and technology* for investigators and prosecutors;
- *apply stricter and fairer punishments* for all, regardless of political influence;
- *deepen international partnerships* for technical support and independent monitoring.

5.6 In Summary

Kosovo is on the right path but still has much to accomplish to ensure a *sustainable anti-corruption system* and *governance based on integrity*.

References

Anti-Corruption Fund. (2023, May 30). *ACF's Annual monitoring report 2022: Institutions remain blind to high-level political corruption*. https://acf.bg/en/godishniyat-monitoringov-doklad-na-akf-4/

Assembly of the Republic of Kosovo. (2023). *Law No. 08/L-188 on Amending and supplementing the criminal code of the Republic of Kosovo No. 04/L-082*. https://gzk.rks-gov.net/ActDetail.aspx?ActID=2834&langid=2

Assembly of the Republic of Kosovo. (2008a). *Law No. 03/L-002 on the provisional criminal code of Kosovo*. Official Gazette of the Republic of Kosovo. https://gzk.rks-gov.net/ActDocumentDetail.aspx?ActID=2767

Assembly of the Republic of Kosovo. (2008b). *Law No. 03/L-003 on amendment and supplementation of the Kosovo provisional criminal procedure code No. 2003/26*. https://gzk.rks-gov.net/ActDetail.aspx?ActID=2602&langid=2GazetaZyrtare+1Gazeta Zyrtare+1

Assembly of the Republic of Kosovo. (2008c). *Law No. 03/L-052 on the special Prosecutor's office of the Republic of Kosovo*. https://gzk.rks-gov.net/ActDetail.aspx?ActID=2834&langid=2

Assembly of the Republic of Kosovo. (2010a). *Law No. 03/L-223 on the Kosovo judicial council*. https://gzk.rks-gov.net/ActDetail.aspx?ActID=2834&langid=2

Assembly of the Republic of Kosovo. (2010b). *Law No. 03/L-224 on the Kosovo prosecutorial council*. https://gzk.rks-gov.net/ActDetail.aspx?ActID=2834&langid=2

Assembly of the Republic of Kosovo. (2010c). *Law No. 03/L-225 on the state prosecutor*. https://gzk.rks-gov.net/ActDetail.aspx?ActID=2834&langid=2

Assembly of the Republic of Kosovo. (2010d). *Law No. 03/L-199 on courts*. https://gzk.rks-gov.net/ActDetail.aspx?ActID=2834&langid=2

Assembly of the Republic of Kosovo. (2010e). *Law No. 03/L-223 on the Kosovo judicial council*. https://gzk.rks-gov.net/ActDetail.aspx?ActID=2834&langid=2

Assembly of the Republic of Kosovo. (2011a). *Law No. 04/L-051 on prevention of conflict of interest in the exercise of public functions.* https://gzk.rks-gov.net/ActDetail.aspx?ActID=2834&langid=2
Assembly of the Republic of Kosovo. (2011b). *Law no. 04/L-050 on declaration, origin, and control of property of senior public officials and declaration of gifts.* https://gzk.rks-gov.net/ActDetail.aspx?ActID=2834&langid=2
Assembly of the Republic of Kosovo. (2012a). *Criminal code of the Republic of Kosovo No. 04/L-082.* https://www.refworld.org/legal/legislation/natlegbod/2012/en/123445
Assembly of the Republic of Kosovo. (2012b). *Criminal procedure code no. 04/L-123.* https://gzk.rks-gov.net/ActDetail.aspx?ActID=2861&langid=2
Assembly of the Republic of Kosovo. (2012c). *Criminal code of the Republic of Kosovo No. 04/L-082.* https://gzk.rks-gov.net/ActDetail.aspx?ActID=2834&langid=2
Assembly of the Republic of Kosovo. (2012d). *Law No. 04/L-129 on amending and supplementing the criminal code of the Republic of Kosovo No. 04/L-082.* https://gzk.rks-gov.net/ActDetail.aspx?ActID=2834&langid=2
Assembly of the Republic of Kosovo. (2014). *Law No. 04/L-273 on Amending and supplementing the laws related to the mandate of the European Union rule of Law mission in the Republic of Kosovo.* https://gzk.rks-gov.net/ActDetail.aspx?ActID=2834&langid=2Gazeta Zyrtare
Assembly of the Republic of Kosovo. (2019). *Criminal code of the Republic of Kosovo No. 06/L-074.* https://www.refworld.org/docid/6012e70d4.htmlecoi.net
Assembly of the Republic of Kosovo. (2019). *Law no. 06/L-074 on amending and supplementing the criminal code of the Republic of Kosovo no. 04/L-082.* https://gzk.rks-gov.net/ActDetail.aspx?ActID=2834&langid=2
Assembly of the Republic of Kosovo. (2022). *Law No. 08/L-032 on amending and supplementing the criminal procedure code No. 04/L-123.* https://gzk.rks-gov.net/ActDetail.aspx?ActID=2861&langid=2Kryeministrii Kosovës+2Gazeta Zyrtare+2Gazeta Zyrtare+2
Assembly of the Republic of Kosovo. (2023). *Criminal code of the Republic of Kosovo No. 08/L-188.* https://md.rks-gov.net/desk/inc/media/D63E0C47-F3DF-42E2-B138-D23402018A92.pdf
Assembly of the Republic of Kosovo. (2023). *Law No. 08/L-188 on amending and supplementing the criminal procedure code No. 04/L-123.* https://gzk.rks-gov.net/ActDetail.aspx?ActID=2861&langid=2
Balkan Investigative Reporting Network (BIRN). (2023, May 30). *BIRN Kosovo publishes report on justice system's handling of corruption cases in 2022.* https://birn.eu.com/news-and-events/birn-kosovo-publishes-report-on-justice-systems-handling-of-corruption-cases-in-2022/
Council of Europe. (2023). *Newsroom PECK III Kosovo.* https://coe.int/en/web/corruption/projects/newsroom-peck-iii
European Commission. (2023). *Kosovo report 2023.* https://eur-lex.europa.eu/legal-content/EN/TXT/?uri=CELEX%3A52023SC0692
European Commission. (2023, October 31). *Key findings of the 2023 report on Kosovo.* https://europeanwesternbalkans.com/2023/10/31/key-findings-of-the-2023-report-on-kosovo/
European Commission. (2024, July 24). *2024 Rule of law report: EU better equipped to face rule of law challenges.* https://commission.europa.eu/news/2024-rule-law-report-eu-better-equipped-face-rule-law-challenges-2024-07-24_en

European Commission. (2024, October 30). *Kosovo report 2024*. Directorate-General for Neighborhood and Enlargement Negotiations.https://enlargement.ec.europa.eu/kosovo-report-2024_en

GAN Integrity. (2023). *Kosovo country risk report*. https://www.ganintegrity.com/country-profiles/kosovo/

Human Rights Watch. (2006). *Not on the agenda: The continuing failure to address accountability in Kosovo post-March 2004*. https://www.hrw.org/reports/2006/kosovo0506/6.htm

Kosovo Anti-Corruption Agency. (2023). *For the Agency—APK - Agjencia për Parandalimin e Korrupsionit*. https://apk-rks.net/en/for-the-agency/

Kosovo Democratic Institute (KDI). (2015). *New study shows that anti-corruption progress in Kosovo is limited*. https://kdi-kosova.org/en/activities/new-study-shows-that-anti-corruption-progress-in-kosovo-is-limited/

Kosovo Democratic Institute (KDI). (2018). *CPI 2018: The fight against corruption IN KOSOVO goes into decline*. https://kdi-kosova.org/en/activities/cpi-2018-kosova-peson-regres-ne-luften-kunder-korrupsionit/

Kosovo Democratic Institute (KDI). (2025a). *Kosovo rises 10 places in the corruption perceptions index*. . https://www.koha.net/en/lajmet-e-mbremjes-ktv/kosova-she-non-rritje-per-10-vende-ne-indeksin-e-perceptimit-te-korrupsionit

Kosovo Democratic Institute (KDI). (2025b). *Despite the progress on corruption perceptions index (CPI), Kosovo remains the most corrupted country in the region*. https://kdi-kosova.org/en/activities/despite-the-progress-on-corruption-perceptions-index-cpi-kosovo-remains-the-most-corrupted-country-in-the-region/

Kosovo Law Institute. (2024, August 28). *New civil society report on Kosovo: Need for stronger accountability, better implementation, and judicial independence*. UNCAC Coalition. https://uncaccoalition.org/uncacparallelreportkosovo/

Kosovo Law Institute. (2024, August 28). *New Civil society report on Kosovo: Need for stronger accountability, better implementation, and judicial independence*. UNCAC Coalition. https://uncaccoalition.org/uncacparallelreportkosovo/

PubAffairs Bruxelles. (2022). *Key findings of the 2022 report on Kosovo*. https://www.pubaffairsbruxelles.eu/eu-institution-news/key-findings-of-the-2022-report-on-kosovo/

Transparency International. (2025). *Corruption perceptions index 2024*. https://www.transparency.org/en/countries/kosovo

UNCAC Coalition. (2024). *New Civil Society report on Kosovo: Need for stronger accountability, better implementation, and judicial independence*. https://uncaccoalition.org/uncacparallelreportkosovo/

United Nations. (1999, June 10). *Security council resolution 1244 (1999) on the situation relating to Kosovo*. https://undocs.org/S/RES/1244

United Nations Development Programme. (2024). *Support to anti-corruption efforts in Kosovo (SAEK III)*. https://www.undp.org/kosovo/projects/support-anti-corruption-efforts-kosovo-saek-iii

UNMIK. (2003). *UNMIK regulation no. 2003/25 on the provisional criminal code of Kosovo*. https://unmik.unmissions.org/sites/default/files/regulations/02english/E2003regs/E2003regs.htm

Chapter 14

Fraud Audit in Taxation and the Case of Turkey

Funda Karakoyun[a] *and Serdar Karaağin*[b]

[a]Dokuz Eylul University, Turkey
[b]Crowe, Turkey

Abstract

Fraudulent and corrupt behaviors in businesses not only harm the sustainable growth of the business but also cause an important problem that threatens the general economic order in the country. These behaviors are based on two tendencies. The first is to present the business differently from the reality against investors and financial resource providers. The second is to create misleading information for the relevant units of the government to reduce the tax burden. In this study, fraud auditing on the basis of taxation is addressed by considering the scope limitation. While detecting abnormal (unusual) economic and administrative actions in fraud audit, Article 3 of the Tax Procedure Law No. 213 of the Turkish Tax Law is applied. Accordingly, if there is suspicion of fraud in the recording of actions and transactions that are not in line with the natural course of life and cannot be related to commercial activities, the taxpayer is required to provide proof. So, the distinction between error and fraud is important in suspicious transactions subject to tax inspection. In the audit of the compliance of the transactions with the tax legislation, data obtained from the risk analysis with the high rate and deliberate repetition of transactions that can be characterized as errors are evaluated. As a result, the issues that are considered as accounting fraud based on their effect on the tax base are clarified, and the issues considered as accounting fraud in terms of Turkish Tax Legislation are explained with case studies.

Keywords: Accounting frauds; tax evasion; tax balance sheet; forged document; legally disallowable expense

Corruption and Crime in Finance, 305–326

doi:10.1108/978-1-83708-170-720261036

1. Introduction

Accounting is an information system that meets the needs of those concerned in the field without being based on taxation. Therefore, in order for accounting to provide accurate, reliable, and common language information, it must be realized and applied in accordance with generally accepted accounting principles. In this application process, it should be applied in a way to fulfill an accurate information system without considering tax concerns. Tax transactions, on the other hand, will be carried out on the basis of accounting theory and principles in order to ensure that taxpayers are not subject to penalized assessments in fulfilling their obligations (Akin, 2018, p. 53).

1.1 Some Concepts Expressed in Tax Laws

These expressions were specifically chosen by the legislator because they express different entities. These concepts, which are systematically preserved in various tax laws and remain faithful to their content (Akin, 2016, p. 84–85), and some important concepts in terms of determining the amount to be taken as basis in tax calculation are explained below (Kumkale, 2013, p. 75).

> Revenue: It is the benefits related to the main activity or obtained as a result of the interest of the capital. Revenue is the money received in return for the sale of commodities, the sale of depreciable economic assets, legal services and renting an apartment.
>
> Expenses: Expenditures made, or sacrifices incurred/borrowed to obtain revenue.
>
> Income: It is the sum of the earnings and revenues subject to taxation as specified in the relevant law. In other words, income is the sum of earnings derived from activities and of revenues derived from capital. Income may be realized as profit or loss as a result of the comparison of revenue and expenses.

Balance Sheet Profit: It is used to mean profit before tax.

Balance Sheet Make-up: Artificially changing the concepts in the balance sheet through illegal interventions. If the error affecting the balance sheet is made to make the company look worse than it is, the balance sheet is "masked."

1.2 Errors and Cheating Concepts

Accounting records should be made in accordance with the basic concepts of personality, primacy of substance, periodicity, and social responsibility as defined in accounting theory and business science, and in accordance with the principles of the uniform chart of accounts. In tracing records, accounting errors and fraud can often be difficult to distinguish from one another. The main objective and subject of controls related to accounting transactions are expressed as examining the accounting system and detecting irregularities and corruption.

Errors may arise due to a lack of full understanding of accounting principles or personal negligence. An error is defined as an *"unconscious or unintentional mistake, miscalculation, or misunderstanding"* (Bayraklı et al., 2012, p. 19).

> According to Turkish Accounting Standards 8 (TAS) and International Accounting Standards 8 (IAS), accounting errors occur without acting consciously during the identification, measurement, presentation and disclosure of accounts in the financial statements used to inform users of financial information. In accounting errors, there is no intent to violate laws, generally accepted accounting principles and standards, business policies, or other principles and rules adopted by the business; rather, there is ignorance or negligence. Errors in accounting are usually caused by forgetfulness, carelessness, negligence, ignorance, or inexperience. (Demir, & Yildiz, 2022, pp. 91–141)

For example, recording a machine, which should be recorded in fixed assets, as a general expense in accounting is an accounting error. The concepts of fraud and irregularities are used in Section 6 of the Communiqué on Auditing Standards, titled *"Responsibility of the Independent Auditor for Fraud and Irregularities in the Independent Audit of Financial Statements."* In the relevant context, fraud and irregularities *are expressed as "the intentional deception to obtain an unfair or illegal advantage by persons responsible for the management, employees of the entity or third parties."* Although fraud and irregularity are very general legal concepts, in the application of this Communiqué, *"the independent auditor should consider fraud and irregular acts and transactions that may cause significant misstatements in the financial statements."* In addition, in the same Section, it is clearly stated that misstatements in the financial statements may arise not only from fraud and irregularities but also from errors, and that the main element that distinguishes them from each other is "intention" (Yalcinkaya, 2019).

Fraud is defined by various authors as unlawful acts;

> It is to act in bad faith, encourage others to act or participate in a crime in violation of national and international legislation, in printed and digital media, in a way that will cause material damage to interested parties without their knowledge, during the formation, documentation, recording, and reporting of accounting-related events to interested parties related to the business. (Açıkgöz, 2025)

If the fraudulent transactions are carried out by the employees, owners and beneficiaries of the business, the financial data are generally designed to make the business look better than it actually is. The objectives of financial statement fraud in these transactions include manipulating prices and contract terms to influence investors' decisions, creating a positive perception of the market, increasing the amount of funds to be obtained in capital increases, avoiding political and legal risks, and obtaining tax advantages through tax planning (Aksoy, 2021, p. 32). In fraud detection, generally concealed erroneous transactions are examined. Intentional or repetitive mistakes give these transactions a fraudulent nature. It is difficult to justify the existence of intent; however, in unusual situations, like deviations from the norm, irregularities in general accounting practices, actions contradictory to business activities, etc., the existence of intent can be accepted. The fact that financial statements do not reflect the truth and the irregularities encountered are expressed in various ways in Turkey. Concepts such as balance sheet embellishment, masking, financial information manipulation are frequently used (Yalcinkaya, 2019). This study, however, is limited to accounting fraud within the framework of tax accounting.

1.3 Cheating Methods

Common behaviors associated with fraudulent transactions are observed. These are mainly incorrect preparation, alteration, or manipulation of financial records, documents, or commercial transactions. Also, there is non-disclosure or misstatement of events, transactions, accounts or other material information on which financial statements are based. Additionally, accounting principles, policies, and procedures used to measure, accrue, report, and disclose economic events and commercial transactions are incorrectly applied. Consequently, the element of intent is important in the methods used in these behaviors (Ceylan, 2013, p. 24).

The concept of document fraud corresponds to the concept of "Misleading Document in Terms of Content and Forged Document" in the Tax Procedure Law (TPL). Here, a "Forged Document" is defined as "a document prepared as if a real transaction or situation existed, even though it does not," while a "Misleading Document in Terms of Content" is defined as "a document that is based on a real transaction or situation but reflects this transaction or situation in a manner that is contrary to the truth in terms of its nature or quantity." The preparation and use of forged documents are among the most common accounting fraud methods that often occur on invoices. In this way, organizations can be formed for the purpose of tax fraud, invoices can be obtained in exchange for commission, and the tax base can be reduced with false expense records (Tolga, 2020, p. 99). Forgeries made on invoices are not considered as the crime of forgery of private documents but as the crime of tax evasion under the TPL and Supreme Court decisions. A false document can be created by different individuals. However, when used for tax fraud, this crime is seen as taxpayer-centered (Tekin, 2023, p. 123).

If accounting errors are made intentionally with a specific purpose, that is, with intent, the transaction should be defined as an accounting fraud rather than an error. Some of them are, for example, frequent repetition of the error, significant irregularities other than extraordinary circumstances (undocumented sales are quite large compared to the annual turnover), detection of errors made in the records in accounting but covering them up with another erroneous record. Businesses must provide all transactions and records on documents. Unrecorded transactions in the form of undocumented transactions or not being recorded in the legal books are usually done for tax evasion purposes. Another practice is recording transactions before or after the actual transaction date. Businesses are required by various legal regulations to record and report their business and transactions within certain periods of time. The basic recording time is regulated in tax laws, and some recording times are also specified in different legal regulations. Businesses may record their transactions and operations before or after the required time, thereby attempting to misinform and gain an advantage. Another fraudulent method involves opening accounts under fictitious names or falsely representing non-existent transactions to appear as if they exist. In this way, it can be aimed to achieve results such as tax evasion, concealing corruption, creating low profits, concealing unrecorded transactions, etc. (Ceylan, 2013, pp. 24–25).

One of the fraudulent methods used to misrepresent the financial condition of a business is the masking of the balance sheet during the end-of-period inventory procedures. When the recorded assets of the enterprise are valued, the balance sheet is manipulated to make it look worse than it is for tax accounting purposes. For example, recorded assets and inventories are valued lower than they should be. Furthermore, by allocating high depreciation and provisions, the expense account is increased, the amount of liquidity is reduced, and debts are increased (Bayraklı et al., 2012, p. 85).

1.4 Fraud Detection

Public institutions and organizations inform about the criteria considered as accounting fraud in their bulletins with regulatory articles. General and specific regulations in the tax legislation are discussed under separate headings.

Some of the issues that the Capital Markets Board has made a criminal complaint regarding financial statement fraud are as follows: (Aksoy, 2021, p. 40).

- Failure to keep the legal books in accordance with the legislation and failure of the records to reflect the truth fully and accurately,
- Issuing unrealistic accounting records, and forged payment receipts,
- Incurring debts the company through unrealistic accounting records,
- Causing losses to the company by unrecorded sales of the company's commercial goods, or by recording lower revenue to the official books than actual sales revenue of the assets,

- Reducing profits or assets of the company by entering into agreements with persons with whom the company has a relationship, or with its peers, that contain terms contrary to market practices and the principles of prudence and integrity in commercial life,
- Failure to include information about the checks and collection of the company in the records.

Some of the suspicious transaction types considered in the banking sector are listed below (Aykın, 2020).

- Recording the company's activities as individual transactions for the transactions that require ordinary repetition or, conversely, recording the continuous repetition of transactions that do not occur frequently in ordinary commercial life,
- Dividing financial transactions, which require continuous and collective actions, without a reasonable justification in order to avoid detection and notification,
- Having no reasonable legal or economic justification for the action taken,
- Difficulty in disclosing or refraining from disclosing information about the purpose of the transaction or the source of the funds subject to the transaction,
- Existence of the customer wishing to open accounts in the name of a large number of domestic or foreign residents, or continuously to deposit or to withdraw cash into accounts opened in the name of third parties, without a reasonable and valid reason,
- Seemingly independent customers that provide the same address, telephone and similar contact information, send remittances to the same beneficiaries, receive remittances from the same supervisors, or authorize the same person or persons to sign the accounts they have opened,
- Existence of the customers making or attempting to make transactions by dividing the money subject to the transaction into multiple accounts, transfer or cash in order to avoid notification procedures,
- The customer having a large number of accounts in various branches of the same bank in which similar transactions are made on his/her own behalf or on behalf of third parties on whose behalf he/she acts, or it is understood from the account movements that similar accounts have been opened in other banks,
- Transferring the cash deposited in the account to another account in Turkey or abroad in installments and without a reasonable explanation, or the account remains inactive for a long period of time after such transactions have been made for a certain period,
- Depositing or withdrawing cash to accounts opened in the name of the enterprise by persons who do not have a clear connection with the commercial enterprise, in an amount that is clearly not made for commercial reasons,
- Performing usually money transfers or electronic fund transfers transactions to a specific name by a customer who may or may not have an account with the bank.

The aforementioned issues are investigated as a priority in fraud detection by the authorized examiners. In the research conducted in risk analysis techniques, these criteria are included in the software and the detection is strengthened with techniques such as cross-checking.

2. Fraud in Turkish Tax Law and Practices

Tax crimes are one of the most important issues addressed within the scope of the informal economy. Tax evasion, which is one of these crimes, causes both damage to the social benefit by negatively affecting the collection of public revenues and damage to the treasury with its disruptive effect on public order. According to the data of the study conducted in Turkey, the estimated informality between 2006 and 2023 is found to be between 16% and 68% of the national income. In the work, the estimated level of the informal economy, which has been on a decreasing trend since 2015, is found around 16% of the national income in 2023. Thus, tax loss is estimated in between 3% and 11%, depending on the size of the informal economy (Gümüş, 2025, p. 36).

Prevention of taxes, which are the basic financial needs of the state, by resorting to fraudulent methods is considered as a public case in terms of tax criminal law. There is no agreed definition of "accounting fraud" in Turkish tax law. However, in order for a transaction to be considered as an accounting fraud, it must affect the financial statements and this effect must be significant and large enough to affect the decisions of those who will make decisions based on the financial statements. In terms of tax law, if there is no tax loss due to the act, even if this act is an accounting fraud in the sense of accounting and auditing sciences, it is not considered as a smuggling crime since it does not affect the State treasury interest (Şentürk & Alpaslan, 2009, p. 104). However, it should be investigated whether the transactions made on the account books and documents not stipulated by the tax law are crimes according to the general criminal provisions. Although, they are not acts of smuggling offenses, it is also evaluated whether there are crimes such as forgery of documents, abuse of trust or fraud (Şenyüz, 2017, p. 409). In this case, for example, transactions that increase the profit for the period by issuing high invoices to the consumer, not allocating depreciation or capitalizing some expenses that can be written off as expenses are accounting cheat but will not constitute an accounting fraud (smuggling) crime in terms of tax law since there is no tax loss (Şentürk & Alpaslan, 2009, p. 104).

2.1 Fraud in Terms of Tax Procedure Law

Although accounting fraud is regulated in Article 359/a-1 of the TPL No. 213, the concept of accounting fraud is not defined in the law. Yet, the phrase, "accounting and accounting fraud" is listed among the acts of smuggling offenses in Article 359/a-1 of the TPL. In the offenses in Article 359 of the TPL, the presence of the intent element of the perpetrator is required. In criminal proceedings, it is essential to find the material truth. Proof is also important in finding the truth. The perpetrator can prove the absence of intent (Taştan, 2018, p. 9). According to the provision of this article, the first behavior sought for the existence of the crime of tax evasion is determined as "making accounting and accounting frauds in books and records." These books and records are kept or organized in accordance with tax laws and obliged to be kept and submitted. Under Articles 359/a-1 and 359/a-2 of the TPL No. 213, persons who keep or prepare documents in accordance with tax laws and are subject to the obligation to keep and present such documents shall be subject to monetary penalties and imprisonment if they commit the following offenses: (Şenyüz, 2017, pp. 406–411)

- Those who commit account and accounting fraud in books and records,
- Those who open accounts in the name of persons who are not real or who are not related to the transactions subject to registration,
- Those who record the accounts and transactions, which should be recorded in the books, in whole or in part in other books, documents or other recording media in a way that results in a decrease in the tax base,
- Those who manipulate books, records and documents,
- Those who conceal books, records and documents,
- Those who issue or use misleading documents in terms of their content.

The first behavior sought for the existence of the crime of tax evasion under the law is determined as "committing accounting frauds in books and records," which must be recorded or arranged and kept and presented. In order to impose a penalty for the offense of transferring the accounts and transactions that must be recorded in the books to other books and records, the tax base must be reduced as a result of the act committed. This distinguishes it from other tax evasion offenses, i.e., the tax base can be concealed by differentiating income and expense records from the real ones in order to pay less tax.

The crime of tax evasion is a deliberate crime. Even if the perpetrator does not perform a certain behavior with the aim of tax evasion, if he/she does it willingly and causes tax loss as a result, the existence of intent should be accepted in this case. One of the behaviors that are among the tax crimes and frequently subject to disputes between the taxpayer and the administration is the issuance and use of forged documents. One of the ways used by those who plan the act of forging documents is to show that the business belongs to someone else, although they are themselves in the background, indeed they actually do all the transactions themselves (Taştan, 2018, p. 131).

Companies can create accounting frauds with acts that reduce income, increase expenses and costs for reducing the tax base. When the actions considered as fraud within the scope of tax evasion are examined, the following pattern is generally observed (Ceylan, 2013, p. 27; Özçelik, 2018, p. 497).

- Using shell companies or individuals to pass off the proceeds as belonging to someone else and to benefit from taxpayer advantages,
- Creating false records of sales of goods and services by issuing forged invoices,

- To carry out transactions with companies that have real commercial activity, although they do not have real commercial activity, in return for commission by issuing forged invoices,
- Recording of documents in the books with missing amounts,
- Shifting income for the current period to the next period,
- Recognizing a "closed invoice" as an "open invoice" or not recording a part of the collections,
- Concealment of the quantity of goods produced by techniques used to determine the cost of production, e.g. yield analysis does not reflect reality,
- Failure to account for exchange rate differences on foreign currency receivables or failure to record credit finance charges received from customers for installment sales or late payments,
- Presentation of a fixed asset, sold at a high price, as if it was sold at a low price,
- De-recording of income from stocks and bonds,
- Presentation of collected receivables as uncollected,
- Continuing to recognize sales revenue in advance even though it has been received, to conceal the revenue or to defer the period,
- Concealment of cash withdrawn by shareholders for their personal needs and stocks withdrawn free of charge,
- Failure to record money given as collateral, interest accrued by third parties, and indirect income elements such as turnover premiums,
- Recording an expense for a future period in the current period,
- Opening accounts and making transactions in names that do not exist,
- Recording installment purchases as cash outflows as if they were paid in advance,
- Excluding incidental income other than those related to the ongoing activities of the enterprises from the legal records,
- Recording expenses for doubtful receivables in violation of the legislation or considering them as worthless receivables,
- Depreciation in violation of the legislation,
- Recording the fictitious advances to partners or relatives,
- Recording installment debts as if they had been paid,
- Duplication of expense records.

These actions may occur with the purpose and intention of tax evasion. In addition, transactions involving bad faith and tax fraud for aggressive planning for tax deductions, refunds, and incentive mechanisms that do not comply with the legislation may be observed.

2.2 Use of Forged Documents

When it is concluded that the forged documents are used intentionally, the value added tax included in the forged documents is demanded back together with the default interest. Additionally, a triple tax loss penalty is imposed in accordance with Article 344/2 paragraph of TPL. When it is concluded that the goods or services subject to the forged document were not actually received, expenses and costs are rejected in accordance with Income Tax Law No. 193 or Corporate Tax Law (CTL) No. 5520, and if it is concluded that expenses and costs are incurred, a special irregularity penalty is imposed in accordance with TPL 353/1. This situation, which is considered within the scope of tax crimes, is reported to the relevant prosecutor's office within the scope of crimes subject to imprisonment from three to eight years pursuant to paragraph (b) of Article 359 of the TPL, and then it is faced with the right to benefit from the pre-assessment reconciliation provision within the scope of tax loss (Canayakın & Türker, 2025, p. 9).

3. Fraud in Terms of Its Effect on Financial Statements

In the Turkish Tax System, in addition to general regulations for the prevention of fraud, there are also specific regulations to prevent the erosion of the tax base and to provide security in tax receivables. Compliance with the legislation is monitored by applying data analysis techniques and carried out in an expanding scope of tax audits on the accounts reflected in the period-end financial statements and at an increasing rate. The tax administration requests explanations from the taxpayer on suspicious transactions. In particular, the issue of "*Legally Disallowable Expenses*" (LDE) that should be added to the tax base is among the special regulations and discussed below with sample applications in this study.

3.1 Financing Expense Restriction

With the Presidential Decree (Official Gazette, 2021), the Financing Expense restriction will be applied to the taxation period starting from January 01, 2021 and subsequent earnings; *Financing Expense restriction,* "in enterprises whose foreign resources used exceed their equity, 10% of the total of expenses and cost elements incurred under the names of interest, commission, maturity difference, profit share, exchange rate difference and similar, related to the foreign resources used in the business (excluding those added to the cost of investment), cannot be taken into account as expenses in determining the profit by income and corporate taxpayers, so that, it will be LDE."

The scenario for the calculation of the financing expense limitation is given in Table 14.1 below.

Organizations that do not consider the financing expense restriction incompletely or incorrectly or businesses that request a refund in value added tax receive an invitation to explanation letter by the Finance Administration. As a matter of fact, in the tax inspection, unallowable expenses are checked in accordance with the financing expense restriction over the accounts numbered 656 and 780 Finance expense.

Table 14.1. Financing Expense Limitation Table in Turkish Lira (TL).

(A)	Total equity	3,600,000.00 TL
(B)	Total short-term liabilities	1,980,000.00 TL
(C)	Total long-term liabilities	2,820,000.00 TL
(D)	Amount in excess of equity [(B + C)−A]	1,200,000.00 TL
(E)	Interest paid (780 interest expense)	600,000.00 TL
(F)	Finance expense ratio [D/(B + C)]	%25
(G)	Total finance expense corresponding to the excess (ExF)	150,000.00 TL
(H)	Financing expense limitation (G*%10) (150,000.00TL*0.10)	(LDE) 15,000.00 TL

Source: Prepared by us.

3.2 The Thin Capitalization

Enterprises search for methods that reduce their costs in financial planning. Tax shield is an advantageous method that reduces the tax burden of interest arising from borrowing and has an impact on capital structures. The methods applied in terms of tax shield effect may have different effects on value of corporation, cost of capital, and debt financing. While the application of these methods within the limits that are in accordance with the laws provides financial resource support to businesses, resorting to transactions that are considered fraudulent for tax fraud purposes constitutes a crime (Gül, 2024, pp. 217–222). It is detected in financial audits and causes penalized calculation of the taxable base amount of the enterprise. In addition to the tax shield effect in the effects of tax analysis on the financial resources of the enterprise, the reflection of the borrowing cost arising from the relationship with the partners on the financial statements is examined. Accordingly, enterprises can meet their financing needs through borrowing at a high rate compared to their equity capital. The reflection of borrowing costs in the financial statements and their expensing in corporate tax returns are limited by the provision of the Law. Here, the legal regulation is aimed to "prevent companies from paying the borrowing costs obtained from both the companies they are partners with and the real and legal persons who are partners with them under the name of financing expenses and deducting these payments from corporate income as expenses." It is based on the understanding that expenses such as interest, maturity difference, exchange rate difference paid for borrowings are actually considered as monetary values that should be paid to shareholders as dividends (Arslaner, 2013, p. 37).

The thin capitalization, regulated under Article 12 of the CTL, is one of the regulations in the Turkish tax legislation. In paragraph 1 of Article 12, the thin capitalization is defined as follows. "The portion of the debts that the corporations use in the enterprise by obtaining directly or indirectly from their partners or persons related to the partners, which exceeds three times the equity capital of the corporation at any time during the accounting period, is considered as implicit capital for the relevant accounting period." The concept of equity capital here is the difference between the total assets (assets and receivables) and liabilities.

In the application of the thin capitalization, a person related to a shareholder refers to an institution in which the shareholder is directly or indirectly a shareholder of at least 10%, or an institution in which the shareholder has at least 10% of the voting or dividend rights, or a natural person or an institution that directly or indirectly holds at least 10% of the capital, voting or dividend shares of the shareholder or the institution related to the shareholder (Şimşek et al., 2015, pp. 374–376). According to paragraph 1 of Article 11 of the CTL, interest and foreign exchange differences, and similar expenses paid or calculated over the hidden capital cannot be deducted in the determination of corporate income. While borrowings up to 3 times the equity capital are used as a tax planning method, borrowings in excess of 3 times the equity capital are considered as thin capitalization as a form of tax evasion. In the thin capitalization, the owners of the capital can lend the amounts that they should put as capital to the company in various ways. Malicious advantage is obtained according to the dividend to be received in case of capitalization and profit (Dogan & Sayan, 2022, p. 35).

Example 1: Equity capital of XYZ Joint Stock Company: 10,000,000 TL and the total debt received from related parties is 40,000,000 TL, the limit of 10,000,000 × 3 = 30,000,000 TL is exceeded. In this case, the portion of 10,000,000 TL is considered as thin capitalization.

Example 2: ABC Joint Stock Company's equity capital at the beginning of the period is 1,500,000 TL. The amounts of foreign resources used by the company and the cost information to the enterprise are given in Table 14.2.

Thin capitalization amount is calculated as: (Foreign currency debt amount − (Equity at the beginning of the period × 3)).

$$\text{Thin capitalization amount} := 6{,}300{,}000 - (1{,}500{,}000 \times 3) = 1{,}800{,}000 \text{ TL}$$

Table 14.2. ABC Joint Stock Company Foreign Resource Debt Amounts and Costs.

Foreign Resources Lending Partner	**Debt Amount (TL)**	**Interest (TL)**
Received from Company X	1,200,000	454,080
Received from Company Y	2,100,000	813,120
Received from partner Q bank	(6,000,000[a]) 3,000,000	1,161,600
Total	6,300,000	2,428,800

Source: Prepared by us.

[a]50% of 6,000,000 TL will be taken into consideration in accordance with Article 12, paragraph 2 of the CTL.

The amount of thin capitalization attributable to each shareholder given in Table 14.3 is calculated as follows:

$$\text{Thin Capitalization Attributable to each shareholder} = \frac{\text{Disguised capital attributable to each shareholder}}{\text{Total debt to be considered in the calculation of thin capitalization}} \times \text{Disguised capital}$$

Table 14.3. The Thin Capitalization Amount Attributable to Each Shareholder.

Lending Partner	**Thin Capitalization Account (TL)**	**Thin Capitalization Amount (TL)**
Received from Company X	(1,200,000/6,300,000) × 1,800,000	342,857
Received from Company Y	(2,100,000/6,300,000) × 1,800,000	600,000
Received from partner Q bank	(3,000,000/6,300,000) × 1,800,000	857,143
	Total	1,800,000

Source: Prepared by us.

The amount of interest expense to be considered as unallowable expense due to the implicit capital of ABC Company amounting to 1,800,000 TL used in the period January 01, 2025–May 31, 2025 is as follows:

$$((1,800,000/6,300,000) \times 2,428,800) = 693,943 \text{ TL}$$

ABC Company wanted to reduce its tax burden in the calculation of corporate tax in violation of the legislation by deducting the entire amount of 693,943 TL of the financing expense corresponding to the debt of 1,800,000 TL, which is the amount of implicit capital.

The accounting record at the end of the period is as follows:

---31.05.2025---

971 Amounts to be added to the Base 693,943.00 TL

971.01. Thin capitalization Financing Expense (LDE)

972 Amounts to be aded to the Base 693,943.00 TL

972.01. Thin capitalization Financing Expense (LDE)

--/--

In the event that a loan is borrowed from a shareholder, or a person related to a shareholder and any interest or foreign exchange difference is paid to this person/persons, the portion corresponding to the implicit capital is an LDE. The interest paid by the user of the thin capitalization is considered as distributed dividend provided that the tax is finalized and paid by the counterparty (Arslaner, 2013, p. 50).

3.3 Expense Restriction on Passenger Car Purchase

According to the legislation, it is restricted that the expenditures made for passenger cars used in the enterprises can be taken into consideration by showing an expense record in the tax base. In the purpose of the law, it is understood on the basis of preventing abuses that passenger cars are suitable for use for personal needs outside the activities of the enterprise. In 2025, passenger car expense restriction, there are varying amounts according to leasing and purchasing preferences. Accordingly, the legal amount of annual depreciation is limited if taxes are added to the cost or if the passenger car is purchased second-hand. In the purchase of passenger cars, VAT and special consumption tax (SCT) can be shown as an expense for vehicles exceeding the passenger car cost limit (including second-hand vehicle purchase) of 2,100,000 TL, including VAT and SCT. In this case, the total of the passenger car cost limit excluding VAT and SCT should not exceed 1,100,000 TL and a prorated depreciation calculation should be made. Therefore, the amount that can be deducted as depreciation in case of purchasing a passenger car is 1,100,000 TL excluding SCT and VAT for the year 2025. If SCT and VAT are recorded directly as expenses by not adding to the cost price of the vehicle, the legal limit for the total of these taxes paid is 990,000 TL. Therefore, if SCT and VAT are included in the cost of the vehicle, the legal limit for the total cost record for 2025 is 2,100,000 TL (TÜRMOB, 2024).

Example: (XYZ) Joint Stock Company purchased a passenger car with a tax-free sales price of 1,800,000.00 TL in 2024. Assuming that the SCT of the vehicle in question is 100% and VAT is 20%, the total amounts paid for the vehicle are given in Table 14.4. The accounting record to be prepared by the entity regarding the invoice including SCT and VAT is shown separately.

Table 14.4. Passenger Car Vehicle Cost Account.

Vehicle cost	1,800,000 TL
Special consumption tax (SCT): 100%	1,800,000 TL
VAT (1,800,000 + 1,800,000) × 20%	720,000 TL
SCT + VAT total	2,520,000 TL
Total vehicle cost:	4,320,000 TL

Source: Prepared by us.

The purchase price of the vehicle is 1,800,000 TL, the invoice amount including SCT and VAT and the total amount owed to the seller is 4,320,000 TL. However, in the case where SCT and VAT are added to the cost price, the maximum legal amount accepted for passenger car registration is 2,100,000 TL and the difference between the total amount paid to the seller is shown in the accounting record as LDE.

---1 January 2025---

254 Vehicles	2,100,000 TL	
-Passenger Car Maximum Amount		
254 Vehicles	2,220,000	
-Amortization Amount to be LDE		
320 Sellers		4,320,000 TL

---/---

The other application on the same example regarding the acquisition of a passenger car is given in detail in Table 14.5. Accordingly, when the SCT and VAT of the vehicle are directly recognized as expense, the legal limit for the sum of these taxes is applied as 990,000TL. In this case, the cost of the vehicle is limited to 1,100,000TL and recorded. Accordingly, the difference between the total amount of the invoice amount and the legally permissible limits is calculated as LDE and shown in the accounting record.

Table 14.5. Passenger Car Cost When SCT and VAT Expense Is Directly Applied.

Vehicle cost	1,100,000 TL
Vehicle cost (LDE)	700,000 TL
Total cost	1,800,000 TL
SCT and VAT expense	990,000 TL
SCT + VAT (LDE)	1,530,000 TL
Total vehicle cost:	4,320,000 TL

Source: Prepared by us.

The accounting record is as follows:

In this application, the enterprise should allocate depreciation of 1,100,000TL and write off the depreciation as much as the amount corresponding to the relevant year, but based on the total vehicle purchase cost, it allocated

---/--

254 Vehicle Cost	1,100,000 TL	
254 Vehicle cost (LDE)	700,000	
770 Excise and VAT Expense	990,000	
770 SCT and VAT (LDE)	1,530,000	
320 Sellers		4,320,000 TL

---/--

depreciation of 1,800,000TL and recorded as an expense. The company, which has unlawfully reduced its tax burden by disregarding the maximum depreciation allocation limit for passenger cars, claims that it is a one-time error caused by carelessness for the illegal transaction, which is revealed in the audit. If the further auditing reveals that this situation is repeated, this transaction, which causes tax loss, is treated as tax fraud.

The LDE amounts calculated in the examples should be taken into account as the amount to be added to the tax base in the tax calculation and should be shown in the accounting record.

4. Tax Fraud and Its Reflection on Balance Sheet Data

In order to reduce the tax burden of the enterprise in violation of tax laws, it is seen that various transactions such as issuing and/or using forged documents, leaving transactions unrecorded, opening unreal current accounts, creating records different from the truth. In transactions aimed at reducing the tax base, it is often aimed to conceal sales from the truth and to show costs and expenses more than the actual amount. Consequently, the profit obtained in the income statement is reflected different from the real one in the balance sheet. In this study, the details of fraudulent transactions that create tax losses are shown on examples.

As of the beginning of the period, the balance sheet of Z Joint Stock Company dated January 01, 2024 is given in Table 14.6. In the scenario where 7 fraudulent transactions are studied in the fiscal period, the underestimated tax base and therefore the under-accrued corporate tax is shown. At the end of the period, the balance sheet of the company is also given in Table 14.7. Here, the corporate tax rate is considered as 20%.

(1) Under-declaration of income: The company has recorded the sales transaction of 1,000,000 TL as 800,000 TL. Assuming that the related expense in the sales transaction is 700,000 TL, the company has reflected its profit, which should be 300,000 TL, as 100,000 TL in its final accounts. Due to the undeclared revenue of 200,000 TL, Corporate Tax (200,000 $\times$ 0.2 =) 40,000 TL has been under-accrued.

Table 14.6. Balance Sheet of Company Z at the Beginning of the Period.

Balance Sheet of Z Co. As of January 01, 2024			
Assets	**Amount (TL)**	**Liabilities**	**Amount (TL)**
Safe deposit box	50,000	Bank loans	100,000
Bank	150,000	Sellers	100,000
Trade receivables	200,000		
Stocks	300,000		
Current assets	*700,000*	*Short-term liabilities*	*200,000*
Tangible fixed assets	200,000	Sellers	100,000
Fixed assets	*200,000*	*Long-term liabilities*	*100,000*
		Capital	500,000
		Retained earnings	100,000
		Equity	*600,000*
Total assets	*900,000*	*Total liabilities*	*900,000*

Source: Prepared by us.

Table 14.7. Balance Sheet of Z Joint Stock Company at the End of the Period.

Balance Sheet of Z Co. As of December 31, 2024			
Active	**Amount (TL)**	**Passive**	**Amount (TL)**
Safe deposit box	432,000	Bank loans	100,000
Bank	100,000	Sellers	100,000
Trade receivables	250,000		
Stocks	200,000		
Current assets	*982,000*	*Short-term liabilities*	*200,000*

(Continued)

Table 14.7. *(Continued)*

Balance Sheet of Z Co. As of December 31, 2024			
Active	**Amount (TL)**	**Passive**	**Amount (TL)**
Tangible fixed assets	180,000	Sellers	110,000
Fixed assets	*180,000*	*Long-term liabilities*	*110,000*
		Capital	500,000
		Retained earnings	100,000
		Net profit for the period (Resulting from fraudulent transactions)	252,000
		Equity	*852,000*
Total assets	*1,162,000*	*Passive total*	*1,162,000*

Source: Prepared by us.

(2) Over-declaration of expense/cost: The Company has over-recorded the expense/cost of 200,000 TL for the sales transaction of 1,000,000 TL, which is actually 700,000 TL. The declared excess expense/cost of 200,000 TL (200,000 × 0.2 =) leads to a loss of 40,000 TL tax.
(3) Misleading invoice: The company asked the counterparty company, with which it has an agreement in return for commission, to issue more invoices than the actual commercial transaction and created a record over this amount. The transaction, which is considered a crime as an accounting fraud within the scope of the use of false and misleading invoices in terms of its content, was recorded as 200,000 TL more expense in the result accounts. This leads to (200,000 × 0.2 =) 40,000 TL loss in the tax, due to the excess expense/cost of 200,000 TL (penalized assessment in terms of VAT is also subject to penalty)
(4) Over-allocation of depreciation expense: The amount of depreciation that should have been allocated for the above-mentioned fixed asset was allocated by 20,000 TL more and thus (20,000 × 0.2 =) 4,000 TL less tax was accrued.
(5) Derecognition: In order to derecognize the cash surplus generated by the sales revenues, the company has realized sales amounting to 250,000 TL unrecorded. Due to the undeclared tax revenue of 250,000 TL, (250,000 × 0.2 =) 50,000 TL has been under-accrued.

(6) Personnel expense inflation: The Company has issued payrolls in the name of two people who are not actually working. For each of them, a salary expense of 10,000 TL per month was recorded and an excess expense record was created in order to erode the tax base amount to 10,000 × 12 × 2 = 240,000 TL per year, and the corporate tax was under-accrued by (240,000 × 0.2 =) 48,000 TL.

(7) Excess cost/expense: A purchase record was created for a product/good that was not actually sold in the enterprise. An extra cost/expense amounting to 150,000 TL was created. As a result of this transaction, the company has accrued a shortfall of (150,000 × 0.2 =) 30,000 TL tax since a fictitious expense of 150,000 TL was recorded.

In the case study, only tax loss in corporate tax was calculated due to working constraints. However, VAT is also frequently subject to penalized assessments in tax audits aimed at detecting fraud through books, records, and documents. In particular, in case of detection of the act of issuing and using forged documents, both fines and imprisonment sentences are imposed.

As seen in the application example, 7 (seven) fraudulent transactions were made within the company, the corporate tax base was made lower than it should be, and a tax loss of 252,000 TL was created. In the balance sheet dated December 31, 2024, it is emphasized that the financial statement does not reflect the truth by stating the under-reflection of the company's net profit for the period in the balance sheet.

5. Conclusion

This study is prepared with the accounting for tax approach in fraud audit. If actions and transactions contrary to tax legislation on accounting documents, book records, and declarations are carried out with the element of intent, it is seen that the tax evasion mechanism is operating.

Fraudulent transactions damage the working capital. In order to protect businesses and prevent fraud, tax authorities have accelerated their efforts to make risk analysis techniques effective in audits. In national and international trade, businesses carry out transactions that reduce the tax burden or postpone the tax on the transaction by concealing sales, unrecorded revenues, using or issuing forged documents, overstating costs and expenses. These transactions erode the tax base for the State Treasury and cause tax losses.

It is possible for businesses to make unintentional mistakes in tax planning due to lack of knowledge and attention. However, repetition of transactions to conceal the truth for the purpose of aggressive tax planning, contradictions to the ordinary course of commercial life, situations that are not explained for economic and technical reasons are scrutinized as suspicious transactions and are seen as fraud risk factors.

Although accounting fraud is not defined in the Turkish tax legislation, situations that are accepted as accounting fraud are counted among tax offenses. While detecting fraud in tax audits, many data such as purchases, sales, payments, capacity utilization, yield analysis, inventory counts, worker utilization and actual control practices, association of invoices with the main activity of the enterprise, borrowing, income and expense records arising from the relationship of the enterprise with partners are examined. For these examinations, there are special regulatory provisions in addition to the general regulatory provisions in the laws.

In the tax legislation, some issues are specifically explained within the scope of expenses not accepted by law. The finance administration asks taxpayers who act contrary to these regulations to provide explanations. Some of these issues; financing expense restriction, implicit capital, and expense restriction for passenger car vehicles are examined in the study and shown in sample applications. Conditions and restrictions are determined in the expense recording of the cost of borrowing foreign resources for the activities of the enterprises and the cost of borrowing from persons related to the shareholders. Although it is in the assets of the enterprise, there are also expense recognition restrictions for passenger cars. In case of violation of these regulations based on the prevention of abuses, the tax base is negatively affected. In particular, the issuance of forged invoices for transactions such as obtaining unfair value-added tax refunds from the state or obtaining expense invoices in return for commissions often causes penalty assessments in tax audits within the scope of accounting frauds. Considering the limitations of the study, the effects of accounting fraud are reflected on the balance sheet calculated in terms of corporate tax.

In the light of our findings and evaluations; it is seen that businesses need to act proactively, plan strategies, identify fraud risk factors, and conduct good governance studies in the field of managing risks. The control of business records and declarations by experts in tax accounting on fraud auditing is also important in terms of avoiding heavy penalties in tax audits.

References

Açıkgöz, H. (2025, February 17). Cheating audit in businesses. *MuhasebeTR*. https://www.muhasebetr.com/yazarlarimiz/harunacikgoz/037/

Akin, E. (2016). *Tax technique and opinion* (pp. 84–85). Bakı Kulu Press.

Akin, E. (2018). *Accounting revision in tax inspections* (p. 53). Bakı Kulu Press.

Aksoy, B. (2021). Prediction of financial statement frauds using machine learning methods and logistic regression: The case of Borsa Istanbul. *Journal of Finance Letters*, (115), 29–60. https://doi.org/10.33203/mfy.733855

Arslaner, H. (2013). Financial expenses and correcting entry paid on thin capitalization. *Journal of Accounting and Taxation Studies*, (2), 37–54. https://dergipark.org.tr/tr/pub/muvu/issue/59866/865424

Aykın, H. (2020, May 14). Pay attention to your financial business and transactions to avoid unnecessary Masak Radar! *Tax File*. https://vergidosyasi.wordpress.com/2020/05/14/gereksiz-yere-masak-radarina-girmemek-icin-finansal-is-ve-islemlerinize-dikkat/

Bayraklı, H. H., Erkan, M., & Elitaş, C. (2012). *Accounting errors and frauds in accounting and tax audit*. Ekin Publishing House.

Canayakın, H., & Türker, C. (2025). Without force majeure in the scope of using forged documents books and documents not submitted to tax inspection problems arising in case of submission to the court. *Journal of Tax Report*, *305*, 7–14. https://vergiraporu.com.tr/upImage/org/1a7c924.PDF

Ceylan, T. (2013). Accounting frauds and indications for detection of accounting frauds in the audit process. *Tax Report Journal*, *165*, 24. https://vergiraporu.com.tr/upImage/org/2013-165-Muhasebe_Hileleri_Ve_Denetim_Surecinde_Muhasebe_Hilelerinin_Tespitine_Yonelik_Belirtiler-Tugrul_Ceylan%20.pdf

Demir, C., & Yildiz, A. (2022). Accounting errors and frauds and the forensic accounting profession in detecting fraud. *Journal of Individual & Society*, *12*(1), 91–141. https://doi.org/10.20493/birtop.1090835

Dogan, A., & Sayan, B. (2022). Tax security practices: Turkey evaluation. *Journal of Tax Report*, *277*, 35. https://vergiraporu.com.tr/ReadArticle.aspx?Id=83377e36-27a9-4b94-bf6d-552c40fae00b#

Gül, O. S. (2024). Tax shield and its impact on capital structure decisions. In *2nd international congress of finance and tax November 08-10, 2024 Konya, Turkey, Proceedings Book* (pp. 218–222). IKSAD Publishing House. https://www.iksadinstitute.org/_files/ugd/614b1f_bd4ce9f07ab047fa9972b74019c50a6e.pdf

Gümüş, M. (2025). An evaluation on tax evasion and its causes in Turkey. In Ş. Ay (Ed.), *Maliye Teorisi Çalışmaları* (pp. 31–56). İKSAD Publishing House. https://iksadyayinevi.com/wp-content/uploads/2025/03/MALIYE-TEORISI-CALISMALARI.pdf

Kumkale, R. (2013). *Tax and accounting dictionary* (3rd ed., p. 75). Seçkin Publishing.

Official Gazette. (2021, February 4). *The presidential decree (03.02.2021, and No 3490)*. Official Gazette No 31385. https://www.resmigazete.gov.tr/eskiler/2021/02/20210204-11.pdf

Özçelik, M. K. (2018). An investigation on tax evasion oriented fraudulent cases in accounting practice. *World of Accounting Science*, (Special Issue 20), 493–517. https://dergipark.org.tr/en/download/article-file/634153

Şentürk, A. G., & Alpaslan, M. (2009). *A phenomenon in tax criminal law practice: Account and accounting fraud* (p. 104). Etki Publications.

Senyüz, D. (2017). *Tax criminal law* (10th ed., p. 409). Ekin Publishing.

Şimşek, A., Özkök, S., & Gündüz, N. K. (2015). *Tax accounting* (5th ed., pp. 374–376). Oluş Publishing.

Taştan, H. (2018). *Tax crimes and penalties*. Istanbul Chamber of Certified Public Accountants Publishing.

Tekin, A. (2023). Investigation of the crime of using fake invoice and handling it in terms of current changes. *Tax Report*, *280*, 123. https://vergiraporu.com.tr/ReadArticle.aspx?Id=2bde7295-037c-4342-8ee7-2bc761e77ce7

Tolga, S. (2020). On the basic problems of the Turkish Tax System. *Tax Report*, *248*, 99. https://vergiraporu.com.tr/ReadArticle.aspx?Id=f984a686-323d-4bd2-a04e-4bfe4065c481

TÜRMOB. (2024). Expense restriction calculation tool for passenger car acquisition. *Calculations.* https://www.turmob.org.tr/hesaplamalar/Binek-Oto-Gider-Kisitlama

Yalcinkaya, D. (2019, February 25). Accounting tricks and irregularities. *Muhasebe TR.* https://www.muhasebetr.com/yazarlarimiz/doganyalcinkaya/002/

Printed and bound by CPI Group (UK) Ltd, Croydon, CR0 4YY
15/09/2026
14962483-0008